14
Conflict
and Cooperation
in Divided Cities

Thematicon

Wissenschaftliche Reihe
des Collegium Polonicum

Band 14

Collegium Polonicum (Słubice)
Europa-Universität Viadrina Frankfurt (Oder)
Uniwersytet im. Adama Mickiewicza w Poznaniu

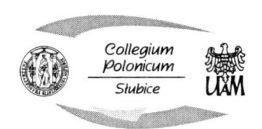

Jarosław Jańczak (ed.)

Conflict and Cooperation in Divided Cities

λογος

Herausgeber der Reihe:
Janine Nuyken, Krzysztof Krasowski, Krzysztof Wojciechowski

Redaktion dieses Bandes:
Jarosław Jańczak

Rezensiert von:
Prof. dr hab. Andrzej Gałganek

Satz und Umschlaggestaltung:
Ryszard Skrzeczyński

Titelbild:
Adam Czerneńko

Postadresse:

In Deutschland:
Europa Universität Viadrina
Collegium Polonicum
PF 1786
15207 Frankfurt (Oder)

W Polsce:
Collegium Polonicum
ul. Kościuszki 1
69-100 Słubice

www.cp.euv-frankfurt-o.de
E-Mail: colpol@euv-frankfurt-o.de

Logos Verlag Berlin
Gubener Str. 47, 10243 Berlin, Tel.: 030-42851090
www.logos-verlag.de

© Copyright by Collegium Polonicum & Logos Verlag 2009
Alle Rechte vorbehalten

ISBN 978-3-8325-2354-1
ISSN 1610-4277

Bibliografische Information der Deutschen Bibliothek

Die Deutsche Bibliothek verzeichnet diese Publikation in der
Deutschen Nationalbibliografie; detaillierte bibliografische Daten
sind im Internet über http://dnb.ddb.de abrufbar.

Table of Contents

Introduction 7

Heino Nyyssönen: Jerusalem. Nations and Their Others:
Memory and Political Tourism 9

Eda Derhemi: Kosovo's Mitrovica. The Symbolic Paradise of
an Ethnic Apartheid 25

Michał Łuszczuk: Ceuta and Melilla. Divisions in the Shadow of
a Border Fence 49

Anna Potyrała: Sarajevo. From the Ashes of Conflict to Cold
Coexistence 62

Marcin Galent: Belfast. An Ambiguous Heritage in a Difficult
Neighborhood 76

Przemysław Osiewicz: Nicosia. Conflict and Cooperation
in the Divided Capital City 88

Cezary Trosiak: Opole. A Stranger at Home. A Study of Inter-Group
Distance 98

Thomas Lundén, Anders Mellbourn, Joachim v. Wedel, Péter Balogh:
Szczecin. A Cross-Border Center of Conflict and Cooperation . . 109

Jarosław Jańczak: Gorizia-Nova Gorica. Between Unification
and Reunification 122

Thomas Lundén: Valga-Valka, Narva-Ivangorod. Estonia's Divided
Border Cities – Co-operation and Conflict Within and Beyond
the EU 133

Magdalena Musiał-Karg: Słubice-Frankfurt (Oder). Cooperation in
a Divided City on the Polish-German Border 150

Agnieszka Wójcicka: Copenhagen-Malmö. Different Sides
of Integration in a Hybrid City? 167

Tomasz Brańka: Tornio-Haparanda. A Unique Result of Neighboring
Towns' Collaboration 191

Alexander Tölle: Berlin. Urban Imagery in a Former No-man's Land
– the Wall Strip Two Decades Later 205

Tom Vandenkendelaere, Lien Warmenbol: Brussels. Cooperation
in Theory, Conflict in Practice? 220

Emilia Palonen: Helsinki. A Divided City? 239

Monica Bajan: Luxembourg. Multiculturalism Revisited
– The Case of the Labor Market 257

Personal Notes 271

Introduction

The world today is an area of simultaneous conflicts and cooperation between cultures, regions, international organizations, states, national and ethnic groups, political parties and other subjects. Conflict is estimated as unfruitful and undesired, whereby cooperation is perceived as an advantageous and wanted state, yet frequently difficult and time-consuming to initiate and strengthen. The analysis of the transition from conflict to cooperation, on the other hand, seems to be an invaluable source of experience that comes in useful for other cases.

Both conflict and cooperation are usually concentrated in particular locations where they are most intensive, observable, and where they are the most interesting to study. These locations involve divided, partitioned or cleavaged cities. These divisions are embodied by state borders, lines of demarcation, as well as by fences and walls, but also by informal rules and invisible lines. Fragmentations within towns reflect national, ethnical, religious, language and other differences. Cases of conflict and cooperation can refer to history, concern the towns where conflict prevails, where both these forms of interaction occur, or where collaboration dominates.

The aim of this publication is to analyze the processes of conflict and cooperation using cities as examples. The authors analyze case studies showing different forms and phases of conflict and cooperation concentrating in urban space. They also represent different academic disciplines and approaches, resulting in an interdisciplinary approach to conflict and cooperation in border studies. This book thus contains analyses of Belfast, Berlin, Brussels, Ceuta and Melilla, Copenhagen-Malmö, Gorizia-Nova Gorica, Helsinki, Jerusalem, Kosovo Mitrovica, Luxembourg, Narva-Ivangorod, Nicosia, Opole, Sarajevo, Słubice-Frankfurt (Oder), Szczecin, Tornio-Haparanda and Valga-Valka.

This book was prepared by 20 authors representing 10 universities from Belgium, Poland, Finland, Luxemburg, Sweden, the UK and the US. It will also be a subsequent research project in the field of border studies conducted jointly by the Faculty of Political Science and Journalism at the Adam Mickiewicz University (AMU) in Poznań, Poland and the Collegium Polonicum in Słubice, Poland – a joint institution of the AMU and the European University Viadrina in Frankfurt (Oder), Germany.

Jerusalem
Nations and Their Others: Memory and Political Tourism
Heino Nyyssönen

Once divided and once to be divided?

Next to the town hall in Jerusalem a copy of a 16th century artistic map reminds people of the old status of the city. It shows the city as the naval of the world, connecting the old continents of Europe, Asia and Africa, like a clover leaf. As the centre of three world religions this "eternal" city is of a special kind, one of the oldest in the world, a city of conflict for its residents and for the rest of the world. It is a town, in which the dead have had more influence on power struggles, thoughts and religion than the living[1]. Recently, between 1948 and 1967 Jerusalem was literally a divided city, in which a "municipal borderline" separated the eastern and the western parts of the city.

The purpose of this essay is to study conflict and co-operation in Jerusalem, particularly from the point of view of memory. I focus especially on places and how different groups and fractions could contest the same sites. The article will make a journey starting from the theoretical and historical discussion, entering Jerusalem and sporadically going forth to the holy of the holiest, the Temple Mount of Jerusalem. The journey ends on a small hill, the source of many wars, which reminds one of an old children's game called King of the Hill. In the game boys challenged the "king" and the one on the top of the hill who then tried to push the others down to maintain his power. My method is based both on my own observations in the city in December 2008 and textual analysis before and after the trip. Hereafter, I call the method political travelling and develop a few tentative ideas connected to it.

Studying Jerusalem is like reading a classic: it has many stratums, and is impossible to explicate them all. At the same the reading experience matters, as almost everything seems to have been said already. As Pierre Nora's realm of memory, lieux of memóire, the city and its status make their appearance in less evident cases in international relations, too. It is known that the origins of the Crimean War were based on the schism of who has the right to protect two churches in Bethlehem and Jerusalem. Instead of mere power politics – as was found in the straits of Turkey in the Crimean cases – this point of view stresses the role of memory and commemora-

---

[1] S. Kahan, *Ikkuna Jerusalemiin: Kulttuuria, katuja, kulkijoita*, Helsinki 2004, p. 29.

tion in international relations. Due to the city's particular status in the world, I have a number of doubts about the city's role either as a potentially partitioned city or as a capital in general.

Memory in international relations

History matters, with even many central works in international relations being based on historiography. However, memory – a close relative to history in Antique mythology – has been a highly neglected topic in this field. On the one hand, this is based on domestic analogy, which underestimated domestic policies in IR and their significance to the present. On the other hand, memory is easily condemned as being of a subjective nature. Still, subjectivity matters in politics: it has often been said that generals fight their previous wars in the beginning of new ones.

Particularly in ethnic conflicts the role of historical roots, use of memory and historical reasons cannot be underestimated. Memory has also to do with questions and arguments concerning so-called historical justice, an obscure concept for avoiding inequities, justice based on dictation and other wrong doings. Moreover, former experiences are used to maintain nations, which might be even more important, to particular groups in their construction of identities, identifications and identity policies. Although the past does not repeat itself, people compare the present to the past, try to get rid of it, nostalgise or even want to repeat the most successful parts of it[2].

According to sociologist Maurice Halbwachs memory depends on social context and ritualistic commemoration, and is activated when people find answers to questions posed to them by others. Halbwachs coined a concept of collective memory; as a part of these collective memories a community also forgets something so as to maintain its coherency and existence[3]. In this sense Halbwachs comes close to Ernest Renan, who argued that nations are based on certain forgetting and a will to stay together instead of militaristic memories of the origins of the nation. Collective memory is a fiction, if taken literally, but the question of the frames of political group making remains. There I think the *process*, how memories are constructed and claimed to be collective, is the most interesting. Politics enter when groups with different memories claim hegemonic positions for the same events and places. The question is not anymore about the object, the identity of the remembered, but of the rememberer[4].

---

[2] H. Nyyssönen, *Time, Political Analogies and the 1956 Hungarian Revolution*, "KronoScope", vol. 6, no 1, 2006, pp. 43-67; E. Cairns, M.D. Roe (eds.), *The Role of Memory in Ethnic Conflict*, Basingstoke, New York 2003; J.-W. Müller, *Memory and Power in Post-War Europe: Studies in the Presence of the Past*, Cambridge 2002.
[3] M. Halbwachs, *On Collective Memory*, Chicago–London 1992.
[4] L. Niethammer, *Maurice Halbwachs: Memory and the Feeling of identity*, [in:] B. Stråth (ed.), *Myth and Memory in the Construction of Community: Historical Patterns in Europe and Beyond*, Stockholm 2000, p. 87.

One form of memory is to find histories and analogies from the past. Here the point is not whether two historical events are finally analogical, but instead is to study with associative rhetorical strategies the monopolisation of the good ones and how to slander the opponent with the negative ones[5]. For example, in August 2008 Georgian President Saakashvili compared the ongoing conflict with Russia to Finland's Winter War in 1939-1940. For Saakashvili a cleavage between "the big" and "the small", David and Goliath, was a sufficient component, although there were no such separatists in Finland in 1939 as in Georgia in 2008.

There is no doubt, as to whether memory, and in particular politics of memory, play a role in the city of Jerusalem. A city, *Marktansiedlung*, in Weberian terms, is a stratum of memory: the same places have different memories and therefore could lead to a conflict of representation. In general, the role of the city and the metropolis is increasing: for the first time in history in 2007, a majority of human beings are living in cities. At its best the city could represent a patrimony and a cultural heritage of the whole of mankind. According to Pierre Nora, patrimony, however, takes place only in sites, in which nationalism is declining or is already *passé* – perhaps true in the present France but, unfortunately, this is not the case in Jerusalem, far from it. In addition to Israelis, also Palestinians are claiming them as part of their national identity[6].

Political tourism

One can argue that all travelling is political in the sense that it has an impact on world views. There are three kinds of journeys separated here: physical, mental and as a metaphor. The first refers to a trip literally, whilst the second can be done comfortably in an arm-chair or on the internet. Georges Remi, alias Hergé, for example, carefully studied the places, which he used in his comics. Among many books dealing with Jerusalem we could mention *Master and Margarita* written by Mikhail Bulgakov in Moscow between 1928 and 1940, with parts of the book located at the sites of Jerusalem.

With particularly Jerusalem in mind I have separated three kinds of ideal types in political tourism: Firstly, a pilgrim comes to strengthen his faith, either to ask forgiveness or just to get a glimpse of the object of admiration. Especially Jerusalem and Rome have been popular for pilgrims, who were also the first "tourists". Secondly, an agnostic is a skeptic, laying the whole thing in context to understand the situation. Finally we have an opponent at hand, a critic, who reads the city like the devil reads the Bible. From the political point of view a journey could be a discovery at its best, but might deteriorate into becoming an Odyssey, a failure, as well.

---

[5] H. Nyyssönen, *Time, Political Analogies and the 1956 Hungarian Revolution...*, op. cit., pp. 43-58.
[6] P. Nora, *The Era of Commemoration*, [in:] *Realms of Memory: The Construction of the French Past. Volume III: Symbols*, New York 1998, pp. 621-634; M. Billig, *Banal Nationalism*, London 2006, p. 70.

Walter Benjamin referred also to memory in his writings and evaluated an idea of a *flaneur* in the study of Baudelaire. Moreover, in his historical philosophical theses he discussed the presence of the past about tiger's leap into the past. There the French Revolution viewed itself as Rome incarnate and evoked ancient Rome the way fashion evokes costumes of the past. In addition to a leap we can compare the relation of an action and a former experience to photography. One may plan in advance and afterwards as much as one can, but at the time of the act anything can happen. First impressions matter, for example, photographer Annie Leibowich has stated she is framing the world all the time. Also pictures are interpretations, cut and framed, based not only on the frames of a photographer but on experiences, too. I dare to argue that most "original" places are a big disappointment when compared to the images of them based on former studies and photographs. However, the political tourist can see the material as such, so can make up his mind and create an interpretation to broaden the present understanding with potential antenarratives, too[7]. Thus, the method for dealing with political tourism is based on earlier reading and own observations in the field – such as the city-text or other political phenomena – and then studying the literature again.

In contrast to a cultural traveller a political traveller concentrates first and foremost on politics and the political. The passenger perceives politics as an historical-rhetorical phenomenon with discontinuities, certain contingencies and problems of classifications – this means political reading. A political tourist might have tentative ideas in mind but frequently the in-depth argument is put forward later. Alexis de Tocqueville, for example, went to study conditions in US prisons but on the basis of his exploration finally wrote a book about the whole of democracy in America. Compared to a resident, a political tourist is an outsider and reads the phenomenon consciously from this point of view, from division lines to political co-operation, from statues and spaces to architecture, from street names to a city even being considered a place for potential guerilla warfare. Well-known is the idea of how Baron Hausmann constructed new boulevards in Paris in order to handle potential uprisings there. Even a week of field work matters as a "weapon of precision", when it is consciously done with former experiences. In this sense, the political traveller might open new perspectives on politics and be even more political than a proper politician, a professional, who usually is bound to tight and official schedules.

Nations and their others

Nations and their others could refer as much to politics on the national level, as to neighbouring states or to great powers. In Israel "us" and "them" is found inside the state but also in relation to the neighbouring states and to the whole world. It is said that Jewish politicians have cleverly allied with great powers of the time. At first the British filled this position, then the Soviet Union, France and finally the

---

[7] D. Boje, *Narrative Methods for Organizational & Communication Research*, London 2001.

United States. Already in Theodor Herzl's political thought, the political centre was in London to guarantee a piece of land, assured by international law. For Herzl the time had come for a return of the Jewish nation, not necessarily in Palestine but, as Herzl mentioned in *Der Judenstaat*, in Argentina. For a man from an imperialist age, there was nothing wrong in taking the land. Instead, according to Ratzelian's geopolitics, powerful nations were created to grow and expand – even Herzl's term *Die Landergreifung* is later translated to occupation.

In Herzl's opinion the new exodus was to take place with scientific methods analogised to Transvaal, and contrasted to mistakes in coal mining in California, where new desperadoes looted the earth from its border. In Herzl's opinion the revolutionary vanguard was seen in *die Society of Jews*, the great gestor, politically analogized to new Moses. "*As soon as we have secured the land, a ship [Landnahmeschiff, HN] will sail to take possession of it...These pioneers [Landnehmer, HN] will have three tasks: first, the exact scientific investigation of all natural properties of the land; second, the establishment of a tightly centralized administration; third, the distribution of land*"[8].

Herzl, however, obviously underestimated other nations and the power of nationalism: "*Every man will be as free and as unrestricted in his belief or unbelief as he is in his nationality. And should it happen that men of other creeds and other nationalities come to live among us, we shall accord them honorable protection and equality before the law*". Herzl opposed theocracy and democracy without a balancing monarchy. Instead he made an analogy to historical Venice, which he considered an aristocratic republic[9]. Herzl believed that the state could be created in a way, which was unknown in history until then.

Nowadays, there is a Jewish majority of ca. two-thirds and a growing Arab minority in Jerusalem. In the 1967 census their relation was ca. 74%-26%, and has altered to ca. 66%-34% in forty years. In the demography of Jerusalem, fertility and immigration are definitely political: for example a Jewish voter in 2009, who considered supporting either Likud or the extreme right, commented that one of Israel's main current problems is a subsequent Muslim majority in Jerusalem, because of Arab fertility. There is an extraordinarily high birth rate in the Jerusalem's ultra-Orthodox population, too: an average *hared* family has more than seven children. According to some estimates, about a half of the Jewish majority in Jerusalem belongs to Orthodox Jews and another half to secular[10].

Representatives of Israel define the state officially as a Jewish state, which as such is a problematic definition. In Israel, there is not, for example, a constitution to define minority rights. On the basis of a law from 1950 all those, who declare to be of

---

[8] T. Herzl, *Der Judenstaat*, [in:] *Zionistische Schriften. Dritte, veränderte und erweiterte Auflage*, Tel Aviv 1934, pp. 88-91, English quotations: *The Jewish State*, New York 1970, pp. 94-96.
[9] *Ibidem*, pp. 93-95.
[10] G. Myre, *Israeli Riddle: Love Jerusalem, Hate Living There*, "New York Times" 13 May, 2007, http://www.nytimes.com/2007/05/13/weekinreview/13myre.html?_r=1, 11.02.2009; "Helsingin Sanomat" 10 Feb. 2009; U. Heilman, *Jerusalem elects secular mayor*, http://jta.org/news/article/2008/11/11/1000898/jerusalem-elects-secular-mayor, 11.02.2009.

Jewish origin, could settle to the state of Israel. Jewish, either in the ethnic or religious sense, form a majority, almost 80% of the whole population, and the last ca. 20% belong to Arabs and other minorities – with the occupied territories the relation is more equal, something like 4.5 to 5.5 million[11]. Although we should not rely too much on statistics, numbers reveal the frame. Since the 1990s extensive immigration has taken place from the former Soviet Union. In Israel former Soviet citizens form the largest immigrant group, equal to the Arab population. Therefore it is no wonder that a tourist, like me, was asked to speak Russian on the street of Jerusalem.

A rapidly growing number of Russians have features of otherness as it changes the present power structure. For example, in the legislative elections of 2009 an extreme *Israel Beiteinu* party demanded to bind the gaining of citizenship to a loyalty declaration to the state. The proposal was directed against the Arab population but also the loyalty of some religious Jewish groups, and the Russian newcomers themselves has been questioned. In East Jerusalem only ca. 5% of the Arab population had Israeli citizenship in 2005. The vast majority were permanent residents of the city, a position conducted on the basis of participating in the 1967 census. They have the right to vote in municipal elections and an accession to social security and state health care. They could lose the status being abroad more than seven years or by not visiting Israel once in every three years. Those who are married to residents of the West Bank or Gaza have to leave the city.

On the footsteps of Halbwachs and others

Maurice Halbwachs, an opponent in my terms, was physically present in Jerusalem in the late 1930s and travelled by car at a time, when the first great Arab rebellion had taken place. For him Palestine meant first of all Jews and Christians; he was critical to Ernest Renan's identifications of Palestine looking similar like in the time of the Bible. In Jerusalem this statement could not be more wrong, as for example, the present great walls around the old city were built by Suleiman the Magnificent in the 16th century – altogether amounting to 4.5 kilometers with seven presently open gates.

In his *La topographie légendaire des évangiles on terre sainte* (1941) Halbwachs used historical documentation of pilgrims' testimonies to tear down the re-appropriation, dedication, new constructions and growth of the holy sites. In political terms Halbwachs indicated, how older traditions became a part of a new movement and those who remember. I think, reading politically, that even a radical movement, cannot make a total break with the past but has to re-read and absorb existing traditions to gain popularity. Thus, Christianity would not have become as powerful without adopting essential elements of Jewish history, and thus rechristening the cultural sites of Jews.

---

[11] S. Peres, *One Region, Two States*, "Washington Post", 10 Feb, 2009, http://www.washingtonpost.com, 15.02.2009.

Christians who returned to Jerusalem considered the city as the same as it was during the time of Jesus. First pilgrims visited places which were connected to the life of Jesus, and particularly to his violent death. When crusaders entered the city, they were disappointed as the city did not correspond to their images. Europeans had been living in the past by believing in the glory of the city, but which in fact had historically demolished a lot[12]. From the point of view of political travelling this Halbwachs' finding reveals the risks of great expectations. They even discuss about the gap between expectations and empirical experiences known as the Jerusalem syndrome, which could cause even physical symptoms. Among others, Mark Twain was deeply disappointed in the city, as was Selma Lagerlöf, a pilgrim, who later wrote a novel entitled *Jerusalem* based on her own experiences.

During their rule crusaders changed the cityscape a lot by building churches and other constructions. Action was based on historical legitimisation i.e. supposing that the memory of the dead, the older generations would give the right for present actions. New representatives of groups like emperors and crusaders created new places and reinterpreted old ones. In this sense Halbwachs turned the focus from historical truth to mechanisms of tradition formation. These religious sites of memory, such as Via Dolorosa, were social artifacts and a subtle critique of the civil religions of the 1930s[13].

In 2008 Via Dolorosa has its name written in Latin and both in Hebrew and Arabic. A procession takes place at three o'clock on Fridays from the Monastery of the Flagellation to Calvary. All 14 commemorative stops, such as where Jesus fell for the third time, are well-detailed in many travel guides. However, as one travel guide admits, because of 2000 years of subsequent building, Via Dolorosa is unlikely to be the precise path that Jesus walked[14]. From the point of view of conflict the former Minister of Defense Moshe Dayan might have a point by saying that there is not any location in Israel without Arabic footsteps. When people follow footsteps, whose do they actually follow?

Via Dolorosa terminates in the Church of the Holy Sepulcher, in which there are the five last stations, including the supposed Golgotha and the tomb of Jesus itself. Crusaders rebuilt this focal point in the 12th century and it has been renovated many times. The governance of the church, including the schism in the background of the Crimean War, is still complex. In November 2008 the church made its appearance in international news, when Armenian and Orthodox Christians had a fight there. Visiting the procession and the Holy Sepulcher in 2008 revealed an international "us" of religious tourism, and particularly the presence of Russians, both tourists and residences, was striking into an eye.

---

[12] M. Halbwachs, *La topographie légendaire des évangiles en terre sainte*, Paris 1971; M. Halbwachs, *On Collective Memory...*, op. cit., pp. 228-232.
[13] L. Niethammer, *Maurice Halbwachs: Memory and the Feeling of identity...*, op. cit., p. 78.
[14] S. Bryant, *Travel guide Israel*, London 2006, p. 39.

Divided Jerusalem

East Jerusalem includes the Old City and some of the holiest places of three world religions such as the Temple Mount, Al-Aqsa Mosque, Western Wall and the Church of the Holy Sepulcher. East Jerusalem refers also to territories under Jordan rule until 1967 and then under the administration of Israel. The Israeli government supports Jewish migration to the area, so as to maintain a Jewish majority in the city. Muslims populate the eastern side, with there seeming to be a slight Muslim majority of 53% in the East, but there is also a significant Jewish population of 43%. The vast majority of Christians live in the eastern side, but their population in the whole city is very small, ca. 2%[15]. In 1988 Jordan, still rejecting Israeli sovereignty over East Jerusalem, withdrew all claims to it.

The 1949 armistice left the Old City and vast majority of the holy places in Jordanian hands. Israel declared unilaterally West Jerusalem to be its capital, which led to a first clash with the United Nations. The eastern part of the city became a part of Jordan in 1950 and its second capital ten years later. All this was a huge loss for the young state of Israel after the 1948 war, which according to new historians, as such was not inevitable. The western part developed rapidly during the partition but also meant a life in a divided city, which Amos Oz has depicted in his novel *My Michael*[16]. To some extent the division resembled Berlin after 1961, I think: the historic centre belonged to the East and the commercial part to the West. As such West Berlin, however, formed an enclave inside the GDR. On this level only Mount Scopus is comparable to Berlin i.e. a small area in the North East, which Jordanians could not occupy. The enclave had only one gateway, the Mandelbaum Gate, to the Jewish populated West Jerusalem. Moreover, next to Mount Scopus is Ammunition Hill, one of the most important basins of Jordanian troops until 1967. During the early hours of June 7, 1967 Israeli paratroopers captured the hill following the Old City later on that day. The trenches and tanks were still there as is a former Jordanian pillbox, which has been turned in to a museum to propagate the "re-unification" and with current visitors a part of ideological education in the Israeli army.

Finally, in 1980 the Israeli Parliament, the Knesset, officially "united" the city by enacting the Jerusalem law. According to the first paragraph "*Jerusalem, complete and united, is the capital of Israel*". Secondly, it is the seat of the President of the State, the Knesset, the Government and Supreme Court. In the third paragraph they declared that the "*Holy Places shall be protected from desecration and any other violation and from*

---

[15] *Statistical Yearbook of Jerusalem 2006/7*, Table III/10, Population of Jerusalem. By age, Population Group and Geographical Spreading, 2003, http://www.jiis.org.il/imageBank/File/shnaton_2004/shnaton_c1004.pdf, 24.03.2009.

[16] J. Feldt, *The Israeli Memory Struggle: History and Identity in the Age of Globaliszation*, Odense 2007, p. 210; B. Wasserstein, *Divided Jerusalem: The Struggle for the Holy City*, New Haven 2002, pp. 136-190; A. Elon, *Jerusalem: Battleground of Memory*, New York 1995, pp. 38-42; A. Oz, *My Michael*, London 2001.

anything likely to violate the freedom of access of the members of the different religions to the places sacred to them or their feelings towards those places"[17]. According to the UN's Security Council the law violated international law, a resolution accepted in the Security Council only with the abstention of the United States.

The Eastern and the Western side have their others, too. Roughly speaking, Jerusalem belongs to cities, in which the rich live in the West and the poor in the East. In particular, since the Second Intifada, the economy in the Eastern side has declined, forcing people to leave the city. At the airport Ben Gurion, a collective taxi driver *sherut* was reluctant to recognise my address in the Eastern side. The first glimpse of the hotel, next to the Herod gate, referred to Palestine instead of Israel: there were no Israeli TV-channels but *al Jazeera*, CNN, a Lebanese one and a leaflet Palestine This Week. There, politics of appearance was evident: no *kipa*s but almost all women were wearing a scarf. The vast majority of children were visible, and particularly boys, subsequent kings of the hill, playing with toy guns on the streets, a phenomenon, which has vanished from many more politically correct sites. Some taxi-divers avoid narrow streets in the area, and also in the core of East Jerusalem, only five minutes to the corner of Saladin Street. An Arabic taxi driver, however, "defended" the area on the basis of safety, by stating that all suicide bombers operate on the Western side.

During the partition a "municipal border", based on the ceasefire agreement, cut the city into two. Remnants of it could still be seen as a certain open area and a wide road next to the Damascus gate. In 2008 big construction works took place also in this area due to the forthcoming Jerusalem Light Rail, partly planned on annexed land, according to critics. There are still different border lines, for example, two transport systems or, like one resident complained, the *Jerusalem Post* was not delivered to him because the address is on the "wrong" side of the street[18].

Topography of the Old City

First of all Jerusalem means the Old City, having an area of less than one square kilometer (0.9 km²). This was the whole space of Jerusalem until the 1860s, when the population started to expand outside the city walls. Already the Bible described Jerusalem as a heavily fortified city – it has been captured ca. 40 times. Since 1948 the walls formed a defense line of Jordanians, and there were heavy fights in 1967 at the Lion and Jaffa Gates, when Israeli troops took the city. There is a famous picture, when the victorious commanders had just entered inside the Lions Gate. As an important symbolic act they raised the Israeli flag to full mast, when the troops reached the Western Wall. Since 1981 the old city is a part of the UNESCO World

---

[17] *Basic Law: Jerusalem, Capital of Israel*, http://knesset.gov.il/laws/special/eng/basic10_eng.htm, 24.03.2009.
[18] R.W. Gee, *Jerusalem divided*, www.coxwashington.com, 11.02.2009.

Heritage Site List, and a little later, a heritage that is considered to be in constant danger.

In Weberian classification – *Konsumentenstadt, Prozentenstdt, Händlerstadt* – Jerusalem's divisions are, however, complicated to explore. No doubt there is a market, artisans, but the manufacturing sector is two times smaller than in other cities. The tourist sector has traditionally been strong; in education and public administration, too, the level is higher than the average in Israel. However, the religious dimension is the most visible: there are more than 70 religious red-letter days in the city[19]. The crucial role of religion is visible even in the names and the topography of the Old City. In addition to the Temple Mount there are four Quarters side by side: Muslim, Christian, Jewish and the Armenian Quarters. The Muslim Quarter – next to the Damascus gate – is the largest and the most populated. Before the 1929 revolts the population was still mixed but now entering from the Damascus gate the first image was very Arabic in nature, a labyrinth of souks resembling other old city centers in the Muslim world.

Next to the Muslim Quarter is the Christian Quarter with the Church of the Holy Sepulcher. According to tradition Saint Helena found the tomb of Jesus ca. 300 years later, and a church was built on a supposed former temple. The church maintained its Christian role for a long time but during the Seldzukkian rule religious tourism turned more dangerous and the Pope instructed Christians to start a holy war to protect the holy sites. Crusaders first recaptured the city in 1099, causing a bloody memory by killing the Muslim and Jewish residents. Instead of crowning himself king, the leader of the crusaders, Godefroy de Bouillon, became *Advocatus Sancti Sepulchri*.

The Armenian Quarter is the smallest and to some extent was the most quiet, too. Its function is more obscure compared to the three others, although it is usually mentioned that Armenia is the oldest Christian nation of the world. From politics of memory it is worth reminding that they have commemorated – and at the same time reminded politically – of the atrocities in Turkey during the First World War.

Finally, there is the Jewish Quarter in the South-Eastern corner, which has a particular history of its own, with a large square in front of the Western wall. This "Wailing Wall" is the holiest site in Jewish religion and the only relic of the Jewish Temple. As one travel guide mentioned, the walls represent, literally, layer upon layer of history[20]. According to British reports signs of conflict emerged already in the 1920s as Jews could enter the wall only along the narrow King David Street leading to locals complaining of the noise. In the1948 war there were struggles next to the Quarter, which was finally captured by Jordanian troops. As a consequence Jews were forced to leave; and Arab refugees were resettled in the Old City. Jews could not enter the Old City until 1967 – an Israeli flag on the Western Wall symbolically ended the war but also reminded of the hegemony in the city.

---

[19] M. Weber, *Wirtschaft und Gesellschaft. Grundriss der verstehenden Soziologie*, Fünfte revidiete Auflage, Tübingen 1980, pp. 727-730; S. Kahan, *Ikkuna Jerusalemiin…*, op. cit., p. 35.
[20] S. Bryant, *Travel guide Israel…*, op. cit., p. 33.

During their rule Jordanians demolished the Jewish Quarter and some graveyards. After the siege Israelis took revenge and deported Arabs from the Quarter, giving them only a few hours notice. The whole Moroccoan (Mughrabi) Quarter was bulldozed to an open plaza in front of the wall for prayers and civic rituals – among them the former provisional home of Yasser Arafat. From the Israeli viewpoint the Quarter had turned to a slum and the site was too narrow to host the expected crowds coming to the wall due to the "liberation". In its present form the square, beside Mount Herzl and the tomb of Herzl himself, is a site of civic rituals, and in my view belong to sites, in which an individual is psychologically manipulated so as to consider him or herself as being only a small part of a larger entity.

Holy of holies: the Temple Mount / Haram es-Sharif

Politically Israel has the upper hand in Jerusalem, but in the game of the King of the Hill the situation is more problematic. De facto Muslims rule the Mount although political power in principle is in the hand of the Israelis[21]. The Western Wall is downwards from the Mount and a particular wooden corridor from the square leads to the Mount. The site is not that simple to visit as the Mount is open only in the mornings from Sunday to Thursday. For a non-Muslim there are several exits, but the wooden corridor is the only way to enter, after a second electronic security control.

In politics centre means power, and this site on the hill represents ultimate power. In principle Jews, Muslims and Christians believe that the creation of the world started here, thus Adam was created on the Mount. Even the first murder, Cain and Abel, is supposed to have occurred on the hill as the story of how Abraham was to sacrifice his own son Isaac. Standing in the "naval" of the world, less than 500 x 300 meters, was a confusing experience. No doubt this is a place for all political travelers: for a pilgrim, an agnostic and an opponent. However, it should not be visited by the very young and in big groups. According to the Bible, King David bought the place to build an altar in honour of the Lord – and he might have known about a cultic nature of the place. Solomon raised the first Temple on the same site, pulled down by Babylonians in 586 BC. After the Babylonian captivity Jews constructed the second Temple, which existed until its destruction in 70 AD. The destruction has led Jews to mourn, to build synagogues facing Jerusalem and to pray that in the next year, next year in Jerusalem they will build a new Temple.

According to Talmud Israel was the naval of the word, Jerusalem the centre of the land and the Temple the centre of Jerusalem. Although this ethno-centrist view is as obscure as recent ideas for finding out the geographic centre point of Europe, in the religious sense the view has been very powerful. Also Christians adopted the

---

[21] H. Juusola, *Juutalaisuus, Pyhä maa ja valtio*, [in:] H. Juusola, H. Huuhtanen (eds.), *Uskonto ja politiikka Lähi-idässä*, Helsinki 2002, p. 34.

idea, and medieval *orbis terrae*, T-O maps, depicted Asia on the top half of the map. In Jewish eschatological expectation there will be a third Temple on the site before the end of the world, a prediction, which has encouraged immigration to Palestine as some of God's commitments could only be carried out in the land of Israel. Politically, the problem has been to find the right *kairos* and not to "force" the end of the world upon people by returning too early to a promised land. The idea to promote "the inevitable" has led some fundamentalist Christians to unite and to understand politically militant Jews, who think that the time for the third Temple has come.

The seeds for the present conflict were sown in the 7th century, when Muslims constructed two Mosques on the hill. According to tradition Calif Umar ibn al-Khattab was conscious about the sacred history of the hill and ordered a construction of a Mosque on the same spot. Had Umar prayed at Golgotha, subsequent generations might have built a Mosque on that site. The Temple Mount represented political power, and the former Jewish temple was already in ruins. The proper Dome of the Rock was commissioned later in that century to compete with the magnificent churches of the city. Inside the dome is the former peak of the hill, the "Foundation Stone", the Kubbet es-Sakhra, on which Abraham – a prophet also in Islam – was supposed to sacrifice his son.

Also Christians have favoured the naval principle, and for them the focal point was not far away, at Golgotha. It almost seems as if every important location next to Jerusalem and Bethlehem is commemorated with a church. Moreover, conquistadors constructed new buildings on earlier cultic sites for example, in Cusco Peru, in which Inca Temples were demolished and churches rose on the site. In Jerusalem, Christian rule ended with a compromise of memory. After Saladin captured the city in 1187, the most authoritative third crusade took place. At first Richard the Lionheart had an upper hand, but finally an agreement was made between them in 1192, in which Christian pilgrims had the right to visit Saint Sepulcher, and the city was to be open.

There can be no doubt, that the two Mosques on the hill, Al Aqsa and the Dome of the Rock with a golden roof, are landmarks of Jerusalem. The Mount is a site of numerous facts and fiction, from the murder of Jordanian King Abdullah to a tourist site for a detective story by Agatha Christie – in which the tourists still could enter the Dome of the Rock. But this is not possible anymore, although a travel guide can make reservations that longer visit hours and permission to enter the buildings may be restored during the time span[22]. Thus, the conflict is not merely historical. For example, during the 1967 war the leading rabbi in the Israeli army favoured even demolishing the buildings on the Mount. In the 1980s two Israelis planned to blow up the buildings to promote the third Temple, and in 1990 another group caused more than 20 deaths there.

---

[22] R. Ullian, *Frommer's Israel*, Hoboken 2006, p. 162.

An attempt to partite Jerusalem

One of the most famous political tourists was Ariel Sharon, who had moved to the Muslim Quarter next to the Damascus gate in 1987 – a provocation as such, according to one travel guide[23]. In September 2000 Sharon, an opponent, catalysed the second intifada, known also as al-Aqsa Intifada due to the Mosque on the Mount. According to Muslim belief Mohammad had visited the site on his Night Journey in 620 AD, and Caliph Umar founded a Mosque on the site. At first Sharon's visit seemed to be only an episode in the shadow of Slobodan Milosevic's fall and the Olympic Games but soon turned to long lasting front page news. According to Reuters and AFP, the struggle began after Sharon visited a territory in the Old City, which is sacred to both Jews and Muslims. According to Israelis, police surrounded Al Aqsa Mosque and used rubber bullets against Palestinian youngsters, who threw stones against the Jewish prayers. Palestinians argued that a struggle of Jerusalem and the occupied territories had begun and demanded that Israel retreat from their own subsequent capital in East Jerusalem[24].

Later, the picture became more focused, with even the starting point of the intifada being questioned. There is a mutual understanding that in the background there were failed negotiations and a deep disappointment in Camp David. The political status of Jerusalem had been one of the most difficult parts in the peace agreement, and therefore its fate had been left to be one of the last topics in the negotiation. Finally Prime Minister Ehud Barak had broken a taboo and, as an Israeli negotiator, was for the first time ready to discuss the partition of Jerusalem. Traditionally the left had favoured giving up territories for peace, but Jerusalem had been out of the question. According to one plan, also the Old City would have been divided: Christian and Muslim Quarters would have become a part of the forthcoming Palestinian state, including certain rights to the Temple Mount and free access for Jews to the Mount. According to another proposal even the Mount would be partitioned: sites on the ground for Palestinians and underground archeological sites for Israelis[25].

It seems that Yasser Arafat did not do his best to prevent the conflict from escalating. For Palestinians and Arafat, Bill Clinton's mediated proposals were inadequate, as they demanded the whole of East Jerusalem. Although they postponed the declaration of statehood for an independent state, planned for 13 September, they also commemorated the memory of Shabra and Shatila massacres three days later – also to remind that Sharon was involved at that time. Thus, Sharon went to the Temple Mount to demonstrate that the Likud opposition will not give up the holy sites of Jerusalem. With a Likud delegation Sharon made his politics of appearance dur-

---

[23] *Marco Polo Israel*, Helsinki–Jyväskylä 1993, p. 63.
[24] "Helsingin Sanomat", Sep 30–Oct 2, 2000.
[25] H. Juusola, *Israelin historia*, Helsinki 2005, pp. 247-250; H. Huuhtanen, *Sionismi Israelin ulkopolitiikassa ja konflikti miehitetyissä maissa*, [in:] H. Juusola, H. Huuhtanen (eds.), *Uskonto ja politiikka Lähi-idässä*, Helsinki 2002, p. 53; *Barak's Proposal to Divide Jerusalem*, www.iris.org.il/divided_jerusalem.html, 11.02.2009.

ing the tourist time and did not visit the Mosque. As a part of the deal, there was to be no praying or public statements there. Moreover, he had a police escort and a permit from the Prime Minister Ehud Barak[26].

There can be no doubt, that as a former general, Sharon, who had studied history, made a provocation even by just appearing on the Mount. At the same time the act as such revealed a deep disagreement in the Israeli's domestic politics concerning the peace agreement in general and the status of Jerusalem in particular. What is less known is that at the Taba summit of January 2001 both parties still accepted divided sovereignty in principle and favoured the idea of an open city. However, Clinton's and Barak's *kairos* was over. The new candidate for Prime Minister, Ariel Sharon, refused to resume the negotiations in the case of his victory.

After the Gaza operation

Although the idea here was to study Jerusalem, I cannot avoid dealing with the Gaza Strip and the West Bank, as Israel was once again in the headlines in December 2008. The fragile ceasefire ended on the 19 December and Hamas continued their rocket strikes. On the basis of earlier cases the Israelis revenge was expected: Israel struck back and launched the Operation Cast Lead on the 27 December, bombing at first and then starting a land offensive a week later. After 22 days, Israel announced a unilateral ceasefire on January 18, 2009. Up until 22 January, 13 Israelis had been killed during the conflict, including three civilians. Palestinian estimates of their deaths toll was 1300, including 700 civilians, with more than 460 children being among them[27].

The campaign and its brutality surprised many observers in the world. Gaza has even awoken provocative analogies to the Third Reich, too, for example the writer Jonathan Littell and the MP Sir Gerard Kaufman have criticised the actions of the Israelis from this perspective. The government timed the operation for Christmas time, with the international community being paralysed due to the US presidential transition. Cynically, the Israeli government in Jerusalem, the new Herod, launched the operation next to the Holy Innocents Day, which is commemorated by West Syrians on the 27th December and a day later by Catholics and Lutherans. Israel did not take the UN or international law into consideration, but on the contrary, as after the operation had been finished Ehud Olmert let slip that there was no more diplomatic space for the campaign.

There were riots also in Jerusalem but otherwise the war did not immediately touch the city – even travel agencies continued their trips to Israel. Nevertheless, Gaza and the latest elections were the newest burdens for the integration of the city. Moreover, on the municipal level religious Jewish parties have a say in the city's affairs, whilst the Arabs have not really been interested in the municipal administra-

---

[26] H. Juusola, *Israelin historia...*, op. cit., pp. 250-251.
[27] *Helsingin Sanomat*, 20 & 24 Jan, 2009.

tion. On the city council the Orthodox United Torah Judaism is the largest group represented followed by Nir Barkat's list Jerusalem Shall Succeed. A secular and a self-made businessman, Barkat succeeded the first ultra-Orthodox *haredi* mayor in the 2008 municipal elections[28].

According to Meir Ben-Dov, even those politicians who raise their voices for a unified Jerusalem understand that there can be no peace agreement without first relinquishing the one city under one rule concept. The dream about one city under one rule would mean de facto division of the city. A "security" wall, which Ben-Dov analogises to the former Berlin Wall "is mainly a placebo for those who still refuse to accept partition as part of the annals of Jerusalem"[29]. In fact they have already separated East Jerusalem from the West Bank suburbs by a security barrier. In despite of arguments of its preliminary nature, parts of it, such as the area next to Bethlehem, refer to a more permanent structure.

Idealists argue for one state, whilst realists prefer two, and in principle both entities – as has the present US leadership – have committed to the latter. However, in history enclaves have turned out to be preliminary solutions, either in Jerusalem or elsewhere. In the two state model there are two separated territories, Gaza and the West Bank and in the West Bank there are areas under Palestinian control, under joint administration and under Israeli control. Nevertheless, also the policy of one state is problematic. A rough analogy with Bosnia reveals a very fragile combination of Serb majority on the one hand and Muslim and Croat majority on the other hand in a joint federal state[30].

There are two great question marks in the Middle-East now: how to integrate Iran and Hamas to this picture and secondly, how to prevent extreme groups from sabotaging peace talks between Israel and the Palestinians. In his *Audacity of Hope*, Barack Obama, perhaps an agnostic, referred also to the area and how he saw "this small plot of land" viewed from a helicopter when pondering the US's role. Obama did not particularly raise his voice during the Gaza campaign, but since then another Clinton has come to office and the question is whether both can do something in the long run. There is still much to do to convince domestic audiences, too, frightened by Samuel P. Huntington's cultural theories and to turn around the pro-Israel opinion. As Edward W. Said (1978) has noted, no academically involved person in the US has wholeheartedly identified himself with the Arabs in the way liberal America has done with Zionism[31].

After visiting Jerusalem, it is hard to imagine the Old City to be divided. It is said that in addition to Rome and Athens, Jerusalem forms one corner in a triangle of the

---

[28] U. Heilman, *Jerusalem elects secular mayor...*
[29] M. Ben-Dov, *Carta's Illustrated History of Jerusalem*, Second Updated Edition, Jerusalem 2006, p. 376.
[30] H. Nyyssönen, *Muuri epäilyttää Jerusalemin jakajia*, "Kaleva", 11 Feb, 2009; H. Fendel, *Olmert: Rabin Would Have Divided Jerusalem*, www.israelnationalnews.com, 11.02.2009.
[31] B. Obama, *Audacity of Hope*, New York 2008, p. 381; E. W. Said, *Orientalism*, London 2003, p. 27.

birth places of Western civilization. On the basis of its religious character and pilgrimage tourism it is an ultimate international city, which is spoiled by ideas of a political hegemony. Following Pierre Nora's line of thought and the idea of patrimony, Jerusalem belongs to a global patrimony and tourism. At the same time this kind of status raises doubts about its role either as being potentially partitioned or as a capital in general. In the 1947 UN Partition Plan the aim was *corpus separatum*, an international administrated zone. In the Resolution 194 (1948) the General Assembly demanded effective UN control and a permanent international regime for the area. Due to all the events and censuses since then this is difficult to implement and it would be easier to transfer the Israel capital, as to move some offices, out of Jerusalem. It might sound idealistic but, for example, in Chile the Presidential palace is located in Santiago and the Parliament in Valparaiso. The US could start to revise its 1995 Act, which preferred the moving of its Embassy to Jerusalem, the capital of Israel. At present the US Embassy, as most other Embassies, is in Tel Aviv.

Kosovo[1]'s Mitrovica
The Symbolic Paradise of an Ethnic Apartheid
Eda Derhemi

Prologue: Some incomplete and unreliable facts about Mitrovica e Kosovës or Kosovska Mitrovica

"After the Kosovo war of 1999, Mitrovica, with most of its Serbian population north of the Ibar river, and most of its Albanian population south, precipitated towards an almost complete ethnic separation of these two groups. The formation of two demographically homogeneous parts expressed the growing fear and hatred the two groups felt for each other. The separation during the ten years after the Kosovo War has made the division deeper, and has furthered the belief that the two groups will never again be together, especially among the Serbs, who see themselves as the victims of Kosovar independence.

Kosovo today has 2,150,000 people, 120,000 of them Serbs. 12,000 Albanians who previously lived in the northern part of the city rented houses in the southern part and still live there today. A smaller number of Serbs left the southern part for the north.. Almost 4000 Albanians and Muslim Boshnjaks live an isolated life in a small neighborhood next to the northern line of the Iber. Uncertain sources claim that today 60,000 Serbs live in the northern part of Mitrovica. In the 1991 censuses Mitrovica county had circa 105,000 inhabitants, Mitrovica city circa 65,000. In the 1998 OSCE census for the county of Mitrovica, the Albanian population was around 95,000, the Serbian about 10,000, while inside the city there were 68,000 Albanians and 10,000 Serbs, which shows that between 1991 and 1998 the city grew by about 13,000 inhabitants, apparently all of them Albanians. Wikipedia refers to the most recent data regarding Mitrovica: "In 2003 the city had an estimated total population of 75,600 and the municipality's population was estimated to be around 105,000." According to these data the population of the municipality in 1991 and 2003 was the same, and the population of the city from 1998 to 2003 must have fallen. Neither logical extrapolations is verified in reality. Obviously the statistical data are incorrect. In fact, the population of the Serbian and Albanian parts of Mitrovica has grown significantly, with people from the countryside and other smaller cities that join their ethnic group in Mitrovica. More than ten

---

[1] The author acknowledges the symbolic struggle for the institutionalization of the Albanian form "Kosova", but she will use the toponym "Kosovo" throughout the study as the form used in English. Nonetheless, as she claims in the section on methodology, the author is a supporter of Kosovo's independence and of the coexistence of Albanians and Serbs in the independent Kosovo.

journalists from Kosovo, Albania and Serbia, and from both sides of Mitrovica, were asked by the author to provide demographic data, and most of the answers were 'we do not know'. The few data that were collected are all reflected in this part of the paper, but the sources themselves claim there are no certainties regarding statistics about Mitrovica. The website of Mitrovica municipality does not work. Some of the International Organizations working in Kosovo give only sporadic and incomplete data regarding Mitrovica. The statistical data that circulates on different internet sources fluctuates a great deal, showing very large discrepancies. The same discrepancies are present in the accounts of the Mitrovica clashes between the two main ethnic groups, the people hurt or killed, the number of houses or churches burned or destroyed, and the accounts of the whos, hows and whys regarding any events. There are, in fact, no reliable official systematic data on the city in any regards.

The nearby Trepça mines and metallurgical complex once employed 25,000 people; today about 2000 still work there. The mines and factories in the north and south do not communicate, being controlled by different ethnic groups, and are rapidly approaching a complete collapse. The level of unemployment in both parts is very high, but there are no reliable statistics. In Mitrovica, like everywhere in Kosovo, there are still functioning units and offices of UNMIK (the UN Kosovo Mission), of KFOR (the NATO force in Kosovo), of EULEX (European Union Rule of Law), of the new Kosovar government, and offices of the Serbian government. UNMIK is supposedly is on its way out of Kosovo, to be replaced by EULEX. KFOR has drastically reduced its numbers in the recent period. The Kosovar government tries to reach the northern part of the city, but has not yet succeeded. The Serbian government in fact controls northern Mitrovica by providing help to build and maintain its parallel structures that function as an interim government for northern Mitrovica."

Picture 1. Map of Kosovo and Mitrovica

Source: CIA The world factbook – Kosovo.

Introduction

The symbolic Mitrovica, its apparent and hidden socially constructed meanings of division and hostility, the symbolically built environment[2] that effects and shapes its inhabitants' behavior and actions as a permanent, still invisible background, are at the center of this study. Imagining the "other" as the person or group that is innately and essentially different and at the same time valueless, is also tackled in this study. The "othering" is understood as a process in which "*the more powerful group creates and names another group as less worthy typically based on some single aspect of identity*"[3]. This atmosphere of hostility, kept alive and reinforced by Mitrovica's population, is not necessarily the result of a conscious process. The inhabitants of both sides are trapped in a system that hurts them. They function as small unconscious mechanisms of a larger machine that generates ethnic hate. This is old and fertile ground in the Balkans, a continuum of ideologies and social practices that govern above and inside people, which only in the aftermath of communism caused several wars in the ex-Yugoslavia, and that today reinforces patterns of ethnic segregation and otherness in Mitrovica.

The city is held hostage by hate and is a hell for its own citizens. Their life is not only affected by unemployment and other social problems of the Western Balkans in general, but it is also unhealthy due to the level of tension, negative communication with the other, and total lack of order and functionality. The uninterrupted circular transaction of negative symbols, verbal or not, is inherent in every cell of the city and is the only way its two main ethnic groups communicate with each other. Margaret Cavin[4] calls it "*the total effect of the symbolic framing*", and referring to Burke[5], she envisions the perpetuation of symbolic action in culture as a chain in which "*symbolic acts of power may lead to physical action… which may lead to further symbolic acts…*" Consequences of this symbol-action chain has been demonstrated more than once in the fights, riots, and bloodshed by both ethnic communities in Mitrovica.

The main purpose of this study is to describe the intense negative symbolic communication of the two sides of Mitrovica with each other and the world, and to underline the vicious circle effect symbols, even words, could have on the future life of the community and in possible further unrest and loss of lives. Another purpose is to highlight similarities among the two communities, in spite of their perception, as often is the case with hostile ethnic groups that have lived for a long time next to each other, in similar socio-historical environments. Finally, it aims to raise among

---

[2] For the concept of "built environment" and its influence on the community, see V. O'Donnell, *The influence of the built environment*, [in:] C. Jowett, V. O'Donnell, *Readings in propaganda and persuasion*, 2006, pp. 213-225.
[3] F. Jandt (ed.), *Intercultural Communication: a global reader*, Sage Publications, US 2004, p. 203.
[4] M. Cavin, *Evening gowns to burqas: the propaganda of fame*, [in:] G. Jowett, V. O'Donnell, *Readings in propaganda and persuasion*, 2006, p. 266.
[5] K. Burke, *On symbols and society*, University of Chicago Press, Chicago 1989, p 77.

the people of Mitrovica independently of ethnicity, and among people in divided cities in general, a "critical awareness"[6], to make them more capable of recognizing the similarities in their lives and in their interests and more resistant to instrumentalization by institutional propaganda.

Personal narrative: "Mitrovica on a Fall day of 2007"

Getting to know Kosovo has been fascinating, not only because of the media project I am working on, but also because I knew so much and at the same time so little about the Albanians and Serbs of Kosovo. During the decades of harsh communist rule in Albania, little or nothing was ever said about the Kosovar Albanians. We were informed only rarely, and then only vaguely, about the Serbian discrimination against Kosovar Albanians and the controversial position of Tito towards Kosovo. For most of that period the Albanian government seemed to behave as if the over two million Albanians of Kosovo, just on the other side of our northeastern boundary, did not exist. At school we learned that Kosovo was unjustly passed to Serbia in the 20th century after the collapse of the Turkish control of the Balkans, and we learned bits and pieces of early Kosovar wars and rebellions against Serbian control and occupation (especially the resistance of the Kaçak movement between 1918-1922), but little was said about post-WWII or current events in Kosovo. I know now that Serbs of our generation were taught that Kosovo is the cradle of Serbian culture, because their national hero Tsar Lazar, who led the Serbian army was killed in Kosovo in a remote battle (1389) against the invading Turks and because of many important Orthodox monasteries in Kosovo. On the other hand, the Albanian thesis is that Kosovo is the Albanian connection with our ancient ancestors: Albanians lived in Kosovo long before the Serbs started arriving in the Balkans in the 6th and 7th centuries AD. And alongside the Serbian army, there were armies of Albanians, Hungarians and other south Slavs that fought and lost against the Turks in that legendary battle that took place in the field of Kosovo. But Albanians counter that they celebrate the battles they have won, not the ones they have lost. Albanians and Serbs both believe the animosity between them has been continuous since that famous battle. But in fact the persistent organized effort to reinforce nationalistic and chauvinistic feelings among the younger generations is mostly a 20th century phenomenon, with particularly sad outcomes in the region of ex-Yugoslavia, like the genocides against the Muslims in Bosnia and against the Albanians of Kosovo. Unfortunately, modern historiography and media in the Balkans have generally reinforced nationalistic ideologies instead of critically approaching them and contributing to building a peaceful multiethnic region.

In Prishtina, the city I live in right now, I am surrounded by Kosovar Albanians who are surprisingly calm, given the tense diplomatic negotiations between Serbs

---

[6] Fairclough coins this expression in 1992 as he argues that the study of language and power is a question of democracy.

and Kosovar Albanians for Kosovo's status in these last months of 2007. I know there are Serbs still living in the outskirts of Prishtina and elsewhere in Kosovo, but they are scattered in small communities that make up less than 5% of the largely Albanian population of Kosovo. My curiosity about the Serbs of Kosovo and their relations with the Albanian majority led me a few months ago to Mitrovica, a city in northern Kosovo with a purely Albanian side and a purely Serbian one, joined only by an infamous bridge over the river Iber: Mitrovica Bridge. I decided to go to Mitrovica, and personally see how divided this city really was and what the ethnic division felt like.

In the morning I took a taxi to the bus station. As we drove along the main street of Prishtina towards the bus station, we passed the site of destruction from a TNT explosion of two nights before, which left two dead and 11 wounded. The taxi-driver mumbled some insults towards the perpetrators. I asked him who he thought was responsible. He replied, "*I don't know, but it was not Serbs who did it this time. Just some of our criminals with no love for themselves or their country. They should all be sent to America and put in the electric chair. These people are our shame. They are the reason we still are not independent from the Serbs*". I am often amazed with the political passion of the taxi drivers in Prishtina. For that matter, every citizen here seems to be politically well-informed, perhaps by necessity, after living in political turmoil and struggle for at least three decades. They connect everything in life to the drive for independence: their prosperity, their children's schooling, their next vacation, hospitalization of a sick mother, the new passport request; everything is postponed to the day independence comes. Life seems suspended in mid-air, hanging there waiting for the cure of all ills.

The taxi passed three large trash containers with the painted label "Ahtisaari's package", displaying the opinion of one part of the population that sees Ahtisaari's package as giving too many rights to Serbian minorities in Kosovo that make up less than five percent of the population. But I know from experience that most of the Kosovars wish that Ahtisaari's proposals for independence could come true soon. On the walls of the line of stores we pass, there are slogans painted in red: "Jo negociata. Vetevendosje!" ("No negotiations. Self-determination!"). This is also the position of Albin Kurti, one of the most active leaders of the peaceful student movement against Serbian occupation of the schools and universities and against Serbian oppression of Kosovo Albanians in Milosevic's time. Once upon a time Albin Kurti was beaten and continuously threatened by the Serbian police, and now he has been put under house arrest by the temporary Kosovar institutions, for disorderly conduct during recent demonstrations. Once Kurti was considered a champion of civil resistance, but now he is being tried for violent behavior, apparently disappointed and frustrated at the endless negotiations with the Serbs and the endless foreign administration of the state-less Kosovo. He and others in Kosovo, unlike the Kosovar Albanian politicians that represent Kosovo in the talks with the Serbians, have lost their trust in the political process, and want the recognition of the results of a massive referendum of the Kosovo population in September 1991, in which 99% of the

Albanian majority voted for independence. A referendum held today would doubtless yield a similar result. Facing an international community that seems undecided and vacillating in the face of Serb pressure turned bold after Russian support, the Albanian community appears to be tired of the endless talks. Kosovar Albanians have no faith in the good will of the Serbian state, which for so many years has discriminated against them.

When we arrived at the bus station, the bus to Mitrovica was waiting. On the way to Mitrovica, from the windows of the bus I could see on both sides of the road large stretches of uncultivated land, interrupted by huge unfinished buildings: the windows and doors, some times the whole upper floor was unfinished, while the family was settled in a finished part of the house. In the entrance to Mitrovica from the Albanian side, like everywhere else in Kosovo, all the street signs are in both Albanian and Serbo-Croation using the Roman alphabet.

As we entered Mitrovica, the bus driver, who already had realized that I was not from Mitrovica, asked me where I wanted to stop. I replied in standard Albanian, "*Anywhere near the center of the city*". Noticing my accent, he asked whether I was from Tirana. When I admitted that I was, the driver decided that I required special care. He accompanied me off the bus, repeating with a worried expression: "*Here you can go anywhere, just do not cross the bridge; never cross the bridge! Ok? You understand? Never go to the other side!*" I smiled, and said "*I understand. You think the Serbs on the other side are going to hurt me*". "*Hurt you?*" he repeated with an ironical tone of voice. As he climbed back into the driver's seat of the bus he gestured to show me that 'hurt' was the least I could expect. Then as he started the bus he said "*not to the bridge!*" and drove away.

I asked some passers-by where the bridge was, and headed in the direction they gave me, leaving them looking at me with puzzled faces. This large modern bridge that was built to connect the two sides of the city has witnessed pain, violence and hate, and is in fact today the symbol of division of the Serbian part of the city from the Albanian one. A friend in Prishtina had told me that the KFOR (Kosovo Force) international forces that patrol the bridge on Iber river do not let people cross the bridge; she had tried to cross a month ago and was not allowed to pass. As I walked toward the bridge, the Albanian side seemed calm and quiet. I passed the KFOR garrison and the UN Mitrovica headquarters. I encountered only soldiers speaking French and a few Albanians who work in this part of the city. On the wall the slogan "*Jo negociata. Vetevendosje!*" had been partially covered with banners that called for peace: "Every day should be a day for peace". In the middle of the boulevard there was a brand new slogan that called the citizens to save water, in Albanian, English and the Serbian 'Stedi vodu' at the end. I approached the bridge, strangely empty for that sunny day, and saw about ten soldiers and police on both sides of the bridge. At the entrance to the bridge I saw instructions for citizens written in all three languages: "*Gatherings are prohibited. Malicious or provocative behavior will be repressed immediately*". I walked slowly and tried to appear indifferent and relaxed, as if I didn't want to disturb the perfect equilibrium the bridge gave to the people in both sides. I was hoping nobody would disturb me either. I could feel the soldiers watching me closely, but nobody said anything.

At the center of the bridge I saw three women coming toward me from the other side of the bridge. I asked whether they were Albanians. They stopped and said 'yes'. "So, were you in the Serbian part of Mitrovica?" I asked. "What are you talking about? We cannot go there! We were in the Bosnian neighborhood, right across the river. There are a few Albanians and Bosnians living there, but that neighborhood is separated from the Serbian area." I love this solidarity that women can very easily establish anywhere, thousand of miles above the earth or in the public bathrooms of a movie theater. Women talk and connect... perhaps a strategy for survival and against the hardship of life. Could women change Mitrovica? They asked me where I was going. I said just to check the other side of the bridge. "Be careful," the women said. "You are Albanian, from Tirana, right?" – "Right" I said. "Then stay away from the Serbian part!" I nodded, saying thanks, and continued.

Crossing the bridge I could see the Iber river, beautiful, clear and peaceful. There is no sign that in March 2004 this river witnessed violent clashes between Albanians and Serbs after the drowning in it of three Albanian children, allegedly chased away by Serbians (children?) with dogs. After that incident, the bridge became the site of trouble and the symbol of confrontation. The division of the city deepened: old neighbors moved to "*the friendly part where they ethnically belonged*": the Serbs left the southern part and the Albanians left the northern part. The beauty of an ethnically mixed city, once so common in the Balkans, is for now unimaginable for Mitrovica. The bridge is there just to be used by the international forces and the indispensable commercial vehicles. The bridge is there to keep the people apart.

I said hello to two French soldiers standing at the Serbian end of the bridge and crossed into the Serbian part. After crossing the car lanes in the main street next to the bridge, I found myself in the middle of very busy pedestrian traffic of young and old people speaking in Serbo-Croatian. I can understand some, but I cannot speak it. I walked as if I was one of them, but I felt a little worried. All those warnings not to pass to the other side made me feel like a hero of an old Balkan legend, who was not supposed to go to the mountain of the fire-breathing dragon with seven heads who had blocked the water springs. But it was a very beautiful day, and the students' faces shined brightly in the warm sun. The cafés on both sides of the street were full. The walk was becoming almost enjoyable. There was nothing telling me these people could be hostile: the same faces of young girls with naked midriff and black-lined eyes as on the Albanian side, the same long thin leeks in the farmer's market, the same smell of grilling kebabs wrapped with the same type of bread, the same dull beige socialist-era buildings. The only visible difference was that everything was in Serbian, all the signs were in the Cyrillic alphabet. Hundreds of people passed by me, but not even once did I hear Albanian spoken. They didn't know where I was from.

I stopped in a bar called Incognito, and asked in English whether I could have a sandwich and a beer. They said they didn't sell food. The waiter wasn't very friendly, (maybe because I spoke English?), so I continued walking and reached the center of the city. Only here was I reminded that this could be a hostile place for me. In large banners crossing from one side of the square to the other I read a slogan in English: "*In the name of God and justice do not make our holy land a present to Albanians!*" I could easily feel the repulsion toward "Albanians" from whomever "*with law and God*" wrote that banner. Underneath it somebody added "*Long live Serbia*". Next to this slogan there were others thanking Russia and asking for its help. There were some portraits of Vladimir Putin with messages of thanks and praise. I continued to walk, with a less confident pace. At a point where the road narrowed and there were fewer people, I turned back. Walking back I found a relatively quiet point to take pictures of the banners. From every little street that connected to the main road I was on, one could see a very large Orthodox church on the main hill. A church of this size, with its high cupolas and large cross, might make sense in Belgrade, but not in this city. I asked some middle school girls what the church was called. They said they didn't know the name of the church, and they added that it was very new. Next to me I saw the same sign about saving water that I saw in the Albanian part of the city, but here the sign was in only Serbian and English, without Albanian.

I continued to walk on another street, but every time I left the main boulevard where the little shops from both sides created a tunnel for the walker, I came back immediately. Now I could see the bridge again. The cars with UN logo written on them that drove around continuously made me feel safer. Only 50 meters from the bridge, still on the Serbian side, I stopped at the café Dolce Vita and ordered a fresh-squeezed orange juice. I asked whether I could pay in Euros. The waiter, a very polite, good-looking boy, said I could. I had read many stories about alleged massive poisoning of Albanian students in Mitrovica in the spring of 1990. I pushed my paranoia away and waited patiently for my drink, sitting in the beautiful sun next to happy, noisy Serbian youngsters. When I finished my juice I paid and walked towards the bridge. Right at the entrance to the bridge there was a large stone monument with the Orthodox cross, on which there were about 50 or so names of Serbian martyrs. Martyrs of what wars? Religious wars? The recent fights? I had no idea. Now that my short visit was finished, I could ask the police women at the entrance of the bridge. "*What wars and martyrs does this monument commemorate?*" One of the women said to me in Kosovar Albanian: "*Let me ask my Serbian colleague*". The Serbian colleague had no idea. Then I asked her about the name of the large church I saw on the Serbian side, overlooking the Albanian Muslim half of the city. She wasn't sure, but perhaps it was called Cveti Dimitr, she said. I suspect that the church must have been built recently only for symbolic political purposes, since not even the Serbs seemed to know much about it.

I crossed back over the bridge with a sense of relief, which I was a little ashamed to admit to myself. On the bridge two men were talking, not in Albanian. I stopped and took pictures of the river. They finished their conversation, and said "ditën e mirë" ("goodby" in Albanian) to each other. I asked the man walking towards the Albanian side why they spoke in Serbian and then ended their conversation with a 'good bye' in Albanian. He immediately reacted: "*No! It was Bosnian, not Serbian!*" I smiled and asked whether he was a Kosovar Albanian. He said yes. His name was Enver. I asked about the big Serbian church. He said it was built just recently to lay claim to the city of Mitrovica, and that the Serbs illuminate it all night long so that Albanians on the other side of the river can see it. I said goodbye to Enver and continued. I was starved, I needed to find a restaurant, but everything I saw in the street was unappealing. Now I could see that the Serbian side seemed more prosperous and happy than the Albanian side I had returned to. I started talking with a few girls, whom I asked for directions to a restaurant. They said they were seniors from Frang Bardhi high school. I told them I saw many Serbian girls that looked just like them in the other side of the city. They said they would never dare to go in that part of town. They said "*we look different. They can recognize us*". I tried to explain how untrue this was. I was coming just now from the other side. But, no way... One of them told me her house was in fact in the Serbian part of Mitrovica, but now she couldn't even go to see it. Her family was forced to rent an apartment on this side of the river. She looked sad as she told me this. She said she liked living on the other side better.

I stopped to eat something and drink a beer at an outside table of a bar next to the UN headquarters. Everybody around me was speaking French or English. I asked the Kosovar waiter about the name of the Serbian church. He said he didn't know, and that he was sorry I didn't arrive just a few moments before when he still had some of his Serbian clients. I asked whether this was common. The waiter said, "*not very common. Still they can come here, but they don't let us cross*". Perhaps I would have had the same reply if I had asked a Serbian waiter in the other side. But perhaps not. Every time I read press releases from the Serbian high official, I can feel and even linguistically analyze the arrogance of the 'superior'. Every time I talk with simple Kosovar Albanians I read fear and inferiority complexes in their speech. Still today, after seven years of freedom, they have not been able to get rid of the long self-depreciation that seems to have entered their bones.

I left the restaurant, looking for the bus station to go back to Prishtina. I saw a little boy with a gyros sandwich in one hand, leaking oil all over his shirt, as he tried with the other hand to put a toy gun in his belt. I asked him why he carried a gun. He said "*to protect myself*". "*From whom?*" I asked. "*From the enemy*", the boy said. "*And who is the enemy?*" – I asked again. The boy looked at me with indifference, and ignoring my intrusive question, ran away, still eating his gyros sandwich.

On my way back to Prishtina I had a feeling of deep sadness. I had seen the river Iber on a warm, beautiful fall day. But the way the city was artificially cut in two was sad, inhuman. I had a more realistic understanding of the political tension in this divided city. Will Mitrovica become one city again? Will more children and adults from this city be hated, even killed, by 'the enemies from the other side of the river', or will they learn to live together in peace? I know the soldiers on the bridge will have to be there for a long time in order for both parts of the city to be calm. Hasim Thaci promises he will include all minorities in the process for the democratic development of Kosovo. During his campaign for the last elections, he never said how though, and from what I experienced here, I cannot imagine how the integration of northern Mitrovica will occur. On the other hand, the partition of Mitrovica has never been a possibility for the Kosovar leaders, because of the other Kosovar territory north of Mitrovica that cannot be abandoned with Mitrovica. But this does not mean partition will not be reconsidered in the future, especially if there is unrest. The parallel governing structures in the northern part of Mitrovica are strong and have strong political and financial support from Belgrade. Such parallel structures cannot be anything but a source of new antagonism and violence. Certainly the lack of a decision on the status of Kosovo will prolong and even reinforce the current state of affairs: hate, hostility and lack of communication. But will the solution of status, even with sincere goodwill from Thaçi, finally allow the citizens of both sides to use the bridge and walk over to the other side?

November 2007

Methodological notes

The author and Mitrovica

As the narrative shows, in a beautiful day in Fall 2007, I visited Mitrovica[7], strictly[8] and innocently divided by the river Ibar/Ibër between Kosovar Serbs on the northern side, and Kosovar Albanians on the southern side. At the time I was living in Albania and Kosovo, as an IREX advanced research fellow. It was not an extremely calm period, since it was obvious at that time that Kosovo would soon proclaim its independence with or without the consent of Serbia. The fact is that nobody expected Serbia to agree, and nobody cared. This greatly irritated the Serbian population in northern Mitrovica, who have always seen their Albanian co-citizens as lower than them, therefore unacceptable as governors. This circumstance, and the continuous and growing manipulation from Belgrade politics, had made the Serbian population of Mitrovica insecure and fatigued, unable to be calm and reasonable. Still today they see Kosovo's new institutions as symbolizing the unfair legitimization of the hated "other".

The Kosovar Albanian population is also disappointed by poverty, unemployment, lack of economic prospects and especially by a government that does not seem to be able to do much for them with or without the threat from the Serbian military, without or with independence. In the way they construct the Serbian "other",

---

[7] The name of the city in Serbian is 'Kosovska Mitrovica', and in Albanian is 'Mitrovica e Kosovës'.
[8] Although there is a small neighborhood in the very southern part of the northern division of the city, called The Boshnjak neighborhood, where there are still some Albanian and Boshnjak families living. In the first months of 2009, there was unrest and small incidents of burning and destruction in this part.

they follow a completely different path based on different ideologies and socio-historical circumstances. After the war of 1999, and especially after the independence of Kosovo in February 2008 and its recognition by 59 countries (as of May 3, 2009), Albanians are the passive group, more satisfied than the Serbs with the developments of the last decade, although little has changed in their lives besides the fact that they are no longer directly oppressed by Serbs; while the Serbian community is the active group fighting for change, that perceives itself as the group that has lost ground and power after the war and also as the group which has on its shoulders the all-Serbian symbolic resistance to the new Kosovar state. But, in spite of their differences, both groups feed and support the same system of "ethnic apartheid". Without their contribution, such a divisive system would not exist.

The period of my visit in Mitrovica was not politically turbulent, compared to other times, especially those of March 2004, when violent clashes exploded on both sides of the Mitrovica bridge and angry crowds attacked each other, leaving a total of 19 dead from both parts. The fact is that there is no real peace in Mitrovica: there is only pause and preparation for the next turbulence and explosion of hate. Certainly it is hard to deny past continuous and systematic massacres, often with an institutional agenda, against the Albanians of Kosovo. But this is not a paper about finding "the guilty community", or who started it all. It is about pointing out that the same ideologies that have hurt both communities in the past, are still active and dominating in Mitrovica, as shown in its symbolic landscape. The symbolic abuse analyzed, verbal or not, occurs in all Mitrovica, and is perpetrated by both communities in passive or active ways. But on the Kosovar side, as shown in the encounters with people, it is still nurtured by sentiments of fear and inferiority, while on the Serbian side, it appears arrogant, characterized by denial and mythical entitlement. In spite of the motives, both positions generate hate for the other and sustain the same primitive status quo of the region.

In a random visit, outsiders might not realize the explosive nature of the dynamics of group perceptions and group relations of this city, but the people from both sides of the bridge know and feel this very well. In my personal narrative of one day in Mitrovica, I try to give a concrete sense of this tension that the place and the people of these two halves of one city emanate, feeding their own long misery. An analysis of the symbolic discursive sites of the city and the way the image of the "other" is built by both sides, follows. Besides the analytical description of the symbolic landscape in both parts of the city, I discursively interpret the specific interactions with community members.

The author's "situated knowledges"[9]

In the first paragraph of the personal narrative I fully and directly introduce myself, as an Albanian from Albania with a certain background, who is eager to learn about Kosovo, and who supports the Kosovar Albanians' dream for independence from

---

[9] D. Haraway, *Situated knowledges: The science question in feminism and the privilege of partial perspective*, "Feminist Studies" 14, no. 3 (Fall 1988), pp. 577-599.

Serbia. My position, although that of an outsider in Kosovo and Mitrovica, is vulnerable to bias in favor of Kosovar Albanians, the group with whom I share my ethnic roots. But isn't the written text *"always situated in culture"* and *"shaped implicitly and explicitly by the social and cultural background, class and gender of the author"*[10]? This paper is in fact my double narrative, a reportage and an academic paper. In these fluidly connected expressions, my goal is to first represent what I see and then interpret what I represent, with open eyes, open mind and with the purpose of discovering and offering ways to bring this city together. I have also been implicitly and explicitly *"self-reflective*[11]*"* during my work, and have tried to control any tendency for selective representation of truth. But the narrative expresses a worldview, and the analysis itself also incorporates and enacts a worldview – my worldview. The best an author can do is to openly and fully express her position. And I try to do it in both the personal narrative and the discursive critical analysis of the narrative. It is for this reason that any bias embodied in the worldview of the author in the case of critical studies, is much less manipulative. It is appropriate here to quote the linguist Skutnabb-Kangas[12] who claims *"the only kind of objectivity one can aim for is to attempt to describe as openly as possible one's own position and the criteria one has adopted, instead of appearing to be neutral..."* As Fisher[13] maintains referring to narrative criticism, it is a *"reliable, trustworthy, and desirable guide to belief and action"*.

Furthermore, when reliable data and any sort of official statistics are scarce and, even when they exist, are political products, often serving simply as a means for black propaganda rather than a representation of reality (as it happens in Mitrovica), the bringing of immediate and personal experiences and the self-reflection in the form of the critical qualitative research, are not only indications of a *"science in flux"*[14], but also the best way to account for the human conditions and for the social practices that occur in places like Mitrovica. The narrative criticism in this study helps *"to view and understand the world being represented, the argument being made and the perspective it presents"*[15]. On the other hand, the method of critical discourse analysis[16], also used in this study, connects the story and the events with the structure of

---

[10] Ibidem.
[11] S. Holman Jones, *The way we were, are and might be: Torchsinging as autoethnography*, [in:] Y. Lincoln, N. Denzin (eds), *Turning points in qualitative research: tying knots in a handkerchief*, Alta Mira Press 2003, pp. 105-119. He sees the self-reflection of the author as a means towards the legitimization of personal narratives.
[12] T. Skutnabb-Kangas, *Bilingualism or not: the education of minorities*, "Multilingual Matters" 1981, p. xiii.
[13] W. R. Fisher, *Human communication as narration: toward a philosophy of reason, value and action*, University of South Carolina Press, Columbia 1987, p. 75.
[14] Y. Lincoln, N. Denzin (eds), *Turning points in qualitative research: tying knots in a handkerchief*, Alta Mira Press 2003, p. 2.
[15] S. K. Foss, *Rhetorical criticism: exploration and practice* (3rd edition), Waveland, Long Grove IL 2004, p. 400.
[16] N. Fairclough, *Introduction*, [in:] N. Fairclough (ed.), *Critical Language Awareness*, Longman, London 1992; N. Fairclough, *Critical Discourse Analysis: The critical study of language*, Longman, London 1995.

power relations in society and with particular institutional interests. Last, the forms of critical inquiry keep an open door between science and social practices and change. They all are engaged forms of doing science, and foresee a practical use of the research for a better future of the society.

The symbolic landscape of the city: division and hate

Mitrovica itself is the symbol of ethnic division in Kosovo. Every part of it is positioned in relation to the discourse of division and hostility, and every event is seen with that hostility as a background. It is an unusual city, because the usual objects exist not to serve their common purpose, but another symbolic purpose. Mitrovica is empty of normal objects that one finds in a normal city, and it is a frightening city for this. Because of the ubiquitous presence of an exaggerated ethnic symbolism, the everyday life of the common citizens is totally controlled by political rhetoric. In fact Mitrovica is a rhetorical city whose main function is propaganda, rather than a real, populated center with its normal functions in service of citizens. And the northern part is much more inclined to active rhetoric than the southern part, which recently participates in this rhetorical war in a passive way. Its industrial and prosperous past and its life as one unit are weakened and almost dead, not just because the mine industry was abandoned, but also because, like everything else, it is shaded by the strong and institutionally supported rhetoric of division.

For the Kosovar government and international institutions Mitrovica has become a nightmare, with which they deal very carefully as with a wild beast, trying to appease it by using euphemistic references. Their help generally is intended to push the problem towards the future, when things could get better somehow. In the days before and after February 17, 2009, the first anniversary of the independence of Kosovo, and in March 17, the 5th anniversary of the Mitrovica riots, all institutional voices inside Kosovo loudly claimed that *"Mitrovica is calm"*, *"there will be no unrest"* and *"the situation is under control"*. The chairman of Mitrovica Commune (and previous prime minister of Kosovo), Bajram Rexhepi, claimed for the Albanian TV network, ALSAT, that *"the Serbs of Mitrovica have started to understand the new reality of Kosovo. Only Serbs that are sent from outside cause trouble in the city now"*[17]. The head of EULEX Yves De Kermabon also claimed that the troubles in Mitrovica in January 2009 were *"not linked to political tensions"*[18]. Certainly in Mitrovica, every word and step of citizens or outsiders can turn into a ticking bomb, as shown by the seemingly casual, yet continuous agitation during all this first part of 2009; even if originally it was not, it can always become political. There is no rule of law and order in northern Mitrovica, there is no cooperation with or control of any Kosovar institutions or jurisdiction. Even EULEX, the new European Mission in Kosovo which intended to replace the UN mission there, has not been successful in this part of the new country

---

[17] ALSAT TV News, February 21, 2009.
[18] BIRN News, January, 2009.

yet. The restoration after one year of two customs points near the city, and the fact that six Serbians joined the Kosovo Force, the new unit intended to become the army of Kosovo with 2500 active members and 800 reservists, was hailed as a great success by these desperate institutions and pathetically overplayed by the media[19]. For the government and most political players in Belgrade, Mitrovica has been a site of political manipulation (electoral, postelectoral and preelectoral), disguised as interest and concern for its citizens. After all, this kind of propaganda is no news in the area that once was Yugoslavia. *"Through the control of all radio, television and newspapers, the competing governments have blatantly propagandized to exhort their populations to violence and nationalistic fervor"*[20] claim two scholars of propaganda in their study on propaganda and ethnic cleansing in the post-socialist Yugoslavia. The political and financial support of Belgrade for Mitrovica, and the parallel system built and supported by Belgrade, intend to keep alive the dysfunctional state and the image of unrest in Mitrovica, and to use it as a demonstration of the local Kosovar state-building inability, and as a failure in general of the new Kosovar institutions. Mitrovica is the only significant active base to destabilize Kosovo, and since this is the main goal of the Serbian government after the independence of Kosovo (even more than their political wish for integration in the EU), they will continue to manipulate Mitrovica and support hostile behavior and militant groups in all ways possible. Therefore, among Serbs in the Balkans Mitrovica is increasingly seen as the symbol of resistance, of not giving up a Kosovo that is part of Serbia. In this tense and hostile background, Mitrovica's denaturalization of common objects occurs: they start serving exclusively as symbols of division, hate and otherness. Their real function is lost as if it never existed, and nobody notices it. Everybody is under the spell of the new negative symbols.

While analyzing the symbolic sites of the city, the right thing to do is to start from the symbolic heart of the city: the bridge (picture 2). A very special bridge, one that is not there to connect people with each other, but to separate them, therefore an anti-bridge, the infamous Mitrovica bridge. It is the chief symbol of division and hostility. And division and hostility are the master narrative that determines all the other smaller and subordinate narratives in this city. The bridge tells the population of Mitrovica a story of hate and fighting with each other, especially as an association with the riots of 2004. It tells the story of how bad "the other" is. The modern steel and concrete bridge on the Ibër, controlled on both sides by soldiers and police, and often visited by vehicles with authority signs on them, bears the institutional mark of power, authority, obligation, punishment. Its narrative enacts a powerful discourse that naturally will cause human resistance. The warning at both entrances of the bridge clearly uses international authority to threaten that "malicious or provocative" citizens would be "repressed immediately". In fact it uses an impersonal form and is directed not to the people but to the "behaviors", units without agency.

---

[19] BIRN, Belgrade, February 11, 2009.
[20] C. Jowett, V. O'Donnell (eds), *Readings in propaganda and persuasion*, Sage, Thousand Oaks 2006, p. 260.

Picture 2. The entrance to Mitrovica bridge

Source: Author's photograph

But it obviously reflects to the citizens of both sides how small and ugly they look from the authority's perspective, and how dangerous they could be if not for the repressive power of this symbolic bridge. It implies that if there is peace, it is because of this bridge, hence the institutions that make it function as an "anti-bridge". So the underlying message is: obey the bridge of division, venerate it! It is your only salvation. Without it there is chaos and death. And the citizens reinforce the same message, which needless to say, is a discourse not generated by the citizens and not in their interest. The soldiers on both sides of the bridge, are always there, armed and ready. There at the bridge, the "master narrative" is loudly and dramatically sung, like in the old folklore of Serbians and Albanians, in "guslas" or 'lahutas' high tone crying background, and its Circean sound has thrown a spell over the communities on both sides of the river. All the "sub-narratives"[21] told by other symbolic sites in the city serve and buttress this spell. Hence, the rest of the city's symbolic

---

[21] For more on "narrative", see S. K. Foss, *Rhetorical criticism: exploration…, op. cit.*, and for an application of the notions "master-narrative" and "sub-narrative", see A. Di Lellio, *The narrative of genocide as cosmopolitan memory and its humanitarian intervention*, Paper presented in the workshop on "Collective memory and collective knowledge in a global age", June 17-18, 2007, London.

images and discourses echo the dark mood set by the principal symbolic metaphor of the bridge. In Fairclough's[22] terms, the bridge, as a discursive site of division and hatred, sets the dominant ideological discursive formation (IDF[23]) which has institutional power and expresses the interests of dominant institutions. It is the ideology capable of 'naturalizing itself' among people, as common sense, as the only way of being and doing, which has always existed and will last forever.

Picture 3. Saint Demeter Church

Source: Author's photograph

The Church of Saint Demeter (picture 3), only recently built, is one of those sites that endorse the main IDF. It stands on the most dominant part of the hill of northern Mitrovica, but is seen well only from the other side of the river, since the apartment buildings of Mitrovica block its view. In fact, this important building, a recent investment by Belgrade, is not principally meant for the Serbian population. All the Serbian passersby I asked had no idea what its name was, and had never visited it.

---

[22] N. Fairclough, *Introduction ...*, op. cit., p. 27.
[23] The concept of dominant IDF of Fairclough is very similar to the concept of "habitus" of Bourdieu (P. Bourdieu, *Language and symbolic power*, Policy Press, Cambridge 1991), namely internalised group norms and dispositions that are the basis (generators and regulators) of our social practices/activities, perceptions and representations.

They all knew it was directed as a symbol to the Albanian side of the city. I finally learned its name from the Albanian journalist Andoni[24] who recently had conducted some interviews with Serbian people from the northern Mitrovica and who visited the church. The Albanian people I asked told me that even when the Serbian Mitrovica is in a black-out moment, *they* make sure the church is lit very well, so that *we*, in the other side of the river, can see how strong and present *they* are in Mitrovica, and that *they* have the control, and not *us*.

The discourse built around the church metaphor reinforces the dominant IDF by attempting to provide the cause of hostility and division in this city. Its narrative is shaped around the "why": why do the two parts of Mitrovica have to be enemies of each other? The meaning this discourse aims to foster is that there is an irreconcilable difference between the two ethnicities: one is Orthodox Christian and the other is Muslim. But this is only the rhetorical claim, symbolically supported by the unused orthodox church in the top of the northern hill, and the empty mosques in the southern part. Growing up in the Balkans, one knows that religion is not what makes people hate and fight each other. The religiosity of the population is in fact far from any sort of fundamentalism, and it is unusual to encounter sincerely fanatic religious groups. This is even more so after the ideological traces left by decades of the communist regime, undergone by both populations. The Orthodox church in northern Mitrovica is a political symbol, disguised as a religious one. The mosques in the Albanian side are forgotten in darkness and silence as historical reliques of a long ago occupation. Both symbols' role is to emphasize the differences between the communities.

The pompous metaphor of the Orthodox Church, on the other hand, also attempts to recall the historical narrative that in the form of myth and history is the classical basis of Serbian nationalism of the last century: their "*centuries of martyrdom in defense of the orthodox faith*" from its enemies, Turks, Albanians, or whatever. The negative role of myth and "*imagined past*" is in fact one significant factor in the formation of an abusive Serbian national consciousness as maintained by Malcolm[25] and Mertus[26]. This symbolic mythical[27] sense of duty and sacrifice for an ideal cause that transcends time, and life and death, gives to the Mitrovica Serbs today a feeling of empowerment and entitlement towards all Kosovo and certainly Mitrovica. Again, the history told by Malcolm[28] about where and when Sava's autocephalous Serbian Church had its cradle (trying to bring evidence that in fact it was not Kosovo), is completely worthless. It is the symbols that reign in Mitrovica! "*For it's*

---

[24] Who visited Mitrovica on February 14-16, 2009 and reported on it in the socio-political Albanian magazine Mapo.
[25] N. Malcolm, *Kosovo, a short history*, Harper Perennial, NY 1999, p. 1.
[26] J. Mertus, *Kosovo: How Myths and Truths Started a War*, University of California Press, Berkeley CA 1999, p. 19.
[27] These factors are not unusual in other cultures either, especially in the Balkans, but both authors notice among Serbs a larger number of nationalistic myths and imagined truths that are still strong and active today.
[28] N. Malcolm, *Kosovo, a short...*, *op. cit.*, p. 44.

clear enough that under certain conditions men respond as powerfully to fictions as they do to realities, and that in many cases they help to create the very fictions to which they respond"[29]. As for the Albanians in southern Mitrovica, they relax in disappointment and occasionally build hopes in the shade of mosques that they rarely notice, without jobs or any clear future, ironical about the Serbs' surreal determination to still live in the Middle Ages, expecting the International forces to defend for them what they are sure they deserve, in the same way they hoped Turks, Austrians, the Catholic church, Germans, Tito, Hoxha etc. would protect them from the Serbs.

The social reality here is made of these ideological pieces of a larger mosaic of power. Each tiny piece of the mosaic is indexed under the pressure of the dominant IDF. The UNMIK cars that run with the UN symbols around both parts of the city remind people of their hostility and the possible punishment. The grandiose monument of Serbian martyrs just next to the bridge in the Serbian side, and that of Avni Haradinaj (a martyr of the Albanians who died protecting them from the Serbs in one of Mitrovica's uneasy moments) in the Boshnjak neighborhood, the still destroyed church along the road to Prishtina, the destroyed houses of Albanians who once used to live in the northern part, are semantically redefined to claim rhetorical hostility and desire for vindication[30].

As Bourdieu[31] maintains, "*Language is a locus of struggle for power.*" The linguistic landscape on both sides of the city demonstrates this struggle in every bit of it. Linguistically the institutions in southern Mitrovica express a superficial multi-ethnic harmony through the use of three languages in the entrance of every office: English, Albanian and Serbo-Croatian[32], although this last one, in Latin and not Cyrillic script. No doubt the order of the languages and the use of Latin script demonstrates order of power and of discourses shaped by each of the languages used. In the northern part of the city there is only Serbo-Croatian, almost always in the Cyrillic alphabet. Nowhere, not even once, in the northern linguistic landscape is Albanian used or seen. Interesting enough, the same advertisement displayed in the streets of southern Mitrovica in three languages (Save water!) in the northern part appears in only two: Serbo-Croatian and English. But the formal use of Serbo-Croatian by the Albanian side is simply an institutional concession the Albanians have made to the international community through whom they see the path to independence. At the level of the common citizen, the two sides have no respect for each other, nor tolerance, nor willingness to cooperate. In fact the private offices and businesses in the southern part do not carry any signs in 'the language of the Serbs'. They obviously are not expected as clients.

---

[29] W. Lippmann, *Public opinion*, Biblio Bazaar Publication 2007 (1922), p. 23.
[30] The last two facts are taken from the report of Andoni, B. Andoni, *Në Mitrovicë koha ka ngrirë* (Time is frozen in Mitrovica), "Revista Mapo", February, 2009 (http://revistamapo.com/index.php?faqe=detail&kat=Reportazh&id=1639).
[31] P. Bourdieu, *Language and symbolic...*, op. cit., p. 60.
[32] I use this term instead of just Serbian, because from a linguistic perspective, the division has no meaning. It is another political empty choice which I resist.

The frequent linguistic reference to the bridge as I was traveling towards it, is another demonstration of language as a site of social struggle. Every instance of use of the word enacted and enforced the same discourse of hostility explained above. Indeed, notice how many times the bridge appears in the personal narrative, as the point in which good becomes bad, hospitable turns to hostile, friends are replaced by enemies. *"Do not cross the bridge! Do not go to the other side! Stay away from the bridge!"* The linguistic expressions were indexically marked for fear, danger and hostility, and bore an extreme dramatical accent, characteristic in the legends of the region. But in an environment of aggressive negative rhetoric and hostility discourses, *"one's rhetoric no longer only indexes reality; It shapes it*[33]*"*. It becomes pure, old-fashioned direct propaganda, and *"The circumstance no longer controls rhetorical expression; rather the rhetorical expression dictates the meaning of circumstance*[34]*"*. This is exactly the case of Mitrovica.

But how true is all this difference and to what extent is the hostility justified by difference? As shown in the personal narrative, the differences and hostility are rhetorically built. But does the real state of affairs matter? No! Now it is the rhetoric that has the power. As shown in the personal narrative, although they use different languages, Serbs and Albanians on both sides of Mitrovica are people with very similar everyday lives, life styles, environments, tastes, (even looks) and historical background. They even share the conviction that they are extremely different from each other, and that they hate each other. Both populations have a non-fanatic religious behavior which is very loose among people under 50. In fact, it was hard to find a person in northern Mitrovica who knew the name of the most obvious church of the town, just as it was hard in the south to find a woman under 60 that had a shawl on her head.

As the rhetorical becomes the actual, Walter Lippman's words come to mind: People respond to the pseudo-environment and not to the real environment; they deal with mental images of events and not with events themselves. It is the pseudo-environment that stimulates their behavior[35]. In the case of Mitrovica, this is the environment created by both ethnic groups, an environment of which they have become slaves. The same point is made by O'Donnell[36] who emphasizes the difference between *"perceived environment"* and *"real environment"*. She emphasizes that environment communicates meanings and influences human behavior. But why would intelligent and educated citizens fall into the trap of a symbolic environment that hurt them, and uncritically take *"the pictures in our heads"* as totems that lead them to hate the other? As Lippmann himself answers, first there is no chance to be in touch with reality in a world fully controlled by media and strong institutions, and *"the fiction is taken for truth because the fiction is badly needed"*[37].

---

[33] W. Starosta, *On Intercultural rhetoric*, [in:] F. Jandt (ed.), *Intercultural Communication: a global reader*, Sage Publications, US 2004, p. 312.
[34] *Ibidem.*
[35] W. Lippmann, *Public opinion...*, op. cit., p. 23.
[36] *Readings in propaganda...*, op. cit., p. 214.
[37] *Readings in propaganda...*, op. cit., p. 26.

Constructing "the other" in Mitrovica

A strong discourse of otherness that thrives in both communities is the consequence of the dominant IDF fed by the symbolic meanings, environment and by the narratives they provide for Mitrovica's people. *"Do not cross the bridge! Never cross the bridge!"* – Certainly. *The other* is on *the other* side, sharpening his teeth. Long segregation is the path to hate; *"it makes both groups a target of phobias of all kinds"*[38] that grow from the lack of direct communication in a climate of negative symbolism. All the verbal references attempt to emphasize the distance between "us" and "them"; all the anaphors used by Kosovar Albanians during my trip, their intonation, gestures, facial expressions underlined how different and unimaginably bad the other was. Even the river Ibar/Ibër, an innocent victim traditionally known to bring prosperity and peace to people, as much as the bridge on it, a lifelong symbol of connection and communication, are both trapped by new discourses of hate, and semantically re-framed to become symbols of otherness.

The personal narrative with the experiences and interactions I had that day on both sides of the river, clearly brought to my eyes the feeling of fear and inferiority of the Albanians and the sense of arrogance and superiority of the Serbs, different expressions of the same discourse of otherness, both containing hate and lack of tolerance, and both probably interchangeable, depending on the political situation of each group. The eyes and expression of the driver, the young Albanian girls from the Frang Bardhi high school, the waiter in the bar, the ladies crossing the bridge all expressed a strong sense of fear and of being less than "the other". The slogans in the middle of Serbian Mitrovica cry loudly of superiority and entitlement. Mertus claims that for Albanians in Kosovo the feeling of inferiority and fear rests on decades of institutionally and media-supported Serbian campaigns of "dehumanization" of the Albanians (derogatorily called 'shiftars'),[39] racism and abuse of all forms. That ideology, although non-aggressive for now, is still there, but it has mutated[40]. On the other side, the Serbian slogan in English in the middle of Mitrovica square (picture 4) endorses an overt, direct, total and maximal expression of otherness: "In the name of God and Justice do not make our holy land a present to Albanians!" There are two sides clearly delineated in this message: "Us" and "them". "Us" includes Serbs and the international community (that speaks English), the ones who respect the correct "God and Justice". This category, so inclusive and still so exclusive towards "the Albanians", is purposefully large and holy. It is not because of its land, mines, water etc, that the Serbs want Kosovo, and they do

---

[38] Carlbom, A. 2003: 25, *The imagined versus the real other: multiculturalism and the representation of Muslims in Sweden.*

[39] J. Mertus, *The role of racism as a cause or factor in wars and civil conflict: Rwanda and Kosovo*, International Council on Human Rights Policy Consultation on Racism and Human Rights, Geneva 1999.

[40] Mertus' contribution in 1999 meeting (December 3-4) of the "International Council of Human Rights Policy".

not even want it because there is a small population of Serbs living there. The slogan claims a completely idealistic reason: Serbs claim Kosovo because it is "their holy land." It could not belong to the un-holy Albanians. Who would not sympathize with such a rhetorical statement!?

"The other" in the slogans is not described. It is self-sufficiently bad: "the Albanians". It stands for anything opposing the first part of the slogan: "*the unGodly, unjust, whose land, this holy one, is not*". This is a perfect cliché that replicates Said's analysis about the tendency in Western tradition to represent the Muslims as dangerous to the West, and no specifics matter. This ideological tendency is enacted in the slogan, identifying the Serbs with the West and also as victims of Muslim Albanians who want to steal their holy land. Said is also borne out by this case study in maintaining that this kind of representation is embedded in a larger political field, in this case a political field that centers in Belgrade and that is influenced by other international developments of the moment. It is interesting that to the slogan is added in Serbian: "*Help us Russia*", and "*Help us Putin*". To this side of the international community the slogan chooses to communicate in a Slavic language activating a higher level of identification in the power stratification of "us", that of Slavic brotherhood.

Picture 4. Slogans in a square in northern Mitrovica

Author's photograph

The dramatic narrative of the slogan perfectly exemplifies Burke's[41] map of "*polar symbolic constructs*" with three principal positions: "*the villain victimizer*" (in this case the Albanians), "*the victim*" (the Serbs) and the "*heroic avenger*" (in this case the Russians). The use of such simplified constructs according to Burke significantly limits the participants' perceptions and critical views, and makes the statement ideal for propagandistic purposes. However, a parallel construct is recently used frequently by Kosovar Albanians, where the role of the hero goes to the United States and the NATO forces, as the Albanians and Serbs exchange places. If we analyze the content of the slogans, the idea that the solution comes from a powerful force from outside is equally strong in both ethnic groups, and encourages the lack of agency in taking their fates in their own hands. It is also an open door for institutional manipulation of both groups.

It is relevant that the slogan above is a structural calque filled with new content, and then recontextualized, of the slogan the Serbs used in 1989 in the political love affair between the Serbian population "*victimized by the Albanians*" and the then-new hero-defender Slobodan Milosevic. That slogan said: "*Slobodan! Kosovo is ours! Don't let Enver Hoxha[42] take it away!*"[43]. It is the same mold that produces otherness and hate, just filled with new characters. Kosovar Albanians even here are the enemy that is not worth even mentioning, another sign of the deep contempt the Serbs show towards "the pariah of their land". The repetition of the same model in two completely different moments, both of which are characterized by a fiery use of division symbols, shows that although the concrete political and social context play a role in the representation of the Other (Said. E. 1993), the ideologies that shape the traditional and perpetual "other" are above such concrete events and make use of them to further reinforce themselves. Similar situations of fear and vindication, institutionally perpetrated, activate the same ideological mold, or, in Fairclough's words, the same institutionally generated dominant IDF. The Albanian side is not trying to resist or to break these symbolic expression of otherness created by the Serbian side. They are thankful consumers of these ideologies, which they themselves keep alive and reinforce. No side makes an effort to break the negative cycle that has enslaved and paralyzed the whole community.

Both sides have traditionally attempted to convince themselves and the outside world that they are the victims of the situation. For the sake of truth I need to say, the Albanians of Kosovo have frequently been the real victims of Serbian state terror, popular contempt and racist campaigns, and this is so not just in the recent decades[44]. But they also have learned with time that playing the victim could bring more attention. However the victimization of Serbs has been discussed as a stable

---

[41] K. Burke, *On symbols and...*, op. cit., p. 42.
[42] The communist leader of Albania for 45 years.
[43] J. Mertus, *The role of...*, op. cit., p. 178.
[44] N. Malcolm, *Kosovo, a short...*, op. cit.; J. Mertus, *The role of...*, op. cit.; H. Clark, *Civil Resistance in Kosovo*, Pluto Press, London 2000; R. Kaplan, *Balkan Ghosts: a journey through history*, Saint Martin's Press, NY 1993.

feature of cultural politics in Serbia. Mertus[45] sees the nationalistic myth of a "Greater Serbia", the strongest in the region, as parallel with the growing feeling of victimization or being sacrificed, developed among Serbs. In both slogans above there is implied association of Serbs with Christ's sacrifices. Di Lellio,[46] discussing the use of "cosmopolitan memory", underlines the role of Draskovic, Serbian poet and politician, in establishing an identity of shared suffering for Serbs and Jews. And the Serbian journalist Julijana Mojsilovic[47] notices the same institutional trend of victimization, in her recent article "*Serbs recall NATO raids in mood of self-pity*".

The problem with the discourse of victimization is in its consequences: it fosters otherness and division in a very prolific way, because it uses deep emotional tendencies of self-pity and of blaming "the other" as a bait to promote hostility. It creates new enemies, and "*easy templates of new conflicts simplifying them into struggles between good and evil*"[48]. Mertus claims that it was not difficult to move from a particular case to the propagandistic argument that Serbs everywhere are oppressed, and the need to do something about their survival as an ethnic group. The feeling of being sacrificed "*can be all at once turned into hatred against everybody else*"[49]. Serbian and Kosovar relations demonstrate this over and over again: the 1985 Martinovic case, the Serb supposedly "impaled with a bottle" by Albanians; the case of the two Albanian children from Çabër that drowned in the river Iber, allegedly pursued by angry Serbs, which started the Mitrovica clashes of March 2004. These events were never verified, although there was hysterical use of the "facts" by the media and the politicians and sustained use and replication of the ideologies behind them among the people.

The Albanians and the Serbs of Mitrovica live two completely different realities, although as shown in the personal narrative, for the eye of the outsider both groups and both realities might look alike. The differences are carefully and consistently built by the whole society and all the actors have been assigned roles of extreme characters, good or bad, as in an ancient tragedy. As Burke[50] says, settings characterized by "*extreme symbolic constructs and demonizing the other, bring critical blindness*", and perpetuate otherness. While the communities live in a state of denial[51], there is little hope for change, especially since the state institutions are doing very little to break the cycle of "otherness": the Kosovar government not being active and creative in finding solutions for the interruption of this hostility chain, and the Serbian government trying with all its means to make Mitrovica an explosive zone that

---

[45] J. Mertus, *The role of…*, op. cit.
[46] A. Di Lellio, *The narrative of…*, op. cit.
[47] J. Mojsilovic, *Serbs recall NATO raids in mood of self-pity*, published in Balkan Investigative Reporting Network, March 25, 2009, http://balkaninsight.com/en/main/analysis/17686/.
[48] A. Di Lellio, *The narrative of…*, op. cit., p. 5.
[49] J. Mertus, *Kosovo: How Myths and…*, op. cit., p. 113.
[50] K. Burke, *On symbols and…*, op. cit., p. 42.
[51] For more on the meaning and expressions of the state of denial as an in-group social behavior, see T. A. Van Dijk, *Discourse and the denial of racism*, "Discourse and Society", no. 3 (1), 1992.

shows the failure of the new state of Kosovo and returns Kosovo to Serbia. The painful efforts of EULEX demonstrated in its positioning against violence during the events of reconstruction of Albanian houses once destroyed by the Serbs in the neighborhood "Kroi i Vitakut" (or Brdzani) in May 2009,[52] show once more that the solutions for a sustainable long-lasting peace should come from the two communities of the city themselves, and cannot be forced from outside. Understanding and recognizing how "otherness" is built in everyday life is a good beginning towards resistance to the manipulation, and towards distancing the self from the language of hatred. Therefore it is a first step towards tolerance and peaceful communication.

---

[52] *Voice of Amerika*, Albanian News, May 3, 2009, and ALSAT News, the whole first week of May, 2009.

Ceuta and Melilla
Divisions in the Shadow of a Border Fence
Michał Łuszczuk

Ceuta and Melilla, two Spanish cities on the Moroccan coast are in geopolitical terms the only European (costal) enclaves on the African continent. At the same time they are the only representatives of the European Union on the North African coast. This geographical position has a lot of consequence for both cities, which are quite well recognized in the world for several reasons. Primarily, they have, for many years, been objects of the continuous dispute of matters concerning sovereignty between Spain and Morocco[1]. Recently, Ceuta and Melilla have been well covered in the media due to accidents at the border fences not only separating them from the Moroccan surrounding areas, but primarily protecting Europe from the emigrant flow from the African continent. In Gold's words: *"as the only territories which provide a land border between the EU and Africa, the Spanish enclaves of Ceuta and Melilla act as magnets for would-be illegal migrants to continental Europe from all over the African continent"*[2].

At the same time both cities, perceived for many years as a major international 'gateway' to Europe for migrants, face new-old 'internal' divisions. As Enríquez points out, *"a new ethnic conflict is emerging, as the Muslim population of Moroccan origin gains demographic weight. The conflict manifests itself in terms of social segregation and demands for cultural rights and positive discrimination, but this takes place within the framework of the anxiety of the population of Spanish origin regarding the future of Spanish sovereignty over the towns"*[3]. Study of this double challenge is subject of the following considerations, in which notions of *divided city* and *frontier city* are used as theoretical foundations of the analysis.

---

[1] Spain relations with Morocco, its southern neighbour have always been tough. The agenda has been dominated by highly fragile issues such as drug trafficking, illegal immigration, fishing rights, the status of the Western Sahara, Islamic fundamentalism, human rights and the last but no t least dispute over the cities. See: R. Gillespie, *Spain and Morocco: Towards a Reform Agenda?*, Paper presented at the FRIDE Workshop on 'Barcelona + 10' and the European Neighborhood Policy, Madrid, 14-16th January 2005, Fundación para las Relaciones Internacionales y el Diálogo Exterior (FRIDE), www.fride.org, 20.02.2009.
[2] P. Gold, *Europe or Africa? A contemporary study of the Spanish North-African enclaves of Ceuta and Melilla*, Liverpool University Press, Liverpool 2000, p. 120.
[3] C. G. Enríquez, *Ceuta and Melilla: Clouds over the African Spanish Towns. Muslim Minorities, Spaniards' Fears and Morocco–Spain Mutual Dependence*, "The Journal of North African Studies", vol. 12, no. 2, 2007, p. 219.

Location, history and legal status of Ceuta and Melilla

Ceuta and Melilla are very often studied as one due to the fact that they share similar situations. They are related by their history (both have been the residuals of the former Spanish colonial system), their identity, their economic dependence and political status to Spain, but separated form the mainland by the Mediterranean Sea. However, at the same time these two Spanish exclaves differ in major ways. This difference has increased in the last few years by the considerable influx of Muslims into Melilla and subsequent "africanisation" of the city[4]. Additionally, Ceuta seems to have greater economic importance for Spain than does Melilla, which is often described at best as a secondary transit hub. Though these factors increase the possibility that the cities will develop along separate paths in the future, they are, as Nice argues, *"inseparable in the Spanish mind"* and *"for this reason the enclaves may have a more similar development after all"*[5].

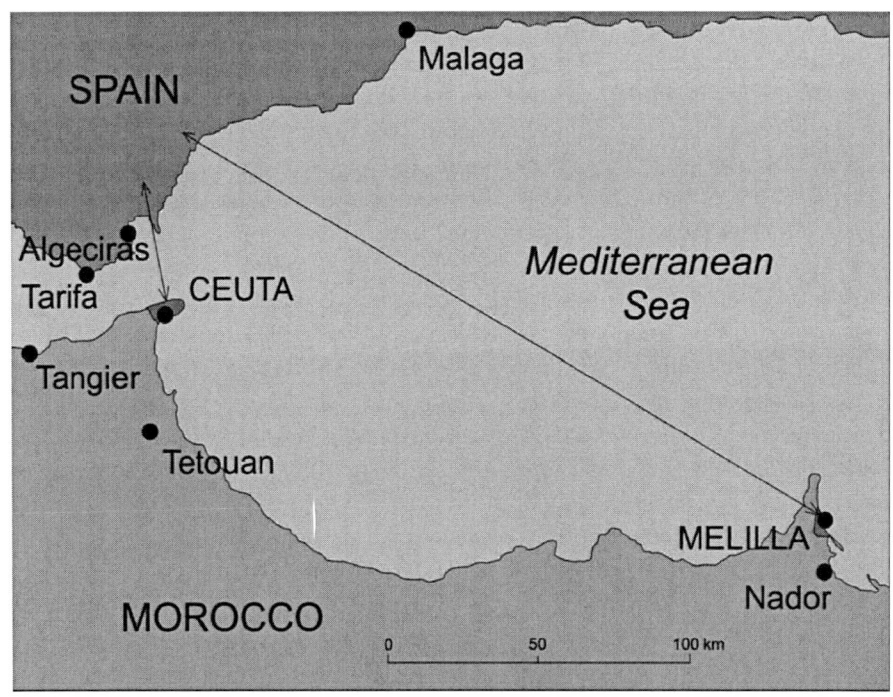

Figure 1. Ceuta and Melilla

Source: E. Vinokurov, *Enclaves and Exclaves of the World: Setting the Framework for a Theory of Enclaves*, p. 38, www.zdes.spb.ru/text/Enclaves%20and%20Exclaves%20of%20the%20World.pdf.

---

[4] A. Toasije, *The Africanity of Spain. Identity and Problematization*, "Journal of Black Studies", vol. 39, no. 3, 2009, pp. 348-355.
[5] S. Nies, *Sand in the Works. Enclaves challenging Metropolitan States. A comparative Study on the Governance of Cabinda, Ceuta, Kaliningrad, Nagorno Karabakh, Nakhchivan, Melilla and Gibraltar*, GRIN Verlag fur Akademische Texte, http://www.grin.com/e-book/109517/sand-in-the--works-enclaves-challenging-metropolitan-states-a-comparative#, p. 55.

Ceuta, covering some 19,5 square kilometers, is situated on the Yebala Peninsula, which is located some 25 kilometers across the Strait of Gibraltar from Gibraltar. A ninety-minute ferry ride connects the town with the Spanish port of Algeciras. The population of Ceuta was nearly 76,000 in 2002. The population density is 4 008 per km^2, while the average density in Spain is 82.69 per km^2. Melilla lies on the Guelaia Peninsula, some 250 km to the east of Ceuta. It had over 62,000 inhabitants in 2002 and covered an area of 12.5 km^2. The direct shortest distance from the mainland is approximately 158 km. The ferry needs about eight hours to cross the sea on the way to Malaga on the Spanish mainland. Furthermore, both cities are mutually isolated as the distance between them (almost 250 km by sea and about 500 by road) makes transport and communication difficult.

Ceuta was originally conquered by Portugal in 1415 and formally ceded to Spain under the 1668 Treaty of Lisbon, following the end of the Spanish-Portuguese Union of 1540. Melilla has been in Spanish hands since 1497. Both cities, Spanish by population and administered as integral parts of the Spanish state (not colonies and not dependent territories), for centuries were socially isolated from Moroccan territory[6]. At the same time their existence as geopolitical enclaves (as well as six other micro-enclaves) called the *plazas de soberanía* ("places of sovereignty"), formerly referred as "*África Septentrional Española*" (Spanish North Africa) or simply "*África Española*" (Spanish Africa) had begun with the independence of Morocco in 1956. Today disagreement about the consequences of Morocco's founding for the two cities still exists, which has not been included by the UN Special Committee of 24 on Decolonization[7] on the list of (former) colonies. Until now, no treaty has been signed between Rabat and Madrid concerning the issue of both enclaves, however the problem has been transferred into the unresolved question of territorial waters and

---

[6] The last partition of Morocco between Spain and France left the Mediterranean coast in Spanish hands and until 1868 Spanish rules forbade Moroccans from living inside the towns although Moroccan farmers from the surrounding areas came to Ceuta and Melilla to put their products on the market. In fact, until then, the towns were almost mono-ethnic, with a very small population reduced to military staff and their families. Moroccans from the hinterlands of both towns began to settle down inside them in the last decades of the nineteenth century, working mainly as soldiers or servicemen in the barracks. Most of them had no access to Spanish nationality and they were not even registered in the Local Registers. See more: P. La Porte, *Civil-Military Relations in the Spanish Protectorate in Morocco: The Road to the Spanish Civil War, 1912-1936*, "Armed Forces & Society", vol. 30, no. 2, 2004, pp. 203-226. Until the end of the 1980's their only Spanish document was the 'statistical card', a document for the family (not the individuals), which enabled them to stay in Ceuta or Melilla, and which lacked any legal force. See: C.G. Enríquez, *Ceuta and Melilla: Clouds over…, op. cit.*, p. 220.

[7] The Special Committee on the Situation with regard to the Implementation of the Declaration on the Granting of Independence to Colonial Countries and Peoples was established by the General Assembly pursuant to its resolution 1654 (XVI) of 27 November 1961. The Special Committee was requested to examine the application of the Declaration on the Granting of Independence to Colonial Countries and Peoples, contained in Assembly resolution 1514 (XV) of 14 December 1960, and to make suggestions and recommendations on the progress and extent of the implementation of the Declaration.

small, uninhabited islands. Spain has persistently rejected the suggestion that the tiny islands Perejil, Chaffarine, Penon, and Alhucemas should be exchanged for recognition of Ceuta and Melilla's status as Spanish enclaves and their right to the exclusive use of the territorial waters. The dispute sometimes transforms into open conflict, as it did in 2002, when two military operations were run on Isla Perejil[8].

Administratively, the enclaves were part of Andalusia until 1978, when the new Constitution was adopted and accepted the devolution of power to the newly established Autonomous Communities[9]. The Councils of Ceuta and Melilla, supported vastly by the inhabitants, in 1981 passed resolutions regarding their autonomous status from national Parliament. However, due to the fact that offering such status to the enclaves could damage the bilateral relations with Morocco, it took almost fifteen year for legislation to be put in force. The Bill, passed finally on 15 February 1995, granted *ceutís* and *melillenses* with the status of Autonomous Towns but not Autonomous Communities. It was only a partial success, since it meant an effective enlargement of right but no legislative power. Madrit decided not to satisfy all the aspirations of the inhabitants of both cities, but at the same time to limit possible Moroccan protests[10]. It also needs to be stressed that Ceuta and Melilla have been treated differently from the rest of Spain not only economically or administratively but also in the sphere of defence. When Spain joined NATO in 1981, the enclaves were explicitly assigned outside the NATO defensive area[11].

Ceuta and Melilla as frontier cities

As J. Kotek argues, frontier cities are ones that are not only polarised on an ethnic or ideological basis, but are, above all, disputed over because of their location on fault-lines between ethnic, religious or ideological wholes. Three elements are features of any frontier-city, namely: sovereignty's quarrel, double legitimacy and conflict. Furthermore, it should be noticed that the notion of frontier-city cannot be

---

[8] R. Gillespie, *'This Stupid Little Island': A Neighbourhood Confrontation in the Western Mediterranean*, "International Politics", vol. 43, no. 1, 2006, pp. 110-132.
[9] J. Botella, *The Spanish "New" Regions: Territorial and Political Pluralism*, "International Political Science Review", vol. 10, no. 3, 1989, pp. 263-271.
[10] See: R. Agranoff, J.A. Ramos Gallarín, *Toward Federal Democracy in Spain: An Examination of Intergovernmental Relations*, "The Journal of Federalism", vol. 27, no. 4, 1997, pp. 1-38.
[11] As Vinkurov argues: "*The NATO members and particularly USA were not willing to sign up for the defence of the territories in North Africa, as it would have caused the risk of escalating into a wider conflict on the Middle East*". See: E. Vinokurov, *Enclaves and Exclaves...*, op. cit., p. 39. It meant that Spain, having to bear defensive responsibility for Ceuta and Melilla on its own, has the military garrisons in both towns making up about 10 per cent of their total population. It should be also noted that 30 per cent of professional soldiers in Ceuta and Melilla are Muslims, what sometimes rises some doubts as regards the loyalty of the troops in the eventual case of a confrontation with Morocco. See: C.G. Enríquez, *Ceuta and Melilla: Clouds over...*, op. cit., p. 225; K. von Hippel, *Domestic pressures in irredentist disputes: the Spanish army and its hold on Ceuta and Melilla*, "The Journal of North African Studies", vol. 1, no. 2, 1996, pp. 157-171.

mistaken with the notions of multicultural or multiethnic cities, however both notions are distinct, a city can be both at the same time[12]. This in the case of Ceuta and Melilla.

When dealing with social political events and the phenomena related to the cities, it is necessary to take into consideration that Ceuta and Melilla have always been two border cities free from any material barriers disrupting communication with their hinterland (but there were formal and administrative barriers), and sensitive to migratory flows coming mainly from the nearby Rif Mountains. As Soddu writes, *"in Ceuta and Melilla the northern and southern worlds have coexisted for over a century, during which time they have attempted to erase the cultural, economic and religious gap separating Europe and Africa. Here the northern and southern shores come together, and Europe and Africa are indissolubly linked"*[13]. However, this has gone – at the beginning of the 1990's, a new phenomenon started to appear at the gates of Ceuta and Melilla: sub-Saharan immigration[14].

Migration to Europe from Africa is not something unprecedented – it can be traced to the 19th century, during colonial times, and also the last (20th) century, when European countries attracted many Africans with job opportunities. Of course, colonial ties also have played a foremost role in this migration. With regard to the issue of migration between Europe and Africa (especially the Maghreb countries), one can distinguish five main phases of this process[15].

The first phase was a North-South movement at the end of the 19th century (1870-1900), when West European countries, especially France, the United Kingdom, Portugal, Belgium and Germany, colonized Africa. Europeans settlement caused many farmers to loose their land and thus these were forced to move within their own country. These were the first large internal migration moves. In the second phase (1900-1945) the South to North migration movement started. This is a wave that has continued until today. Africans have been hired mainly as cheap labor in European countries, and they were also enlisted as soldiers in the two world wars. The third phase started after World War II and lasted until 1970 (1945-1970). In

---

[12] J. Kotek, *Divided cities in the European cultural context*, "Progress in Planning", vol. 52, no. 3, 1999, pp. 227-237.
[13] P. Soddu, *Ceuta and Melilla: Security, Human Rights and Frontier Control*, http://www.iemed.org/anuari /2006/aarticles/aSoddu.pdf (20.02.2009).
[14] See: P. Gold, *Immigration into the European Union via the Spanish enclaves of Ceuta and Melilla: A reflection of regional economic disparities*, "Mediterranean Politics", vol. 4, no. 3, 1999, pp. 23-36.
[15] I. Stacher, K. Demel, *Migration aus dem Maghreb nach Europa – neue Formen, neue Zielländer*, [in:] K. Husa, Ch. Parnreiter, I. Stacher (eds), *Internationale Migration. Die globale Herausforderung des 21. Jahrhunderts*, Brandes &Apsel/Südwind, Frankfurt–Wien 2000. As in: D. van Moppes, *The African Migration Movement: Routes to Europe*, Working papers, Migration and Development Series, Report no. 5, Research Group Migration and Development, Radboud University, Nijmegen, 2006, http://socgeo.ruhosting.nl/html/files/migration/migration5.pdf (20.02.2009).

this period, the time of decolonization, many Africans were hired as cheap labour, particularly in France, the Netherlands, Belgium and Germany.

The fourth phase lasted from the early 1970s up to the beginning of the 1990s (1970-1990). In this period, European countries decided to start applying more restrictive immigration policies. However, despite this, the stream of migrants from Africa to Europe persisted. Due to better conditions and opportunities on the labor markets in Europe, it was no longer only men who come to Europe, but also, and even more frequently, family members of guest workers, asylum seekers and other people who tried to enter a country illegally. In the 1980s, Italy and Spain also become favorite countries of destination for Africans, and no longer acted as transit countries to North-western Europe. And between 1974 and 1997, the number of migrants from the Maghreb countries almost doubled.

The fifth and last phase began in the early 1990s, and it is still continuing today. In this period, European immigration policies have been characterized by serious efforts to reduce the number of immigrants. The governments of European countries and the European Union try to exercise more control over those who want to enter the country, and those who actually are allowed into a country. Closely linked to this, countries also want to put an end to undocumented and illegal immigration. Moreover, governments also try to get migrants to voluntarily return to their country of origin. Migrants who stay are required to integrate better into the society they line in. Some measures are also taken to reduce the number of refugees by changing the rules and conditions under which refugees are allowed to seek asylum. Additionally, on a bilateral level, European countries also try to form agreements with African countries in order to exercise more control over the migration issue[16]. Considering the economic and demographic conditions and trends in most African countries, however, the stream of migrants keeps growing.

In this perspective the border between Spain and Morocco gains more significance and attention[17]. In regard to the mentioned before African pressure, this border is becoming a frontier. As Ferrer-Gallardo argues, it's starting to be perceived as a *"built upon a complex amalgamation of clashes and alliances: Spain and Morocco; Christianity and Islam; Europe and Africa; EU territory and non-EU territory; prosperous north and impoverished south; former colonizer and formerly colonized. A wide range of geographical, historical, political, social, cultural, and economic factors are at play on the Spanish Moroccan border landscape"*[18].

---

[16] M. Gil-Bazo, *The Practice of Mediterranean States in the context of the European Union's Justice and Home Affairs External Dimension. The Safe Third Country Concept Revisited*, "International Journal of Refugee Law", vol. 18, no. 1-2, 2006, pp. 571-600.

[17] M. Baldwin-Edwards, *'Between a rock & a hard place': North Africa as a region of emigration, immigration & transit migration*, "Review of African Political Economy", vol. 33, no. 108, 2006, pp. 311-324.

[18] X. Ferrer-Gallardo, *The Spanish Moroccan border complex: Processes of geopolitical, functional and symbolic rebordering*, "Political Geography", vol. 27, no. 3, 2008, p. 302.

Figure 2. Border fence between Spain and Morocco

Source: *European Security Fencing*, http://www.europeansf.com/en/referencias.html.

This border landscape has been transformed in 1995 into a real demarcation zone with *las vallas de Ceuta y Melilla*. The Ceuta border fence is a separation barrier constructed by Spain and co-financed by th EU. It consists of 8 kilometers of 3-metre fences topped with barbed wire, with regular watchtowers and a road running between them, to accommodate police patrols. Underground cables connect spotlights, noise, movement and infrared sensors and video cameras to a central control booth. The Melilla border fence is a separation barrier consisting of 10 kilometers of parallel 3-metre fences, closely resembling the Ceuta fence. The height of both the Ceuta and Melilla fences has been raised recently to 6 meters.

However, the fences are only a part of the Spanish-Maroccan border, they rightly express the idea of building barrier on a EU-African frontier[19]. According to Ferrer-Gallardo, "*the functional reconfiguration and securitization of the Spanish-Moroccan border and its new role as a regulator of flows is characterized by the 'selective permeability' of borders and their 'differential filtering effects'*". On the one hand, the border is becoming more open or rather permeable to the flow of goods and capital, due to the logic of globalization and the prospective Euro-Mediterranean Free Trade Area. On the other hand, the border is becoming less permeable to the flow of some types

---

[19] See: J. Carling, *Unauthorized Migration from Africa to Spain*, "International Migration", vol. 45, no. 4, 2007, pp. 3-37.

of labor migration[20], especially in the context of development of the 'Fortress Europe', e.g. via the implementation of SIVE[21]. Additionally, other security measures are now coordinated at EU level by the European Agency for the Management of Operational Cooperation at the External Borders (FRONTEX)[22].

Ceuta and Melilla as divided cities[23]

According to models presented by J. Kotek[24], Ceuta and Melilla are not only frontier cities, they are also multicultural cities – unfortunately, this feature has become a source of problems. Here comes the issue of divided cities and separate communities living together in shadow of the frontier fence.

The population of Moroccan origin in both cities traditionally call themselves Muslims. The inhabitants of Spanish origin call themselves 'españoles' (Spaniards) or Christians to distinguish themselves from the population of Moroccan origin. As a matter of fact, religion nowadays seems to have no influence on their lives (like in the mainland of Spain), and they use this phrase primarily as a cultural and historical sign of identification.

Population in both cities grew gradually during the first half of the twentieth century and increased quickly in the 1960's when trade with Morocco unfolded. This development changed the social landscape of the towns, as a new middle class appeared, composed mainly of Spaniards and Moroccans, with a small but remarkable presence of Sephardic Jews (today they represent around 2% of Melilla population) and Hindu community. Public employment is still the most important occupational group, mainly for Spaniards. Besides the retail market, Moroccans work in restaurants and hotels, construction or the small agricultural sector.

Actually, since the beginning of 1990's, the percentage of the population of Moroccan origin in the cities has increased remarkably, mainly due to continuous

---

[20] See more: G. W. White, *Sovereignty and international labor migration: The 'security mentality' in Spanish–Moroccan relations as an assertion of sovereignty*, "Review of International Political Economy", vol. 14, no. 4, 2007, pp. 690-718.

[21] System of Integrated External Surveillance is a coordinated system of radars and video cameras to control the first 20 kilometres of Mediterranean coastline. It is connected directly with a coordination centre that directs rescue and immigration forces along the entire Andalusian coast and during the last years notably has reduced the attempts to cross the Mediterranean Sea by illegal immigrants. See: M. Lorca-Susino, *Immigration to the EU Through Spain*, "MPRA Paper", no. 7949, 2006, http://mpra.ub.uni-uenchen.de/7949/1/MPRA_paper_7949.pdf (20.02.2009); G. Cimadomo, P. Martínez Ponce, *Ceuta and Melilla Fences: A Defensive System?*, "Sarai Reader 06: Turbulence", no. 1, 2006, pp. 336-334, http://www.sarai.net/publications/readers/06-turbulence/10_guido.pdf (20.02.2009).

[22] E. Berg, P. Ehin, *What Kind of Border Regime is in the Making? Towards a Differentiated and Uneven Border Strategy*, "Cooperation and Conflict", vol. 41, no. 1, 2006, pp. 53-71.

[23] This part of the article is mostly based on fine analysis by C.G. Enríquez, *Ceuta and Melilla: Clouds over...*, op. cit.

[24] J. Kotek, *Divided cities...*, op. cit.

immigration and to a birth rate higher than the Spanish one. Furthermore they frequently marry Moroccan partners who, according to Spanish norms, can then legally migrate and acquire Spanish citizenship. It is hard to estimate precisely the size of this minority as neither the Census nor the Local Registers include religion and many people of Moroccan origin do not register[25]. According to socio-demographic research carried out in 2000, 53% of families in Melilla were of Spanish origin, 38% were of Moroccan origin and 8% were mixed. Estimations based on names and family names show that around 40 per cent of the total population is now of Moroccan origin, however it must be highlighted that a percentage is much higher among children and teenagers–around 60% of school children are Muslims–and demographic projections show that, around 2015 Muslims will be in the majority in both towns[26]. Apart from the Muslim population who stay on a permanent basis in the towns, every day around 20,000-30,000 people from neighboring provinces of Nador, Tangier and Tetouan come to the cities and trade. This trade, estimated to be around 1,000 mln euros per year, has become the main financial source for both cities and one of the most important activities in the three mentioned border regions[27].

The presence of this Muslim and Moroccan community in Ceuta and Melilla was largely disregarded by Madrit until 1985, when the approval of the first Spanish Law on Aliens, a regulatory act directed to control irregular migration as Spain was entering the European Community, put the Moroccan population of Ceuta and Melilla in a new situation. To be born in the towns was not enough to obtain Spanish citizenship as, according to the new Spanish rules, nationality is acquired only if at least one of the parents was also born in Spain. Muslim and Moroccan community in the cities had to decide between becoming regular migrant in their own place or to risk expulsion. According to Enríquez, *"the difficulties facing the Moroccan popula-*

---

[25] According to first, and, until now, the only statistical study of the Muslim population in the cities, in 1987 in Melilla lived 17,000 Muslims (32% of the total population) while in Ceuta there were 12,000 (18% of the total). Most of them were born in the towns, 75% in the case of Muslims in Ceuta and 70% in Melilla. The distribution of this population in the cities was irregular with a high concentration in the case of Ceuta (87 per cent of Muslims living in three districts).

[26] Discussing the ordinary relation within the cities, one more issue should be raised – there is namely an important cultural and political difference between the Muslim population in Ceuta and Melilla, as the Muslims in Ceuta speak Arabic while those in Melilla use Tamazight, the Berber language. Berbers form the most important cultural minority in Morocco, where they inhabit the Rif area. They were not arabised during the Arab expansion in the Middle Ages and have maintained a distinct identity which is now promoting a kind of autonomist movement in the Rif, repressed until now by the Moroccan regime. The Berber identity of the Muslim population in Melilla weakens the influence of the Moroccan State over this community, an influence which is in turn stronger in Ceuta.

[27] This trade is mostly a kind of smuggling, Moroccans who enter each of the towns daily have a special document provided by the Spanish authorities to the inhabitants of the Nador, Tetouan and Tangier provinces which allows them to enter Melilla and Ceuta on condition that they leave by midnight, a condition which no authority tries to enforce.

tion were an unintended result of the legislative change, as legislators had not taken into account the special situation of this minority on Spanish territory"[28].

Conflict occurred, when Muslims in both cities refused to ask for the residence permit that would describe them as 'aliens' in their home towns and then force them to wait for the next ten years to apply for Spanish nationality. Protest gatherings and demonstrations at the turn of 1985 and 1986 against the application of the Law in Ceuta and Melilla were the first politically visible acts of this minority and the first occasion on which a political confrontation between Christians and Muslims was manifest. Regrettably, Spanish authorities, supported by the Spaniards, not only did not support the Muslim postulates, but on the contrary decided to suppress these demands[29]. Additionally, the protests against the Law on Aliens also marked the ethnic division of the political and social forces[30].

These Muslim protests were used by the Moroccan nationalist party, Istiqlal, in order to pressure the Moroccan government to vindicate the 'decolonisation' of the enclaves and their return to Morocco, and this domestic and international pressure led the Spanish Socialist government to reconsider the application of the Law on Aliens in Ceuta and Melilla and to finally draft a much more favorable and flexible norm which allowed Muslims with a long presence on Spanish soil to acquire Spanish citizenship.

Since the beginning of the 1990s, some Muslim leaders have been indicating the 'marginalisation' of the Muslim population in the cities and urge for social measures to improve their conditions. This marginal situation is so apparent that the Statutes of Autonomy of both cities include 'the elimination of economic, social and cultural elements which provoke the uprooting of some population groups' as basic objectives of institutions. There are serious problems with education – Muslim children get very low grades at school, what can be explained by the high percentage of illiteracy among parents and the difference between their mother language (regardless of whether this is Arabic or Tamazight) and that of the school (Spanish)[31]. Very few Muslims can reach intermediate or high posts in the

---

[28] C.G. Enríquez, *Ceuta and Melilla: Clouds over...*, op. cit., p. 220.

[29] The escalation of Muslim protests against the Law on Aliens during 1986 and the appearance at these protests of demands for separation culminated in January 1987 with a confrontation between Muslims and Christians in Melilla which led to four persons being wounded by gunshots (one of them, a Muslim, died) and 32 were arrested. This was the first occasion that violence between both communities reached such a serious level.

[30] Muslims left the socialist trade union, UGT (Unio'n General de Trabajadores), and joined the pro-communist one, CC.OO (Comisiones Obreras), as Christians moved from CC.OO to UGT. CC.OO was the only organised social force which supported the Muslim demands.

[31] Students in Ceuta and Melilla obtain the worst academic qualifications in Spain. Around 50% of children in Ceuta and Melilla did not gain the certificate of obligatory secondary education (ESO) when finishing this high school period in 2004, in comparison with 26% in Spain as a whole. In Melilla the failure rate at school among Berber children is five times higher than that of the rest. Sixty per cent of pupils at school in Melilla are Berber and 46% in Ceuta, and they make up more than 80% of the students who do not achieve the ESO certificate. Only 4% of teenagers who did the University Selection exam in Ceuta in 2000 were Muslims.

institutions, mainly due to their failure in the educational system. This is the setting for growing unemployment, drug dealing and Islamic radicalism which are common among young Muslims. Police do not willingly enter some Muslim quarters, where they are frequently attack with stones thrown from windows. Some districts in both towns are inhabited exclusively by Muslims, such as La Cañada de la Muerte in Melilla and El Príncipe, Benzû and Jadū in Ceuta. The social integration of both communities, Muslims and Christians, is weak as shown by the small number of mixed marriages[32], the lack of common festivals, urban segregation and the tendency of parents of Spanish origin to avoid schools with high percentages of Muslim children.

Until very recently the political climate on the Peninsula was dominated by the mistrust, lack of interest and the voluntary silence on the existence of any kind of conflict in Ceuta and Melilla, partially due to the intention to avoid confrontation with Morocco and historical role played by these two towns in supporting the military uprising against the Spanish Republic in 1936 and next the Francoist regime.

However, this climate of voluntary silence about the Muslim presence in Spain had to be broken after the terrorist attack of 11 March 2004 in Madrid, carried out by Moroccan immigrants. This tragedy provoked an increase in islamophobic feelings on the Peninsula and opened the door to the publication in the mass media of reports about the political and cultural life of Moroccans living in Spain, suggesting that the Muslim, non-integrated population from Ceuta and Melilla can be seen as a threat to Spanish sovereignty[33]. Additionally, the demands to 'liberate' the towns from the 'infidel' Spanish State recently voiced on radical Islamic webs and the arrest in 2006 a group of 11 Muslims – 10 of them of Spanish nationality – supposedly members of Salafia Yihadia related to Al Qaeda planning terrorist attacks in the town, has confirmed the Islamic threat.

These vindication and threats induce deep insecurity among the population of Spanish origin, provoke a strong feeling of nationalism (which is demonstrated in the symbols in public areas: statues, names of streets and squares, etc.) and give the army a specially relevant social rank. Although Spanish government has always guaranteed that Ceuta and Melilla will remain Spanish, from time to time, some politicians, mainly leftist or nationalist from Spanish regions with separatist aspirations (Catalonia or the Basque Country), suggest that Spain should 'return' the cit-

---

See also: M. Cuevas López, *School management in multicultural contexts*, "International Journal of Leadership in Education", vol. 11, no. 1, 2008, pp. 63-82.

[32] In Ceuta, from a total of 243 weddings in 2003, only 28 were between a Muslim and a non-Muslim. In 81 cases a Muslim with Spanish citizenship married a Moroccan, which is one of the ways more frequently used by Moroccans to legally migrate to Spain and acquire Spanish citizenship. These data imply a high social segregation of both communities and the tendency of the population of Moroccan origin to maintain and strengthen social relations with Morocco.

[33] A.N. Celso, *Al Qaeda in the Maghreb: The "Newest" Front in the War on Terror*, "Mediterranean Quarterly", vol. 19, no. 1, 2008, pp. 80-96.

ies. In this situation, exacerbated by the loss of their military value, the fear of a dramatic decrease in commercial activity with Morocco and the rapid increase in the population of Moroccan origin, the population of Spanish origin in both towns feel pessimistic about the future and fear of being abandoned by the Spanish State.

This anxiety obstructs relations between both social groups, as Christians perceive any advancement of the public presence of the population of Moroccan origin as a danger. The fear of the population of Spanish origin to become a minority in coming years has two implications: (1) their apprehension regarding an eventual islamisation of social life; (2) the fear that the Kingdom of Morocco could seize the sovereignty over the towns when the population of Moroccan origin is in the majority[34], just appealing to the 'right to self-determination' and requesting a referendum.

The strong pressure of demographic data has forced the political authorities and elite in Ceuta and Melilla to formally recognize the presence in the towns of another cultural community. Thus, the Preambles of both Statutes of Autonomy mention 'cultural plurality' as a common good to be defended, however it does it without explicit reference to the population of Moroccan origin or Muslims. This requirement, being no more then a declaration, has not been translated into political measures, and the demands raised by Muslim organizations asking for official recognition of their languages (a local dialect of Arab in Ceuta and Tamazight in Melilla), and their use in the schools and in administrative practice, has been systematically rejected until now by Christian political parties in the towns[35]. Muslim demands for positive discrimination policies regarding access to administrative posts have been denied by Christian parties arguing that Spanish legislation does not allow positive discrimination[36]. The political discourse of Muslim parties (called *'partidos de corte musulmán'* – parties of Muslim persuasion) mainly deals with social affairs related to poverty, unemployment and the lack of infrastructures in the Muslim districts, and second, with cultural issues such as the demand for the official use of Arabic or Tamazight. They ran for the first time in elections in 1995 and have since then substantially increased their share of the total vote cast in local elections, but this is still

---

[34] Despite of the fact that most Muslims in the towns have Spanish nationality, non-Muslims distrust their loyalty to the Spanish state. According to research carried out by the Spanish Military Information Services, 40% of Muslims in the cities are clearly in favour of maintaining Spanish sovereignty of Ceuta and Melilla, 10% would be clearly against it, while the rest, 50% (!!!) are undecided. Many Spaniards suspect that development gap between Spain and Morocco is the main reason for Muslims preferring Spanish citizenship as the Spanish welfare state offers more and better services than the Moroccan one – and they consider this 'instrumental' national identity as weak and non-reliable.

[35] By rejecting the use of Arabic or Tamazight at school, the Spanish authorities are failing to observe the agreements on protection of minorities and minority languages signed and ratified by Spain and promoted by the Council of Europe.

[36] See also: C. Guarnieri, *Courts and marginalized groups: Perspectives from Continental Europe*, "International Journal of Constitutional Law", vol. 5, no. 2, 2007, pp. 187-210.

far from the percentage of the Muslim population in the towns, as abstention is high in Muslim districts[37].

Conclusion: Modern *convivencia* requested

Ceuta and Melilla as frontier cities sometimes look like a broken bridge between the global North and South from where thousands of Maghreb and Sub-Saharan migrants desperately attempt to complete their journey to rich Europe. Ceuta and Melilla as the divided cities may be seen as a place where former colonizer and formerly colonized meet and where Islam meets the West. The multiple boundaries and continuities that shape the social and political landscape of the cities may however be perceived as their anathema and opportunity at the same time.

Since the early 1990's, in spite of the differences and challenges describe here, both communities: Muslims and Spaniards, calling themselves together as *Ceutíes* ("people of Ceuta") try to make use of a concept borrowed from the historians trying to describe a time during the Middle Ages when Christians, Muslims, and Jews lived peacefully, although not equally, on the Iberian Peninsula – *convivencia* ("cohabitation," "coexistence," or "living together"). However, Spaniards and Morrocan Muslims do not understand *convivencia* in the same way, yet the concept is significant in shaping how *Ceutíes* communally remember the past, think about the present, and hope for the future. Most *Ceutíes* understand that they should negotiate their inter-communitarian struggles otherwise they degenerate into feuding factions and jeopardize the future of the exclave as an integral part of Spain.

Additionally, this scenario can realized by the developing economic and political relationships between Spain and Morocco which weave a complex web composed of mutual dependencies and of possibilities of influence over Ceuta and Melilla and other fields of common interests. This network of economic and strategic interests is a guarantee against any temptation to escalate the present social conflict and elevate it to the category of a violent ethnic and international confrontation. Spain and Morocco have many reasons to avoid confrontation and little to gain by fuelling the conflict, and this fact leaves much room for co-operation and a peaceful resolution.

---

[37] E. Arigita, *Representing Islam in Spain: Muslim Identities and the Contestation of Leadership*, "The Muslim World", vol. 96, no. 4, 2006, pp. 563-584.

Sarajevo
From the Ashes of Conflict to Cold Coexistence
Anna Potyrała

Sarajevo has occurred many times in history. The city was a place where on June 28, 1914 Archduke of Austria-Hungary Franz Ferdinand was assassinated; where in 1984 the XXIII Olympic Games took place; where during the Balkan wars the so-called sniper campaign started. Since the Dayton Peace Agreement of 1995, which ended the war in Bosnia and Herzegovina, a new chapter of history of this city has been written by inhabitants and authorities – Muslim, Serb and Croat. In 1991, before the Balkan wars started, Bosnia and Herzegovina had a population of about 4 million. That number comprised 43.5% of Muslims, 31.2% of Serbs and 17.4% of Croats. Sarajevo was inhabited by 540,000 people, with 40% of Muslims, 30% of Serbs, and 20% of Croats[1]. As of 2008, the city's population is about 400,000. The city ethnic composition has also changed and Sarajevo is now inhabited by 80% of Muslims/Bosniaks. The essence of Sarajevo as a multiethnic city expired despite international and local efforts to guarantee a fair representation of the three ethnic groups. The reason of such a visible change was the war, as well as provisions of the Dayton Peace Agreement of 1995.

The aim of this paper is to analyse the post-war situation of Sarajevo and to focus on examples of cooperation among Muslim, Serb and Croat populations, as well as on signs of tensions still visible in Sarajevo. The realisation of this aim is dependent upon presentation of the city's history, especially during the Bosnian war, as well as the legal status of Sarajevo, approved after 1995. The main assumption of this paper is that despite total change in the ethnic structure, the city is still the point of interests of competing ethnic groups, because of historical, political and even religious reasons. The principal reason for cooperation is the will to overcome the war past of Sarajevo. The main cause of tensions is the experience of the war of 1992-1995, connected with tendencies to revenge observed in all ethnic groups. Sarajevo is an ex-

---

[1] S.A. Bollens, *City and Soul. Sarajevo, Johannesburg, Jerusalem, Nicosia*, "City – Analysis of Urban Trends, Culture, Theory, Policy, Action", vol. 5, no. 2, 2001, p. 171. Other numbers are given by Apostolis Fotiadis in his article *To the Future, with the Past Following*. According to the author, Sarajevo had a population of 427,000 with 45% of Muslims, 38% of Serbs, and 7% of Croats. See: A. Fotiadis, *To the Future, with the Past Following*, available at: http://www.ipsnews.net, 28.02.2009.

ample of a polarized city where group identity is a primary driver[2]. In such cities the main difficulty is to reconcile ethnic groups of inhabitants and to guarantee equal participation in governing. Majoritarian democracy may intensify potential conflicts. Therefore, other forms of local democracy must be introduced. There are two methods for managing ethnic differences, both aimed at power-sharing: decentralisation and consociation. "*Mechanisms used comprise decentralization of city authority to neighborhoods, minority vetoes on issues of particular importance to group, proportionality requirements in areas such as budgeting and civil service appointments, and the use of power-sharing grand coalitions to govern the city*"[3]. Hegemonic control, regarded by some authors[4] as another way of managing ethnic differences, cannot be an example of ethnic conflict resolution. It focuses on domination of one particular group which is favored in all spheres of public live: political, economical, even cultural.

Conflict arising – Sarajevo during the Bosnian war

The Bosnian war arose out after the death of Josip Broz Tito in 1980 and was the result of the collapse of the idea of multiethnic state. Collective identity was replaced by ethnic nationalism and a deep-rooted rivalry among different ethnic groups leaded to a struggle for control of territory[5]. After the proclamation of independence of Bosnia and Herzegovina, Croats and especially Serbs became ethnic minorities in the new state.

The war in Bosnia and Herzegovina started on March 1, 1992. Events taking place in Croatia and Slovenia and ethnic tensions among Serbs, Croats and Muslims (Bosniaks) led to first attempts aimed at Bosnia and Herzegovina independence. On February 29 and on March 1, 1992 national referendum, boycotted by Serbs, took place. 99.43% of voters opted for independence[6]. As a result, on March 3, 1992 president Alia Izetbegović declared independence. The new state was recognized on April 6, 1992 by the European Community and its member states, and by the United States. On May 22, 1992 the state was admitted to the United Nations. On April 7, 1992 the independence of the Republika Srpska of Bosnia and Herzegovina was declared by Radovan Karadić.

---

[2] S.A. Bollens, *Governing Polarized Cities*, Swyer Seminar, University of Pennsilvania, October 28, 2008, available at: http://www.polisci.upenn.edu, 26.02.2009, p. 3.
[3] *Ibidem*.
[4] See: B. O'Leary, B. McGarry, J. McGarry, *Regulating Nations and Ethnic Communities*, [in:] A. Breton, G. Galeotti, P. Salmon, R. Wintrobe (eds), *Nationalism and Rationality*, Cambridge 1995, pp. 245-289.
[5] J.A. Slack, R.R. Doyon, *Population Dynamics and Susceptibility for Ethnic Conflict: The Case of Bosnia and Herzegovina*, "Journal of Peace Research", vol. 38, no. 2, 2002, pp. 140 and 143.
[6] S. Wojciechowski, *Wojna w Bośni i Hercegowinie*, [in:] W. Malendowski (ed.), *Zbrojne konflikty i spory międzynarodowe u progu XXI wieku. Analiza problemów i studia przypadków*, Wrocław 2003, p. 320.

From the beginning, Sarajevo became the theater of war. It was valuable for all ethnic groups, not only because of its history, but mostly because of the fact that it was proclaimed the capital of the new state. On March 1, barricades were constructed in Serb and Muslim parts of the city. On April 5, 1992 the siege of Sarajevo started, demolishing the city's structure and infrastructure, and destroying lives of inhabitants. It lasted 1395 days and resulted in killing over 10,000 persons, wounding over 56,000 and destruction of 64% of the city's buildings[7], including cultural and religious property. The Sarajevo Romanija Corps within the Bosnian Serb Army (established in May 1992 and commanded by major general Tomislav Sipcić and later by major general Stanislav Galić) of almost 13,000 soldiers formed into eight brigades took up positions in the hills around the exposed city and started bombardment. Over the course of the siege Sarajevo has been hit by an average of approximately 329 shell impacts per day, with a high of 3,777 shell impacts on July 22, 1993[8]. Public buildings such as the Parliament, the Presidency building, the Sarajevo Courthouse and the town hall, were among the first to be destroyed. The target for Serb artillery was the Library in the Institue for Oriental Studies which contained over 5,200 historical and literary manuscripts of the Ottoman-era (Arabic, Persian, Turkish) of primary importance to Muslim population. During the siege the National Museum and Olympic Museum were destroyed and the National Library partly destructed. University buildings, the Islamic Theological School, the Veterinary College and other educational centres were shelled. Mosques and religious buildings, as well as hospitals and medical centres (the Kosevo Hospital, the Military Hospital, called the French Hospital, the Jezero Hospital, the Institute for Physical Therapy and Rehabilitation) were among the next military targets. Moreover, media and communication centres (radio and television buildings, television tower), hotels (Bristol, Europa, Bosna, Holiday Inn) and Olympic sites were shelled. The main military aim however, was to divide Sarajevo into two parts and destroy communication between them. The siege and the so-called sniper campaign focused on the major road (known as *Sniper Alley*) that linked the centre of Sarajevo with business and residential district. Daily death victims numbered between 15 and 30.

Taking those events into consideration, on June 8, 1992, the UN Security Council in resolution 758 warned that UN peace forces – UNPROFOR would be sent to Sarajevo to protect the airport and to guarantee food supplies. The first blue helmets arrived to the city on July 1. Atrocities still could have been observed. The Serb artillery attacked the Sarajevo airport and the United Nations buildings such as UNHCR and UNPROFOR facilities and personnel. The most tragic incident was shooting down an Italian plane on September 3, 1992. Therefore, in order to protect international military personnel and civilian population of Sarajevo, on May 6, 1993

---

[7] *Study of the battle and siege of Sarajevo. Final Report of the United Nations Commission of Experts established pursuant to Security Council resolution no. 780 (1992)*, Annex VI, S/1994/674/ Add. 2 (vol. 2), 27 May 1994.
[8] *Ibidem*.

the United Nations Security Council adopted resolution 824, proclaiming Sarajevo a safe area, *free from armed attacks and from any other hostile act*[9]. Serb military and paramilitary forces were demanded to cease hostilities and withdraw to a distance at which they no longer constituted a menace to civilians. Nevertheless, the siege continued, using an important instrument – the blockade of humanitarian aid. In May 1993 Ratko Mladić, the general commander of the Bosnian Serb Army in Bosnia and Herzegovina announced that his intention was to cut off water and power supplies[10]. The city was without electricity for weeks, water supplies were blocked, the sewage system had broken down, there was danger of epidemics. Reports estimated that almost 430,000 persons in Sarajevo and surroundings were dependent on food aid. Meanwhile, because of shelling and sniping attacks, the Sarajevo airport was closed and humanitarian aid was suspended. The international community condemned the blockade of the city. The UN Security Council, in its resolution 859, demanded all parties to the conflict to *"facilitate the unhindered flow of humanitarian assistance, including the provision of food, water, electricity, fuel and communications"*[11]. On July 20, 1993 the Owen-Stoltenberg Plan was presented, proposing a special status of Sarajevo as a separate entity under the international governance. The SC resolution 859 was taken into consideration, as the document provided the need to guarantee *multicultural, multi-ethnic and pluri-religious* character of Sarajevo[12]. On August 29, under international pressure, the Bosnian parliament conditionally approved the Plan. The proposal was subject to negotiations, leading to the Plan of 1994 which recommended UN administration over the city. Unfortunately, that Plan has been dismissed by all parties of the conflict.

On February 9, 1994 NATO member states issued an ultimatum to Serb forces to withdraw artillery beyond a 20 km-wide *total exclusion zone* or face air strikes. The decision however, was not taken. Military action on Serb positions around Sarajevo started on August 30, 1995 as a direct response to an attack on the Markale market of August 28 in which 37 persons died and 89 were wounded[13]. On September 9, 1995 Serb leaders started to withdraw their weapons and agreed to peace proposals. The Dayton Peace Accords (General Framework Agreement for Peace in Bosnia and

---

[9] Point 3, *Resolution no. 824 (1993) adopted by the Security Council at its 3208th meeting on 6 May 1993*, S/RES/824 (1993), 6 May 1993.

[10] More: R. Donia, *Sarajevo in the Twentieth Century*, London 2005. Ratko Mladić is accused by the International Criminal Tribunal for the Former Yugoslavia of crimes against humanity (committed during the siege of Sarajevo) and genocide (perpetrated in Srebrenica in July 1995). As of December 2009, he is still at large.

[11] Point 3, *Resolution no. 859 (1993) adopted by the Security Council at its 3269th meeting on 24 August 1993*, S/RES/859 (1993), 24 August 1993.

[12] Point 6e, *Resolution no. 859 (1993) adopted by the Security Council at its 3269th meeting on 24 August 1993*, op. cit.

[13] M. Kuczyński, *Krwawiąca Europa. Konflikty zbrojne i punkty zapalne w latach 1990-2000. Tło historyczne i stan obecny*, Warszawa 2001, p. 227, and C.S. King, *The Siege of Sarajevo, 1992-1995*, [in:] W.G. Robertson, A. Lawrence (eds), *Block by block: the challenge of urban operations*, Fort Leavenworth 2003, p. 272.

Herzegovina), concluded on November 21, 1995, provided a *de facto* partition of Bosnia and Herzegovina into the Federation of BiH and the Republika Srpska. As to the future of Sarajevo, the idea of international administration of the city has been overtaken by the decision on a partition.

Sarajevo – the multifunctional city

The need for decentralisation in ethnonational states is connected with the necessity to find mechanisms to distribute political power among minorities, to ensure their influence upon the decision-making process, to guartantee efficiency in governing, and, what is the most important, to avoid the majority dictatorship[14]. As a result, a system of checks and balances is created in order to achieve stability and regulate post-conflict situation. On the other hand however, decentralisation is regarded as a power legitimising ethnic divisions and questioning the idea of one multiethnic state.

From among four known types of decentralisation[15], Bosnia and Herzegovina is the example of a quasi-confederacy, formed by three main ethnic groups: Bosniaks, Serbs and Croats (therefore BiH is called by many "Little Yugoslavia"). The country is divided into two, ethnonationalist *unique and indivisible constitutional* entities: the Federation inhabited mainly by Bosniaks and Croats, and the so-called Republika Srpska (the Serb Republic) inhabited by Bosnian Serbs. The first forms 51% of territory, the second – 49% (see: Map 1). The two entities, connected by a new road, have separate constitutions, authorities and are entitled to decide about citizenship. There is also one special district of Brcko (with own assembly), responsible for economy, finance, customs, public property, health and social protection, police, administration of justice, urbanism and planning.

The political structure of the Federation is divided into three levels: 1) the entity level, 2) the canton level, 3) the municipal level[16]. On the first level, the administration is comprised of a two-house parliament with legislative powers, a president and two vice presidents, and a government presided by a prime minister with executive powers. The canton level is composed of ten cantons, each with its own constitution, a parliament and a government presided by a prime minister. Canton competencies include guaranteeing and enforcing human rights, education, cul-

---

[14] C.A. Monteux, *Decentralisation: The New Delusion of Ethnic Conflict Regulation*, "International Journal on Multicultural Studies" vol. 8, no. 2, 2006, p. 164.

[15] These are: confederation (a very loose association of independent, sovereign territorial entities), federation (an association of independent, but not sovereign entities, which posses certain competences in international law), autonomy (a constitutional status guaranteed to a particular group to administer itself); local self-government (the lowest degree of autonomy from central authorities).

[16] *Bosnia and Herzegovina Public Administration Country Profile*, Division for Public Administration and Development Management, Department of Economic and Social Affairs, New York 2003, p. 1.

Map 1. Bosnia and Herzegovina – inner border between the Federation and the Republika Srpska

Source: T. Levitas, *A Tale of Two Entities: How Finance Reform Builds Democracy in Bosnia and Herzegovina*, "DAIdeas – Democracy Briefs", no. 1, 2007, p. 2.

ture, social welfare policy, public services, environmental policy, health, police, use of natural resources[17]. On the municipal level, there are 81 local municipalities (*općine, opštine*), each with its own assembly, a governing council and a local government. Republika Srpska is divided into two levels: 1) the entity level, and 2) the municipal level. Within the first, the legislative powers are fulfilled by a parliament, executive powers – by a president, two vice presidents, a government and a prime

---

[17] See: Article 2 and 4, Part III of the *Constitution of the Federation of Bosnia and Herzegovina*, Official Gazette 1/94, 13/97, 16/02, 22/02, 52/02, 60/02, 18/03, 63/03.

minister. The second level is of municipal character. The Republic is divided into 62 municipalities (there are no cantons), all having separate assemblies and governments.

Figure 1. Bosnia and Herzegovina administrative, government and parliamentary division

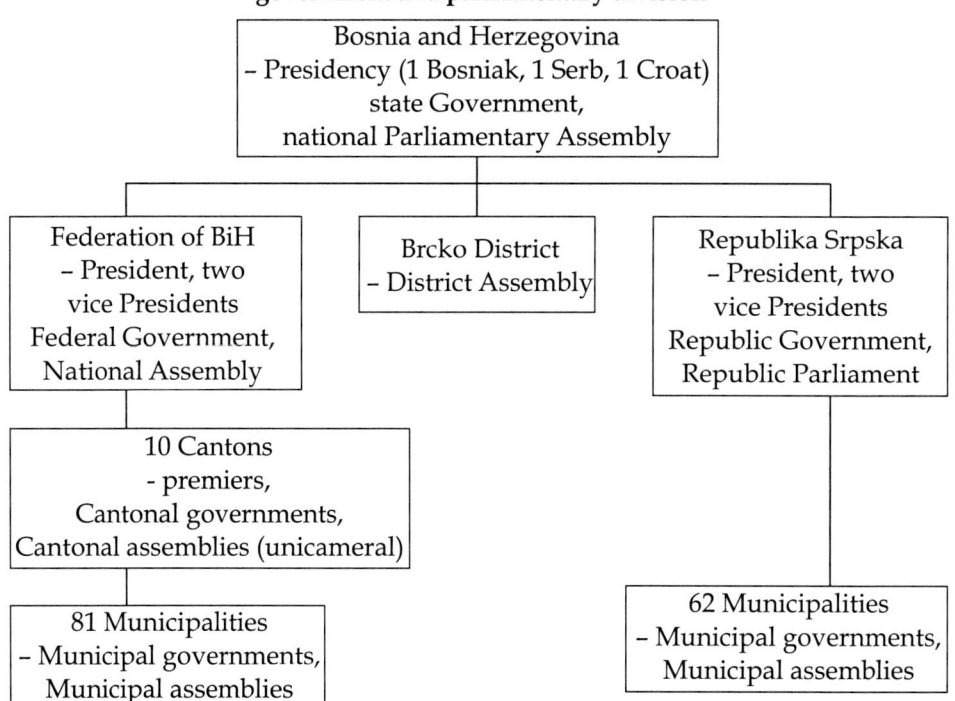

```
                    Bosnia and Herzegovina
          – Presidency (1 Bosniak, 1 Serb, 1 Croat)
                       state Government,
                  national Parliamentary Assembly

  Federation of BiH         Brcko District          Republika Srpska
  – President, two        – District Assembly       – President, two
   vice Presidents                                   vice Presidents
  Federal Government,                              Republic Government,
  National Assembly                                Republic Parliament

     10 Cantons
     – premiers,
  Cantonal governments,
Cantonal assemblies (unicameral)

                                                   62 Municipalities
   81 Municipalities                             – Municipal governments,
 – Municipal governments,                          Municipal assemblies
   Municipal assemblies
```

Source: Author's own concept based upon Article 2, Part I, Article 5, Part V, Article 3, Part VI of the *Constitution of the Federation of Bosnia and Herzegovina*, Official Gazette 1/94, 13/97, 16/02, 22/02, 52/02, 60/02, 18/03, 63/03; and Article 69, and Article 102 of the *Constitution of Republika Srpska*, CDL (2008) 047.

Such a division (of territorial and political character) was introduced by the Dayton Peace Agreement of 1995, and is described as "*one of the most complicated and wasteful systems of government ever devised*"[18], being expensive and characterised by inefficiency. The aim was to separate ethnic minorities to avoid possible tensions and conflicts. According to some critics however, the Dayton Peace Agreement (described as a *Frankenstein agreement*) legally solidified the war's ethnic cleansing policy by dividing the country into two entities[19].

---

[18] I. Traynor, *Revealed: US Plans for Bosnian Constitution*, "The Guardian", 10.11.2005. In October, 2005, Olli Rehn, the EU commissioner for enlargement, stated that the constitutional structure is too complex and fiscally unsustainable.

[19] R. Wilkinson, *The 'miracle' of Dayton – 10 years later*, "Refugees", vol. 3, no. 140, 2005, p. 16. On proposals for reform of the territorial and political division of Bosnia and Herzegovina

Within this complicated territorial and political division of Bosnia and Herzegovina, there was a need to regulate the status of Sarajevo, together with relations among three main ethnic groups of inhabitants.

Three possibilities may be taken into consideration in order to avoid or eliminate ethnic conflicts in urban areas. The first is aimed at forced population transfers, the second – on political partitioning of urban space, the last – on integration or assimilation[20]. In order to ensure a better balance among Serb, Croat and Muslim interests, the decision on partitioning of Sarajevo was taken. According to the Dayton Peace Agreement, eastern parts of the city, comprising 35.7% of the aglomeration's territory, were incorporated to the Republika Srpska. The official name of the parts transferred to the Republika Srpska was *Srpsko Sarajevo*, however, in 2004 the name *Istočno/Istočni Sarajevo* was introduced as a result of the decision of the Constitutional Court of Bosnia and Herzegovina. This city consists of six municipalities: Kasindo (the former Srpska Ilidza), Lukavica (the former Srpsko Novo Sarajevo), Pale, Sokolac, Istočni Stari Grad (the former Srpski Stari Grad) and Trnovo, and is inhabited by about 70,000. The rest of the territory of the pre-war Sarajevo (64.3%), including Serb districts, was incorporated to the Federation of Bosnia and Herzegovina (see: Figure 2). The aim of such a decision was to avoid ethnic fragmentation of the city and to guarantee that Sarajevo was inhabited by all major ethnic groups. Paradoxically, that caused a mass population transfer of about 62,000 Serb inhabitants who did not want to live in the Federation composed mostly by Bosniaks and Croats.

The city, officially named *Sarajevo*, is inhabited by around 400,000 and is the largest city in Bosnia and Herzegovina. The city is situated in the Sarajevo plain, surrounded by Bjelasnica, Igman and Trebević mountains, and functions as:
– the capital of Bosnia and Herzegovina,
– the capital of the Federation of Bosnia and Herzegovina,
– the *de iure* capital of the Republika Srpska,
– the capital city of Canton Sarajevo,
– four municipalities, and
– a frontier city.

Sarajevo is a frontier city, located in the Federation near to the Inter-Entity Boundary Lines with the Republika Srpska. The Lines, decided and guaranteed in the Agreement attached as Annex 2 to the Dayton Peace Accords, are situated outside the city's southeastern parts. Within the new political division, Sarajevo as the capital of Bosnia and Herzegovina (according to Article 1 Paragraph 5 of the Constitution of Bosnia and Herzegovina), is the seat of state authorities: the state government and the Parliamentary Assembly. Sarajevo is also the capital of the Federation of Bosnia and Herzegovina, according to Article 4, Part I of the Constitution of the Federation. Simultaneously, according to Article 9 of the Constitution of the

---

read: *Making Federalism Work – A Radical Proposal for Practical Reform*, European Stability Initiative, Berlin–Brussels–Sarajevo 2004; and S. Sebastian, *Leaving Dayton Behind: Constitutional Reform in Bosnia and Herzegovina*, FRIDE Working Paper no. 46, November 2007.

[20] S.A. Bollens, *Governing Polarized Cities*, op. cit., pp. 4-5.

Republika Srpska, Sarajevo is the capital of the Republic, although the city is not within its territory (only eastern parts of the pre-war Sarajevo, as it was emphasized above, are located in the Republic, forming a separate city of Istočno/Istočni Sarajevo). Therefore, the *de facto* capital of the Republika Srpska is Banja Luka, the seat of authorities. As the capital city of Canton Sarajevo – the most populous in the country, with 419,000 inhabitants – Sarajevo has a special status as *a unit of the local self-government*[21], being an example of consociational character[22]. The Constitution of Canton Sarajevo regulates the composition of city authorities, as well as municipal composition and territorial organization of Sarajevo. The legal status of Sarajevo is also governed by the Law on Principles of Local Self-Government in the Federation of Bosnia and Herzegovina. Sarajevo is administratively divided into four municipalities: Centar, Stari Grad, Novi Grad, and Novo Sarajevo (see: Figure 2).

Figure 2. Municipalities in Canton Sarajevo
(with the Inter-Entity Boundary Lines)

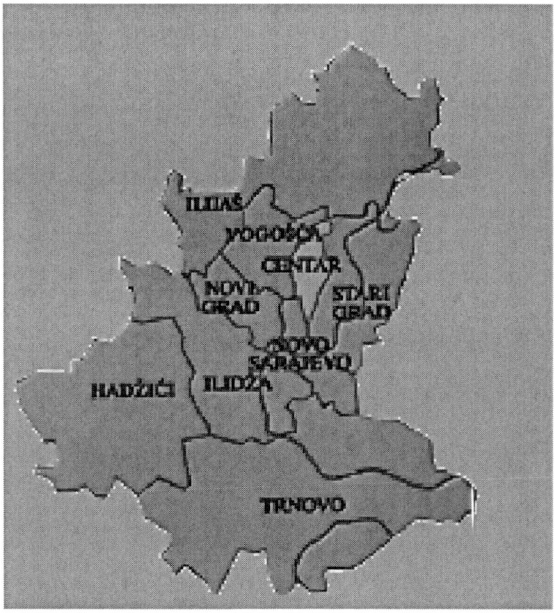

Source: available online at: http://www.pksa.com.ba, 3.04.2009.

Centar is a municipality of central Sarajevo, located between the old parts of the city (which form Stari Grad) and modern parts (which form Novi Grad and Novo

---

[21] Part VI.B., *Constitution of the Federation of Bosnia and Herzegovina*, op. cit.
[22] More: M. Bouda, *A City Divided: Jerusalem in Comparative Perspective*, "Sound Politicks – Journal of Political Science at the University of Pennsylvania", vol. XIV, no. 1, Fall 2007, pp. 12-13.

Sarajevo). The municipality of 33 km² is inhabited by 80,000 (82% of Bosniaks, 12% of Croats, 4% of Serbs and 2% of other ethnic groups)[23]. Stari Grad is the oldest part of Sarajevo, with the territory of 51.4 km² and 50,000 of inhabitants. Novi Grad has over 296,000 residents and occupies the territory of 47.2 km². Novo Sarajevo is a municipality located between Centar and Novi Grad, inhabited by almost 75,000 people of whom 88% are Bosniaks. The municipality occupies the territory of 9.9 km².

Furthermore, architecturally, Sarajevo is comprised of three towns: centre of the city of oriental (Turkish) character, surrounded by the Art Nouveau Viennese city and the contemporary city with blocks of flats, apartments and industrial plants[24]. The first was constructed in the 16th century and is full of mosques, bridges and market places. This part of Sarajevo was severely damaged during the Bosnian war and the siege of the city. The second is the result of the history of Sarajevo within the Austrian empire in the 19th century. The third was constructed in the Tito era and was reshaped because of the Winter Olympic Games of 1984.

Sarajevo – the city of ethnic cooperation, the city of ethnic tensions

The Dayton Peace Agreement of 1995 was aimed at ending the conflict and establishing political framework for the new state with its two entities (by adopting constitution of BiH, and deciding about the Inter-Entity Boundary Lines). The fundamental problem however, was to guarantee reconciliation and justice and to give basis for socio-economic development of Bosnia and Herzegovina. These were of primary importance especially in Sarajevo. Without dialogue among ethnic groups, return of refugees and internally displaced persons, as well as reconstruction of infrastructure (economic, health, education), it was impossible to rebuild the state and the city. Considering the necessity to regulate the post-war situation in Sarajevo, on February 3, 1998, principles concerning the status of the city were adopted. Multi-ethnic character of the city was emphasized, as well as the obligation of equal treatment of all ethnic groups.

The most crucial for the future of Sarajevo and cooperation among ethnic groups was the return of refugees. During the war in Bosnia over 1.2 million persons were forced to leave their homes. As of January 1, 2005, almost 95,000 of persons remained outside Bosnia and Herzegovina as refugees. In 1996, 62,000 Serbs left Sarajevo as their neighborhoods became parts of the Federation of Bosnia and Herzegovina. According to Annex 7 to the Dayton Peace Agreement, the United Nations High Commissioner for Refugees is primarily responsible for *early, peaceful* repatriation of persons forced to leave their homes during and after the war. The Agency was entrusted "*with the role of coordinating among all agencies assisting with the*

---

[23] *Centar Municipality*, available at: http://www.pksa.com.ba, 29.03.2009.
[24] L. Cordall, *The Role of the Landscape Architect in the Rebuilding of a War-torn City*, 1998, available at: http://www.friends-partners.org, 16.03.2009.

repatriation and relief of refugees and displaced persons"[25]. Consequently, the Coalition for Return has been established (with the International Committee of the Red Cross), responsible for promoting the idea of repatriation, assistance for persons who would like to return home and collaboration with local authorities in facilitating return[26]. In March 1997, the High Commssioner introduced the Open Cities Initiative aimed at promoting openness to minority return in exchange for international aid. As a result, the Sarajevo Housing Commission was established with representatives of the High Commissioner, the UN Stabilization Force, the UN Police Task Force, the Organization for Security and Cooperation in Europe, the Coalition for Return (the only non-governmental partner), the Sarajevo Canton Housing Department and the Sarajevo Canton Ministry for Refugees. Between January and August 2001, 13,445 persons returned to the Canton Sarajevo (11,668 were Serbs)[27]. The Commission main responsibility is to resolve problems related to repossession of property as Annex 7 to the Dayton Peace Agreement provides the right of refugees to have their property restored and to be compensated for property which cannot be restored to them. Therefore, alternative housing must be provided for persons who after the war were placed there. Such a situation often leads to ethnic tensions, although its aim is to guarantee equal opportunities for returnees and possibilities to participate in the life of the Sarajevo society.

One of the most important aspects of cooperation is the reconstruction of the city which is regarded as a force that fosters multiethnicism and multiculturalism[28]. Reconstruction projects focused on rebuilding the Sarajevo University (by adapting the Marshall Tito Army barracks) and a network of pedestrian links and public parks – elements of a sustainably city. The creation of a pedestrian orientated society encourages daily face to face contact and frequent interaction among ethnic groups in the streets, market places, squares and parks[29]. Therefore, it guarantees multiethnic character of the city. The need for reconstruction and rehabilitation of the city in order to preserve multiethnic and multicultural Sarajevo, is perceived by UNESCO. The Organization provided financial support for reconstructing the National Mu-

---

[25] Article III.1, Annex 7, *Dayton Peace Accords – General Framework Agreement for Peace in Bosnia and Herzegovina*, Paris 21.11.1995, Lilian Goldman Law Library 2008, The Avalon Project Documents in Law, *History and Diplomacy*, available at: http://www.avalon.yale.edu, 4.04.2009. During the Bosnian war the UNHCR provided humanitarian aid for the city and medical evacuation.

[26] P. Lippman, *Promoting Return of Refugees: Sarajevo and Zvornik in Bosnia and Herzegovina*, [in:] N. Dimitrijević, P. Kovacs (eds), *Managing Hatered and Distrust: The Prognosis for Post-Conflict Settlement in Multiethnic Communities in the Former Yugoslavia*, Budapest 2004, p. 9.

[27] *Ibidem*, p. 12.

[28] Cited after: L. Cordall, *The Role of the Landscape Architect in the Rebuilding of a War-torn City*, op. cit.

[29] L. Cordall, *The Role of the Landscape Architect in the Rebuilding of a War-torn City*, op. cit. Another reason for the reconstruction of parks and squares is the need to overcome the recent history of the city – during the war, parks and the Olympic playing fields were pressed into service as graveyards.

seum in 1996 and 1998, as well as the 16th century Sheik Magribija Mosque minaret in 2000[30]. A special Commission for the Preservation of National Monuments in Bosnia and Herzegovina has been established according to the Dayton Peace Agreement. In 1996, the European Union started a 35 million euro – programme "Europe for Sarajevo" aimed at supporting the economy, reconciling ethnic groups and rehabilitation. Through the programme housing rehabilitation, school rehabilitation, water supply rehabilitation, public health, preservation of civil and cultural landmarks, are supported.

The significance of rehabilitation in Sarajevo was appreciated in 2005 when the Council of Europe awared Sarajevo with the 2006 European Region of the Year. The aims were *"to increase knowledge and recognition of European regional affairs, to make new contributions to regional construction and European integration and, finally, to project the regions designated as European Region of the Year onto the European and international scene, in all their aspects, such as the social, cultural, economic and tourism aspects"*[31]. The neccessity to support initiatives focused on cooperation of ethnic groups, was of a crucial meaning. In September 2005, Sarajevo was accepted to the International Association of Peace Messenger Cities. The Association, founded in 1982 by the mayors of Hiroshima and Nagasaki, is aimed at strengthening the role of cities in creating peace culture. In November 2005, the city joined the European Cities' Network – established to promote cultural and social development and cooperation in economy and technology.

Although 80% of inhabitants of Sarajevo are Bosniaks, the city still witnesses ethnic tensions. The fact that Sarajevo is inhabited mostly by Bosniaks, is oftenly regarded as a proof of the city's intolerance towards Serb and Croat residents. In 2008, the non-governmental organization Croatia Libertas condemned the coloring of pavements in two streets of Sarajevo downtown into green, stating that green pavements cannot be found even in Teheran. *"Every year, Sarajevo is less and less multiethnic, and it increasingly becomes Bosniak capital. And this is not the case only in demographic sense, but also in political, religious, educational and every other"*[32]. The primary problem is the fact that all ethnic groups insist on remaining separate. There are three incompatible models of education (influenced by political elites) with different school curricula, which reinforce ethnic tensions, blame the other groups, and glorify their own mitology, and introduce religious instructions in schools[33].

---

[30] B. Goodey, W. Desimpelaere, *External Evaluation of UNESCO's Action in the Preservation of Cultural Heritage Damaged by Conflict: Bosnia-Herzegovina 1996-2003*, IOS/EVS/PI/24, 2003, pp. 8 and 14-15.
[31] Cited after: A. Crevar, *Peace Signs in Sarajevo. After the War, the Capital Rises from the Ruins*, "The Washington Post", 26.03.2006.
[32] V. Selimbegovic, *Sarajevo in not Teheran*, "Dani" August 2008, pp. 20-27. Cited after: *Sarajevo, city of intolerance for non-Bosniaks: justified criticism or pre-election campaign?*, MIA Archive and Research Report, 3 August 2008 - 26 August 2008.
[33] *Social Inclusion in Bosnia and Herzegovina. National Human Development Report*, United Nations Development Programme, New York 2007, p. 50; and J. Lyon, *Bosnia and Herzegovina: an impossible reconciliation, 1999*, available at: http://www.unesco.org, 4.04.2009.

Cooperation signs as well as ethnic tensions are visible not only in the every-day life of the city, but mostly when political aspects are taken into consideration. In order to guarantee the balance of interests of all ethnic groups and their full integration, ethnic quotas were introduced to all city's authorities. The history of distribution of seats among different ethnic, religious and political groups in various administration bodies in Sarajevo dates back to 1919. In the Provisional Sarajevo Council there were 9 Muslims, 9 Catholics, 9 Serbian Ortodox, 4 Jews and 9 socialists[34]. According to the constitution of Sarajevo of 1997, the city had a joint governance and administration structures. Twenty-eight seats in a legislative Assembly (each municipality of Sarajevo represented by seven persons) were occupied by Bosniaks, Croats and other nationalities. Each group was guaranteed with at least 20% of seats. Ethnic quotas were also guaranteed in the executive Council composed of a mayor and two deputies, each being a representative of a different ethnic group. The lower posts in the administration, were also distributed fairly among all ethnic groups. On March 27, 2002 the so-called Sarajevo Agreement was signed by representatives of all ethnic minorities from Bosnia and Herzegovina. The document established symmetrical limits on arrangements for sharing power among and safeguarding the vital interests of ethnic groups[35], regarded as the constituent peoples. All governmental, legislative, judicial and administration structures in the Federation of Bosnia and Herzegovina, the Republika Srpska, as well as in all cantons and municipalities must follow power-sharing mechanisms among Bosniaks, Croats, Serbs and others. In the Federation government eight ministerial posts are taken by Bosniaks, five – by Croats and three by Serbs. The prime minister and two deputies represent three ethnic groups, as well as the president and two vice-presidents. The Sarajevo Agreement maintains the consociational structure of Sarajevo. It guarantees representation of all ethnic groups in the administration, the judiciary, the police, public companies, schools, public health institutions and other public authorities (ethnic quotas), as well as neccesity to adopt legislation concerning vital national interests by concurrent majority. This step was of a crucial meaning as in 2001 the new Election Law was adopted, liquidating quotas (seats in the Sarajevo Assembly and the Council were to be allocated proportionately to votes obtained).

Conclusions

Since the era of the Austrian empire, Sarajevo has had the multiethnic and multireligious character with mosques, catholic churches, Orthodox shrines and Jewish

---

[34] C. Simmons, *A Multicultural, Multiethnic, and Multiconfessional Bosnia and Herzegovina: Myth and Reality*, "Nationalities Papers", no. 4, 2002, p. 627. The ethnic-quota requirement has integrative aspects, since decisionmaking is majoritarian. N. Caspersen, *Good Fences make Good Neighbours? A Comparison of Conflict Regulation Strategies in Postwar Bosnia*, "Journal of Peace Research", vol. 41, no. 5, 2004, p. 583.

[35] *Implementing Equality: the "Constituent Peoples" Decision in Bosnia & Herzegovina*, ICG Balkan Report, no. 128, Sarajevo–Brussels, 16 April 2002, p. 12.

synagogues. After the war in Bosnia, the city was divided. Consequently, its nature has changed. The aim was to avoid possible ethnic conflicts. Instead, ethnic distance has created isolation of each ethnic group, leading to more tensions.

Thankfully, despite ethnic tensions, no violence has erupted. Without any doubt the reason is the international presence in Sarajevo – the Office of the High Representative, the Organization for Security and Cooperation in Europe, SFOR and EUFOR peacekeeping forces, and international aid institutions such as UNHCR and ICRC. Another reason is the system of checks and balance in Sarajevo's political and administration institutions, guaranteeing representation of all ethnic groups. The real cooperation however, is dependent on mutual understanding of differences: ethnic, historical, religious and political. Therefore, civic education and tolerance training is crucial, as well as common addressing the past. Otherwise, the only example of cooperation despite ethnic and religious differences will be FK Sarajevo football team.

Belfast
An Ambiguous Heritage in a Difficult Neighborhood
Marcin Galent

When Tony Blair and the Prime Minister of the Republic of Ireland Bertie Ahern signed an agreement in Belfast in 1998 many believed that it was the ultimate end of one of the bloodiest conflicts in Europe after WWII. The Good Friday Agreement, as it was subsequently dubbed, brought about a long awaited official end to the conflict between Protestant and Catholic political and paramilitary groups which had struggled openly for dominance and independence in Northern Ireland since the end of the 60s. The fact that the two fighting sides managed to reach a compromise and agreed to sit together around a table in order to find a solution through peaceful talks was massively supported and widely applauded by the prevailing majorities of Irishmen and Britons. It is enough to mention that during two referendums conducted in Northern Ireland and the Republic of Ireland 71 and 94 per cent of voters respectively supported the Agreement.

Alas, this first success did not mean that sectarian conflict and violence was definitely over. As it quickly transpired, it was just a first step in a long and thorny process of building cross community trust, dialogue and co-operation. Paradoxically, this long awaited reconciliation between most important political and military actors was challenged on the streets of Northern Ireland's cities where still frequent spontaneous clashes and skirmishes between Catholic and Protestants show that underlying tensions are still very much present. These acts of hostility and aggression not only cause havoc among ordinary citizens, but also stir up violent emotions and give support to these paramilitary organizations who do not want to reconcile themselves with the fact that the leaders of the two communities have definitely abandoned military struggle as a means of inter community rivalry.

The list of the off-shoots of the main republican and loyalist organizations is long on both sides. What makes them similar is the fact that they do not want to acknowledge the end of the "civil war". Such self-appointed representatives compete for public opinion and, by new acts of terrorism, try to polarize the two communities in order to win over those inhabitants of Ulster who refuse to participate in dialogue and co-operation. They openly admit that their main goal is to try to derail the most recent conflict solution achievements in the Northern Ireland conflict and bring back the logic of war.

Realistic versus nonrealistic. Official versus everyday life

What may probably help in understanding these most recent developments in the peace process and its disturbances is the taking into consideration of the distinction which is often made by social scientists while analyzing the dynamics of social conflicts. They usually talk about their realistic and nonrealistic dimensions[1]. Realistic in this theory means such conflicts where the confrontation between the sides of the conflict is based on identified imbalances of the distribution of certain precious social goods like wealth, power and prestige. In other words there is an identifiable pool of resources which can be the subject of competition. The nonrealistic dimension of conflicts has to do not with imbalanced distribution but rather on prejudices, social distances, and is not fully identified undercurrent emotions which drive hatred towards "the other".

Although these two dimensions can characterize different conflicts at the same time, it seems that the former is much better controllable if there are institutionalized sides which are potentially able to renegotiate the imbalanced distribution of different resources and, by this token, reach a conflict resolution. The latter kind of conflict is much more fluid, unpredictable and difficult to deal with. Irrationality rarely comes from the official and institutional level and its roots are usually deeply ingrained in personal horizons of experience. This is why it is of such importance to look at the features of everyday experience, since as Piotr Sztompka says it may give answers to the most important questions about: "*subjective and intersubjective meaning of peoples' activities in personal and collective life*"[2].

The memory of tragic events, spontaneously constructed and the often one-sided mythology of suffering and represented in a subjective manner are an important aspect in building group solidarity and the creation of social boundaries[3]. The memory of heroes and their acts is a very important constituent of social groups. Myths, tombs and rituals produce feelings of belonging and identity. These memories may fade away, be institutionalized or located in a special sphere which constitutes a sacred sphere of certain communities. But they rarely inspire their members to act on a daily basis and contribute to the perpetuation of the conflict. However, when we take a look at the everyday life of the inhabitants of certain districts of Northern Ireland's cities, we realize that the tragic history of the bloody conflict is constantly present among them. It is represented by thousands of murals which cover the walls of houses inhabited by those who are socially the most disadvantaged and historically the most experienced and harmed. The role of the murals in the reproduction of hostile attitudes among people in Northern Ireland has recently become

---

[1] L. Coser, *Społeczne funkcje konfliktu*, [in:] W. Derczyński, A. Jasińska-Kania, J. Szacki (eds), *Elementy teorii socjologicznych. Materiały do dziejów współczesnej socjologii zachodniej*, PWN, Warszawa 1975.
[2] P. Sztompka, *Życie codzienne – temat najnowszej socjologii*, [in:] P. Sztompka, M. Bogunia-Borowska (eds), *Socjologia codzienności*, Kraków 2009, p. 36.
[3] Z. Mach, *Symbols, Conflict and Identity*, SUNY, Albany 1993.

one of the most hotly debated issues. Recent initiatives undertaken in order to diminish their potentially negative effects, encountered mixed feelings on both sides. The last attempt which aimed at getting rid of them completely surprisingly united voices from both sides, regardless of their basic identifications and loyalties. The visual legacy of the Troubles allowed some observers to talk about emergence of a common Northern Ireland heritage shared by the two communities and, by this token, about the universalization of so far separated social memories.

The roots and character of the conflict

The roots of the conflict stem from as early as the beginning of the 17th century. From 1608, British settlers, known as planters, were given land confiscated from the native Irish in the Plantation of Ulster. Prior to the process of colonization, Ulster had been the most Gaelic part of Ireland. Such symbolic places as Armagh, the town of Saint Patrick, are located there. This strong cultural difference was also supported by feudal independence which meant that until the end of the 16th century it existed largely outside of English control.

This relative autonomy was a bone of contention between Irish lords and the English crown. Ulster was the most resistant of Ireland's provinces to the English invasion. The last blow to the ambition of Irish independence came with The Nine Years War which ended in 1603. The Irish rebels surrendered to the English crown and the whole island became subordinated to James I, king of England, Scotland and Ireland. In order to weaken resistance and to prevent future rebellions from the native Irishmen, the English prepared a detailed plan for the colonization of Northern Ireland. Huge areas of land in Ulster were confiscated and devoted to the creation of dense settlements of British immigrants. New towns and garrisons were funded and inhabitant by English-speaking Protestants. The surrounding lands were distributed to wealthy men from England and Scotland. These new landowners were banned from taking Irish tenants and had to important tenants from England and Scotland. Each of new colonizers was given around 3000 acres, provided that they settled a minimum of 48 adult males and 20 families. The settlers also had to be English-speaking and Protestant. The remaining Irish landowners were to be granted around one quarter of the land in Ulster and the peasant Irish population was to be resettled to live near the British centres of power and religion. This process of colonization led to two bloody conflicts in 1641-1653 and 1689-1691, each resulting in Protestant victories and further laws aimed at the exclusion of Catholics and Dissenters[4].

What was also very important was the fact that the Irish supported James II against William of Orange during the Glorious Revolution. It was the famous siege of Derry (Londonderry) where British Protestant loyalists fought for their king un-

---

[4] http://www.bbc.co.uk/history/british/plantation, 20.04.2009.

der the slogan "No Surrender" for the first time. The slogan is one of the most often painted loyalist inscriptions among unionist estates in contemporary Northern Irish cities.

Photo 1.

Source: Author's photograph.

These events drew deep lines between the two communities along religious and ethnic lines, where the Protestant's showed their allegiance and loyalty towards the British crown, and Catholics who sought some form of autonomy and eventually independence. By the end of the 19th century attitudes were so entrenched that the terms 'Catholic' and 'nationalist' were interchangeable, as were 'Protestant' and 'unionist'[5]. It is important to remember here that when the Irish Parliament was abolished in 1801 and Ireland was completely incorporated into the United Kingdom, Catholics constituted around 75 per cent of Ireland's population. In 1798 the Orange Order was founded, with its stated goal of upholding the Protestant faith and loyalty to William of Orange and his heirs. It was founded as a: "*means of mobilizing lower-class Protestants for the defense of the institutions of the state, the established Church of Ireland and landed property*"[6]. The Orange Order remains active to this day, especially among the Protestant working class. The Order organizes a series of parades held annually during the summer in many cities and towns of Northern Ire-

---

[5] C. Pilkington, *Devolution in Britain Today*, Manchster University Press 2002, p. 74.
[6] A. Aughey, D. Morrow, *Northern Ireland Politics*, Longman, Harlow 1996, p. 3.

land. Most of them are to commemorate events related to Protestantism and links with the British Crown. The peak of the marches comes on the 12th of July where the Protestant community celebrations mark William of Orange's victory over king James II at the Battle of Boyne in 1690. These parades have often been perceived by Catholics and nationalists as offensive and triumphalist and are treated as a manifestation of the victory over Irish Catholicism. Many times they have provoked clashes between the two communities and, in the late 1990's, led to severe rioting. These forms of celebration of Protestant identity are especially contentious in those places where the routes of the marches cross Catholic dominated areas. Currently, there are nearly 2000 marches organized across Ulster, but only around a dozen of them are considered to be contentious. Nonetheless, they still polarize the communities and are often captured by extremists who seek to stir up sectarian tensions.

For the first thirty years of the 19th century the main issue in Irish politics was that of Catholic emancipation. The Catholic Association achieved its goal in 1829 with the Catholic Emancipation Act that was passed in the same year. The Association was dissolved quickly afterwards, but the attention of the people turned towards social and economic concerns and particularly to the question of land tenure. A growing awareness of discrimination was saturated by the most important event in the 19th century Irish history which was the potato famine. This tragic catastrophe brought a radical change in Ireland towards British rule. The Irish population was nearly totally dependent on the potato and when the potato crop failed, the family starved. In 1845 nearly half of the total crop became diseased and rotted in the fields. As an immediate effect of the famine about one million people died in Ireland and three million immigrated to Britain, about two million of whom went on to the United States.

What was critical during the crisis was the fact that the British authorities, led by a doctrine driven government, stuck to the rules of free trade and kept exporting meat and grain from Northern Ireland to Great Britain while thousands were starving in the south and west of the island. The famine and emigration was of lasting importance to Irish nationalism. For the next 65 years the main goal of the Irish elite was to secure a form of self-governance for Ireland. The struggle for the Home Rule was near to success, with the Home Rule Bill passed in 1912 by the British Parliament dominated by liberals. The devolved power in response united unionists, mostly Protestants concentrated in Ulster, who fiercely resisted both self-government and the independence of Ireland, fearing for their future in an overwhelmingly Catholic country. In 1912, unionists led by Edward Carson signed the Ulster Covenant and pledged to resist Home Rule by force if necessary. To mobilize the Protestant population, they formed the paramilitary Ulster Volunteers and imported arms from Germany. These actions sent a clear sign to Westminster that they would not obey its decision on giving political autonomy to Ireland, would stay loyal to the crown, wanted to stay in the union and that they would "never surrender". As a response, nationalists formed the Irish Volunteers who announced that they would oppose the Protestant militants. Northern Ireland was on the brink of civil war, and only the outbreak of the WWI prevented both sides from bloody conflict.

The Easter Rising in Dublin in 1916 began the five year long struggle of the Irish nationalists for independence which was eventually gained in 1921. But in Ulster, and particularly the six counties which became Northern Ireland, support for nationalists in the 1918 election was very weak, with the majority of votes going to Unionists who won a strong majority. That fact could not be ignored by Westminster. The British government supported the northern counties during the Irish Civil War and in 1920 partitioned the island of Ireland into two separate entities. This partition of Ireland was confirmed when the Parliament of Northern Ireland exercised its right and under the Anglo-Irish Treaty of 1921 decided to leave the newly established Irish Free State and remain a part of the United Kingdom.

The British government had wanted to include all of the nine traditional counties of Ulster, since it was believed that partition would only be temporary. But the Protestant leaders were afraid of accepting three counties with an overwhelming majority of Catholics. They realized that the threat it posed to the size of the overall Protestant majority and the unionists therefore forced the government to accept a six-county solution. There were no popular votes in the particular counties, as it was very probably that some counties would want to join the Free State. This process did not avoid political and sectarian violence. Northern Ireland came into being in a violent manner with casualties on both sides, but it was mainly Catholics, who in Belfast referred to the period of 1920-1922 as a 'pogrom' against their community[7].

Northern Ireland has remained within the United Kingdom, but a devolved Parliament and government were created as an acknowledgement of regional autonomy. The whole structure of government has become known as Stormont with the name being taken from Stormont Castle where the parliament is located. The castle is a grandiose building on the outskirts of Belfast, set in a huge park which amplified the feeling of separation and distance from the real life of both communities. The first prime minister of Northern Ireland defined the nature of Stormont by stating that he wished to create a 'Protestant parliament in a Protestant state'. From the beginning, the Northern Irish authorities were dominated by the Unionist party, the Orange Order and the Royal Ulster Constabulary, the regional police dominated by Protestants. Although the 1920 Act established that voting in Northern Ireland should be based on a system of proportional representation so as to ensure cross-community representation, in 1922 the proportional system was abolished and simple majority voting reintroduced. As a consequence, from that year on every election returned a Protestant majority and the institutions of the state ensured that the Catholic minority would neither gain power nor achieve parity of representation; the more so given that Catholics were discriminated against in their voting rights. The franchise in local elections did not include the whole adult population and a so called 'business vote' gave some people the right to up to six votes. Except

---

[7] C. Pilkington, *Evolution in Britain Today*, Manchester University Press 2002, pp. 80-81.

for political discrimination, members of the Catholic minority were also discriminated against in the labor market, when applying for council houses and often intimidated by a paramilitary part-time police force recruited from the ranks of the Ulster Volunteer Force, who were notorious for their discriminatory use of violence in support of Protestantism. This undemocratic situation was completely tolerated by Westminster which did not devote much time in dealing with Northern Irish matters. As one of the experts on this issue has shown, during the entire fifty-year period that Stormont was in existence, between 1922 and 1972, Westminster devoted a mere two hours a year to the discussion of Northern Irish issues[8].

A relatively stable situation came to an end in 1966 with the foundation of the Northern Ireland Civil Rights Association (NICRA) which was modeled on the American civil rights movement. The main aim of the NICRA was to show to the world that they suffered from discrimination in a similar way to the blacks in America. This sensational non-violent movement also hoped to attract international support and sympathy, and based its campaigns on peaceful marches and manifestations throughout Ulster.

A Protestant backlash against the protest movement appeared very quickly on the government side which directed brutal police action against the protesters. Counter-demonstrations led by militant Protestants started to end in violence. The situation quickly spiraled out of control and came to a head in 1969 during the summer season of the traditional Orange Order marches. In many cities of the province serious rioting took place and the situation was exacerbated by the fact that these street skirmishes were often supported by off-duty members of the special forces loyal to Stormont. In the wake of the events, the British government sent British soldiers to control the situation. Initially warmly welcomed by Catholics, the army quickly lost its non partisan image and soon became perceived as being one-sided, losing their original support and alienating the Catholics. This fact gave a good argument to these military forces on the nationalist side which declared that they would act as defenders of the Catholic community. In 1971 the first British soldier was killed by an active faction of Irish Republican Army (IRA). The situation deteriorated every month. On 30 January 1972 paratroopers open a fire on a civil march in Derry (officially: Londonderry), killing thirteen unarmed people. This tragic event came to be known to history as Bloody Sunday. The terrified government in Westminster suspended the devolved government of Northern Ireland and two years later dissolved the autonomy and imposed direct rule.

From 1966 till 1998 Northern Ireland was the scene of a violent sectarian struggle known as the Troubles. Between 1969 and 1998 3, 500 people were killed[9]. More than 100 hundred people have been killed since 1998 which raises the question about the durability of the peace process started by the Good Friday Agreement signed in 1998 and renewed by the Saint Andrews Agreement accepted by both sides in 2007. The most recent casualties were two British soldiers killed in March 2009.

---

[8] V. Bogdanor, *Devolution in the United Kingdom*, Opus, Oxford, p. 79.
[9] http://cain.ulst.ac.uk/sutton/tables/Year.html, 20.04.2009.

Divided neighborhoods in the divided city

One of the most critical places of the Northern Ireland conflict has been for a long time two neighboring areas in west Belfast. Located around the shipyards of Belfast, they have mostly been occupied by the working class and still are the most deprived, run-down, and derelict districts in the city. These two areas are known after the name of their main streets: Shankill Road and the Falls Road. The space between Catholic and Protestant communities has been witness to the most terrific acts of violence from both sides. These two main streets have also been areas where most of the paramilitary and their illegal terrorist offshoots headquarters have been located.

It was here where in 1969 a Protestant mob from the Shankill area attacked the neighboring Catholic district, burning and wrecking homes in the process. This outbreak of violence was the mainly due to the decision regarding the army deployment by the government in London. A year later the road was the scene of what became known as the Falls Curfew. At the beginning of July (the season of Orange Order marches) British troops started an arms search among Catholics. Since the nationalist population had completely lost trust in British troop non-partisan attitude, the operation quickly evolved into three days of rioting and gun battles between the Army and Irish republican paramilitaries. Nearly one hundred IRA members exchanged fire with the British troops. Hundreds of local youths also attacked the troops with stones and petrol bombs. Three thousand British soldiers sealed off a whole district populated by ten thousand people, with troops cordoning off the area with barbed wire. During the clashes, four civilians were shot dead in the firing and one more died after being run over by a military vehicle[10].

To prevent further acts of intercommunal violence, the Belfast authorities decided to build one of the first 'peace lines' in Ulster there. These peace lines were thought of as separation barriers between the conflict ridden communities. Their actual constructions differs from just white lines painted on the streets and pavements to tall fences to brick and steel walls up to seven meters high with bribe wire on top of them.

The 'peace line' erected between the Shankill and the Falls Road is one of the longest, highest and most impenetrable. Originally there were only a few such walls in the whole province, and most of them were located in Belfast. The process of separation has sped up in recent years since were only 18 such walls in the 90s and their number has grown rapidly since the beginning of the 21st century. Currently, it is said that there are about 40 walls in Northern Ireland. It was not until 2008, when a public discussion began about their role in the reproduction of intercommunity distances by preventing everyday contacts between two sides, that this was questioned. Some even claim that: "*there is more segregation between Protestants and Catholics since the peace process began then there was before it, and that some of these dividing walls have been built since the peace process got under way in the early 1990s*"[11].

---

[10] E. Moloney, *A secret History of the IRA*, Penguin Books, London 2007, p. 91.
[11] K. Rooney, *Northern Ireland: painting over the cracks*, http://www.spiked-online.com/index.php/site/article/5702/, 9.09.2008.

Although, the British army built a base there, it did not prevent the conflicts. To separate these two dangerous centers of violence from the rest of the city the local government decided to cut off the militant communities from the centre by building a huge dual carriage way in between the Shankill and the Falls and the "normal" districts of Belfast. On the one hand, while this purposely designed separation to some extent prevented the clashes from encompassing the rest of the city, it created a sort of ghetto where everyday life is dominated by a landscape composed of violent images of murals, walls and the barbed wire of separation barriers and abandoned, underinvested council estates. In these economically struggling areas, where people already feel isolated and marginalized, this move only deepens the social exclusion. Both districts are seen as dangerous and no go areas. Entering them is like a journey to a different world known rather from television news on such conflicts like Palestine or the former Yugoslav countries. It is probably one of the very rare European urban spaces where a feeling of danger creeps around every corner of buildings.

Until the end of the 90s the Falls Road and the Shankill were notorious for the actions of various nationalist and loyalist forces. The most terrifying acts were conducted by 'the Shankill Butchers' who operated in the 70s. They killed upwards of thirty people including some members of loyalist community. What was most horrifying was the fact the way they treated their victims. They were usually captured on the streets, tortured and killed by a slashing of the throat. Actually, the leader of this terrorist group had worked as a butcher before he became a regular killer. His actions were so destructive that it is believed that he was executed by IRA members with loyalist consent. But also the Shankill and its residents were subjected to shootings and bombings by Irish republican paramilitary forces. It was in 1993 when a time bomb was exploded in a fish shop where 10, mostly accidental customers, were killed. These two districts, occupied by a population of around 20 thousand people each, are also known for the large number of murals spread across the streets[12].

Heritage and Visual representation

The murals are literally painted on the walls and depict people and events which have had played a role in the construction and maintenance of divisions between the communities. The first mural in Belfast is thought to have gone up in 1908; it was a Loyalist painting of William of Orange's defeat of the Catholics at the Battle of the Boyne in 1690[13]. It is estimated that at the height of the Troubles, there were over 2000 of these sectarian murals in Ulster[14].

They were painted to commemorate dead heroes of both communities, celebrate their victories, or, what is very important from the present perspective, to show who is in charge of the particular territories.

---

[12] http://www.bbc.uk/history/recent/troubles, 20.04.2009.
[13] S. Kuper, *Northern Ireland's murals*, "Financial Times", 29.11.2008.
[14] E. Caesar, *Freeze Frame: Loyalist paramilitary murals, Shankill, Belfast*, "The Independent", 11.07.2006.

The murals converted typical streets built up with terrace houses into Catholic and Loyalist areas. Their role was to build symbolic boundaries dividing two different social worlds inhabited by hostile communities. They were created spontaneously by young and amateur painters and expressed an authentic devotion to mark the area with a visual representation of their collective identities. In the Shankill they often express these moments of the history of Ulster provinces which tied it in a bloody knot with the British crown such as the support for anti-Catholicism during the Glorious Revolution or the heroism of Ulster soldiers in the WWI trenches. On the republican side, they often pay tribute to those who actively fought against Protestant dominance such as, for example, the huge mural depicting Bobby Sands and the other hunger strikers who died in the Maze, an infamous prison where paramilitaries of both sides and political activists have been imprisoned.

These spontaneously created pictures have become a vehicle of collective memory. For people who had to go through all these tragic times they are simple a way of expression of respect and admiration for those who did not hesitate to pay with their own lives in order to protect their fellow citizens.

However, there also only murals which have nothing to do with some form of heroic history and heroes ready to sacrifice their lives. There are pictures, painted relatively recently, which have become a means of competition among different factions of paramilitary organizations on both sides. Some internal rivalries which started many years ago among Catholics and Protestants have brought many conflicts inside the two communities. Frequent divisions and radical ways of operating have led to the situation where some of these groupings have completely lost their local support among ordinary citizens. The peace process meant an end to their previous reality. For most members of smaller organizations which, according to the official government were treated not as freedom fighters but terrorists, starting a new life turned out to be to either too difficult or too humiliating. They spent most of their lives as fighting activists and their lives were quite distant from the daily routines of their working class fellows. To defend their status they started to look for new possibilities of carrying on with their military ethos. In order to maintain the image of violent reality, they started to spread images which are full of violence, glorify hatred and mobilize militant activism. The Catholic Falls Road suddenly seemed to be deeply engaged in supporting terrorist organizations around the globe. There are a series of pictures at the beginning of the street which express solidarity with terrorist organizations in the Basque Country, Palestine or Columbia. Their common feature seems to be support for orthodox international Marxist revolutionary movements whose aim is not only independence but also radical social change. It is worth remembering that for many offshoots of the IRA, the main goal of their fight was not only independence but also the establishment of a united Irish communist republic. Some 20 years after the collapse of the Berlin Wall, the attractiveness of radical violent anti capitalist ideologies has diminished, so the murals are to mobilize the local youth to join already seriously weakened troops. The situation seems to be even worse on the Protestant side. Many paramilitary organizations have started to more resemble criminal gangs than patriotic activists. Members of the most radical groups are very often involved with drug and gun dealing and have little to do with the actual danger caused by neighbouring Catholics. Nonetheless, this gangster-like style of life is still portrayed as a part of civic obligation and is represented by murals depicting hooded men with guns who serve as attractive role models to the Shankill teenagers. There are still freshly burned houses, broken windows and people shot dead in the street in the streets, but they are usually casualties of inter group conflicts and not sectarian violence.

For the extremists on both sides, putting an end to this conflict means losing the last chance to preserve their social status in their communities. There is a very thin line between being a combatant and a criminal and the freshly painted murals which depict these most recent fights and their victims try to capture the past glory of troubled days in order to use it for their own quite cynical and pragmatic purposes.

And these images have been targeted by civic movements who have started different campaigns to remove the provocative manifestations of militaristic images.

The initiative first came from the Reverend Gary Mason, a Methodist pastor, who spent more than year persuading local Protestant paramilitary groups to replace their paramilitary murals with new ones. His blatantly open question has often been recited by many supporters: "*Imagine a 6- or 7-year-old child who gets up every morning, opens the curtains, and the first things he sees are two hooded gunmen painted on the side of the building across the street. Is that healthy?*"[15].

Photo 2.

Source: Author's photograph.

---

[15] K. LaCamera, *Peaceful images replace violent themes on Belfast murals*, http://gbgm-umc.org/global_news/full_article.cfm?articleid=1871, 14.03.2009.

His initiative has found many followers amongst Catholics and Protestants alike. There have been many grassroots initiatives which have taken over the idea and started to replace the violent images to move beyond the violence and brutality of the past. One of them led to the organization of the Summer Mural Festival in 2004. The Festival was widely appreciated for breaking barriers of exclusion and transforming controversial paramilitary murals across the city into positive 'shared spaces'. In 2006 the New Belfast Community Arts Initiative started similar projects in collaboration with local community groups across Belfast. Soon, other cities, towns and villages in Northern Ireland have followed suit and are repainting and creating new, more open, inclusionary and forward looking images which have appeared on their streets.

These activities have also been supported by considerable local authority funding and eventually by the British government which devoted £3.3 m to a project administered by the Arts Council as means of helping communities present themselves in more positive light and develop a "shared future"[16]. That gave a new impetus to the whole idea. Many walls in the Shankill and the Falls Road have been covered with very similar images with the most popular being of George Best. One of the greatest British footballers and a friend of the Beatles were born and bred in west Belfast. A famous novelist was also born in Belfast and it is very common for the two communities to feature characters from C.S Lewis' books.

These initiatives aimed at recreating the public landscapes of the everyday life of Belfast inhabitants and other populations in Ulster have also raised some controversy and criticism. For many of them, murals are a visible sign of their troubled history. They argue that repainting will help to hide tensions, but that they will not remove the reasons which cause them. Besides, they point out that they constitute a vital part of Northern Ireland's heritage. In their view, there is no point in running away from the historic facts – a better solution is to openly face the historical truth, since it could help people cope better to handle contemporary antagonisms.

There is probably no simple answer to the question as whether or not to preserve the symbolic remains of the Troubles. But, the fact that the issue of visual representation has triggered a public debate which mobilized support and actions across both communities is definitely an indicator that the polarized world of Ulster's population is becoming increasingly more complex and nuanced. The confrontational character of both identities is losing its overwhelming power and bringing more space to social communications. This, in turn, allows one to hope that the agreement reached by the political actors will bring peace also at the grassroots level.

---

[16] O. Bowcott, *Gables and murals to be replaced*, "The Guardian", 12.07.2006.

Nicosia
Conflict and Cooperation in the Divided Capital City
Przemysław Osiewicz

The analysis setting

Cyprus, a former British colony, became an independent state in August 1960. The Cypriot independence was a result of compromise between Greece and Turkey. While Greece opted for *enosis*, namely an annexation of Cyprus, Turkey preferred *taksim* – the partition of the island. Unfortunately, complicated constitutional provisions failed to guarantee essential conditions for a peaceful coexistence of two equal Cypriot communities – Greek Cypriots and Turkish Cypriots. Therefore the Cyprus conflict could be defined as an ethnic conflict. Moreover, it is also a religious conflict as Greek Cypriots are predominantly members of the Cypriot Orthodox Church and Turkish Cypriots are mainly Muslims.

As regards proportion of ethnic groups in Cyprus in 1960, there were 448,857 Greek Cypriots (77.7 per cent) and 104,350 Turkish Cypriots[1] (18.1 per cent). On this basis Greek Cypriots claimed that the constitution provided the Turkish Cypriot community with disproportionate representation in the chief organs of the state, for example, in the Cypriot House of Representatives where 15 out of 50 members were Turkish Cypriot (7:3)[2]. The same ratio was applied to the public service. This and similar arguments were used in order to support the idea of amending the constitution in 1963. Then President of the Republic of Cyprus Makarios had proposed Vice-President Fazil Küçük 13 constitutional amendments which were rejected by the Turkish Cypriot community and inflamed ethnic fights in the end of 1963[3]. In Katia Hadjidemetriou's opinion, "*December of 1963 marks the beginning of a government crisis which was followed by endless efforts for the negotiation of a political arrangement. Immediately after the intercommunal clashes all those Turkish Cypriots who were members of the government together with Turkish Cypriots civil servants left and went to stay in the Turkish quarter of Nicosia*"[4]. However, both sides present discrepant views as regards sources of the Cyprus dispute as well as the moment when it began.

---

[1] *Report on the demographic structure of the Cypriot communities of 27 April 1992*, Nicosia 2000, p. 17.
[2] K. Chrysostomides, *The Republic of Cyprus: A Study in International Law*, The Hague 2000, p. 28. According to the above ethnic proportion this ratio should be 8:2 in favour of Greek Cypriots, not 7:3.
[3] T. Potier, *A Functional Cyprus Settlement*, Ruhpolding 2007, p. 16.
[4] K. Hadjidemetriou, *A History of Cyprus*, Nicosia 2002, p. 390.

According to Turkish Cypriots, the Cyprus question has remained unsettled since 1963. In their opinion the dispute began with the de facto fall of the Republic of Cyprus as a unitary state. Violent ethnic clashes in December 1963 resulted in a partial separation of two Cypriot communities. *"British troops began patrolling Nicosia and Larnaca on 24 December and a 'green line' (reminiscent of EOKA days and regularly likened to the more famous Berlin Wall) was subsequently established on 29/30 December 1963 in Nicosia to separate the Greek from the Turkish Cypriot quarters. This demarcation line, guarded by British troops, cut straight across the mixed suburbs of Omorphita and Neapolis and put the entire Armenian quarter as well as the Greek areas of Kermia, Ayios Kasianos and Ayios Iakovos behind Turkish lines"*[5]. It was when the first barricade across Lidras (in Turkish – Lokmaci), the main commercial street of Nicosia, was erected. Soon another barricades appeared within the Walled City of Nicosia. Most of them were built of old barrels, boxes, barbed wire and sacks of sand[6].

On 4 March 1964 the Security Council decided to create a United Nations Peace-keeping Force in Cyprus and recommended *"that the function of the Force should be in the interest of preserving international peace and security, to use its best efforts to prevent a recurrence of fighting and, as necessary, to contribute to the maintenance and restoration of law and order and a return to normal conditions"*[7]. In March 1964 the first UN troops appeared on the island in order to separate both communities and prevent further strife, for example, in the old town of Nicosia. Turkish Cypriots were forced to live in small enclaves or a few poky quarters in bigger cities, for example, in the walled city of Nicosia or Famagusta[8]. The successful coup d'état of 15 July 1974, which was prepared by some right-wing Greek Cypriots and the Greek military junta, provoked the Turkish military operation which was described by Turkey and Turkish Cypriots as the Cyprus Peace Operation[9].

Contrary to the Turkish Cypriot side, Greek Cypriots point to 1974 as the beginning of the dispute when the Turkish government led by Bülent Ecevit took advantage of a political turmoil in Cyprus and decided to invade and occupy a part of the island. The Greek Cypriot authorities do not agree that Turkey had right to take such steps and do not back up an argument that it did so in order to protect Turkish

---

[5] S. Panteli, *The History of Modern Cyprus*, Nicosia 2005, p. 225.
[6] Forty years later Brain Self described the Green Line zone with the following words: *"Negotiating the old cities' narrow street and following the barrier as closely as possible is to witness 30 years of decay. The UN controlled buffer zone – the Green Line – between two armies is a scar of lifeless tissue across a living city. Rotting sandbags, collapsed mud bricks, faded hoardings and broken windows bear silent testimony to an everyday life wrenched brutally from its socket. Abandoned shops and houses are a theatre of the dead"*. See: B. Self, *Untidy Essays: A Journeyman in Cyprus*, Kyrenia 2007, p. 21.
[7] *The Security Council Resolution 186 (1964) of 4 March 1964*, in: *United Nations Security Council and General Assembly Resolutions on Cyprus 1960-2006*, Nicosia 2006, p. 12.
[8] Venhar Keskin presented his recollections from Ktima, a district of Paphos, which became a Turkish Cypriot quarter between 1963-1974. See: V. Keskin, *Besieged*, Nicosia 2000.
[9] S. Ismail, *Cyprus Peace Operation: Reasons – Development – Consequences*, Nicosia 2000.

Cypriots. Greek Cypriots claim that the Turkish invasion resulted in a de facto partition of Cyprus and occupation of its northern part[10].

Both sides intended to settle the problem in a peaceful way, however, lack of mutual trust as well as progress during bilateral negotiations under the UN auspices worked up to the de facto division of Cyprus in 1983. On 15 November the Assembly of Turkish Cypriots proclaimed the unilateral declaration of independence (UDI). Since then the Turkish Cypriot state under the name of the Turkish Republic of Northern Cyprus (TRNC) has been functioning, although so far it has been recognized only by the Republic of Turkey. Greek Cypriots officially condemned this decision and began diplomatic activities aimed at restoration of status quo of 1974. This policy did not prove efficient, however, it resulted in international isolation of the Turkish Cypriot state. *The purported secession of part of the Republic of Cyprus* was officially deplored by the Security Council in its resolution of 18 November 1983[11]. Furthermore, the Security Council considered the UDI as "*legally invalid* and called upon *all states to respect sovereignty, independence, territorial integrity and non-alignment of the Republic of Cyprus*"[12]. The European Parliament also condemned "*the action taken by the Turkish Cypriot sector to declare an independent Turkish Cypriot State in Cyprus* and invited *the Council of Ministers to take all the necessary measures so that this action by the Turkish Cypriot sector remains null and void*"[13]. Nevertheless, the division of the island has remained a fact. According to the Turkish Cypriot position, "*the Turkish Republic of Northern Cyprus has an effectively functioning state mechanism, a democratically elected government and legislature, an independent judiciary and all other institutions of statehood*"[14].

Since 1974 consecutive rounds of negotiations have not led up to comprehensive solution of the Cyprus dispute. Undoubtedly, the Annan Plan, negotiated between 2002 and 2004 under UN auspices, constituted the best opportunity. The European Union also engaged in the process aimed at reunification and accession of a federal Cyprus to the EU[15]. Nevertheless, the simultaneous referenda on the Annan Plan of 24 April 2004 ended in a fiasco. The majority of Greek Cypriots, namely 76 per cent,

---

[10] For more details on the military operation and its consequences see: M.A. Birand, *30 Hot Days*, Nicosia 1985; G. Clerides, *Cyprus: My Deposition*, vol. 4, Nicosia 1992; V. Coufoudakis, *Cyprus and International Politics*, Nicosia 2007; C. Hitchens, *Hostage to History: Cyprus from the Ottomans to Kissinger*, London 2002; S. Ismail, *Cyprus Peace Operation: Reasons – Development – Consequences*, Nicosia 2000; F. Mirbagheri, *Cyprus and International Peacemaking*, London 1998; P. Osiewicz, *Pokojowa regulacja kwestii cypryjskiej*, Toruń 2008; O.P. Richmond, *Mediating in Cyprus: The Cypriot Communities and the United Nations*, London 1998.

[11] *Security Council Resolution 541 (1983) of 18 November 1983*, [in:] *United Nations Security Council...*, op. cit., p. 87.

[12] Ibidem.

[13] *Resolution of the European Parliament of 17 November 1983 on 'the Declaration of Independence' by the Turkish Cypriot Sector of Cyprus*, [in:] *European Stand on the Cyprus Problem*, Nicosia 2003, p. 34.

[14] *Facts About Turkish Republic of Northern Cyprus*, Nicosia 2008, p. 7.

[15] See: A. Theophanous, *The Cyprus Question and the EU: the Challenge and the Promise*, Nicosia 2004.

rejected the plan, while 65 per cent of Turkish Cypriots voted in favour of the comprehensive solution based on the UN initiative as well as the accession of a federal Cyprus to the EU on 1 May 2004[16]. As a consequence, the international community was forced to acknowledge the results and find a way out of the complicated situation. The Republic of Cyprus, precisely Greek Cypriot controlled southern part of Cyprus joined the EU on 1 May 2004. Although *de iure* the whole Cypriot territory constitutes a part of EU territory, *acquis communautaire* is suspended in the northern part of the island dominated by Turkish Cypriots, including the northern part of Nicosia[17]. Such decision created yet another dimension of division on the island.

Since 1974 Greek Cypriots have controlled 59.4 per cent and Turkish Cypriots 35.2 per cent of territory of the island of Cyprus. The rest of territory comprises a buffer zone – 2.6 per cent and British Sovereign Bases – 2.7 per cent[18].

Nicosia as a divided city: One city – two capital cities

The ceasefire line, which is a state border to Turkish Cypriots, divides Cyprus into two parts. It is often called the Attila Line and its name comes from the codename of the Turkish military operation of 1974. Its section in Nicosia is referred to as the Green Line and crosses the city from the west to the east. The Green Line in Nicosia was created in 1964 and marked the division line between two communities within the city after the 1963 ethnic clashes.

Nicosia is the only divided capital city in the world. For Greek Cypriots Nicosia (Lefkosia) is the capital of the Republic of Cyprus. Its population in the sector controlled by the Greek Cypriot administration is 224,500[19]. The Municipal Council consists of 26 members and there are 15 committees. In 2007 Eleni Mavrou was elected the Mayor of Nicosia. As regards international cooperation, the Greek Cypriot administered Nicosia is twinned among others with Athens, Lisbon, Milan, Odessa, Shanghai and Shiraz in Iran. The Nicosia Municipality also cooperates with Helsinki, Zagreb, Moscow and Damascus[20].

The Turkish name of Nicosia is Lefkoşa. Its northern part controlled by the Turkish Cypriot administration is the seat of government of the Turkish Republic of Northern Cyprus. In 2006 the total population was 85,000[21]. It increased rapidly by

---

[16] A. Sözen, *The Cyprus Negotiations and the Basic Parameters: An Overview of the Inter-communal Negotiations*, [in:] A. Sözen (ed.), *The Cyprus Conflict: Looking Ahead*, Famagusta 2008, p. 90. See also: C. Dodd, *Disaccord on Cyprus: the UN Plan and After*, London 2005.
[17] More: P. Osiewicz, *The European Union and Its Attitude towards Turkish Cypriots after 2004: Continuity or Change?*, [in:] J. Jańczak (ed.), *Beyond Borders: External Relations of the European Union*, Poznań 2008.
[18] *Geography – Environment*, [in:] P. Lyssiotis, V. Kokoti (eds), *About Cyprus*, Nicosia 2007, p. 8.
[19] *Ibidem*, p. 9.
[20] *Municipal Council and Committees*, www.nicosia.org.cy/english, 10.02.2009.
[21] *The Press Statement of Prime Minister Ferdi Sabit Soyer on the Tentative Results of 2006 Population and Housing Census, 5 May 2006*, www.trncpio.org, 12.07.2007.

36.3 per cent comparing to the 1996 Population Census (62,000 residents). The annual average growth of population in the Turkish Cypriot part of Nicosia is 3.4 per cent[22]. As regards municipal administration, the Turkish Cypriot part of Nicosia has its own administration. Cemal Metin is the Mayor of the Turkish Nicosia Municipality (Lefkoşa Türk Belediyesi). The Municipal Council has 21 members[23]. As its Greek Cypriot counterpart, the Turkish Cypriot Nicosia is twinned with the following cities: Ankara, Bursa, Kumanova, Comrat (Gaugazia), Gaziantep and Alanya[24].

Areas of conflict

Grey areas

City plans of Nicosia are the best examples of lack of mutual recognition. Both Greek Cypriots and Turkish Cypriots provide tourists with maps which do not include districts of Nicosia controlled by the other side. Instead one can see grey or yellow areas with such inscriptions as 'Area inaccessible because of the Turkish occupation'. That's the reason why tourists have to collect two different city plans if they intend to visit both sides of Nicosia.

On the one hand, Turkish Cypriots perceive the Green Line as a state border. A passport and a Turkish Cypriot visa or a Cypriot origin are required while crossing the border[25]. It should be emphasized that only EU citizens are allowed to cross the line. On the other hand, Greek Cypriots present it as a ceasefire line. Only the police control the Green Line crossing points on the Greek side. There are no border guards.

It should be emphasized that it had been impossible to cross the Green Line until 2003 when both sides lifted the restrictions. Beforehand only tourists could cross from the south to the north just for a few hours and they had to come back before 5 p.m. Otherwise they had to come back home through Turkey. As regards that, nobody was allowed to cross from the north to the south. Although nowadays all Cypriots as well as other EU citizens can cross the line without difficulty, the division still causes problems and encumbers bilateral cooperation as there are just a few crossing points, for example, the Ledra crossing and the Lokmacı crossing.

Provocative nationalistic symbolism

Unfortunately, both sides still use provocative nationalistic symbolism. Turkish Cypriot and Turkish flags or Greek and Greek Cypriot flags can be found along the

---

[22] *Ibidem*.
[23] *Belediye Meclis Üyeleri*, http://www.lefkosabelediyesi.org/index.html, 11.02.2009.
[24] *Kardeş Belediyeler*, http://www.lefkosabelediyesi.org/index.html, 11.02.2009.
[25] A Turkish Cypriot visa can be obtained on the spot while crossing the Green Line or coming to Cyprus via Turkish Cypriot airport Ercan or sea harbours. It is a free of charge sheet of paper which is not required by the Greek Cypriot authorities.

buffer zone almost everywhere. Turkish Cypriots also painted a huge flag of the Turkish Republic of Northern Cyprus on one of the hillsides nearby Nicosia. It can be seen from the southern part of the city even during the night. Furthermore, both sides present banners like 'Turkish Republic of Northern Cyprus: Forever" or provocative posters devoted to various historical events nearby the Green Line crossing points, e.g. at the Ledra crossing. Undoubtedly, such nationalistic symbolism only preserve negative stereotypes[26].

The Nicosia International Airport vs. Ercan

Nicosia is the only capital in Europe, and probably in the world, which possesses two airports, but cannot make any use of any of them. The Nicosia International Airport, located within the UN buffer zone to the west of the city centre, has remained closed since 1974. For that reason Greek Cypriots have to use other Cypriot airports in Larnaca or Paphos. However, this remark applies only to the Greek Cypriot part of Nicosia. Turkish Cypriots built their own airport to the east of the city, namely Ercan. The only problem is that Ercan has not been designated as an international airport yet due to the Greek Cypriot backlash. Therefore the Turkish Cypriot airport is connected directly only with a few Turkish cities like Istanbul, Ankara or Antalya.

"*It is sometimes claimed that foreign states cannot allow direct flights to Northern Cyprus as the government of the Republic of Cyprus has not designated any airport in the north as an international airport. The principle of effective control dictates that the authorities exercising de facto control are in a position to decide on whether or not an airport can be designated as an international airport*"[27]. On this basis, the authorities of the Republic of Cyprus reject any Turkish Cypriot demand for designation of Ercan as an international airport. There are no direct flights from or to Ercan except for a few Turkish cities. In response to the Greek Cypriot policy, Turkish Cypriots do not agree on reopening of the Nicosia International Airport.

As a consequence, these circumstances result in a bizarre situation which affects both sides. Greek Cypriots are forced to fly from the airport in Larnaca, while Turkish Cypriots always have to travel to other countries via Turkey. At the moment nothing indicates that this situation may change in the foreseeable future.

The economic gap

The economic gap between both parts of Cyprus as well as of Nicosia remains one of the most significant problems, however, nowadays it is not as big as it used to be,

---

[26] More about nationalism in Cyprus see: N. Persitianis, *Cypriot Nationalism, Dual Identity, and Politics*, [in:] Y. Papadakis, N. Peristianis, G. Welz (eds), *Divided Cyprus: Modernity, History, and an Island in Conflict*, Bloomington 2006, pp. 100-120.
[27] T. van den Hoogen, S. Tiryaki, M. Akgün (eds), *A Promise to Keep: Time to End the International Isolation of the Turkish Cypriots*, Istanbul 2008, p. 46.

for example, 10 years ago. In 1996 *per capita* income in the North had amounted to 32 per cent of the per capita income in the South, while in 2006 it reached 59 per cent. Yet it should be emphasized that the ratio in 1977 was 67 per cent[28]. According to the TRNC authorities, such decrease is a result of economic isolation of Turkish Cypriots. Its best example is infrastructure condition. The northern part of Nicosia needs far more attention and financial resources than the Greek Cypriot districts. Ongoing bilateral projects can only limit this gap, but they will not liquidate it. Only successful reunification process could result in a gradual equalization of living standards.

On 1 January 2008 the euro became the monetary unit of Cyprus and replaced the Cyprus pound, although in practice only in its Greek Cypriot administered part[29]. Turkish Cypriots still use Turkish Lira. For this reason residents as well as tourists crossing the Green Line from the Turkish Cypriot to the Greek Cypriot part of Nicosia have to exchange money if they want to pay in cash. It does not apply to visitors from the south who come to the northern part of the city as euro is widely accepted there. At the same time such situation boosts trade as prices of a lot of goods in the north are much lower than in the south. Therefore the Greek Cypriot authorities limited quantity as well as value of products which can be purchased in the northern part in order to protect domestic market[30].

Areas of cooperation

The Nicosia Master Plan

United Nations Development Programme (UNDP) has provide assistance to both communities since 1964. *"Since 1981 there have been four UNDP projects, namely the Nicosia Master Plan, the Thalassemia project, and farming and handicraft projects. Funds for three of these project are divided equally between the Greek and Turkish Cypriots. The aid allocated for the period 1983-1986 for the Turkish Cypriots was 658,000 dollars, which was 30 per cent of the total allocated for Cyprus"*[31]. As far as the Nicosia Master Plan is concerned, it is defined as a bi-communal project dedicated to revitalization as well as future development of Nicosia. Officially the project was initiated on 29 October 1979. The team consists of various experts representing both sides, for example, economists, sociologists, architects and civil engineers. Its main aim is to protect architectural and cultural heritage in the Walled City. *"In most of projects within the*

---

[28] Ö. Gökçekuş, *The Economics of the Isolation of Turkish Cypriots*, Kyrenia 2008, p. 12.
[29] *The Republic of Cyprus: An Overview*, Nicosia 2007, p. 68.
[30] According to the Green Line Regulation, *"goods contained in the personal luggage of persons crossing the line shall be from turnover tax and excise duty as well as from other duties provided that they have no commercial character and their total value does not exceed EUR 260 per person. The quantitative limits for these exemptions shall be 40 cigarettes and 1 litre of spirits for personal consumption"*. See: *Conditions for Trading with Regards to the Green Line Regulation*, http://www.ktto.net/english/foreigntrade.html, 10.02.2009.
[31] *North Cyprus Almanack*, London 1987, p. 37.

Nicosia Master Plan emphasis is placed on housing rehabilitation, upgrading or provision of community facilities, landscaping and pedestrianisation schemes. The first twin investment projects that have been implemented were Chrysaliniotissa and Arab Ahmed residential programmes"[32].

The first phase of the plan was being realized between 1981-1984. Then a general development strategy was introduced in order to concentrate and consolidate the city. The second phase lasted from 1984 until 1986 and *"focused on a more detailed operational plan for the central area of Nicosia, including the historic centre and the central business district"*[33]. At the present time the Nicosia Master Plan is in the third phase. Within this phase the priority is given to projects focusing on housing rehabilitation and pedestrianisation. The ongoing projects include:
– Chrysaliniotissa Housing Revitalisation;
– Pedestrianization of the Commercial Area of the Historic Center;
– The improvement of green open spaces;
– The improvement of traffic and parking conditions;
– Rehabilitation of neglected areas[34].

As regards cooperation between governmental institutions and local authorities, the Department of Town Planning and Housing of the Republic of Cyprus deals with urban and spatial planning and cooperates with the Municipality of Nicosia. *"The Department also incorporates the Sectors of Preservation and Planning Schemes, as well as supporting administration, while it provides personnel and advice to the Nicosia Master Plan, a bi-communal institution involving both the Greek and Turkish Cypriot communities of the divided capital"*[35]. Besides, one of the committees of Nicosia Municipality on the Greek Cypriot side is the Committee for the Revitalisation of the Green Line. Its main aims are:
– Submitting suggestions and promoting the implementation of plans and projects for the revitalisation of the areas neighbouring the Green Line;
– Monitoring the implementation of the revitalisation projects in progress;
– Solving the various problems and monitoring the management of the already completed revitalisation projects[36].

Since 1995 Cyprus has participated in the European Heritage Days, which were established by the Council of Europe in 1991. In 2008 Nicosia presented the architectural heritage situated along the buffer zone. *"The cultural richness of the area, so close and yet inaccessible, was presented for the first time through walking tours and exhibitions. The aim was to explore the ways in which common heritage unites people from different com-*

---

[32] A. Petridou, *Nicosia Master Plan: Perspectives for Urban Rehabilitation – Building Bridges Between the Two Communities of the Divided City of Nicosia*, http://www.eukn.org/binaries/cyprus/bulk/practice/2005/10/nicosia-masterplan.pdf, 13.02.2009.
[33] *Nicosia Master Plan: Planning Strategy for the Divided City*, http://www.nicosia.org.cy/english/enniaio_anaviosis.shtm, 27.02.2009.
[34] *Nicosia Master Plan: Priority Projects*, http://www.nicosia.org.cy/english/enniaio_proteraitotitas.shtm, 27.02.2009.
[35] *Administration – Land Use and Planning*, [in:] *About Cyprus*, op. cit., pp. 111-112.
[36] *Committee for the Revitalisation of the Green Line*, www.nicosia.org.cy/english, 9.02.2009.

munities and builds communication bridges between them"[37]. Such initiatives may result in restoration of buildings located within the buffer zone in the future.

Since 2001 UNDP is also responsible for Partnership for the Future, namely an UNDP project funded by the EU, which is also dedicated to restoration of the Walled City of Nicosia. Since then the Nicosia Master Plan has been included in the programme[38].

UNDP Partnership for the Future

UNDP Partnership for the Future deals with comprehensive rehabilitation of Old Nicosia. The programme aimes at:
– Involving the Greek Cypriot and Turkish Cypriot technical teams in an effort to implement the projects for the Nicosia Master Plan;
– Supporting the revitalisation of the Walled City of Nicosia and the conservation of its architectural and cultural heritage, according to the policies and provisions of the Nicosia Master Plan;
– Drawing the attention of Nicosia residents to conservation issues and to the importance of a shared heritage;
– Improving the living environment of Nicosia neighbourhoods[39].

A lot of UNDP projects have been completed or initiated in Cyprus since 2001. So far UNDP Partnership for the Future's main achievements are:
– Revitalization of selected buildings in the Phaneromeni area;
– The Omeriye bath complex;
– Infrastructure and facades restoration in the Selimiye mosque area in Selimiye;
– Saint Nicholas church (the Bedestan) in Selimiye;
– Restoration works in the Samanbahçe area;
– Walled City Info Point – an info point which provides residents as well as tourist with easy access to information related to revitalisation of Old Nicosia;
– Various brochures and other publications on taking care of historical buildings[40].

Among ongoing UNDP projects in Nicosia are:
– Improvement of urban infrastructure and of the public space in Omeriye, Selimiye, Phaneromeni and Samanbahçe districts[41];
– Preservation and restoration of the buildings of architectural and historical value in Selimiye and Phaneromeni;
– Revistalisation of different neighbourhoods in Selimiye and Phaneromeni;
– Restoration of monuments in the area of Omeriye[42].

---

[37] *European Heritage Days*, "Cyprus Today" vol. XLVI, no. 3, 2008, pp. 52-54.
[38] *UNDP Cyprus Portal*, http://mirror.undp.org/cyprus/, 12.02.2009.
[39] *Rehabilitation of Old Nicosia*, http://www.undp-pff.org/index.php?option=com_content&task=view&id=13&Itemid=22, 12.02.2009.
[40] *Ibidem*.
[41] Selimiye and Samanbahçe areas are located in the northern part of Nicosia while Phaneromeni and Omeriye areas are situated in the south.
[42] *On-going Projects*, http://www.undp-pff.org/index.php?option=com_content&task=view&id=82&Itemid=141, 12.02.2009.

The United States also supported the Nicosia Master Plan through the UNDP Bicommunal Development Programme. The project was financed by the United States Agency for International Development (USAID), which *"has been the principal U.S. agency to extend assistance to countries recovering from disaster, trying to escape poverty, and engaging in democratic reforms"*[43]. Between 1997 and 2004 USAID invested in Cyprus more than 16 million dollars. In 2007 the USAID-funded Nicosia Master Plan project won the 2007 Aga Khan Award for Architecture, the world's largest architectural award[44]. Nowadays the United States supports projects in Cyprus through Action for Cooperation and Trust in Cyprus (ACT) – a new UNDP peace building project in Cyprus. *"The ACT project is managed directly by UNDP and has a total budget of 26.5 million dollars for three years (October 2005-October 2008). The project is funded principally by USAID, with additional funding from UNDP"*[45].

The new crossing: Lidras/Lokmacı

One of the examples of bilateral cooperation in Nicosia is a recent opening of the Lidras/Lokmacı crossing point. Both sides decided to pull down the oldest barricade in the Walled City and restore commercial activity in the city centre. As a result, Greek Cypriots and Turkish Cypriots succeeded in reconstructing the most important and historical pedestrian zone in Nicosia.

Conclusions

Undoubtedly, Nicosia is a very interesting as well as exceptional example of a divided city. It is the only divided capital city in the world. Although the division line does not exist according to international law, in practice it functions and effectively separates two Cypriot communities.

Nevertheless, it should be emphasized that the bi-communal cooperation in Nicosia has been developing since 2003. After almost 30 years of complete isolation Turkish Cypriots and Greek Cypriots began cooperating and changing their city. Both communities still face several problems and obstacles, but the future looks promising. Such initiatives as Nicosia Master Plan, UNDP Partnership for the Future or new crossing points create a positive atmosphere. Some sources of conflict like Grey Areas or nationalistic symbolism could be easily eliminated if there was enough political will on both sides. Even economic gap could be decreased thanks to bilateral trade and EU funds.

---

[43] *This is USAID*, http://www.usaid.gov/about_usaid/, 27.02.2009.
[44] *Nicosia Master Plan Wins World's Largest Architectural Award, September 6, 2007*, http://cyprus.usembassy.gov/EmbatWork/NMPsep07.htm, 27.02.2009.
[45] *United Nations Development Programme – Action for Cooperation and Trust in Cyprus*, http://www.undp-act.org/main/default.aspx?tabid=22, 27.02.2009.

Opole
A Stranger at Home. A Study of Inter-Group Distance
Cezary Trosiak

Introductory remarks

The town of Opole is located in a territory which has undergone a process of radical reconfiguration of social, cultural and political space after WWII. When compared to other parts of the Western and Northern Lands, it had a peculiar nature as the 'newcomers' encountered the indigenous population on a greater scale than anywhere else in the lands incorporated to Poland after WWII. By the end of the verification campaign in 1949, 436,000 autochthons remained in the territory of Opole Silesia (*Śląsk Opolski*) accounting for 54% of the total population of the Opole province (*województwo opolskie*) at the time. This was the highest percentage of indigenous population in the Western and Northern Lands. On the basis of statistics obtained from the national census in 2002, at present the Opole province is inhabited by approximately 270,000 individuals who declare to be of a non-Polish (Silesian or German) origin. Around 105,000 of them spend over two months in the Federal Republic of Germany annually[1]. It seems, however, that the actual number of 'autochthons' is higher, as when speaking to the pollsters many of them could conceal their national identity for pragmatic and opportunistic reasons. This was definitely not caused by reasons of security, as used to be in the case between 1949-1989, though.

The role of the town as the center of Polish and German national life

The history of Opole is quite unique in Polish-German relations. This uniqueness is a result of the function the town had been playing in mutual relations over the last century. Right after the end of WWI, Opole was the capital of the regency, and the focal point of Polish national life as it was the site of the most significant institutions of Polish national life in this part of the Upper Silesia that stayed on the German side as a result of the plebiscite and the 3rd German uprising. After 1989, the town became the 'capital' of the German minority in Poland. Paradoxically, the population has

---

[1] R. Rauziński, K. Szczyglewski, *Śląska ludność rodzima w strukturze demograficznej i społecznej Śląska Opolskiego wczoraj i dziś*, Opole 2008, p. 48.

not changed much. In the inter-war period, a considerable proportion of the inhabitants of Opole Silesia opted for Poland, whereas at present a definite majority of their successors choose the German or Silesian option, or at least to keep their distance from the Polish option.

Basic facts concerning Opole

Opole is a town of 127,000 in population, which makes it a medium-sized Polish town. The area amounts to 92 sq. km, and in this respect the town is relatively large when compared to the population. A relatively extensive area was created in the mid-1970s when many villages (Gosławice, Grotowice, Bierkowice, Grudzice, Malina) were included within the urban borders. They are mainly inhabited by the Silesian population who declares a nationality other than Polish. After 1989, services have become the main source of income for the inhabitants of Opole. Formerly, the income used to be provided by the sector of building materials, machinery, metallurgy and food processing. Since 1994, Opole has become an academic center with a university resulting from a merger of the Wyższa Szkoła Pedagogiczna (Higher School of Pedagogy) and a branch of the Katolicki Uniwersytet Lubelski (the Catholic University of Lublin). The University of Opole, alongside the Technical University of Opole and four other schools, make Opole a significant academic center providing education for the youth in the Opole province and elsewhere.

Historical context of the processes under analysis

Readers who are not familiar with the issue of Polish-German relations may find it difficult to understand why the 'conflict' between the Poles and Germans is described using the example of a town which is located over 200 km away from the Polish-German border. Therefore it is necessary to briefly present the processes which have led to the situation where the town has become a venue of encounter for the representatives of various cultures, who have chosen to keep quite a distance from one another.

The beginnings of the town reach back to Medieval times when Opole was the capital of the Piast Duchy. The town was chartered before 1254, it passed under Czech rule after the mid-14th century, in the middle of the 16th century it became a property of the Habsburg dynasty, to fall under Prussian rule in 1742 following the defeat of Austria in the so-called 'first Silesian war'.

The processes and phenomena discussed in the present paper have mainly been shaped by the events of 1922-1945. A whole series of events that were significant for these processes occurred then. Firstly, there was the plebiscite, in which only 1,098 votes were 'for Poland' and 20,818 votes were 'for Germany'. This precisely reflected the structure of ethnic divisions in Opole. *"The inhabitants of Opole were di-*

vided with respect to nationality into Germans, Poles and Jews. According to the German census of 1933, out of 100 inhabitants 96.6% spoke German exclusively. There were 1,368 Poles, 523 Jews [the town's population amounted to 44,680 in 1933 – C.T.]. *The population of Opole was not uniform with respect to religious denomination either. The Catholics accounted for the largest proportion of 77%, the Evangelists for 20.25%, and the Jews for 1.18%"*[2]. After the decisions concerning the division of Upper Silesia had been made, the capital of the regency was moved from Katowice to Opole. Consequently, Opole became a typical clerical town. According to the census of 1933, clerks and white-collar workers accounted for 41.5% of the workforce. *"The character of the town's population was determined by numerous administrative and police officers, the military, teachers, the clergy and representatives of free professions. The percentage of laborers was among the lowest when compared to all the towns enumerated above* [Nysa, Racibórz – C.T.] *and amounted to 37.1% of employees in 1933. According to the statistics of 30 June 1936, out of 16,435 employees there were 7,171 laborers"*[3]. In the inter-war period, the capital of the Opole regency was the center of local authorities, newspapers were printed in German and Polish languages, educational and cultural institutions operated. Opole was the most significant center of the Polish movement in Silesia at that time. The Board of the 1st District of the Association of Poles in Germany, established in Bytom, had its site in Opole.

After the Red Army occupied the town in 1945, by virtue of the decisions the victorious powers had made in Yalta and Potsdam, Opole and the entire Upper Silesia region were incorporated into the Polish state. During the military operations 60% of the town center was destroyed; only around 600 persons remained in the town.

The situation after 1945 – the transfer of people

The first 'new' inhabitants of Opole were railroad workers, who had arrived at the *Zaodrze* (the territory across the Oder river) before the fights ended, in order to start the Opole railroad junction. The first transportation of repatriates from across the Bug river arrived as early as April 1945. According to the statistics collected in 1946, the population of Opole at that time amounted to 24,666. It took ten years from the end of the war to return to the pre-1939 level. Initially, the increase in population was achieved by means of including the adjacent villages into the borders of the town. According to the statistics from 1950, the repatriates accounted for 45% of the inhabitants of Opole, the re-immigrants 1%, the settlers from Central Poland (including the Silesian population from the part of Upper Silesia that was incorporated into Poland after 1922) 30%, and the indigenous population, which mainly inhab-

---

[2] S. Golachowski, *Materiały do statystki narodowościowej Śląska Opolskiego 1910-1939*, Poznań 1950, tab. 1 *Statisisches Jahrbuch deutscher Gemeinden*, Jena 1934, pp. 264-265 [all citations have been translated into English exclusively for the purpose of this paper (translator's note)].

[3] E. Mendel, *Studia nad stosunkami społecznymi i politycznymi w Opolu w latach 1933-1939*, Opole 1988, pp. 7-8.

ited the town's peripheries, accounted for 23%[4] of the total population of Opole. It was probably the highest percentage of native population among the inhabitants of Opole in the post-war history of the town. Population growth in the years to come mainly resulted from the inflow of people from other parts of Poland. They were coming to an Opole which was going through a period of intense industrialization in the 1950s, 60s and 70s. The indigenous population of Opole increased slightly in the mid-1970s when the borders of the town encompassed several nearby villages, inhabited almost entirely by a Silesian population.

The distribution of Silesian population in the Opole province and Opole county

The primary objective of this paper, established with reference to the subject of the conference, was to present the problem of inter-group distance in the town of Opole. However, owing to a limited number of materials which address this issue, the author was forced to slightly modify the topic. The case of Opole is only going to be referred to when describing the concrete instances of Polish and Silesian populations distancing themselves from one another in the period of 1945-1989. This change is justified by the fact that such concrete instances of the Poles and Silesians maintaining mutual distance were in no way unique in the territory of the Opole province and county.

For the purpose of the present paper we will use the notion of **non-Polish population**, applied by Kazimierz Szczygielski, the author of a study into the distribution of the native population in the Opole province. The notion comprises both the individuals who claim to be of German origin, the Silesian population, and that of a so-called 'indeterminate' ethnic origin. All the current statistics referred to by the authors of the study *Śląska ludność rodzima w strukturze demograficznej i społecznej Śląska Opolskiego wczoraj i dziś* [Indigenous Silesian population in the demographic and social structure of Opole Silesia in the past and present] and concerning the demographic composition of the Opole province population are derived from the National Census held in Poland in 2002. However, this source is not necessarily credible in view of the subject of the present paper. Poles strongly disapprove of the population of Opole province declaring themselves to be of German origin. This is a consequence of the ignorance of the realities of the region; the presence of a German minority evokes negative reactions rooted in the last 200 years of Polish-German relations.

The range of the non-Polish population in the Opole province is delineated on Map 1. It clearly shows that this population primarily inhabits the eastern part of the Opole province. What is both interesting and meaningful is the fact that this ter-

---

[4] K. Żygulski, *Małżeństwa mieszane w Opolu*, [in:] A. Kwilecki (ed.), *Ziemie Zachodnie w polskiej literaturze socjologicznej. Wybór tekstów*, Poznań 1970, p. 228.

ritory coincides with the area where the so-called Upper Silesian plebiscite was held on 20 March 1921 (Map 2).

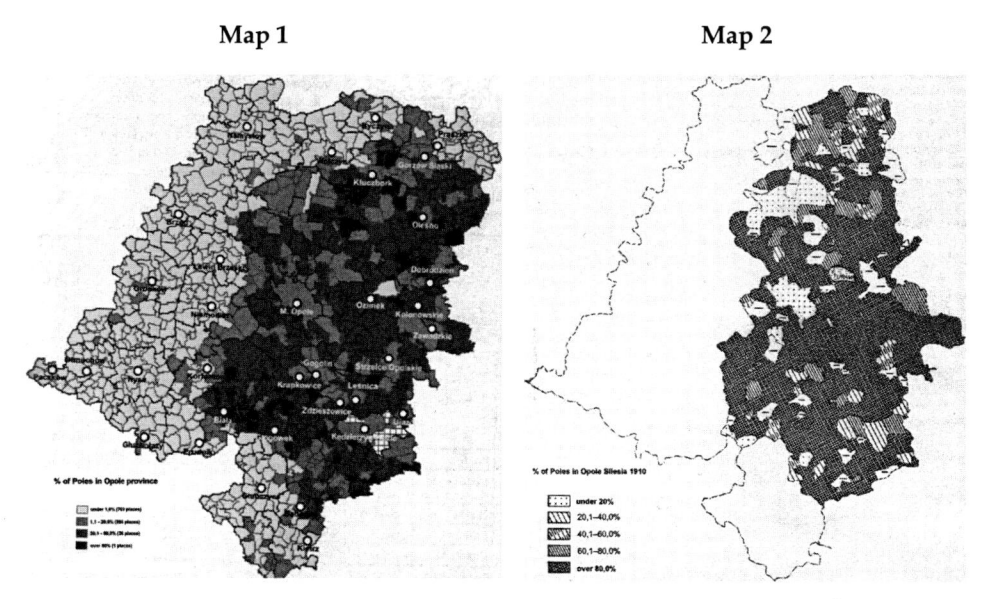

Map 1

Map 2

Source: Author's own analysis, on the basis: R. Rauziński, K. Szczygielski, *Śląska ludność rodzima w strukturze demograficznej i społeczności Śląska Opolskiego wczoraj i dziś*, p. 63, 165.

It is estimated that the votes cast 'for Poland' prevailed in around 30% of what is today the Opole province. If we take into consideration the fact that the German population that had not been subjected to the national verification in 1947 had left, and those who had been verified negatively were forced to leave Opole Silesia, it can justifiably be assumed that in 1945 the 'plebiscite' part of the Opole province was inhabited by the people whose connections with Polishness reached back to the inter-war period.

The same phenomenon is even more evident in the territory of the Opole county (see Map 3).

The statistics collected during the 2002 national census indicate that there were only 3.55% of people of non-Polish origin (4,609 out of 129,946 inhabitants of the town). The situation is quite different when the percentage of non-Polish population in the individual communes[5] (*gmina*) of the Opole county is considered. Then the percentage of non-Polish population in the communes is as follows: Chrząstowice 33%, Dąbrowa Niemodlińska 21%, Dobrzeń Wielki 30%, Komprachcice 39%, Łubiany 35%, Murów 34%, Niemodlin 0.5% (these data seem hardly credible since we know that there are entire 'Silesian villages' located in this county), Ozimek 24%,

---

[5] An unit of administrative division below the county level (translator's note).

Map. 3

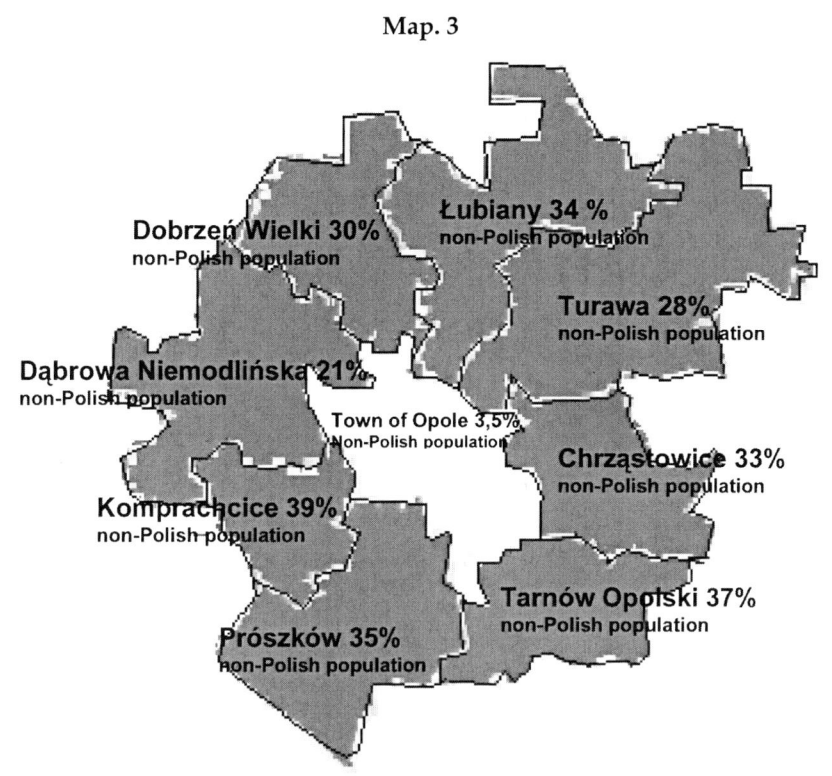

Map showing percentages of non-Polish population in communes around Opole:
- Dobrzeń Wielki 30% non-Polish population
- Łubiany 34% non-Polish population
- Turawa 28% non-Polish population
- Dąbrowa Niemodlińska 21% non-Polish population
- Town of Opole 3,5% non-Polish population
- Chrząstowice 33% non-Polish population
- Komprachcice 39% non-Polish population
- Tarnów Opolski 37% non-Polish population
- Prószków 35% non-Polish population

Source: Author's own analysis, on the basis of: M. Lis, *Polska ludność rodzima na Śląsku Opolskim po II wojnie światowej*, Opole 1991.

Popielów 22%, Prószków 35%, Tarnów Opolski 37%, Turawa 28%. When we compare these data with the results of the by-elections to the Polish Senate of 18 February 1990, in the second round of which a Silesian, Professor Dorota Simonides, competed against the leader of the German minority in Silesia, Henryk Król, we obtain a more credible picture of ethnic divisions in these communes. The same is confirmed by the results of elections to the local government from 2006. Their results, however, are not as equivocal, which is probably a consequence of many factors. Firstly, the German minority had already attained most of their objectives, and the turnout was clearly lower in Silesian communes as over a hundred thousand Silesians were permanently staying in the Federal Republic of Germany.

Mutual contacts in 1945-1989

The arrival of Polish population to the territory of Opole Silesia is best described as a culture shock for both parties. Poles, who mainly came from the Eastern Borderlands (*Kresy*), experienced the strangeness of culture of the Silesian, pertaining to their language, material culture, habits, and attitude to work. On the other hand, the Silesian population felt profoundly hurt by the attitude of the newcomers, who treated them in a highly suspicious and distrustful way. What was most difficult for the autochthons to accept was that the Poles from Western Ukraine transferred their attitude to the Ukrainian rural population onto the Silesians, and consequently treated them paternally, feeling culturally superior, as was the case with Ukrainian peasants. In the conclusion to the survey started as early as August 1945 (sic!) in Giełczyn (Dobrzeń Wielki), S. Ossowski described the social and cultural consequences of this encounter referring to the "sociological law of the background". By virtue of this law *"mixing with the repatriates shortened the social distance between the Silesian population and the Germans as perceived by the latter, and made them remember the Germans as the people of the same culture, as being more like them than these 'Polocs' speaking with a Ukrainian accent and calling the Silesians Germans"*[6]. The concepts of settlement, developed by the then sociologists, assumed that the Silesian population would initiate the egress of a 'new society' in the territories where the 'settlers' were to come into contact with the 'autochthons'. Despite the propagandistic stories of successful integration of the Polish and Silesian populations, the assumptions turned out to be far from realistic. An example of such a story are the recollections of a young Silesian, born in the suburbs of Opole before the war: "*I was born in one of the districts of Opole in 1934. [...] In 1946 we returned to my home town* [in 1945 the respondent was mandatorily evacuated by German authorities – C.T.]. *The most difficult time of my youth began. I could not speak Polish, I could only say a few words I had picked up from the elders, this was a dialect, though. I needed to enroll at school, my mother wanted me to study. I was humiliated and disgraced a lot. I could not understand why they called me a szwab, hanys*[7]*. [...] I wanted to learn Poland and Poles, I learned the language over a relatively short period of time, but I wanted to know everything about the nation I belonged to. [...] In 1951, when I turned seventeen, I joined the 'SP'*[8]*, I worked on a railroad embankment between Cracow and Nowa Huta, which was only expanding at the time. It was for the first time in the brigade that I really started to trust my colleagues, the Poles, the People's Rule. I had forgotten the hanyses and szwabs and all the biting remarks from my childhood years*"[9]. The reality was nowhere near the story from this memoir, however. The Silesian response to such an attitude was to distance themselves from 'Polish matters', closing themselves inside their own group and being reluctant to make inter-group contacts which were limited to the necessary minimum. The number of mixed marriages in Opole is the most adequate indicator of such an attitude. Although the Silesian population accounted for 22% of the total population of the town in 1950, the number of marriages between the Silesian and representatives of

---

[6] St. Ossowski, *O ojczyźnie i narodzie*, Warszawa 1984, p. 122.
[7] A person of Swabian origin (from: Schwabenland), a person of German origin (from: Hans), derogatory nicknames to mock one's German connections (translator's note).
[8] Mass organization 'Service to Poland' (translator's note).
[9] *Już zapomniałem o "hanysach", o "szwabach"*, [in:] Z. Dulczewski (ed.), *Młode pokolenie Ziem Zachodnich. Pamiętniki*, Poznań 1968, p. 460.

other groups inhabiting Opole at that time accounted for only 1.8% of all marriages[10]. Keeping their distance from the problems bothering Polish society was also expressed by avoiding taking sides in disputes. For example, there were no Silesians among the individual farmers protesting in front of the Province Governor's Office in 1980; no Silesians were among the leaders of protest campaigns during the whole period of real socialism, either. This strategy was supposed to protect the Silesians from additional persecution they could experience when applying for permission to leave Poland. A joke was circulating in Opole in the 1970s that the longest line in the town was the line of those waiting in front of the Passport Department of the Province Militia Station.

The institution which was most harmful in maintaining the distance between the Polish and Silesian was school, which from the beginning was the most important institution to return the 'Germanized Silesian people' to the Polish nation. Social endogamy was mainly maintained by family and neighborhood ties whereas school was the necessary evil. Thus, it was a natural attitude for the Silesian to minimize their educational ambitions to the level of vocational education which prepared them to start work as early as possible. Education meant going beyond one's group, a kind of losing of one's national identity. Kazimiera Wódz describes this phenomenon making reference to Pierre Bourdieu's concept of habitus: "*An individual dimension of socialization in a traditional Silesian family and a culturally homogenous local environment meant the acquisition of the dialect combined with a certain level of linguistic and cultural competence, and by this token the formation of a primal habitus, typical of these circles, which frequently turned out to be dysfunctional given the requirements of the educational system. [...] Elementary school frequently – and unfortunately! – was the place where the children from Silesian families experienced the consequences of their mother dialect being stigmatized. For many this experience was so painful that it affected their attitude to school, the teachers and those colleagues who did not have similar problems*"[11].

All that made the Upper Silesians, including the inhabitants of Opole and neighboring communes, 'vote with their feet' and make the decision to move mostly to the Federal Republic of Germany, which they called 'Richtig Fine Germany'[12]. As a result of that, 222,000 people left Silesia in 1950-2005 and the number of Silesians inhabiting Opole Silesia has dropped from 436,000 in 1950 to 270,000 in 2002[13].

The transformation following 1989

When the external circumstances for the discussion on the status of the Silesian population in the Opole province had changed, there immediately emerged leaders who

---

[10] K. Żygulski, *op. cit.*
[11] K. Wódz, *Rewitalizacja śląskiej tożsamości – szanse i zagrożenia*, [in:] K. Wódz (ed.), *"Swoi" i "obcy" na Górnym Śląsku. Z problematyki stosunków etnicznych*, Katowice 1993, pp. 29-30.
[12] Really Fine Germany – a mocking development of the Polish acronym for FRG (translator's note).
[13] R. Rauziński, K. Szczyglewski, *op. cit.*, pp. 118, 121.

demanded that the social and cultural identity of the Silesian people be acknowledged. This demand was based on the claim 'it's us who's at home': "*Throughout the entire period after WWII the indigenous population was treated as second-class citizens. Our land was treated as the source of resources for the rest of the country. The Polish raison d'état made us forget that the hosts of the 'recovered territories' were the people who had been living there for centuries. [...] Until now we have been passive and resigned. Our activity was limited to abandoning our fatherland and searching for our identity abroad*"[14]. The authors of this declaration had no doubts that searching for their identity they would turn to German motifs in the history of Silesia while minimizing, disregarding or plainly neglecting the Polish ones. Such a radical attitude has stirred fears among many Polish inhabitants of Opole Silesia concerning the future of their land and their own future in those localities where the indigenous population was a majority and refused to be called a 'native Polish population'. Such localities were a majority in the communes around Opole (see Map 3). Similar fears were expressed in the entire country, where the claims of some inhabitants of the Opole region to be treated as Germans, and their support by the activists of the Association of Expellees, evoked the worst associations. This confrontation was most 'heated' during the by-elections to the Polish Senate following the demise of Senator Edmund Osmańczyk, who was an ardent advocate of Silesian issues in the Polish Parliament. During this confrontation, two visions of the future and past of Silesia were expressed on the walls of the town's buildings. Dorota Simonides, a Silesian of Polish origin, impersonated one of them, the other one impersonated Henryk Król, a Silesian of German origin. Although it was Dorota Simonides who won, the candidate of the German minority won by a landslide in the territories dominated by the Silesian population. The walls were covered with graffiti demanding that the newcomers go back across the Bug river or that the Germans go to the Reich, offices of national minorities were being demolished, the monuments to commemorate German soldiers in WWI and WWII from a given locality were being desecrated, which illustrated the direction in which the conflict might escalate.

It appears that the atmosphere was calmed mainly by the signing of the Polish-German treaties, and the moderate support of the German authorities for the radical demands concerning the status of the German minority in Poland that were formulated by the activists of the Association of Expellees, and backed by some leaders of German minority organizations. The local government officer (*sołtys*) in the village of Dziewkowice can be used as an example here. At the entrance to the village he placed signs with the name Frauenfeld, although this name was used in the period of 1936-1945, and the former German name of the village was Schewkowitz.

Public feeling changed also as a result of hopes that the German character of the Silesian population would be welcome in the Federal Republic of Germany. This was not the case, however. The authorities in Bonn, and later in Berlin, did not want

---

[14] The platform declaration of the Social and Culture Society of Opole Silesia German Minority, in "Oberschlesische Nachrichten/Wiadomości Górnośląskie", no. 0, 20 April 1990.

to raise conflicts concerning the issue of the German minority so as not to be accused by international public opinion of reviving the ghosts of the past and defending the rights of the German minority in Poland. The Silesians who arrived at the FRG were additionally disappointed to find out that they were no longer treated like their predecessors, who had obtained comprehensive aid in Germany (language courses, employment, accommodation) and – what is more – that their German origin was questioned. This was a result of the belief that the German origin of the Silesian was 'useful' from the point of view of public opinion in Germany, who had a confrontational attitude to Poland, only when it was claimed in Poland. Yet another reason why the radical attitude of the first period was somewhat softened was that the Silesians who claimed to be of German origin were given the right to dual citizenship. This automatically enabled them to leave Poland at any time and settle down in Germany, or to start working there. Consequently, according to the statistics provided by the national census in 2002, over 100,000 individuals stay in Germany and work there for over ten months a year, thus losing the opportunity to exert actual influence on the 'German interests' in Opole Silesia.

The beginnings of the German minority organizations reach back to Gogolin, where one of the first organizations of the German minority in Poland was established after WWII. However, owing to its significance as the capital of the province, Opole became the center of the German minority movement emerging in the Opole region despite the fact that as a result of demographic and migration processes only 3.5% of the town's population declared to be of non-Polish origin in 2002. The most significant institutions of the movement were located in Opole: the Union of German Social and Cultural Societies, Social and Cultural Society of Opole, Silesia Germans, and the editorial office of a German periodical "Schlesische Wochenblatt". Opole is the site of the most important cultural events organized by the German minority. To a certain extent, at present Opole has a similar function for the German minority as it did in the inter-war period for the Polish minority. Another paradox is that the same people, or their successors, live there.

Like every group from the borderlands, the Silesians have developed specific instruments to contact strangers. They maintain the necessary contacts, but without familiarity, they avoid conflicts retreating to their own group rather than fighting, and they tend not to include strangers into their own group. Although the inter-group distance has been maintained after 1989, it has tended to diminish. The change consists in the Silesian population increasingly accepting their neighbors, provided that the latter adopt Silesian cultural patterns. Some statements Maria Szmeja recorded confirm this transformation: "*The children of our neighbor, the one from the mountains, are Silesian as they were born here. […] This neighbor from the mountains, I do not know if she feels Silesian, she was born there. I would already include her among us. She's OK, she already speaks the way we do*"[15].

---

[15] M. Szmeja, *Niemcy?, Polacy?, Ślązacy!*, Kraków 2000, p. 220 [the Polish version is in distinctive Silesian dialect (translator's note)].

For the Polish population the adoption of these standards has become a part of their blending with the Silesian character, one could even attempt to claim that we are faced with a kind of a 'Silesianiziation' process in these territories. This process finds a good illustration in the statement of one of the respondents in a survey conducted in a village near Opole: "*I feel Silesian because I was born here and Silesia feels closer for me. [...] I like the Silesian population and many of the people who were born here and feel Silesian [...] I feel the connection with this village. [...] people are frequently afraid to say that they are Silesian, but who are they if they were born here, the inhabitants of Przemyśl?*"[16] We can follow Maria Śmiełowska's observation that the contacts of the incoming population with the indigenous culture had to lead to the internalization of this culture when some of its aspects were attractive for the Poles who had come to Silesia, e.g. the attitude to work and order, religiousness, and contacts with the Germans. As a result a definition of their own identity may emerge combining the elements 'brought from home' with the 'local' ones.

Future prospects

For the first time the Poles and Silesians met at a joint manifestation of unity at the Opole Monument of Fighters for the Polishness of Opole Silesia (sic!). They were faced by the threat that the Opole province in the shape assumed after the administrative reform in 1999 would be wiped out from the administrative map of Poland. The Poles and Silesians were demonstrating for different reasons (the latter found it particularly difficult to demonstrate in this place as they had a critical attitude to the Silesian uprisings). The Poles demanded that the province be maintained for prestigious and economic reasons. The Silesians feared that they would dissolve in a new Silesian province and thus it would be more difficult for them to formulate and realize their group interests. The question arises whether that encounter was only an opportunistic gesture, or a good forecaster of the future showing that the representatives of both groups are able to act collectively for the benefit of their region?

Both Opole and the entire Opole Silesia area stand a chance of becoming an example of how to avoid conflicts in solving ethnic problems for the whole of Central and Eastern Europe, which has painfully experienced such conflicts following the collapse of the Eastern Bloc. So far, the prevailing approach involves maintaining distance, retaining attitudes and limited trust. It appears that with the rise of a new generation born in the Opole region, who are not burdened by the trauma of the post-war years, it is realistic to assume that this European region can set an example of finding the solutions to achieve the common good.

---

[16] M. Śmiełowska, *Tożsamości etniczne i identyfikacje narodowe wśród mieszkańców Śląska Opolskiego*, [in:] K. Frysztacki (ed.), *Polacy, Ślązacy, Niemcy. Studia nad stosunkami społeczno-kulturowymi na Śląsku Opolskim*, Kraków 1998, p. 214.

Szczecin
A Cross-Border Center of Conflict and Cooperation

Thomas Lundén, Anders Mellbourn, Joachim v. Wedel, Péter Balogh

Since the delineation of the Polish-German boundary in 1945, and the displacement of the original German population, the city of Szczecin (Stettin) has been situated in the periphery of Poland and close to, but inaccessible from, the German territories. Szczecin is by far the largest and most lively city in the area. It has, however, fallen behind comparable Polish cities which share its history of being located in what used to be German territory, e.g. Poznań, Gdańsk and Wrocław. Furthermore, the future of Szczecin's main industry, the shipyards, is bleak – to say the least. In order to flourish, Szczecin needs an economically vigorous hinterland on the German side of the border.

In the seventies the border became more open, a development that was later re-enforced by the events of 1989, and by Poland joining the EU in 2004 and the Schengen Union on December 21, 2007. Possibilities have opened up for cooperation with the neighboring German areas, in matters such as formal politics, trade and personal relations. But this openness has also revealed, resurrected and created old and new conflicts between – and within – the two sides of the border.

The purpose of this paper is to analyze Szczecin's situation, in relation to the possibilities of conflict or cooperation with its cross-border hinterland. Relations to surrounding central places (such as Warsaw and Berlin) will also be taken into account. Three factors that influence border relations will be analyzed: Political relations, market relations and individual relations, as well as their reciprocal linkages. The question is how these factors interrelate, and to what extent existing opportunities and hindrances create the present human, political and market relations in the border area.

Background to the present situation

In 1912, in an early geographical analysis of the cities around the Baltic Sea, the Swedish geographer Sten De Geer described Stettin as a typical, single-river-bank settlement, located on the steep left-hand bank of the Oder. According to De Geer, the lack of urbanization on the other bank was explained by the marshy character of the Oder Valley[1]. However, Stettin was served by a number of railway lines that led in all directions, including a circle line on its western side, which led northwards[2]. Stettin's zone of influence varied according to the type of market and the existing means of transportation. For instance, the shipping routes created contacts further south, while e.g. the Uecker-Randow area, including Pasewalk, belonged to the 'Speckgürtel' (zone of rich commuters) of Stettin[3].

The major German towns and cities, located further west of the border, such as Greifswald and Neubrandenburg, had historical contacts with Berlin, to their direct south. Even before the war, their horizontal ties with Stettin were limited, while Stettin flourished as a port city for Berlin and as an export harbor for Schlesien (Silesia).

So, the northern stretch of the Oder-Neisse line is a state boundary which has no historic precedent. Pomerania was long a German territory, but as its place-names suggest, it has a Slavic past. Over the centuries, the area has been divided into different realms, not least because of Swedish involvement.

The demarcation of the provisional boundary between areas under Polish and Allied (i.e. Soviet) administration as of September 21st, 1945 in Schwerin[4], left Szczecin and the towns of Świnoujście, Police and Nowe Warpno on the Polish side of the border towards the Soviet Occupation Zone of the remaining German territory. The reasons were purely strategic. The Oder, and further south, the Neisse, were meant to constitute a new boundary between Germany and Poland. But it was considered inexpedient to have the two sides share control of the ports and the river access to the Baltic Sea. Thus, the former German ports of Swinemünde and Stettin were incorporated into Poland, as was the territory that separated them. The decision to put the city of Stettin on the Polish side of the new border was the last detail of a post-war agreement on Germany reached by the victors of World War II[5].

During the years that followed the demarcation, the border remained relatively closed, even after the agreement between Poland and the GDR that was signed in Zgorzelec on June 5th, 1950[6].

Analyzing the border and its impact on relations and movements

After a long period of academic disinterest, due to the bad reputation of 'geopolitics', boundary studies are becoming increasingly popular in the social sciences and humanities. In contrast to earlier studies, which concentrated on territorial confron-

---

[1] S. De Geer, *Storstäderna vid Östersjön*, "Ymer", vol. 1912, p. 79.
[2] *Ibidem*, p. 78f and map supplement.
[3] D. Gutgesell, *Landkreis Uecker-Randow*, interview 12.01.2009.
[4] B. Aischmann, *Mecklenburg-Vorpommern, die Stadt Stettin ausgenommen. Eine zeitgeschichtliche Betrachtung*, Schwerin 2008, p. 118ff.
[5] *Ibidem*, p. 125.
[6] *Ibidem*, p. 192f.

tation or the legalities of demarcation, modern studies (at least when the subject matter is Europe) focus on the impact of relatively open boundaries on the local population[7]. One approach to boundary theory is to juxtapose two principles, the state as a limited territorial and hierarchical organization (the authoritative principle), and the theoretically unbounded market of goods and services (the market principle), and to these add mutual closeness and network relations of the inhabitants in a boundary area[8]. In this essay, we will try to show how these principles create incentives for cooperation but also conflicts of interest.

The authoritative principle: The state is a territorial, mostly hierarchical, regulatory organization that claims monopoly on the use of force within its domain. It provides services to its members (citizens and/or residents), e.g. infrastructure, protection and education. In return it demands loyalty, membership fees (taxation) and certain services (e.g. military and civil defense service). In certain respects, the independent state attempts to make its territory homogeneous, in particular with respect to the authority of laws and the responsibilities of the inhabitants, in most cases the state's citizens[9].

The market principle: the Central Place Theory, developed by Walter Christaller and August Lösch[10], presupposes rational behavior which, on the one hand, is based on the friction of distance, and, on the other, on supply and demand. This principle results in a hierarchical and symmetrical ordering of the market places, ranging from low-order village markets to those of the major world cities. Each central place has a market hinterland. The authors realize that their presuppositions – that the central places have equal geographical areas, populations, wealth and accessibility to their hinterlands – are virtually non-existent, but they use them as a starting point for discussions about the factors that make reality deviate from theory. One such factor is the political aspect, especially at a boundary between states with border restrictions and different market regulations. Another factor is accessibility, which, in turn, is greatly influenced by infrastructural arrangements, the latter mostly being planned for the purpose of integrating each individual state's territory.

For any central place, the theoretical region of influence would encompass an area whose boundary reaches as far as to the halfway point between that place and

---

[7] See e.g. V. Kolossov, *Theoretical limology: new analytical approaches*, [in:] T. Lundén (ed.), *Crossing the border. Boundary relations in a changing Europe*, Eslöv 2006, pp. 15-35.
[8] See e.g. T. Lundén, *Valga-Valka, Narva – Ivangorod Estonia's divided border cities – cooperation and conflict within and beyond the EU*, [in:] J. Jańczak (ed.), *Conflict and Cooperation in Divided Towns and Cities*, Logos Verlag, Berlin 2009.
[9] T. Lundén, *Border agglomerations in the Baltic area: obstacles and possibilities for local interaction*, "Geographica Helvetica", vol. 2007:1, p. 22.
[10] W. Christaller, *Central Places in Southern Germany*, Englewood Cliffs (N.J.) 1966 (*Die zentralen Orte in Süddeutschland*, Jena 1933); A. Loesch, *The economics of location*, New Haven 1954 (*Die räumliche Ordnung der Wirtschaft*, Jena 1944). See also: J. Güßefeldt, *Die Raumwirtschaftstheorien von Christaller und Lösch aus der Sicht von Wirtschaftsgeographie und "New Economic Geography"*, Göttingen 2005.

any city of comparable size. The state boundary will always be a hindrance, in time, effort and because of problems caused by custom regulations or differences in political guidelines. In consideration of the above-mentioned imbalances, the political divisions heavily influence the real central place system in the actual area. An article by Professor Stanisław Ciok outlined both the theoretical development of the hinterlands during the periods before and after 1945, in the relative openness of the 1990s and after Poland's entrance into the European Union, and also the theoretical hinterland areas of the main central places Berlin, Szczecin, Poznań and Wrocław.

While Szczecin's suggested periphery of dominance, west of the city, would reach just 10 kilometers east of Stralsund, its boundary towards Berlin would be almost at the suburban outskirts of Szczecin, due to the great attraction of, and easy access to, Berlin[11]. It should be born in mind that central place theories do not attempt to explain other spatial activities of the population, but that market and other relations mutually interact.

The human individual is a creature with biological, social and economical needs and desires that relate to the physical and social environment. As many of these needs and desires are available at specific locations, the individual has to relate to the surrounding world by moving, forming daily, annual and life-time trajectories in time-space[12]. In the relation between the individual and the environment, three sorts of resources are at hand: *physical*, *human* and *social capital*[13]. State boundaries, as well as – but to a lesser extent – other boundaries, mark a change in the 'landscape of opportunities', physically, economically, socially and psychologically. The fact that this landscape looks entirely different according to which side of the border it is seen from, leaves room for potential conflicts and makes cooperation essential.

In order to measure the actual impact of the state boundary as a barrier or incentive, we need the means to measure functional integration. An obvious difficulty is to define reliable and simple measures for this kind of integration and growth. One analytical framework of interest suggests two sets of conditions for overcoming barriers, the degree of *interdependence* and the degree of *transactions*. Interdependence includes both *hardware conditions* (like nature, infrastructure) and *software conditions* (culture, language etc)[14]. Transactions include capital and goods, services, employees, students, customers, tourists etc. but also contacts, e.g. between local and state authorities in the area.

---

[11] S. Ciok, *Oddziaływanie Berlina na pogranicze zachodnie Polski*, [in:] J. Jańczak, M. Musiał-Karg (eds), *Pogranicze polsko-niemieckie po 2004 roku. Nowa jakość sąsiedztwa?*, Toruń 2009, pp. 136, 150. See also: Regionaler Planungsverband Vorpommern, *Zentralörtliche Verflechtungen zwischen Ostmecklenburg/Vorpommern und der Stadt Szczecin. Szenarien*, Berlin Juli 2004.
[12] T. Hägerstrand, *Space, time and human conditions. Dynamic Allocation of Urban Space*, [in:] A. Karlqvist, A. Lundqvist, L. Snickars, F. (eds), Farnborough Hants. Saxon House, Lexington 1975, pp. 3-14.
[13] R.B. Putnam, *Bowling alone. The collapse and revival of American community*, New York 2000, pp. 18-24.
[14] P. Schmitt-Egner, *Cross-border co-operation (CBC) among European regions in different perspectives*, in: H.-Å. Persson, I. Eriksson (eds), *Border Regions in Comparison*, Lund 2001, p. 75.

The impact of German-Polish official relations

The new boundary was soon recognized by the German Democratic Republic (GDR) and the Polish People's Republic, both of which were members of the Warsaw Pact and under Soviet domination during the Cold War. In spite of their mutual membership in the Warsaw Pact, the border contacts between the GDR and Poland were quite limited from 1945 to 1990 (except during occasional political 'thaws') and the attitude was, on both sides, resentful. There was little economic activity and hardly any personal contacts[15]. In the West, the Federal Republic of Germany found it hard to accept that the most eastern quarter of pre-war Germany had to be given over to Poland (or, in the case of the northern part of East Prussia, to the Soviet Union). The Oder-Neisse line was not recognized until 1970, when the treaty between the Federal Republic and the People's Republic of Poland was signed, and again when a treaty was signed by the united Germany in 1990.

The 1990s saw positive developments in German-Polish relations, both in general and in the border areas. The border treaty and the subsequent signing of the German-Polish Friendship and Cooperation Treaty formed the foundation for various contacts, also related to Poland's intention to join the European Union. So-called Euro-Regions were established along the border. By making most bilateral efforts part of the EU pre-membership strategy, PHARE-CBC funding from the EU could support the efforts, and simultaneously dampen Polish fears of a "peaceful Germanization"[16].

However, official Polish-German relations seem to be a perennially sensitive theme[17]. Germany was consistently, from the mid-1990s and onwards, during the negotiations leading up to the Central and Eastern European countries' accession to the EU, the strongest proponent of Polish EU membership. The new open climate on the border culminated in Poland's accession to the EU in 2004, and finally its accession to the Schengen Union in December 2007. However, transitory regulations that, until 2011, limit the free movement of labor into Germany from the new member states, Poland included, constitute impediments to cross-border mobility and interaction.

There are other lateral conflicts as well. During the first decades after the war, those Germans who came from the previously German areas in the east, campaigned quite vigorously for their right to return. Although the border is now finally recognized, claims for compensation, or for the right to return, have not faded away completely[18]. Today, however, the great majority of Germans with eastern

---

[15] See e.g.: K. Stokłosa, *Grenzstädte in Ostmitteleuropa. Guben und Gubin 1945 bis 1995*, Berlin 2003.
[16] B. Morhard, *Das deutsch-polnische Grenzgebiet als Sonderfall europäischer Regionalpolitik: Die institutionelle Ausgestaltung zur Förderung grenzüberschreitender Kooperation im Kontext der EU-Erweiterungsstrategien im Zeitraum von 1989 bis 1998*, Heidelberg 2000.
[17] See e.g. *Eine doppelte Täuschung*, "Der Spiegel", no. 2, 2008.
[18] See e.g. A. Kossert, *Kalte Heimat. Die Geschichte der deutschen Vertriebenen nach 1945*, München 2008, p. 427.

roots are no more than interested visitors to western Poland. Also, EU-involvement, beginning with pre-membership accession funds like PHARE, had a soothing effect on bilateral relations.

A border of hierarchical asymmetry

Poland is a unitary state with a centralized, four-tier administrative system in which the *voivodship* level is characterized by a diarchic structure, having a centrally appointed authority (*wojewoda*) and a regionally elected leader (*marszałek*). The German system has, also, on its lower levels, elements of this sort of double structure. In spite of these similarities, and an almost identical structure at the municipal level in both countries, it is the state quality of the German Länder (with their own governments and – within certain limits – the right to have their own foreign relations) that leads to certain discords in cross-border cooperation. Germany, on the other hand, is a federal state with a four- or five-tier system, and the distribution of authority between its different levels differs greatly from that of Poland[19]. These differences account for hierarchical asymmetries and discords in the lateral relations on a local level[20].

The post-socialist era has so far seen varying degrees of engagement in Polish-German cross-border cooperation in the Szczecin region, with e.g. some of the city's mayors being more interested than others. Certainly the ambitions and orientations of the actors involved are significant, but the current administrative structures are already an impediment to cooperation. Although, in the past two decades, an ongoing decentralization has been taking place in Poland (especially the *gmina*, or municipal level, has been strengthened) it remains a centralized country, in stark contrast to Germany with its great regional autonomy. Hence, many Szczecin-related issues require negotiations between Warsaw and the state of Mecklenburg-Vorpommern (MVP), and this is perhaps one of the more difficult connections: Schwerin (MVP's capital) and Warsaw are 860 kilometers apart, and quite some distance from Szczecin as well.

Also, MVP has two middle-sized port cities, Rostock and Stralsund, and is not particularly interested in encouraging competition from the much larger Szczecin. Because of its location, and because of the attractiveness and dynamism of Hamburg and Lübeck, Schwerin with surroundings, over the past two decades, has been far more engaged in re-establishing its links to the west. There are even those who think that MVP would be better off if it belonged to Brandenburg, but as it is ex-

---

[19] http://www.bundestag.de/parlament/funktion/gesetze/Grundgesetz/index.html, 11.02.2009. See also: S. Marschall, *Das politische System Deutschlands*, Konstanz 2007. Also: M.G. Schmidt, *Das politische System Deutschlands*, München 2007.
[20] T. Lundén, *Valga-Valka, Narva – Ivangorod. Estonia's divided border cities – cooperation and conflict within and beyond the EU*, [in:] J. Jańczak (ed.), *Conflict and Cooperation in Divided Towns and Cities*, Logos Verlag, Berlin 2009.

tremely difficult to modify any *Länder*-boundaries (this would require changing the German constitution[21]), the option has never been seriously discussed. Internally, MVP is going through a lingering administrative-territorial reform process, while, in the Polish *voivodships* (hence, also, in West Pomerania), the roles of the Marshall and the Voivod are still being negotiated. One might assume that these processes also detract attention from cooperation with the respective neighboring areas.

The levels most engaged in cooperation are, then – apart from the EU, of course – the lowest ones. Border contacts and border region developments are driven on a local, regional, state territorial and super-state territorial level through the EU.

Infrastructure and structural economy

The physical infrastructure is part of the 'opportunity landscape' that makes possible – or impossible – movements, contacts and provisions with and to the population of the border area. Much of the infrastructure was damaged at the end of World War II, and from 1944 to 1948, the Red Army even dismantled the railway lines that connected Szczecin to the west and southwest[22]. Due to the non-promotion of cross-border contacts, the remaining roads were, until recently, left to decay and to run into dead ends at the border. As the interest in border contacts was limited, roads that crossed the new border west of the Oder were left unattended. As late as in 1963, GDR maps of the area showed no roads crossing the boundary[23]. Nevertheless, after an apogeum of atomism in the early 1950s, even among the socialist states, the number of cross-border contacts began slowly to increase in the late 1950s, leading to a complete opening of the borders between 1972 and 1980[24].

With the political changes of 1989-90, a number of infrastructural changes were planned and implemented. On the German side, the major road investment was the new Autobahn from Lübeck to the Uckermark (Brandenburg), which also interconnects with the old Berlin-Szczecin Autobahn, which had been built about seventy years earlier.

The new motorway A20 crossing Mecklenburg-Vorpommern is reported to have less traffic than any other German Autobahn and its eastern half has hardly any traffic at all[25]. The Autobahn practically functions as link for transit traffic coming from the east and heading towards Hamburg, not as a means of making regional interconnections.

For Szczecin, the Autobahn and the parallel railway offer quick contacts with Berlin, and thus reinforce the old links to Germany. Berlin is only two hours' drive

---

[21] S. Marschall, *Das politische…*, op. cit. See also: M.G. Schmidt, *Das politische…*, op. cit.
[22] Z. Taylor, *The dismantling and removal of railway lines by Soviet Red Army troops on present-day Polish territory, 1944-1948*, "Journal of Transport Geography", no. 16, 2008, p. 223.
[23] B. Aischmann, *Mecklenburg-Vorpommern…*, op. cit., p. 195. Also: *Verkehrsatlas VEB Hermann Haack*, Gotha 1963.
[24] K. Stokłosa, *Grenzstädte…*, op. cit., p. 56ff.
[25] R. Kirbach, *Bahn frei für den Aufschwung*, "Die Zeit", 14.12.2006.

from Szczecin, and there is regular shuttle service to airports and bus stations[26]. A journey from Szczecin to Warsaw, on the other hand, takes six hours. The Polish authorities seem to have de-prioritized a projected highway between Szczecin and Gdańsk. This reinforces Szczecin's orientation towards the west, or more correctly, towards the south-west.

Today there are three border crossings in Szczecin's immediate surroundings – one serves the "Autobahn" and two serve regional roads on either side of it. Among the local cross-border connections, the regional B104 road in particular, which passes westwards through Linken and Löcknitz in the direction of Pasewalk, would need more attention; this, still very narrow, road has lately become extremely congested as more and more Szczeciners have moved to the German side; most of these commute to Szczecin daily (see below).

Until recently, there was not one border crossing for motor vehicles further to the north of the city. A major road with a border crossing was opened northwest of Szczecin at Hintersee, as part of the Schengen accession, linking Ückermünde and Police. On the German side, the local authorities had long opposed this opening. Immediately after the festivities on December 21, 2007, however, it was closed on the Polish side, because of a missing security procedure ("natura 2000"), and because some repair work remained to be done. The road was finally opened, with half a year's delay, on June 5th 2008[27].

Inside Poland, there are as yet no bridges across the northern Oder, e. g. at Police, to facilitate local or regional cross-border contacts. There are only bridges in the immediate neighborhood of the city for traffic from Szczecin, further east into Poland.

The GDR invested heavily in transforming Rostock into its main port city, while, in the newly reshaped Polish state, this function was filled primarily by Gdańsk. This meant that Szczecin's harbor lost part of its historic hinterland and markets, which again resulted in primarily negative regional development.

On the European level, there were plans to establish a South Baltic transport corridor called 'Via Hanseatica' between St. Petersburg and Lübeck, and the recently finished German motorway A20, connecting Lübeck and Szczecin, is part of this link. But the Szczecin-Gdańsk section of Via Hanseatica has not been included in the transeuropean transport network TEN/TINA. And the evaluation report of the follow-up project does not even mention the Via Hanseatica. A look at Poland's road and railway priorities makes it clear that this passage does not rank highly. Instead, Polish authorities seem to be committed to enlarging the highway from Szczecin to Bydgoszcz[28] and Poznań, which are more centrally located in Poland. These priorities also diminish the potential benefits of the newly (re)built German motorways A11 (Berlin-Szczecin) and A20, since these links do not continue eastwards.

---

[26] See e.g.: www.BERLinia.eu, 16.02.2009.
[27] Amt am Stettiner Haff, telephone message, March 10, 2009.
[28] P. Heise, *Euroregion Pomerania*, interview 14.01.2009.

Infrastructure is crucial to the market situation of Szczecin. The city is unevenly linked to the surrounding areas, with priority given to southern contacts inside of Poland and to Berlin. Szczecin is an attractive goal for shopping- and service trips to the local German hinterland. The city itself, however, does not benefit from the differences in price-levels and regulations. Rather, the profit goes to shopping centers at the border.

Local cross-border relations

On the micro level, border relations on the ground have been studied quite extensively on the central "front" – in divided cities like Frankfurt (Oder) and Słubice and Guben/Gubin[29]. The Szczecin area, by contrast, is less researched and its structure differs from that of river boundary areas further to the south. The area is characterized by imbalances. On the Polish side: dense population, recent (multi)ethnic settlement, industrialized urbanization, religious faith, marginality in relation to the state capital. On the German side: sparse population, an agricultural and recreational profile, unemployment, secularism, and relative proximity to the state capital.

Education

Cooperation was initially limited to initiatives to provide emergency services, coast-guard duties, public health service and water purification. The most ambitious initiatives have been in the school sector, with German-Polish classes in a limited number of German high schools (particularly at Löcknitz: see below). As a result of the population decrease on the German side, the rationale for school cooperation has often been defensive (recruitment from across the border in order to get enough students) rather than oriented towards future development. Unfortunately, the education system does not automatically help fight prejudices. In Poland, the geography and history of the Polish nation has a strong place in the curriculum, whereas in Germany, because of the Federal system, local Länder aspects are highlighted. In none of the school systems does the local trans-boundary reality receive much attention[30].

A project to establish a campus of Szczecin University at Eggesin (Landkreis Uecker-Randow) has not been completed, as a request from the University to the Ministry of Education in Warsaw of 2007 has received no reply. Eggesin has premises, while Szczecin University lacks space[31].

---

[29] See e.g.: K. Stokłosa, *Grenzstädte in Ostmitteleuropa. Guben und Gubin 1945 bis 1995*, Berlin 2003. Also: U. Rada, *Zwischenland. Europäische Geschichten aus dem deutsch-polnischen Grenzgebiet*, Berlin 2004.
[30] P. Bartnik, U. Berlińska, A. Kotula, interview 13.01.2009.
[31] D. Gutgesell, *Landkreis Uecker-Randow*, interview..., op. cit.

Human interaction

The far-reaching political decisions of 1945 severed the strong and close links that for centuries had united the regions east and west of the Oder and Neisse, and which also united Szczecin with the area that today contains the counties of Uecker-Randow, Ostvorpommern and Uckermark. The ethnical "homogenization" east of the border seems to have put an end to any substantial human interaction across the new borderline for the foreseeable future.

Thus, because of the shifts in population after World War II, the German-Polish border is one of the sharpest linguistic boundaries in Europe[32]. There are no significant natural or resident language minorities on either side, with the exception of a small group of recent Polish immigrants on the German side (see below). The lack of linguistic competence, the history of expulsion and settlement, and the present economic problems become the basis both of mutual distrust and of the realization that co-operation is essential. Further south along the river boundary, twin cities, particularly Frankfurt/Oder and Słubice, have developed fruitful co-operation, not least in the university sector. In the Szczecin region, the above-mentioned imbalances make relations more complicated. German-Polish relations are even, by some observers at least, said to be at their very worst in these border areas.

Traditional Polish fears of a new "Germanization" of the area are here mirrored by a growing German fear of a new "Polonization". Far into the new, 21st century, there is, in the city of Szczecin, an underlying and specific suspicion that the Germans have not yet accepted the fact that Szczecin now is a Polish city[33]. Because of poverty and limited population, the northeastern parts of Germany have, to some extent, developed into centers for political extremism. Mecklenburg-Vorpommern has the highest figures for xenophobia (about 64 per cent in recent opinion polls) in all of Germany. In villages in the border area immediately west of Szczecin, for which Stettin, up until the end of World War II, was the obvious metropolis, rightwing nationalists received up to 30 per cent of the vote in recent regional elections. In these groups, there is resistance to increased contacts with Poland. Regional integration is mistrusted as leading to even more of the region being sacrificed to Polish interests. Similarly, on the Polish side, there is skepticism, perhaps even fear of the German neighbor, particularly among lower-class citizens. Anti-Polish acts by German extremists are covered exhaustively in the Polish media[34].

---

[32] T. Lundén, *Language landscapes and static geographies in the Baltic Sea area*, [in:] M. Andrén, T. Lindkvist, I. Söhrman, K. Vajta (eds), *Cultural identities and national borders*, Göteborg 2009, p. 90.

[33] See e.g.: M. Drzonek, *Szczecin – a Polish, German or European City. A portrayal of Szczecin's principal identity and awareness of its borderland status*, [in:] J. Kurczewska (ed.), *Polish Borders and Borderlands in the Making. From the field studies of Polish Sociologists and Anthropologists*, Warszawa 2006, pp. 187-204.

[34] L. Meistring, *Mayor of Löcknitz*, interview 14.01.2009. See also: M. Sontheimer, *Aufbau Ost. Abschied von Vorurteilen*, "Der Spiegel", vol. 9, 2008, 25.02.2008, p. 62 and S. Schmollack, *Bis es knallt. Antipolnische Ressentiments in Vorpommern*, "TAZ", 13.05.2008.

However, the recognition of a common regional problem provides for more constructive initiatives. The existence of the European German-Polish Grammar School Löcknitz has even been so successful that Polish parents have moved to Szczecin in order to send their children there. Pupils from Polish Police commute daily to the school in Löcknitz, in the framework of organized cooperation between the two towns[35].

The most remarkable sign of an emerging, new cross-border culture is the substantial increase, after 2004, of Polish settlers on the German side of the border, in particular after Poland's accession to the Schengen Union in 2007. Germany is otherwise richer than Poland; in this area, however, housing prices are lower than they are in Polish Szczecin. It is estimated that about 2,400 Poles live in the German part of the metropolitan area. Löcknitz has long been able to attract Polish settlers (about 8% of 3,000 inhabitants). But for as long as the German ban on Polish (and other) job-takers is in effect – that is, until 2011 – the number and selection of settlers will be restricted.

Still, on balance, it is surprising to see that the area around Szczecin shows evidence – now, only a few years after Polish accession to the EU – of a new, and old, pattern of cross-border development, which distinguishes this area rather markedly from other parts of the border region. The agglomeration as such seems to be able to restore its own "Speckgürtel", and to once again surround itself with a coherent circle of, somehow dependent, smaller entities. The German side of the border is developing fast, both as a residential and recreational area for the Polish "metropolis". (An odd but delightful case is the Ückermünde Zoo, which has quickly been turned into the local Szczecin Zoo, with the leading local Polish daily, "Kurier Szczeciński", as its primary sponsor[36].) To some extent, the otherwise hard linguistic border[37] is here softening faster, because of the agglomeration's size and economic force. Here, the need to learn the neighboring language seems to become palpable sooner than it does elsewhere. As evidence of this development, one can cite, on the one hand, the advanced German-language courses that are being offered in Szczecin (somewhat reduced, recently, because of the German labor restrictions that are in force until 2011), and, on the other, the increasing demand for Polish lessons on the Western side of the border[38].

Also, with respect to the issue of ethnicity, the pure size of the agglomeration, when combined with the mechanisms of the common market (freedom of movement), apparently make possible a Polish-German mélange that is not seen in other

---

[35] G. Scherer, *Director of European German-Polish Grammar School Löcknitz*, interview 14.01.2009.
[36] Cf. Interview with Bogdan Twardochleb, journalist at "Kurier Szczeciński", Oct 14th, 2008.
[37] T. Lundén, *Language landscapes and static geographies in the Baltic Sea area*, [in:] M. Andrén, T. Lindkvist, I. Söhrman, K. Vajta (eds), *Cultural identities and national borders*, Centre for European Research, Göteborg 2009, p. 90.
[38] Cf. Interview with Rainer Dambach, mayor of Pasewalk, Jan. 12th, 2009; this general tendency is also true for Świnoujście, see Coleen Clement 2003: 79.

Map 1. Szczecin region

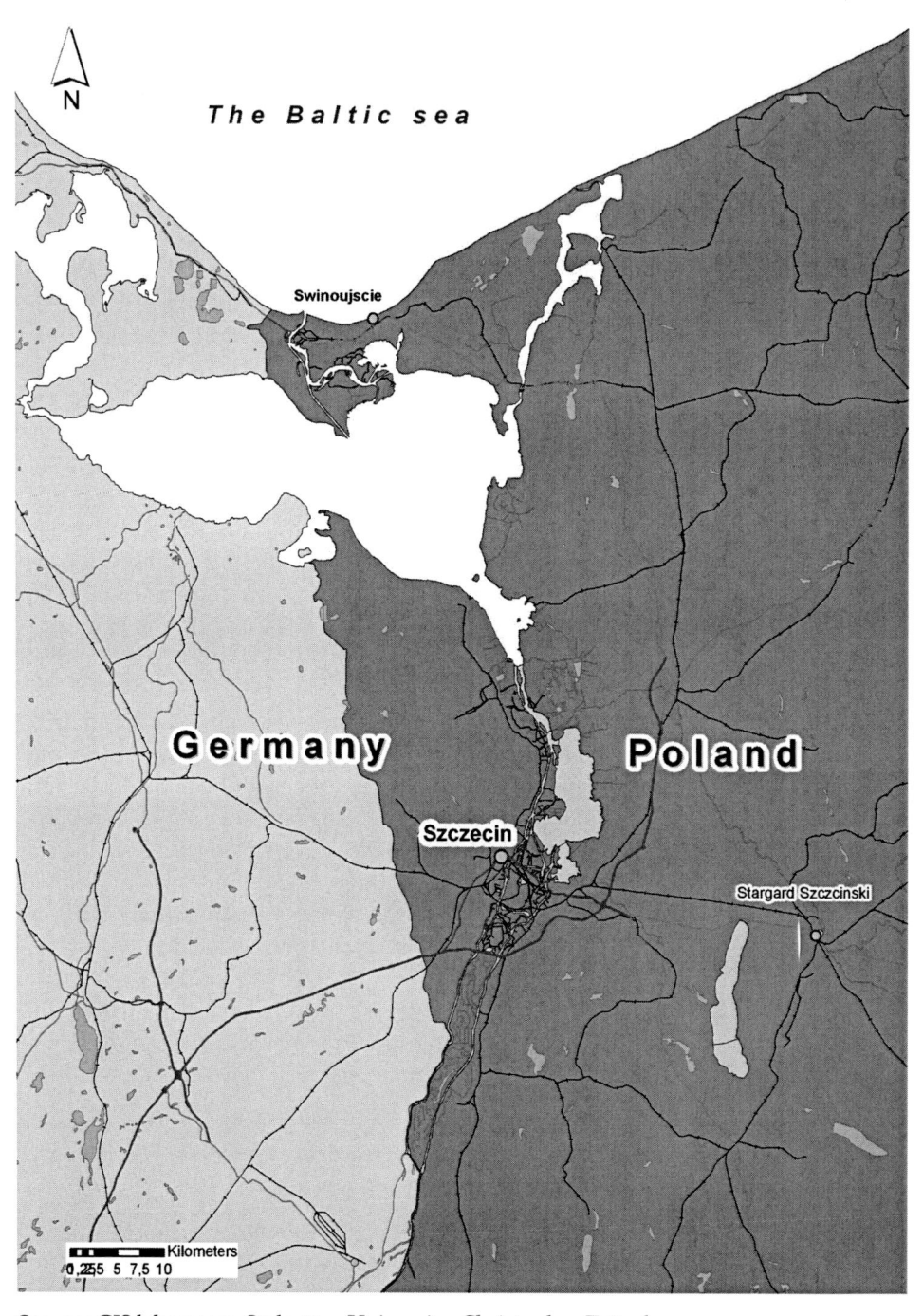

Source: GIS laboratory, Södertörn University, Christopher Zetterberg.

parts of the Oder-Neisse-border. It is less surprising to see local protests against the development, than to observe the fundamental ethnic and political changes that have taken place, and the rapidity with which old settlement and dependency patterns have reappeared on the Western side of the border. As these new settlement and economic activities were not steered from above, they seem to indicate the intense force of certain, apparently inherent patterns of spatial self-organization.

Conclusions

Szczecin has a unique location, as a border city with a weak hinterland on the German side. The infrastructure that used to link the town with its region was destroyed in World War II and its aftermath. After 1989, the unification of Germany, Poland's entry into the EU and the Schengen Zone, the material and legal possibilities for cooperation across the State boundary have increased. However, the level of cooperation is still low, and uneven. Some factors contribute to this situation:
– The administrative-political situation is characterized by hierarchical asymmetry, which hampers cooperative initiatives.
– The different hierarchical levels on both sides have different interests in relation to cross-border contacts and relations. The state level, for example, especially in Poland, has an understandable interest in an infrastructural homogenization of the country, which leaves Szczecin in the periphery.
– The levels most interested in cross-border relations seem to be the local ones, but here the asymmetry with respect to size and political power is most noticeable.
– Szczecin's role as a market centre for the theoretical hinterland is unevenly influenced by the boundary. In some ways, as a result of differences in market regulation, the border itself has attracted consumers of goods and services, but this has not, to any significant degree, led to political or individual contacts.
– Individual relations are, on the whole, peaceful but weak. They do, however, include some examples of interaction and cross-border activities, but also of minor conflicts, often exaggerated by activists and the press.

Gorizia-Nova Gorica
Between Unification and Reunification
Jarosław Jańczak

Introduction

About 10% of the European population lives in one of 1,060 towns located not further then 25 kilometers from one of the European borders[1], making border settlements forerunners of political, social and cultural processes in Europe. The divided town[2] of Gorizia and Nova Gorica represents one the most interesting examples. Located on the Italian-Slovenian border, the town embodies several phenomena characteristic for that sort of settlements in the Old Continent. The towns are located in the center of so-called contested space that – because of its geolocation on the edge of different cultures and empires – has changed its political allegiance several times. As a result, the space has been claimed by different ethnic groups and states as "their own", what was also strengthened by the presence of national minorities there. Additionally, the relatively recent town division meant in practice that new settlements (in the "green field" form) which had already been constructed and attached to the already existing town were now located on the other side of the border. Consequently, Gorizia and Nova Gorica represent both division and unity, as well as conflict and cooperation. The aim of this paper is to present an historical and empirical overview of both conflict and cooperation in the divided town. The paper's intention is not to cover every aspect of those two forms of coexistence. Only chosen elements will be investigated based on research conducted by historians, sociologists, political and European scientists, geographers and urban planers.

---

[1] A. Gasparini, *Do European Border Towns Hold the Key to Cultural Integration, Incubation*, "American Sociological Association Footnotes", December 2008, vol. 36, Issue 9.
[2] Alberto Gasparini defines a twin town as "*a border town in which the border is a division but is also a factor reinforcing identity. The border is part of the town's everyday life, with advantages and disadvantages great and small, cross-border kinship and friendship ties, a relationality that is not only structural and a factor of economic organisation (joint ventures, mergers, cross-border co-option between companies), but also individual and informal in purchases, holidays and cross-border employment*". A. Gasparini, *European Border Towns as Laboratories of Differentiated Integration*, "ISIG Quarterly of International Sociology. Borders in Europe. How Life is Lived in Border Towns, Border Regions and Border Cultures", year VIII-IX, no. 4 December – 1 February 1999-2000, p. 4.

The main questions addressed in the paper are: first of all, what determines a smooth shift from conflict towards cooperation in the case of Gorizia-Nova Gorica relations? The initial assumption will stress a role played by a new and "artificial" division as the decisive factor that, together with the historical tradition of "multiculturness", borderland heritage and European integration, pushed the settlements towards close collaboration. Second, the fact that towns were in fact not divided, but the Slovenian (in terms of state location) part of the town was "joined" to the Italian one creates a problem if both settlements represent reintegration or integration. This paper claims that the towns are in the process of integrating, whereas the region of which they are the main center is reintegrating. In turn, this contributes strongly to the quality and pace of the processes there.

Italy and Yugoslavia/Slovenia – a history of border relations

Conflict and cooperation in the divided town of Gorizia and Nova Gorica has to be analyzed in the regional context of the Italian-Yugoslavian/Slovenian-Austro-Hungarian/Austrian borderland.

The towns are typical of the Upper Adriatic region combining *"Alpine and Mediterranean regions [...] German, Slovene, Friulian, Italian and Croatian linguistic areas, [...] three major European cultural areas – the Romance, the Germanic, and the Slavic"*[3]. The region has been an arena of heavy territorial disputes and shifts in the last 150 years[4]. What is relevant is the fact that it has changed its political-territorial belonging several times. Untill 1947, it has always remained more or less internally undivided. This was reflected in the homogenous and diverse character of the province and its clear characteristics, distinguishing it from the surrounding region/area.

The region has always been multiethnic. In the middle of 19th century, the County of Gorizia and Gradisca was inhabited by 65% Slovenians, 25% Friulians, 8% Italians and 1% Germans. For a long time, the Italian language played a universal role in the region, with German however becoming the language of the Habsburg state. Catholicism dominated the province.

By the end of World War I, the region was part of the Austian-Hungarian Empire as a County of Gorizia and Gradisca with a high level of self-governance. As a result of the war, two autonomy movements started vehemently to express their postulates: the Slovenians inhabiting the Eastern part, and Western – Friulians. As their territories almost did not cross, they were rather anti-Austrian than opposed to each other anti anti-each other oriented. The only exception was the town of Gorizia.

For the region, World War I meant the diminishing of Austrian influences and becoming a playground of Italian-Yugoslavian competition.

---

[3] M. Bufon, *Cross-border Cooperation in the Upper Adriatic*, [in:] J. Anderson, L. O'Dowd, T.M. Wilson (eds), *New Borders for a Changing Europe*, London–Portland 2003, p. 177.
[4] See: A.L. Sanguin, M. Berta Mrak, *The Italian-Slovenian border in the framework of the European Union's enlargement*, "Annales De Géographie", no. 112, (632) (Jul-Aug).

The London Treaty signed by Italy and the Triple Entente resulted in Italian attempts to receive territorial gains on its Northeastern outskirts, especially in Istria and Dalmatia. Internal pressure during the post-war period to compensate war losses pushed Italy into further disputes with Yugoslavia (Kingdom of Serbs, Croats and Slovenians) to gain as much of the border territories as possible.

The disintegration of the Habsburg's empire led to Italy's occupation of the region, resulting in its incorporation in 1920, as confirmed by the Treaties of Rapallo and Saint Germain-en-Laye. The province of Gorizia became part of the centralized Italian state, and was then provincialized through unification with neighboring territories.

Further territorial changes resulted from World War II. Territorial claims of both Yugoslavia and Italy lasted two years, and the province was divided by the so-called Morgan Line with British and American control over its Western part and Yugoslav over the Eastern. What has to be stressed again, is that the Gorizia region has formed a single administrative and functional unit for most of its history since the Middle Ages. In this form, it was a part of the Austrian, then the Italian state. The border that might be observed nowadays was delimitated in 1947. It divided the region, leaving most of the population (about 74%) and only 8% of the territory on the Italian side, and ceding the rest to Yugoslavia as a part of the Socialist Republic of Slovenia. The urban center of Gorizia was separated from its hinterland[5]. The new border divided a previously homogenous region, separating especially the old regional center from its surroundings. It should be pointed out here that no serious population transfers were conducted.

Post-war developments in the region were determined by the Cold War and East-West conflict and then realistic coexistence. Initially, the new border (line of demarcation) – being a southern part of the Iron Curtain – was strongly guarded and marked with wires and fences. The border opening was initiated by the Udine Agreement and resulted in the creation of border crossings for urban areas. The Yugoslav-Italian border became probably the most open part of the Iron Curtain in following years during the Cold War.

A new phase in bilateral relations was marked by the independence of Slovenia in 1991 that pushed this state into the Western direction, making Italy one of its two key partners. This was caused by both economic development chances seen in Western Europe as well as the necessity of overcoming the Balkan heritage. The growing importance of the borderland as a bridge to Western Europe was on the other hand modified by the refortification of the border due to the Schengen agreement, which protected against threats coming from the East – especially immigrants and crime from the Balkans. Finally, the European integration of Slovenia and European financial assistance for border collaboration, together with the enlargement of the Schengen "zone" accelerated the process of reunification of the region.

The Gorizia region has been an important part of Italian-Slovenian relations. For the majority of its history, it has been – albeit with a frequent change of state affilia-

---

[5] M. Bufon, *Cross-border...*, op. cit., p. 182.

tion – a border province with a multicultural population. However, it was only in 1947 that decisions divided it "artificially". The Cold War was characterized by growing collaboration; its time as part of Europe has seen renewed attempts to reintegrate the province.

Gorizia-Nova Gorica – a divided town

The town of Gorizia has a history dating back around a thousand years, having, always been a natural center of the region. The town itself – similar to the province – was also characterized by its multicultural and multilingual character. However, the Slovenian population was, dominating in the rural areas, less represented among the town dwellers. In the inter-war period, the number of Italian and Friulian speakers constituted about 70% of the Gorizia town population, Slovenian about 30%.

According to provisions laid down in the 1947 Paris Peace Treaty, Yugoslavia obtained mainly rural parts of the Gorizia region. The new border was drawn along the Eastern suburbs of the town. Only smaller districts remained in Yugoslavian hands. However, one of them was the central railway station, with the border cutting the square in the front of it in half and preventing Italian inhabitants from using the rail service without considerable difficulty.

Although Yugoslavia won most of the desired territory, there was no urban center that could serve the local administrative, social, economic and cultural needs. As a result, it was decided – with the support of Josip Tito – to construct a new Gorizia on the Yugoslavian side of the border. It was to be the manifestation of the rivalry with the Italian Gorizia, but also as a consequence of local needs of the Slovenian province of Goriška. The new, modern and model park city was designed by Edo Ravnikar and named Nova Gorica.

It is important to note, that the fact that Nova Gorica was built as a new town by Yugoslavia after losing Gorica is, for some scholars not entirely obvious as to why the two areas should be classified as a divided town[6]. However divisions within Gorica were observable even before the creation of Nova Gorica. This was a consequence of multiethnic composition of the town, national movements of Slovenians and Italians and finally Italy's oppression policy during the inter-war period.

Contemporary Gorizia and Nova Gorica form one spatial area located on both sides of the border. Administratively, they are separate towns located in two states, with own separate administrative structures, competences, budgets, etc.

Gorizia is inhabited by about 38,000 people, Nova Gorica by about 20,000. The historical town center is located in Gorizia. About 17% of Gorizia's inhabitants declared in 200 that they belonged to the Slovenian minority, with only 1% of Nova

---

[6] H. Schultz, K. Stokłosa, D. Jajeśniak-Quast, *Twin Towns on the Border as Laboratories of European Integration*, FIT Discussion Paper, no. 4, 2002, p. 5.

Gorica inhabitants declaring themselves to be Italian[7]. The ethnic composition of Gorizia has changed over the last century, with several asymmetries observable between towns. This is especially true in the field of economic development and cultural homogeneity of the Italian part[8].

Conflict in Gorizia-Nova Gorica

Conflict in the divided town of Gorizia-Nova Gorica can be divided into four phases: Habsburg, Inter-war, Cold War and European. The former two periods took place within the town of Gorizia[9] and were not related to the border itself, but more to the cultural and ethnic boundaries. The latter two appeared after the delimitation of the new border and the creation of Nova Gorica was manifested in inter-town relations.

The Habsburg era facilitated the ground for conflict because of the nation formation processes initiated at the time. The Gorizia region was one of the centers of Slovenian culture at the end of 19th century. The Slovenian language was gradually replacing German in public life, numerous cultural institutions were established there, and the language of instruction at among others *the State Gymnasium* (high school) was Slovenian. At the same time, however, the town was also a center of Friulian language and culture and was penetrated by Italian cultural elements. As a result, the main source of conflict were *"overlapping cultural spaces that created difficulties in boundary-making processes which sought ethnically based political borders. As a consequence individual states either tried to adapt the existing ethnic structure to the current political situation or opened irredentist demands towards neighboring countries"*[10].

The Italian inter-war period brought an intensive Italianization of the region addressed at repressing both the Slovenian and German languages and cultures. It was characterized by the oppression of language use, naming, literature publishing, etc., and resulted in an anti-Italian Slovenian resistance. The region was liberated by the Yugoslavian communist guerillas at the end of World War II what was accompanied by oppression on many Italians living there.

The Cold War period solved the territorial disputes, as well as ethnic and cultural problems, in part due to the creation of Nova Gorica. The Italian population of Gorizia started to grow especially in 1950s, when many Italians left territories ceded

---

[7] *Ibidem*, p. 19.
[8] M. Bufon, *Cultural and Social Dimensions of Borderlands: The Case of the Italo-Slovene Trans-border Area*, "GeoJournal" 30.03.1993, p. 239.
[9] Borders within "normal" towns have been observed in e.g. spatial, social, ethical, forms etc. However, this was a relatively new phenomenon resulting from town growth. The consequence of its existence was usually the necessity of protecting some of the areas (e.g. inhabited by higher classes) against the others. G. Amendola, *Border within Cities*, "ISIG Quarterly of International Sociology. Cooperation and Euroregions. For Borders to Became Centers", year XIII, no. 3-4, December 2004, p. 1.
[10] M. Bufon, *Cross-border...*, op. cit., p. 179.

to Yugoslavia. Its younger sister territory was inhabited mainly by Slovenians. However, the new border was part of the Iron Curtain and Gorizia-Nova Gorica were the second biggest border towns situated there after Berlin. Two towns were to represent two realities; capitalist and communist were to compete with each other. One of the consequences of the post-war period was the separation of Gorizia's and Nova Gorica's development strategies.

The last period started together with Slovenian independence and its European aspirations. Here, the problem was that both towns needed the chance to develop their competition against each other or by close collaboration as the best strategy. This dilemma was visible also after the EU accession and was related to border normalization. The disappearance of the border has led to the moderation of the pace in further cooperation. At the same time, the changing position of Slovenia with regard to her economic growth has resulted in an emphasis on the deregionalization of trans-border collaboration.

It is important to highlight two characteristic elements of the conflict in Gorizia-Nova Gorica. First, its intensity has been continuously diminishing throughout the periods analyzed here. This might be explained by disappearing elements fanning the flame of conflict: territory was divided according to specific criteria, minority rights were guaranteed, etc. Second, the manifestation of conflict was usually the most visible in the presence of external factors: the Italian-Yugoslavian territorial conflict, Cold War, Schengen. That would imply that without external factors, the double town tends to collaborate instead of becoming involved in the conflict.

Cooperation in Gorizia-Nova Gorica: towards *Gorizia Nova*?

The Gorizia-Nova Gorica case represents the border that is a natural cooperation space much more then a division line. As Milan Bufon points out, "*the greater were conflicts in political partition of a previously homogeneous administrative, cultural and economic region, the greater are then opportunities for such a divided area to develope into an integrated 'trans- border region'*"[11].

The history of the towns' collaboration was directly related to the creation of Nova Gorica as a natural border partner in the newly divided region of Gorizia. Two factors seem to be decisive here: first of all, the ethnic composition of an artificially divided region, especially the social and family ties as well as a significant Slovenian minority on the Italian side of the border. Second, weakening external obstacles were replaced after 1991 with European support for a transborder collaboration. This resulted among others in self-identity as a symbol of overcoming differences and effective integration.

The divided towns' collaboration might be considered at least two levels: local and central. The former results from functionally driven needs whereas the latter

---

[11] M. Bufon, *Cultural and...*, op. cit., p. 240.

proves and symbolizes good relations between neighboring states[12], also in the European context.

One of the first attempts at cooperation was liberalization of the border control regimes shortly after their introduction in 1949. A threat of the Berlin scenario – the so-called "Berlinization" of the border – forced Italian and Yugoslavian decision makers to sign the Udine Agreement that softened border crossing constraints for property owners in the region. Extended shortly after to the whole Slovenian Italian border, it resulted in a nine-fold increase in border crossing traffic between 1955 and 1960 in the region of Gorizia, then about 95% of total Italian-Yugoslavian traffic[13]. The relaxing of the border regime and the increased possibility of crossing the border was of primary importance for the two border cities: Triest and Gorizia had both been separated from their hinterlands by the new state border.

The border was opened to person traffic in 1955, followed by the construction of several border crossing points. Border normalization was reached by the 1970s in the region. In 1980, an agreement between the European Community and Yugoslavia was signed accelerating economic exchange and – as a result – border crossings.

The first agreements between Gorizia and Nova Gorica were signed in 1963. Very soon, drinking water started to be transferred from Gorizia to Nova Gorica. This showed space for sectoral cooperation based on coexistential pragmatism being more important than ideological conflicts. A similar collaboration was observable in the 1970s and 1980s. The beginning of 1990s primarily meant a cooperation in the field of practical aspects of neighborhood. Both towns were working on a water supply system, the softening of border controls, etc.[14]

Research by Moreno Zago published in 2000 shows that the level of sectoral cooperation in border twin towns on the Italian-Slovenian border was relatively high, especially compared to other European divided towns. What dominated was a collaboration in public administration, then public services for citizens, economic services as well as sports and culture[15].

In the following parts of investigation, social contacts, "public institutions" collaboration and its European context will be analyzed.

Social contacts between both towns

The Gorizia-Nova Gorica contacts and interactions model represents a typical bottom-up process. It was initiated by personal contacts, followed by social ones, com-

---

[12] R. Kosonen, X. Feng, E. Kettunen, *Paired Border Towns or TwinCities from Finland and China*, "Chinese Journal of Population, Resources and Envirnment", vol. 6, no. 1, 2008, p. 3.
[13] M. Bufon, *Cross-border Cooperation...*, op. cit., p. 183.
[14] T. Marušič, G. Valenti, *The Different Ways of Being Common Towns Gorizia (Italy) Nova Gorica (Slovenia)*, "ISIG Quarterly of International Sociology. Borders within Towns, Towns without Borders", year IV, no. 1-2 October 1995, p. 7.
[15] M. Zago, *State of Cooperation between Border Towns*, "ISIG Quarterly of International Sociology. Borders in Europe. How Life is Lived in Border Towns, Border Regions and Border Cultures", year VIII-IX, no 4, December – 1 February 1999-2000, p. 4.

pleted finally by political interactions. This was primarily due to the ethnic and cultural composition of the local population. The trans-border town became a manifestation of a trans-border community[16].

According to research conducted in 1994 by Milan Bufon, the level of cross-border integration amongst the population in the Gorizia region was very high compared to both the Italian-Slovenian border as well as other border areas in Europe. He explained this phenomenon through the young age of the border as well as the fact that the population is mixed in the divided towns area. Chadwic Adler reported in 1995 on several elements of border cooperation in Gorizia-Nova Gorica. He observed and concluded that social boundaries and their overcoming are much more important in divided towns than state borders in the process of cooperation[17].

In Gorizia-Nova Gorica, about four-fifths of both Italians and Slovenians declare they have relatives on the other side of the border; many declared having friends there. This was followed by a high level of declarations related to border commuting. 30% of inhabitants in the Gorizia area declared that they cross the border at least several times a week[18]. Among the main reasons for visiting are not only purchasing cheaper goods and services, work (Slovenians) but also visiting friends and relatives[19].

Language relations may be considered as one of the factors describing the level of cooperation. The role of language and culture proximity on both sides of the divided town for effective communication and collaboration is stressed by Thomas Lundén[20]. According to research conducted at the end of the 1990s, both Italian and Slovenian are widely spoken in Gorizia and Nova Gorica[21]. In Nova Gorica, Slovenian dominates, followed by Serb and Croat. Italian is rarely reported[22]. Altogether, about 85% of the border population reported they are able to communicate in both Italian and Slovenian. This is accompanied by a high level of information flow on what is offered on the other side of the border, as well as use of the neighbors's media[23].

---

[16] M. Bufon, *Cultural and Social...*, op. cit., p. 237.
[17] C.F. Alger, *The Role of Border Towns in Formation of International Relations*, "ISIG Quarterly of International Sociology. Borders within Towns, Towns without Borders", year IV, no. 1-2, October 1995, p. 3.
[18] M. Bufon, *Cross-border...*, op. cit., p. 183.
[19] *Ibidem*.
[20] T. Lundén, *European Twinn Cities: Models, Examples and Problems of Formal and Informal Co-operation*, "ISIG Quarterly of International Sociology. Cooperation and Euregions – for Borders to Become Centers", year XIII, no. 3-4, December 2004, pp. 1-2.
[21] S. Novak-Lukanovic, K. Munda-Hirnök, B. Jesih, I. Verdenik, N. Vodopivec, *Percpetion of cultural and linguistic diversity in two border towns novagorica [SI]/Gorica [IT] – presentation of selected results of the research project [case study]*, "Razprave in Gradivo – Treatises and Documents"(46), 2005.
[22] A. Gasparini, *Situations, Conditions, Styles of Life and Government in Border Towns*, "ISIG Quarterly of International Sociology. Borders in Europe. How Life is Lived in Border Towns, Border Regions and Border Cultures", year VIII-IX, no. 4, Decembcr – 1 February 1999-2000, p. 10.
[23] M. Bufon, *Cultural and Social...*, op. cit., pp. 236-238.

The above paragraphs could be concluded with Milan Bufon's findings that "*social and functional cross-border integration is determined less by the proximity of the border than by a common social, cultural and territorial background of the border population*"[24].

Collaboration amongst public institutions'

Social contacts as well as sectoral collaboration usually leads to the institutionalization of cooperation. Helga Schultz, Katarzyna Stokłosa and Dagmara Jajeśniak-Quast propose a pattern of three steps to evaluate the institutionalization of collaboration of border twin towns: first, the implementation of single joint projects; second, the systematic cooperation and third, the creation of joint bodies[25].

All of them are visible in the case of Gorizia-Nova Gorica. Already in the 1990s, the idea of a common city appeared as a natural continuation of previous forms of collaboration. In 2002, a joint public transportation line was initiated providing both towns with a trans-border service. Another example of cooperation is the rapidly developing hi-tech sector. Projects aiming at the creation of a virtual community in Gorizia and Nova Gorica are proposed at two levels: regional (administration, public services, etc.) and international (business and telematic centers)[26]. Also, cross-border semi-institutions have been created. At the beginning of the 21st century, city mayors were meeting about four times a year; councils once a year.

Common strategies of further development are based on overcoming local weaknesses as well as assessing external opportunities and internal strengths[27]. A regional context seems to be relevant here. A Gorizia-Nova Gorica cooperation could be placed within the wider context of trans-border cooperation in the region containing Italo-Slavon, Italo-Austrian and Austrio-Slovinian borders. Cross-border governance tools have been developed, among others, in the MAREMA (Managing Regional Management) project that involves Austria, Italy and Slovenia[28].

One of the projects that will create an enhanced collaboration and overcome the marginalization of both Gorizia and Nova Gorica is the *Gorizia Nova* project. The name refers to both names as well as to the Italian and Slovenian traditions. The pro-

---

[24] M. Bufon, *Social Integration in the Italo-Slovene Gorizia Transborder Region*, "Tijdschrift voor economische en sociale geografie", vol. 87, Issue 3, 2008, p. 56.

[25] H. Schultz, K. Stokłosa, D. Jajeśniak-Quast, *Twin Towns...*, op. cit., p. 34.

[26] L. Bregantini, M. Zago, *Gorizia-Nova Gorica: a Possible "Virtual" Community Notwithstanding the Border*, "ISIG Quarterly of International Sociology. Virtual Relaity – Designing the Future", year IV, no. 3-4, December 1995, pp. 1-2.

[27] E. Ferluga, A. Gasparini, *SWOT Analysis in Three Cross-Border Areas: Strategies and Actions to Plan Cross-Border Cooperation*, "ISIG Quarterly of International Sociology. Borders in Europe. Governance of Cross-Border Cooperation. Marema. Methods and Contents of Regional Management", year XIV, no. 2, April 2005, p. 16.

[28] A. Gasparini, *Introduction*, "ISIG Quarterly of International Sociology. Borders in Europe. Governance of Cross-Border Cooperation. Marema. Methods and Contents of Regional Management", year XIV, no. 2, April 2005, pp. 1-2.

ject was conducted between 2003 and 2006 by Triest University (Interreg III A framework) and proposed future direction for economic, social and territorial development as well as for urban joint planning[29].

European context

The European integration process has strongly contributed to the acceleration of collaboration between Gorizia and Nova Gorica in several ways.

First of all, the European Union's financial support is crucial for the institutionalization of the towns' cooperation, not only because of its pragmatic meaning but also because it imposes specific mechanisms and procedures[30]. In 1998, Gorizia and Nova Gorica signed a cross-border agreement to achieve Phare-CBC assistance[31]. Interreg Italy-Slovenia enables, for example, hospitals collaboration[32].

Second, collaboration between divided towns, especially on the border between Western and Eastern Europe, has an enormous symbolic meaning, showing a new period of peaceful coexistence in integrating Europe and overcoming different divisions. Gorizia-Nova Gorica's cooperation strategy is strongly based on symbolism. Symbols can be described as *"the crystallization of a linguistic description"*[33] embodying given ideas. Collaboration was defined at local, interstate and pan-European levels[34]. The first one intended to represent the functional interdependence of neighboring settlements inhabited by a culturally close population, yet artificially divided. The second level symbolized effective collaboration between Italy and Slovenia, where both cities were to be gateways, bridges, etc. Finally, Gorizia and Nova Gorica were to symbolize the overcoming of the Iron Curtain, its heritage and, in turn, effective European integration.

The European dimension was also very visible in "European celebrations" in the towns. On the occasion of EU enlargement in 2004, for example, an official Italian-Slovenian fete was organized on May 1 in Gorizia-Nova Gorica with the European Commission President Romano Prodi. The towns hosted different cross-border initiatives, such as a meeting of 40 border mayors (resulting in Gorizia Map), or the Cross-Border Pact in 1998. On the other hand, the Schengen zone enlargement on 21 December 2007 that marked another milestone in cooperation tightening in the twin city, was not celebrated or contested in both towns[35].

---

[29] *Gorizia Nova. The Urban Area Gorizia-Nova Gorica As A Model For Europe. Final Report*, Department of Geographical And Historical Sciences, University of Trieste, Gorizia 2006.
[30] H. Schultz, K. Stokłosa, D. Jajeśniak-Quast, *Twin Towns on…*, op. cit., p. 35.
[31] *Ibidem*, p. 34.
[32] G.M. Apuzzo, *Beyond the Divided City (II)*, "Osservatiorio Balccani", 3.06.2008.
[33] K. Pekonen, *Center-Periphery Relations in the Cycles of Political Symbols: the Problem of Modernity*, [in:] *Transformation of Ideas on a Periphery*, J. Kanerva, K. Palonen, I. Valmisteksti (eds), Helsinki 1987, p. 40.
[34] G.M. Apuzzo, *Beyond the Divided City (I)*, "Osservatiorio Balccani", 26.05.2008.
[35] G.M. Apuzzo, *Beyond the Divided City (I)…*, op. cit.

Conclusion

Goriza-Nova Gorica represents a for Central Europe typical border situation: it consists of changing borders, dominating empires, statehoods, but also of national and ethnic minorities located on the other side of the (new) border as well as a long lasting tradition of coexistance.

As Milan Bufon points out, the studies on borders and borderlands have changed its focus from separating lines in a political and economic sense towards adding to this perspective a binding factor as well as social and cultural elements[36]. This tendency might be explained by the case of Gorizia and Nova Gorica. Twin towns tend to become joint towns by integrating sector by sector. Only then can integration accelerate in the sectors that are of a special relevance for both sides[37], followed by differentiated integration logics[38]. The process is easier in the case of those regions with borderland tractions, multicultural heritage that have been recently artificially divided. The European integration process accelerates the cooperation process by equipping the parties with additional tools. What is also illustrated by the Gorizia-Nova Gorica example is that the collaboration is easier when integration of the towns is accompanied by the reintegration of a previously divided region.

---

[36] M. Bufon, *Cultural and Social...*, op. cit., p. 235.
[37] A. Gasparini, *European Border Towns...*, op. cit., pp. 4-5.
[38] A. Gasparini, *Social and Political Variables for the Solution of Conflict between Minorities and Majorities*, "ISIG Quarterly of International Sociology. How Diplomacy Conceives and Achieves the Protection of Central-Eastern European Minorites", year IX-X, no. 4, December – 1 February 1999-2000, p. 4.

Valga-Valka, Narva-Ivangorod
Estonia's Divided Border Cities – Co-operation and Conflict Within and Beyond the EU

Thomas Lundén

Boundary theory

A boundary is a line, usually in space, at which a certain state of affairs is terminated and replaced by another state of affairs. In nature, boundaries mark the separation of different physical states (molecular configurations), e.g. the boundary between water and air at the surface of the sea, between wood and bark in a tree stem, or bark and air in a forest. The boundaries within an organized society are of a different character. Organization means structuration and direction, i.e. individuals and power resources are directed towards a specific, defined goal. This, in turn, requires delimitations of tasks to be done, as well as of the area in which action is to take place. The organization is defined in a competition for hegemony and markets, and with the aid of technology. But this game of definition and authority is, within the limitations prescribed by nature, governed by human beings.

Political geography

Among the first works to address the relation between a state and its territory was Friedrich Ratzel's *Politische Geographie* (Political Geography), published in 1897[1]. While some aspects of his teaching today seem quite outmoded, others have an actuality that few Cold War scholars would have predicted. The concept of political geography, as defined by Ratzel, encompasses the exigency of power over terrestrial space, irrespective of scale or location. Today, many of the claims made by Ratzel and by his follower, the Swede Rudolf Kjellén, seem dated. Furthermore, both the "German" and Anglo-American schools of politics and geopolitics fell into disrepute at the end of World War II. A new emphasis was eventually placed on trans-boundary communication and the individual's role in the territorial state, especially at 'open' boundaries[2]. This pre-

---

[1] F. Ratzel, *Politische Geographie*, München–Leipzig 1897; see also reflections on Ratzel's work in: M. Antonsich, V. Kolossov, M. Paola Pagnini (eds), *Europe between Political Geography and Geopolitics*, Società Geografica Italiana, Memorie vol. LXIII, Roma 2001.

[2] See e.g. D.E. Reynolds, M. Mc Nulty, *On the analysis of political boundaries as barriers: A perceptual approach*, "East Lakes Geographer", IV, Dec. 1968, pp. 21-38; T. Lundén, *Individens rumsliga beteende i ett gränsområde*, Stockholm 1973.

pared the ground for the revival of a revised political geography, which included not only the discipline of geography but other fields within the social sciences and humanities as well, especially if we include boundary studies on ethnicity, gender relations and cross-border co-operation[3].

Authoritative organization

In a modern society, the most visible type of organization is that of the political institutions. By *political* organization we mean a social institution that has authoritative competence, i.e. that has (been given) the power to regulate conditions within a certain subject area and/or territory[4]. *Regulation* can be described as the array of laws, and other societal forces, that restrict mobility and contacts. Regulation is characterized by definition and delimitation. It is expressed most clearly in a state's border controls, but in a more general manner in censorship laws, age limits, etc. Within all organizations that demand credibility, or whose members' influence is regulated, formal decisions must be reached, and there must be regulations or laws that, in some respects, create reasonably homogenous conditions throughout the domain.

The *state* is a territorial, mostly hierarchical, organization that claims monopoly on the use of force within its domain. It supplies services to its members (citizens and/or residents), e.g. by providing infrastructure, protection and education. In return, it demands loyalty, membership fees (taxation) and certain services (e.g. participation in military and civil defense). In certain respects, the independent state strives to attain homogeneity in its territory. This is especially the case with respect to laws and the rights and responsibilities of those dwelling in the domain, in most cases the state's citizens.

Most state domains incorporate a number of sub-domains that have some measure of local self-determination, but still have to conform to state directives. Municipalities, provinces and autonomous regions form smaller domains where more specific rules apply, e.g. building permits, emission rules or official language(s). As a given function may be handled by the municipality in one state, but on the county- or even central state government level in another, cross-boundary contacts become difficult.

In the vocabulary of Torsten Hägerstrand, a domain is a (spatial) area which, in some manner, is dominated by an individual or an organization. There are thus domains of all sizes – my desk is a domain, as is the territory of a world power. Domains are regulated formally or informally. To each domain applies rules that are valid only within that domain[5]. The independent territorial state is just one level in

---

[3] V. Kolossov, *Theoretical limology: new analytical approaches' Crossing the border*, [in:] T. Lundén (ed.), *Boundary relations in a changing Europe*, Baltic and East European Studies 9, Södertörn University College, Eslöv 2006, pp. 15-35.
[4] D. Easton, *Political Science*, [in:] D.L. Sills (ed.), *International Encyclopedia of the Social Sciences*, New York 1968.
[5] T. Hägerstrand, *Space, time and human conditions*, [in:] A. Karlqvist, L. Lundvist, F. Snickars (eds), *Dynamic Allocation of Urban Space*, Lexington 1975, pp. 3-25.

a hierarchy of domains, each of which has its specific jurisdiction[6]. Clearly, there are levels above the state, e.g. the European Union, the United Nations and other regional and international organizations. But the development of inter-state organizations has been accompanied by a growth in intra- or trans-state power as well. J. Fall[7] speaks of a "new medievalism", by which she means the re-appearance of conglomerate states with internal legal differences and privileges, but also formal and informal regionalism, i.e. the autonomous areas etc. This, she believes, now characterizes even 'ordinary' European states. The organization of public society is thus a construction in which increasingly large units are placed on top of each other, from municipalities and provinces to independent states and supra-state organizations. But the territories of the smaller units almost always add up to the outer limits of the independent state. State legislation and regulations control the reach and the movement patterns of citizens and non-citizen residents.

Where territorial states are in juxtaposition, differences between the jurisdictions of specific hierarchical levels have led to an asymmetry which produces what one could term misfits, or discords[8]. Asymmetries have had a negative influence on authoritative organizations' attempts to create local cross-border communities. An issue that one state treats at a certain level may be handled at a different level in the neighboring state. This, in turn, means that the issue cannot be solved locally, through

Figure 1. Hierarchical asymmetry. The political treatment of a local trans-boundary problem from local level (bottom) to European Union (top). The thick arrows denote the handling of a local trans-boundary problem at different hierarchical levels and the thin arrows indicate attempts to make lateral contacts (based on Lundén, 1973, p. 191)

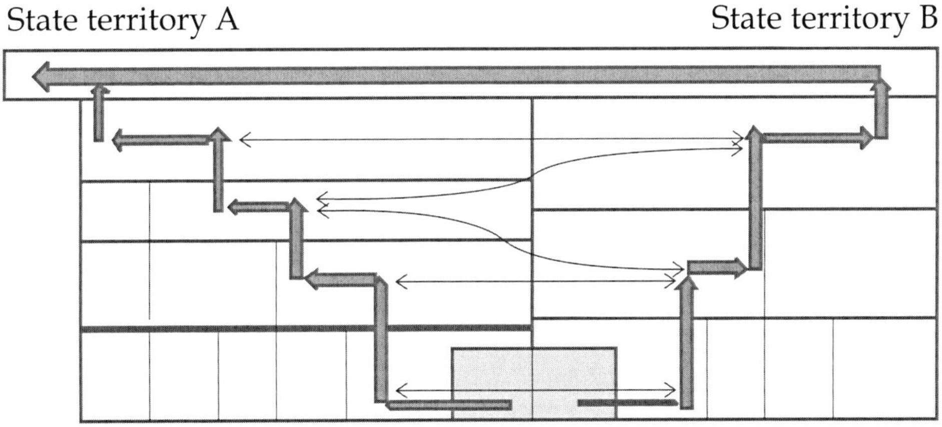

State territory A   State territory B

---

[6] A. Abbott, *The system of professions: An essay on the division of labor*, Chicago 1988.
[7] J. Fall, *Drawing the Line. Nature, Hybridity and Politics in Transboundary Spaces*. Williston 2005.
[8] H. Fichter-Wold, *Hochschulkooperationen in Grenzräumen. Lernfeld für die Entwicklung eines gemeinsamen europäischen Wissenschftsraums. DISP(ETH, Zürich)* 173 2/2008, pp. 34-46, from O.R. Young, *The Institutional Dimensions of Environmental Change: Fit, Interplay, and Scale*, Cambridge Mass.–London 2002.

negotiation between officials at symmetric hierarchical levels. Instead, the matter often has to be referred upwards in the hierarchy, where it is often not prioritized[9].

The state, the market and society

The state, formally characterized by regulation, stands in marked contrast to another type of organization, the *market*, defined as the free exchange of goods and services according to their trade values. Some theorists argue that the market, and even the internal structure of commercial companies, show many characteristics typical of political organizations[10], while others, e.g. representatives of the public-choice school, argue that, in the free economic market, authoritative decisions are made by the individual[11]. As mentioned above, the market economy has, in principle, no boundaries, but every sectorial economy is strongly regulated or subsidized by each state. The fact that a given product must be transported across a boundary may raise its price significantly, even if the transportation cost is negligible. If the boundary is open, or partly open (e.g. through customs restrictions), a situation will ensue where the consumers on the one side and the suppliers on the other will benefit from trans-boundary commerce.

Society, with its mixture of markets and regulations, functions through *communication*, the distribution and exchange of information between individuals and groups. Communication is often organized, directed and structured according to political and market rules, but also according to current technological development. One of the most important means of communication is *language*. Through communication in the form of language and symbols, those common values that determine behavior and attitudes, *culture*, are mediated and reproduced. And before this plethora of facts and ideas stands the reflecting, acting, indivisible human being.

The state and its residents

The individual who lives in a given state and in a given location is, to some degree, influenced by that state's territory of authority. The state authority is sometimes taken for granted. At other times, it is questioned. Those who live in boundary areas may encounter alternative social orders, and may thus become alert to new possibilities, but boundary populations rarely have the demographic strength or political power to influence the territorial center of the population and power.

An array of possibilities and restrictions determine the individual's movement- and contact patterns. Civic society establishes certain configurations of behavior. As stated above, these established configurations also influence our 'spontaneous' behavior.

---

[9] T. Lundén, *Individens rumsliga beteende…, op. cit.*, pp. 188-191; J. Rosenau, *Toward the study of national-international linkages*, [in:] J. Rosenau (ed.), *Linkage Politics*, New York–London 1969.
[10] C. Lindblom, *Politics and markets*, New York 1977.
[11] M. Olson, *Power and prosperity: outgrowing communist and capitalist dictatorships*, New York 2000.

In today's North European welfare state, the citizen has access (reach) to public services localized in different parts of the country. The regional availability of these services often mirrors the civic administration's hierarchy, from municipality to state territory. But in return the citizen is expected to show loyalty to the civic society and to perform his duties. This implies movement and mobility. According to Karl W. Deutsch, one criterion for the success of a 'nation state'[12] is that its residents are 'nationalized'. This means that their communication with 'their' state has led to their accepting that they belong to that particular 'nation state'. This can be achieved in various ways, some voluntary and others coercive. The school curriculum, legislation, military service can serve this purpose, as can the construction of an infrastructure (transport routes, communication networks) that makes it more natural to move and make contacts within, rather than beyond, the state territory. More brutally, it can be achieved through forbidding the citizens to leave the state territory or to have contacts with the outside world. But the point that Deutsch wishes to make is really that a liberal democratic state, through its concern for its citizens, will create a surface upon which most contacts will be made, and that this, in turn, will enforce the need for further development of the domestic infrastructure. The 'nationalizing state', more or less consciously tries to structure itself in such a manner that its residents either assimilate into the state 'nationality', more or less, or choose to 'exit' rather than to show 'loyalty'[13]. *Language* obviously plays an important role in this communication[14]. A 'nationalizing state'[15] will use the language of the 'nation' (in the sense of the state-forming people) for direct communication with its inhabitants, but also as a symbol that unites the population, often at the expense of autochthonous language minorities and immigrant groups. At a state boundary it is reasonable to suppose that the intake of knowledge about the 'own' and 'the other' country is uneven, both in quantitative and qualitative terms[16].

The individual in a bounded society

In the daily life of most people, contacts and movements are a result of personal decisions, biological needs, demands made by the state and its organizations, or reac-

---

[12] K.W. Deutsch, *Nationalism and social communication*, Cambridge Mass. 1953; T. Lundén, *The domain in Time Geography. A focus on Political Geography*, [in:] M. Antonsich, V. Kolossov, M. Paola Pagnini (eds), *Europe between Political Geography and Geopolitics*, Società Geografica Italiana, Memorie vol. LXIII, Roma 2001, pp. 269-277, p. 273. The word 'nation' is used in the more original meaning of a group of people claiming commonness and destiny, in difference to the interpretation of nation as being synonymous to 'state'.
[13] A. Hirschmann, *Exit, voice and loyalty*, Boston Mass. 1970.
[14] T. Lundén, *Language and communication proximity in border areas*, [in:] M. Hurd (ed.), *Borderland Identities: Territory and Belonging in North, Central and East Europe*, Södertörn University College: Baltic & East European Studies 8, 2006, pp. 147-162.
[15] R. Brubaker, *Nationalism reframed. Nationhood and the National Question in the new Europe*, Cambridge 1996.
[16] D.E. Reynolds, M. Mc Nulty, 1968: *On the analysis…, op. cit.*, p. 25f.

tions to social pressure, e.g. acts motivated by pride, family honor and cultural norms. People who live at a boundary, or have other limitations imposed on them, will act under duress more often than those who live closer to the center, where decisions are made. Many civil servants, such as teachers, are attached to the career systems of the state and its chain of *bread-winning positions,* places and domains where individuals have to conform to certain norms in order to survive[17]. Some people have the liberty to live almost anywhere within the state territory but not outside of it, while others live in a world that consists of one small village through which a state boundary runs, without that being a hindrance to their free movement.

Communication between the individual and the surrounding society (in a very wide sense) plays an important role. Individuals have to relate to the surrounding world by moving around, by forming daily, annual and life-time trajectories in time-space[18]. The individual contact and movement field is composed of *voluntary acts*, such as meeting friends and going shopping and *mandatory acts*, such as going to school, doing military service and paying taxes to the state and/or local municipality. In the everyday life of most people, and under ordinary conditions, acts, contacts and movements are a mixture of individual decisions, biological necessities and involuntary acts, imposed either by the state and its organizations, or by "social compulsion", e.g. family matters and cultural norms. M. Schack, among others, has pointed out that different groups may form different networks, thus creating separate 'regions', but within each group there will also be different networks, depending on the type of action or communication, e.g. economical, regulatory, social or cultural[19]. But the various individual and communal projects must be coordinated to fit in with the time and space constraints of the individual lifelines, and different types of networks therefore influence each other[20]. In a state boundary area, the state territory and its organizational and behavioral implications play a particularly important role in determining the individual's choice of lifeline[21]. Obviously, people with a life history of migration, or who belong to an ethnic, social or religious minority, may have a reach that is very skewed. Such groups have developed "virtual checkpoints, boundary markers and monitoring devices that their members employ in order to project the essentiality and primacy of the group's own boundaries"[22]. We

---

[17] T. Lundén, *Linguistic minorities in boundary areas. The case of Northern Europe*, [in:] B. De Marchi, A.M. Boileau (eds), *Boundaries and minorities in Western Europe*, Milano 1982, pp. 149-163.
[18] T. Hägerstrand, *Space, time...*, op. cit.
[19] M. Schack, *On the multicontextual character of border regions*, [in:] M. van der Velde, H. van Houtum (eds), *Borders, regions and People*, London 2000, pp. 202-219, 204ff.
[20] T. Lundén, *The domain in Time Geography...*, op. cit., p. 270ff.
[21] T. Lundén, D. Zalamans, *'National Allegiance' and Spatial Behaviour in Baltic Boundary Twin Towns*, "Journal of Baltic Studies", XXXIII/2, 2002, pp. 177-198, 178ff; T. Lundén, *On the boundary. On human beings at the end of territory*, Södertörn University College, Läromedel från Södertörns högskola 2, Stockholm 2004, p. 22f.
[22] J.S. Migdal, *Mental maps and virtual checkpoints. Struggles to construct and maintain state and social boundaries*, [in:] J.S. Migdal (ed.), *Boundaries and belonging. States and societies in the struggle to shape identities and local practices*, Cambridge 2004, pp. 3-26.

might talk about a differentiation between a homogenizing and a nearness principle. The former unites individuals according to kinship ties or other similarities, irrespective of geographical distance, while the latter unites them according to geographical proximity[23]. In Hägerstrand's words, *"every large group of human beings is subjected to a tension between two principles of integration, the territorial and the functional modes. In the first mode, nearness is the supreme category. Thinking, loyalty and acting are highly place-bound. In the functional mode of integration, similarity is the supreme category"*. *"Thinking loyalty and action become of a 'non-place' kind and unite what is similar in function over wide geographical areas"*[24]. Even if all societies are a mixture of both modes, it is clear that the process, over a long period of time, has favored the functional over the territorial mode. And in this process, technological development and the increasing intervention of formal regulation have been major forces. The latter has been related to the integrating force of the *state*. Even at a very 'open' boundary, it is considered natural to send students far away to a school in their 'own' country rather than to an adjacent school on the other side of the boundary[25]. This is also the case for public services. In certain exceptional cases, students may get their education on the other side of the boundary, but in these cases the children are almost always of a 'mixed' background – or there are other, very specific reasons.

Figure 2. The territorial and the functional principle as theoretical examples. The thin lines are state boundaries

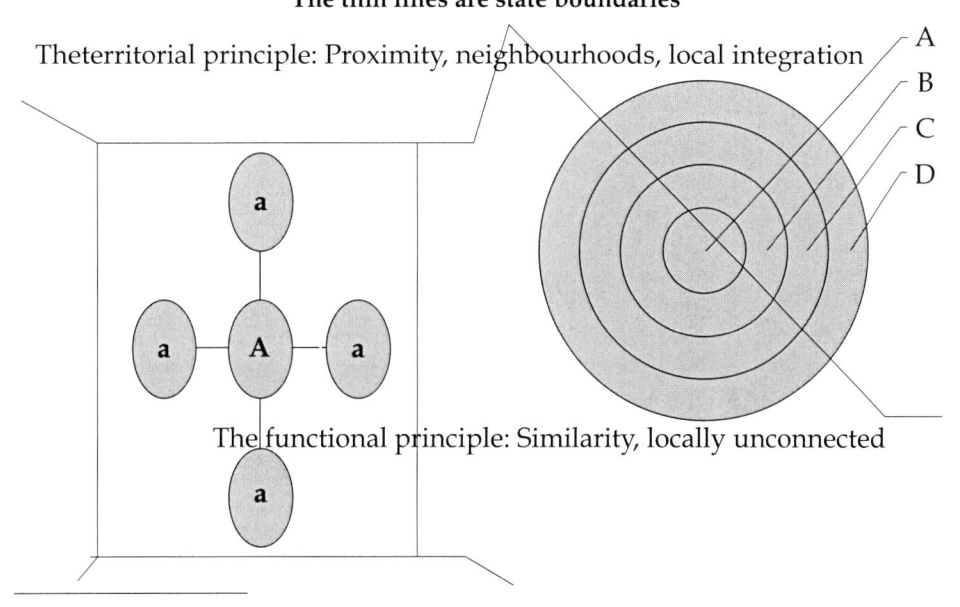

Theterritorial principle: Proximity, neighbourhoods, local integration

The functional principle: Similarity, locally unconnected

---

[23] C. Waack, *Stadträume und Staatsgrenzen*, "Beiträge zur regionalen Geographie 51", Institut für Länderkunde, Leipzig 2000, p. 107; F.-J. Kemper, *Aktionsräumliche Analyse der Sozialkontakte einer städtische Bevölkerung*, "Geographische Zeitschrift" 68, 3, 1980, pp. 199-222.
[24] T. Hägerstrand, *Decentralization and Radio Broadcasting: on the 'possibility space' of a communication technology*, "European Journal of Communication", vol. 1, 1986, 7-26, p. 8.
[25] T. Lundén, *Individens rumsliga beteende...*, op. cit., pp. 141-150.

The state, the individual and the boundary situation

At a state boundary, loyalty towards the state is of extreme importance, and there is always a possible conflict between state and individual, even in cases when the boundary is not contested. The state and its subordinate organizations must try to use the border location to the advantage of its citizens, and preferably to the advantage of the neighboring population as well. On the state level, this can be done through co-operation with the neighbor state in order to improve living conditions at the border. Municipalities and local organizations must work 'upwards' in the authoritative hierarchy in order to accomplish this, but also 'downwards', for and with its residents. This is in order to make the boundary area into an attractive region, and thus secure the loyalty of its residents.

To its inhabitant, the boundary town presents a very special situation in which the 'national' idea of unquestioned allegiance to the state and its territory can be questioned. While some of the above-mentioned factors will work in favor of a homogenous state territory with no supplies or attractions outside of its boundaries, others will emphasize proximities to supplies and attractions beyond that territory. Obviously *regulation factors*, including the state laws, the election system and boundary controls, will work predominantly in favor of the state of domicile. Technical infrastructure is moreover often attuned to the state territory. The economic and communicative activities have no boundaries, in principle, but in reality they are often restricted by state regulation. Furthermore, the 'national's' systems of education and mass communication have a cultural influence that may work to the advantage of the state of residence.

Estonia's borderlands: Eastern conflict and southern indifference

From a geopolitical point of view, Estonia and its neighbors represent different realities. Estonia has two land boundaries, one towards the Russian Federation and one towards Latvia. Although both of these were established as state boundaries in 1991, their historical and geopolitical situations differ greatly. In the Tartu Peace Treaty of 1920, the boundary towards Russia was drawn east of the Narva River, leaving the Narva suburb of Ivangorod/Jaanilinn in Estonia. After Soviet occupation and annexation in 1940 and the German occupation in 1941, the Soviet Union recaptured the area in 1944, and the internal republic boundary was moved to the river, making Ivangorod part of the Russian SFSR. This partition had little impact on the living conditions of the population, until it became a real line of separation with Estonia's independence in 1991. However, as Estonia considered its independence in 1991 a return to the 1920 Tartu Peace after the Soviet Union's occupation and illegal annexation, it saw the Narva River boundary as established *de facto*, as merely awaiting a new boundary treaty. After informally having recognized the river boundary, the Russian Federation rejected it, accusing Estonia of adding a 'preamble' that referred to the legality of the Tartu Peace. While both sides accept the present delineation, there is still no formal treaty between the two states[26].

When the republics of Estonia and Latvia became independent in 1918-1920, the Estonian boundary with Latvia was delineated on ethnic grounds. The only real problem with this division was the railway junction town of Valga/Valka, which had a mixed population of Estonians, Latvians, Russians and others. In 1920, the town was divided according to a British arbitrage[27], which left Estonia with most of the town, including the railway-station area. This Estonian region protruded into the surrounding Latvian suburbia and countryside (as described by the Estonian geographer Edgar Kant in 1932[28]). During the Soviet era, the boundary between the two Soviet republics was kept intact, but in reality the town was integrated and its services coordinated.

Estonia and Latvia have a three-tier structure. Estonia has 15 counties, which are divided into municipalities with fairly great autonomy. The eastern border area, north of Peipsi Lake, is entirely within the County (Estonian: *maakond*) of Ida-Virumaa, which has around 170,000 inhabitants of which an estimated 70% speak Russian. The county is subdivided into municipalities. There are 6 urban municipalities (Estonian: *linnad* – towns) and 16 rural municipalities (Estonian: *vallad* – parishes) in Ida-Viru County. The boundary area consists of two towns, Narva and Narva-Jõesuu, plus three rural municipalities. Valga county, which borders on the Republic of Latvia, has some 35,000 inhabitants and is divided into 13 municipalities. The town of Valga, with around 15,000 inhabitants, is one of two urban municipalities.

The Russian Federation comprises 83 federal subjects. These, however, differ with respect to autonomy: 46 oblasts (provinces), 21 republics, nine krais, four autonomous okrugi, one autonomous oblast, and two federal cities, Moscow and St. Petersburg). *Leningrad Oblast* contains 17 districts (районы) and 31 cities/towns (города). The town of Ivangorod is in the district Kingisepp, which has 9 *volosts* under its jurisdiction, whereas the southern part of the Narva River belongs to the district of Slantsy, which has 7 *volosts* under its jurisdiction. In this system, municipalities of larger cities and *rayons* report to the regional government (smaller cities could also be included in the *rayon* category). Financial dealings with federal government agencies (transfer of funds and redistribution of tax revenues) are executed by branches of the regional governments. This pattern is typical of most Russian regions.

Latvia's administrative division is also complicated, having, on the intermediate level, 26 county municipalities or *rajons* – and 7 city (Latvian: *pilsēta*) municipalities,

---

[26] L. Mälksoo, *Which Continuity: The Tartu Peace Treaty of 2 February 1920, the Estonian–Russian Border Treaties of 18 May 2005, and the Legal Debate about Estonia's Status in International Law*, "Juridica International" 1 ISSN 1406-1082, 2005, pp. 144-149.

[27] *Arbitration Convention between the Esthonian and Latvian Governments, signed at Walk, March 22, 1920*, League of Nations Treaty Series vol. 2, 1920, pp. 188-189. Source: http://www.forost.ungarisches-institut.de/pdf/19200322-1.pdf.

[28] E. Kant, *Valga. Geograafiline ja majanduse ülevade*, Tartu Ülikool Majandusgeograafia Seminari Üllitised, Tartu 1932 (With a summary in French).

453 rural (*pagasts*) municipalities, and 20 *novads*, amalgamated rural and urban municipalities. The city municipalities perform both the basic and intermediate functions. Compared to Estonia, the local government has less autonomy vis-à-vis the central authorities. A municipal reform that called for the merger of smaller municipalities has been postponed. The Valka district has about 32,000 inhabitants, the town of Valka around 6,000.

EU – Russia: Narva – Ivangorod

Narva is a town of approximately 70,000 inhabitants, located on the western bank of the Narva River in north-eastern Estonia. On the opposite bank of the Narva river, in the Russian Federation, lies the town of Ivangorod with its 10,000 inhabitants. At the reestablishment of the Estonian Soviet Republic in 1944, Narva was designated an important union center for textile production, furniture and metal industry, and the extraction of oil shales for the Leningrad market. Russians and other ethnic groups from the Soviet Union replaced the original population. This led to an almost total russification of language use in Narva and the rest of the Ida-Virumaa province. As a result of Russia's economic decline, and complications in communication with Narva, Ivangorod has lost almost all its industry. Narva was also severely affected by the collapse of the command economy that had been characteristic of the entire Soviet Union[29].

Narva and its environs are replete with symbols that refer to the many upheavals the city has undergone. Monuments, graveyards and buildings in e.g. Stalin-era style remind inhabitants and visitors of different, often contradictory, interpretations of the past[30].

The inhabitants of Narva can be divided into three categories of about equal size according to *citizenship*. One third has acquired Estonian citizenship, another third is Russian subjects while the last third consists of those who are considered aliens. The latter are required to have a special permit which, until recently, also functioned as a valid entry permit at the boundary. According to interviews, many Narvaites see little advantage in acquiring Estonian citizenship. Russian citizens have access

---

[29] J.S. Jauhiainen, T. Pikner, *Narva-Ivangorod : integrating and disintegrating transboundary water network and infrastructure*, [in:] T. Pikner, *Evolving cross border urban networks. Case studies in the Baltic Sea areas*, Nordia Geographical Publications, vol. 37:4, Oulu 2008, pp. 6-8; T. Lundén, D. Zalamans, 'National Allegiance'…, op. cit., p. 182 ff; D.J. Smith, *Narva region within the Estonian Republic: From autonomism to accomodation?*, [in:] J. Batt, K. Wolczuk (eds), *Region, state and identity in Central and Eastern Europe*, London–Portland Or. 2002, pp. 89-110.

[30] T. Lundén, *On the boundary*…, op. cit., pp. 109-111, 141; D. Burch, D.J. Smith, *Empty spaces and the value of symbols: Estonia's 'War of monuments 'from another angle*, "Europe-Asia Studies", vol. 59, no. 6, September 2007, pp. 913-936; K. Brüggemann, *Narva. Ein Erinnerungsort der estnischen und russischen Geschichte*, [in:] N. Angermann, M. Garleff, W. Lenz (Hrsg), *Ostseeprovinzen, Baltische Staaten und das Nationale, Festschrift für Gert von Pistohlkors zum 70. Geburtstag* – Schriften der Baltischen Historischen Kommission 14, Münster 2005, pp. 635-661.

Figure 3. Narva and Ivangorod with surroundings. The state boundary mainly follows the Narva River, while the eastern line shows the Tartu Peace delineation

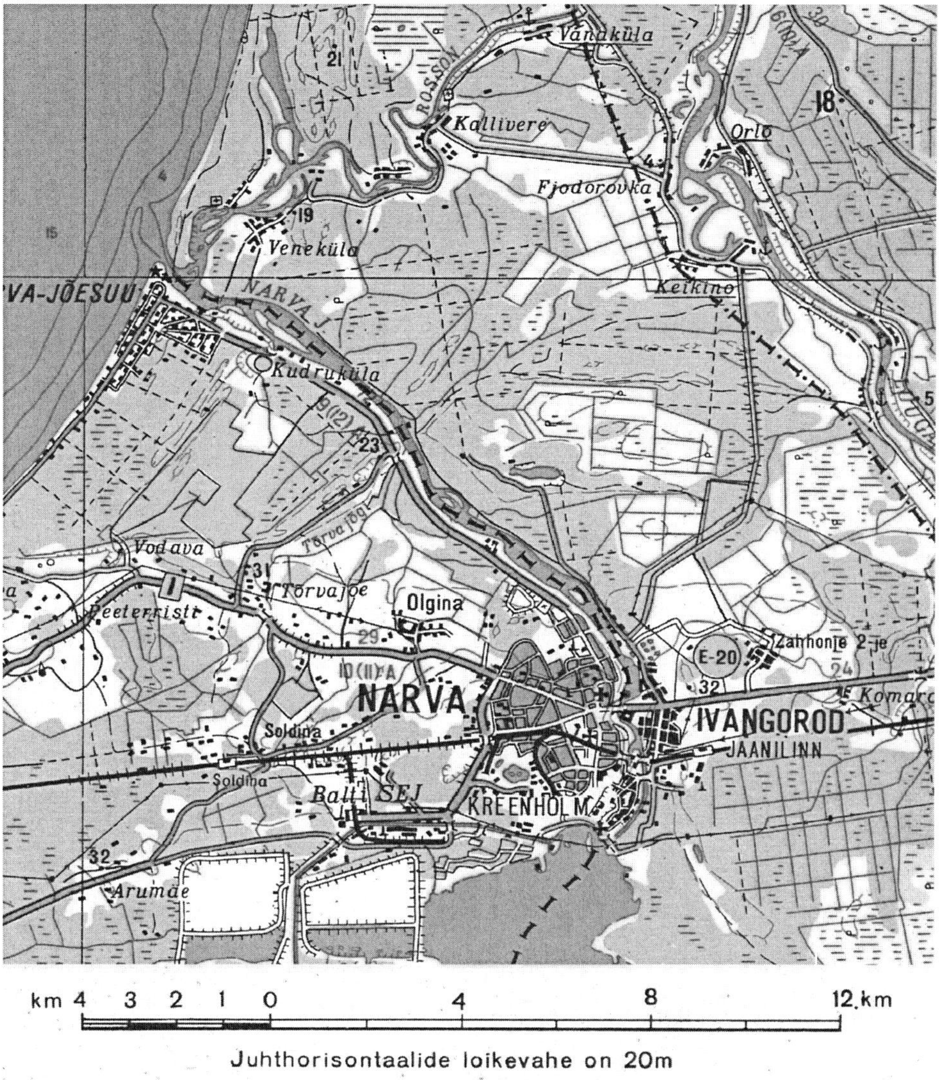

Source: Extract from *Narva. Eesti topograafiline kaart, Leht nr 2*, St. Petersburg 1992.

to free basic medical care in Ivangorod; and until recently, it was easier for a Russian citizen to cross the boundary. Now that Estonia must conform to European Union standards, a visa is required. A number of multi-visit visas were distributed free of charge to a (limited) number of residents, but to get one of these one had to possess a valid passport. However, it is also difficult to be an "alien". The alien must apply for work and residence permits, and the application procedure is slow and tedious. An alien's action radius is circumscribed; it is difficult to travel abroad, to invite relatives to Estonia, to do business and to acquire land in border areas, including, of course, the Narva area. During the Soviet era, criminals were often deported to areas other than their home *oblast'* after their release. Narva was just beyond the Leningrad oblast' and therefore attracted persons from that region. Available statistics show that the rate of violent crime is proportionally high in the north-eastern parts of Estonia. This is not unexpected in an area with border traffic, high unemployment and a class structure characterized by certain types of "visible" crime.

With one exception, all schools teach Russian as the first language. Some schools have begun teaching in Estonian, but there is a great lack of Estonian-speaking teachers, in spite of vigorous recruitment attempts on part of both municipality and state. The Narva schools do not cooperate with those of Ivangorod.

In principle, the population of Narva has access to Estonian- and Russian language *media*, broadcasting from Estonia and Russia. Most people watch Russian TV, and this includes the Russian news. Local Narva radio stations' (FM) broadcasts are mostly in Russian; they try to cover Ivangorod news, as well. Narva has some local newspapers, all in Russian, but the younger people usually do not read newspapers[31].

Trans-Boundary Interaction

In their analysis of Russian-Estonian border relations, Kolosov and Borodulina mention three factors that necessitate at least a minimal level of co-operation[32]:
1) Territorial proximity of the urban settlements;
2) A common interest in the maintenance of the transport infrastructure;
3) The prevention of natural and technological disasters that might result from harnessing the water of the Peipus Lake and Narva River, which border on both states.

Even though the Narva River constituted a boundary between the two Soviet Republics, much of the local infrastructure was managed jointly. In 1991, after the dissolution of the USSR, most of these services were discontinued, starting with public transportation in 1992 and telephone service in 1994. Two years later, the slate-oil powered Baltic Electricity plant near Narva stopped providing Ivangorod with heat[33]. Urban planning has been started in Narva, in compliance with Estonian legislation. There is no co-operation with Ivangorod on this issue, one reason being that the sister town lacks organized city planning. Narva is supplied with water and sewage treatment from a local plant that used to supply Ivangorod as well, but the local water supplier cut off supplies to Ivangorod in November 1998, after sending repeated reminders of overdue payments, and after Ivangorod had been provided with development funding from the EU and Estonia. Eventually, even sewage treat-

---

[31] T. Lundén, D. Zalamans, 'National Allegiance'..., *op. cit.*, pp. 188-189.
[32] V.A. Kolosov, N.A. Borodulina, *Rossiysko-estonskaya granitsa: bar'ery vospriyatiya i prigranichnoe cotrudnichestvo*, Unpublished paper, c. 2004, p. 2.
[33] J. Jauhiainen, T. Pikner, *Narva-Ivangorod...*, *op. cit.*, p. 9 (also in Pikner, 2008).

ment and purification was discontinued, which meant that the effluents were dispersed in the river. This situation has been eased somewhat by the sad fact that most industries on the Russia side now lie idle. A new plant has recently been built, with financial help from Danish development assistance[34].

The Narva hospital has no contact with its counterpart in Russia. On the Russian side, hospitals receive many Russian citizens from Estonia for treatment. This is because they have a right to free care in Russia, whereas the Estonian system requires that they, as aliens, pay a substantial sum for health care insurance. This, together with other real and imagined benefits, explains why so many Estonian Russians have chosen Russian citizenship. To Ivangorod this is a financial problem, another cause of cross-boundary tension[35].

Narva politicians fully accept the fact that the city belongs to Estonia, but complain that the Central Government ignores Narva and that the Estonian Russians are seen as an "alien mass". Narva's intellectuals often express bitterness over Estonia's language legislation, which they (wrongly[36]) consider to be in violation of the Council of Europe National Minority Rights. Even if Narva and Ivangorod form a historical unit and are forced to cooperate on some technical issues (water, cross-border traffic), their coexistence is marked by an absence of official co-operation. This is partly due to hierarchical asymmetries (misfits or discords), partly to frosty relations on the national level.

Baltic Europe: Valga-Valka

Valga (Estonia) and Valka (Latvia) are legally two towns. Morphologically, and to some degree functionally, however, they constitute one unit that is divided by a state boundary. In the Soviet era, Valga/Valka functioned as one city when it came to issues such as health care, planning and the development of infrastructure. During the first years of independence, this situation was reversed. All co-operation was abandoned. Today, access to health care is strictly determined by a person's country of residence. Some years after Estonia's independence, Valga opened its own hospital. Today the Valka hospital is over-dimensioned, which leads to severe problems for an already stressed economy. Both towns have had problems with the quality of their drinking water and they have each constructed their own sewage-treatment plant. Each of these plants is large enough to serve both towns, and both sides have expressed a wish to supply the other side with clean water, as well – which, of course, is now impossible.

---

[34] *Ibidem.*
[35] T. Lundén, D. Zalamans, *'National Allegiance'…, op. cit.*, p. 188f. , Kolosov & Borodulina, *Rossiysko-estonskaya granitsa…, op. cit.*
[36] T. Lundén , *Language landscape and static geographies the Baltic Sea Area*, [in:] *Cultural identities and national borders* , M. Andrén, T. Lindqvist, I. Söhrman, K. Vajta (eds), "Center for European Research", Göteborg University 2009, 85-102, p. 93.

Figure 4. Excerpt from Valka/Valga Town plan, 1994. Savienība Street is seen in the upper middle part of the map, extending from the Estonian side into Latvia

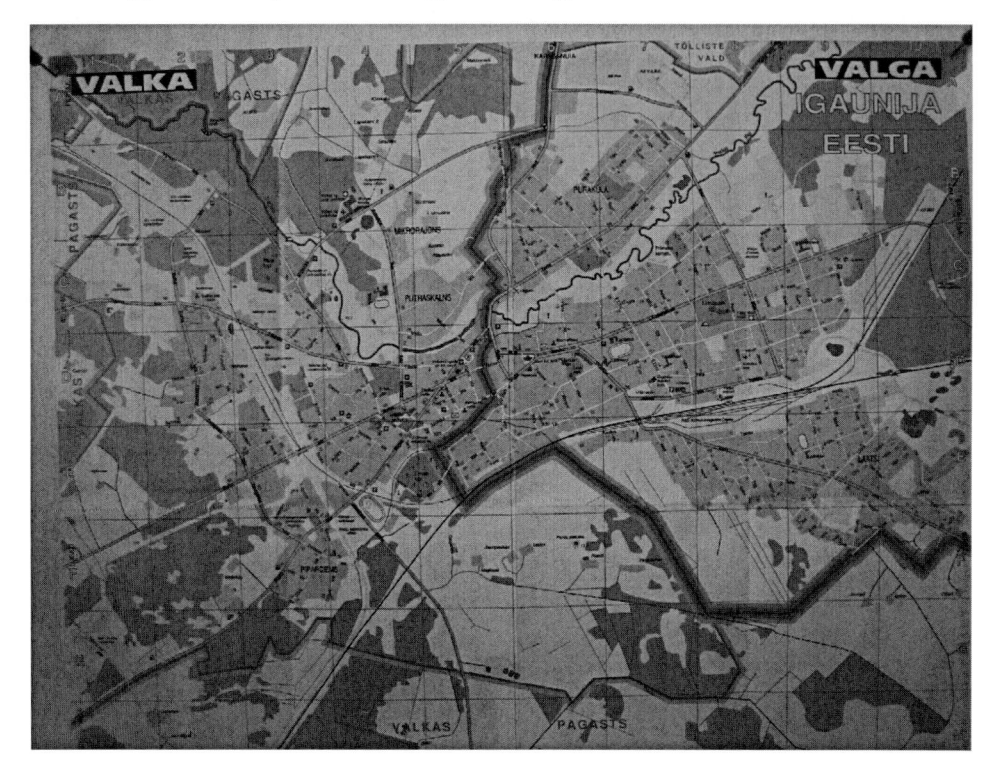

The *education systems* in Estonia and Latvia have roughly the same structure. A few pupils cross the border every day to go to school on the other side, but all of these are Estonian or Latvian citizens, so they encounter no problems at the border. There were Russian-language schools in Valga and Valka that had good contacts with the majority schools on the same side, and which were becoming integrated with the 'national' schools. Contacts between Estonian- and Latvian-language schools across the state boundary are rare, but, it seems that they are non-existent between Russian-language schools. These do not have contacts with schools in Russia either.

Even though Valga/Valka is a twin-town situated on the border, its media are divided into Estonian and Latvian media respectively. Today Latvian pupils, to some extent, use the sports arena and swimming pool in Valga. Apart from the difficulties caused by visa requirements (see below) and language differences, the waiting time at the boundary has been a great problem, especially for non-citizens. When Estonia and Latvia became members of the EU, and particularly after the two had joined the Schengen Union, most of these problems were eliminated. Paradoxically, Valga/Valka is today the 'open' city that it was in during the Soviet era, at least on the surface. But each part is, of course, subjected to the laws, regulations and planning systems of the state to which it belongs, and many of the infrastructural initiatives that were taken separately after independence in 1991 still shape the daily lives of its inhabitants[37].

Savienība[38]

As mentioned above, citizens who had been deported were not allowed to return to their original domicile. On their return form Siberia, some Valga Estonians therefore chose to settle in Latvia, on a street that was, in fact, nothing more than an extension of the Põhja road, close to the center of the town. Savienība is nothing but a small road flanked by a few houses, but it has played an important role in serious negotiations between Latvia and Estonia, which have been without results. Whoever moved to Savienība would have known that there was an old boundary running through the area, but they would not have been able to imagine that the importance of this boundary would become apparent so soon. Until the implementation of the Schengen regime in late 2007, the people in Savienība Street had to choose between three official stations when they wanted to cross the border. This caused great inconvenience. The authorities in Valga/Valka therefore agreed to issue a special permit to cross the part of the border that ran through the street. This permit would be issued to people who had their permanent addresses on Savienība. The problem is, however, that several of the street's inhabitants have their permanent address somewhere else on the Estonian side, even if they are actually living in Savienība. This means that they cannot get the special permit. There are several reasons why these Estonian residents in Savienība prefer to have a permanent address in Estonia, insurance and labor issues ranking high among these.

Ten years after the independence of Latvia and Estonia, some thirty-five people lived in Savienība, in nine houses. Of these, twenty-six were Estonian citizens, seven were Latvian citizens and two were so-called non-citizens. Of the seven Latvian citizens, two are of Estonian origin. These have taken Latvian citizenship in order to make life easier, but they still consider themselves Estonian by nationality. The average age of the Savienība population is relatively high, and there are no school children in the group.

The Estonians in Savienība have been faced with other problems, such as inadequate electricity supply, telephone service, road maintenance and emergency health care. Electricity used to be provided from the Estonian side, but for rather obvious reasons the Latvian authority wants to take over its distribution. The price of electricity is much lower in Estonia than in Latvia, so the Savienība population does not want this change. The telephone system is Latvian, which means that the Estonians make international calls every time they call someone in downtown Valga. They have therefore chosen to have no telephones at all. Some may now have cellular phones, as the Estonian system dominates even in Valka. Road maintenance is con-

---

[37] T. Lundén, D. Zalamans, 'National Allegiance'..., op. cit., pp. 188f, 189ff.
[38] T. Lundén, On the boundary..., op. cit., pp. 160-161.

spicuous by its absence. Neither Estonian nor Latvian authorities maintain the road. The Estonian side sees no reason to cross the state border to do so, and the Latvian side is obviously not interested. Any Estonian on Savienība who needs emergency health care, must cross the border into Valga to receive it. This may lead to fatal delays at the border. A doctor who has to make a house call from Valga to Valka encounters the same problem.

The ownership of land is also a source of uncertainty. It is unclear who owns the land and houses in Savienība. Legally the land belongs to a Latvian citizen who left Valka a long time ago. If this owner should want to sell his land, another problem would arise. According to Latvian law, no foreigner may own land within a two-kilometer zone along the Latvian border. This means that the Estonians in Savienība never will be able to own the land on which they are living. They can only own their houses. Some Estonians on Savienība have, reluctantly, considered selling their houses and moving to Valga, but Savienība is in the 'periphery' of Valka, a 'problem-area' that, apparently, no Latvians wish to move to. The area covered by Savienība, a mere 2.6 acres, seems to be an extremely difficult problem to solve. This unkempt little street with its tidy one-family houses has proven an insoluble problem for the municipalities, the counties and the two states. An exchange of territory has been discussed, and seems reasonable enough, but this is against Latvia's laws. The two presidents had a meting in the twin towns, and promised to reach a solution, but so far nothing has happened[39].

Conclusions

Two Baltic Border Towns: Attempt at a Classification

	Process	Pol. Permeab.	Phys. perm.	Ethnicity	Ethn/state	Pol. coop
Valg/ka	Change	Medium	High	Unit/mixed	Unit/diff.	Medium
Narva/Ivang.	Change	Low	Low	Unit	Different	Low

The two divided cities can be characterized according to process, political permeability, physical permeability, ethnicity, ethnicity in relation to nation state, and to political cross-border co-operation.

Compared to other twin towns in Europe, Valga/Valka is unique in that its two majority populations clearly differ with respect to nationally, while both cities have a large minority of ethnic Russians. On the advice of the Haparanda/Tornio administrations, Valga and Valka have entered a program of contacts and communication that have as their object improved living conditions at and across the boundary. Several difficulties have been reported, however. In most cases, local intentions clash with state legislation and with the 'estonification' or 'latvification' policy of

---

[39] T. Lundén, 2004, *On the boundary...*, op. cit., p. 160f; see also Ch. Waack, *Stadträume und Staatsgrenzen...*, op. cit.

each country. To most of the town's inhabitants, the border does seem an important obstacle, as they see few opportunities on the other side. The ethnic Russians and other Russian speakers appear to be the only group that really has a cross-boundary contact network.

Even if two neighboring municipalities, separated by a state boundary, wish to cooperate and are legally able to do so, they often find that they differ so much with respect to legal competences that other hierarchy levels must get involved. This, for example, is the case for the relations between Estonia and Latvia[40], but also for those between Finland and Sweden, though the latter are culturally similar and are both members of the European Union. In the case of Narva and Ivangorod, obstacles are so great that co-operation is practically impossible, in spite of a common local language and a common history – or perhaps for those very reasons.

---

[40] P. Joenniemi, *Border issues in Europe's North*, [in:] T. Diez, M. Albert, S. Stetter (eds), *The European Union and Border Conflicts: The Power of Integration...*, Cambridge 2008, pp. 129-173.

Słubice-Frankfurt (Oder)
Cooperation in a Divided City
on the Polish-German Border

Magdalena Musiał-Karg

Introduction

The system transformation that had started in Central and Eastern Europe in the late 1980s and early 1990s has involved the border regions in particular. The collapse of the Soviet-bloc in 1989 opened Eastern European borders. The opening of the borders allowed, for the first time since 1945, the opportunity for cross-border cooperation analogous to the Western European integration process.

On the one hand, in Central and East European countries, one could observe a process of "opening" of frontiers (by rescinding the regulations on crossing the borders). This made possible or even caused a rapid growth of trans-border traffic, establishing trans-border relations between authorities of different political levels and between non-governmental organizations, local communities etc. On the other hand – as a result of collapse of some European states such as the Soviet Union, Czechoslovakia, Yugoslavia and the creation of new states in their place – new borders have appeared, which have increasingly separated territories, economies and societies. At the same time the process of integration in the Western part of Europe had burgeoned much deeper and intensively – both parts of Germany were united[1], the Maastricht Treaty came to life, a customs union was created and cooperation in the framework of *Schengen Agreement*[2] was tightened. Those processes marked inter alia vanishing and effacement of borders inside the European Union.

---

[1] During the summer of 1989, rapid changes known as *peaceful revolution* also took place in the Eastern part of Germany, which ultimately led to German reunification.

[2] *The Schengen Agreement* was signed in 1985 between five of the then ten member states of the European Community. It was originally created independently of the European Community law order, in part owing to the lack of compromise amongst EC members, and in part because those ready to implement the idea did not want to wait for others to be ready to join. *The Schengen Agreement* provided for the removal of systematic border controls between the participating countries. Ireland and the United Kingdom opted out of Schengen's border control arrangements, while participating in certain provisions relating to judicial and police cooperation. The borderless zone created by *the Schengen Agreements*, the Schengen Area, currently consists of twenty-five European countries.

After the EU enlargement in May 2004, a new situation has emerged, particularly in Poland. The transformation process as well as EU membership has been affecting the nature of the border-regions in this country. Poland's accession into the European Union and the conversion of the Polish-German border into the EU-internal one, has without a doubt affected the relations and cooperation within the border area. On 21 December 2007 Poland together with eight other new EU Member States, joined the Schengen area. That important European occurrence has changed the functioning of the Polish-German border region to a great extent. Currently the citizens of the border regions of Central and Eastern Europe are optimistically embracing the future of a united Europe. The Schengen area external border has been moved to the Eastern border of Poland. Abolition of customs controls on the Polish-German border (in practice an effacement of the state border between Poland and Germany) has been felt strongly by citizens of Lubuskie Voivodship. It has also affected the lives of all of the people who lived in the area of the Pro Europa Viadrina Euroregion[3].

However, it seems that eliminating of border control has been much more visible and experienced more strongly in so called *divided cities*, where border checkpoints had been located before 21 December 2007. As an example of this type of town on the Polish-German border one may enumerate Frankurt Oder and Słubice, Guben and Guben or Görlitz and Zgorzelec. In these pairs of towns the trans-border cooperation has assumed, to some degree, a more intensified form than in other regions in Poland and Germany.

It is therefore without a doubt that the Polish-German cooperation problems in the border area, contributions of both partners from Poland and Germany and effects of those relations support the thesis about the significance of experiences in Słubice and Frankfurt Oder in the field of trans-border cooperation. These practices prove that the endeavors of political authorities at local levels and of different social organization are considered a great input in international relations and the process of shaping a new Polish-German reality in the border area.

The last 20 years have provided substantial evidence that Polish and German municipal councils, regional authorities (Land, Voivodship) and state institutions treat regions placed by the borders as vitally important territories in shaping good neighborliness and in overall foreign policy – which is the reason for calling the Pol-

---

[3] Euroregion "Pro Europa Viadrina" is situated right within the dynamic East-to-West trade and traffic corridor Rotterdam–Berlin–Warsaw–Moscow. The cities of Frankfurt-on-Oder, Eisenhuettenstadt, Gorzów and Słubice are centers of economic activity. To the West the Euro-region borders with Berlin and offers direct access to the markets of Central and Eastern Europe, a highly educated labor force, and a well developed manufacturing and industrial production base. The total length of the German-Polish border is 461 kilometers. The border section running through Euroregion "Pro Europa Viadrina" is 135 kilometers long. The total number of border checkpoints within Euroregion is six: four road and two railway connections that cross the border. The Polish part of Euroregion consists of 28 communities and is inhabited by 374,000 people. The German part consists of the Frankfurt Oder area and two poviats, it is inhabited by 449,000 people; Stowarzyszenie Gmin Polskich Euroregionu Pro Europa Viadrina, http://www.euroregion-viadrina.pl/viadrina_gb.php, 10.03.2009.

ish-German border area a *laboratory of European integration*. Analyzing trans-border contacts in a divided city like Słubice and Frankfurt Oder contains a number of considerations. First, both of these towns remain a key place of shaping good neighbor relations and an important example of international cooperation for other divided cities. Second, in this pair of towns, special connections and trans-border ties (affiliations extending to the border regions) have been formed and which are evolving and changing the quality of trans-border cooperation. They are mainly the results of intensive efforts of political actors to initiate and to increase trans-border activities in various areas of mutual relations. It should be emphasized that both representatives of Słubice and Frankfurt (Oder) are generally acting of one accord in this context.

Research methodology

The main research subject in this text is the nature of cooperation in the Polish-German border region – paying a special attention to a pair of towns – Słubice and Frankfurt (Oder), that are located in the Lubuskie Voivodship (on the Polish side) and Brandenburg (on the German side).

Using the example of the Polish-German border region (and border towns) I would like to present the view of how the borders can be overcome and how they can evolve into a sphere of contact and cooperation. The Słubice-Frankfurt relationship may be viewed as a very interesting example, because the border in that region has not grown historically, rather it was created under a policy of power. As a consequence of a decision made at the Potsdam conference of the allied powers near the end of World War II and as an effect of the manner it was established, the border was hermetically sealed. *"It had to defend itself so that it kept the neighbors apart"*[4]. For a long time, the border was impermeable to persons, goods and information, and as such it resembled the iron curtain.

This article will answer the following questions: First, what forms of trans-border cooperation may be observed in a divided city – Słubice and Frankfurt (Oder)? Second, what are the main results of mutual contacts in Słubice and Frankfurt (Oder)? Finally, does this cooperation generate any significant problems or difficulties in realizing trans-border undertakings?

The theoretical framework for this research field – that is for problems connected with existing and functioning societies living in the border areas – is based inter alia on the approach of Jerzy Nikitorowicz, who has listed four types of border areas;[5] a border area understood as a territory[6] of contactive or transitive character, a con-

---

[4] H. Schultz, S. Kowal, *Neue Grenzen – alte Nachbarn. Deutsche und Polen im Widerstreit von großer Politik und regionaler Kooperation*, [in:] H.-J. Wagener, F. Heiko (eds), *Im Osten was Neues. Aspekte der EU-Osterweiterung*, Dietz 1998.
[5] J. Nikitorowicz, *Pogranicze. Tożsamość. Edukacja międzykulturowa*, Białystok 1995, pp. 11-15.
[6] A territory, where at least two different culture groups coexist – mostly comprised of different ethnographic features, different language, religion or nationality.

tent-cultural borderland[7], an interaction border area[8] and a borderland of states and acts of individual's awareness[9].

A borderland is identified by Nikitorowicz as an area of contact of two communities (these communities benefit from the fact of living in a neighborhood), where prejudices are weakening or dropping away, which is a result of the creation of a community founded in mutual respect and appreciation[10]. Gordon W. Allport confirms Nikitorowicz's opinions. He states that mutual prejudices can be reduced only by the mutual contact of groups of the same status in order to reach common objectives[11]. It allows us to reach the conclusion that divided cities located in the Polish-German border area seem to function in circumstances mentioned above.

Słubice and Frankfurt (Oder) – a divided city on Polish-German border

Before analyzing the trans-border relations between Frankfurt and Słubice, some general information on both towns needs to be presented.

Towns located directly on the international border of the European Union are usually called "laboratories" of the European integration[12]. This is particularly visible in the divided cities – placed on the former Schengen zone border: Frankfurt Oder (Germany) and Słubice (Poland). This pair of towns is also one of the main urban centers of the Pro Europa Viadrina Euroregion about 80 km east of Berlin and 180 km west of Poznań. Because the relations and interactions in the border area of Słubice and Frankfurt (Oder) are much more intensive than in other regions, theoretically in this pair of towns "integration" and "convergence" of the EU can be "first observed, and should act as a leading indicator" of the effectiveness of the Polish-German cooperation[13].

---

[7] In a territorial borderland people "produce" a wide range of customs that make their co-existence much easier. That process helps to create a cultural specificity of a certain community, where it is possible for individuals to choose and shape values based on multicultural features.
[8] It is a process and its effect on people's communication, which is based on moving from monolog to dialog of cultures, from stereotypes and prejudices to mutual understanding, negotiations and caring about the borderland culture.
[9] Territory and thought and research area, that was unwanted, forbidden, isolated and neglected. Life on the crossing of cultures allows to mentally pass out of area that is qualified by the subsidence. It is so because territorial location activates comparative scales, which work like impulses.
[10] J. Nikitrowicz, *Pogranicze, tożsamość…, op. cit.*, p. 15; M. Musiał-Karg, J. Jańczak, *Położenie przygraniczne a mapa polityczna województwa lubuskiego*, [in:] M. Dajnowicz (ed.), *Oblicze polityczne regionów Polski*, Białystok 2007, pp. 239-256.
[11] G. Allport, *The nature of prejudice*, Addison-Wesley, Reading 1954, p. 281.
[12] A.D. Asher, *In the laboratory of Europe: governing the "Europe of Regions" on the Polish/German frontier*, University of Illinois at Urbana-Champaign, February 2004, p. 1, http://aei.pitt.edu/2033/01/ASHERWPSP2004.pdf, 12.03.2009.
[13] *Ibidem*.

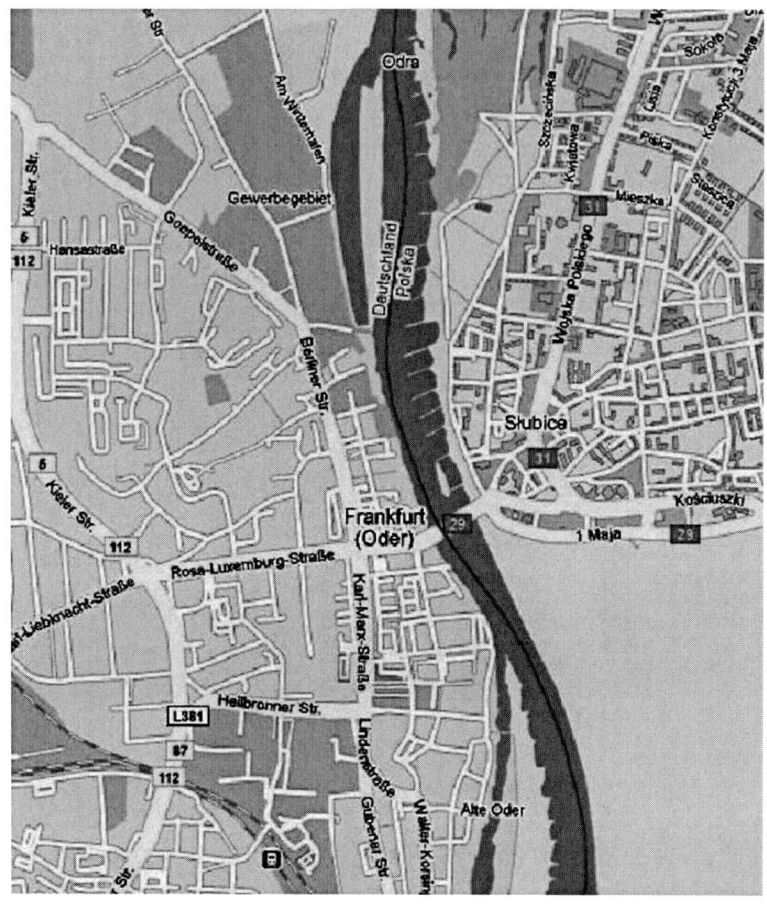

Map 1. Map of Frankfurt (Oder) and Słubice

Source: Mapy Google, http://mapy.google.pl/, 5.01.2010.

The term *divided city* is related to the existence and functioning of towns that earlier had made up one urban organism and are currently separated by a national border. Establishment of these two towns had been preceded by shifting the frontier between Poland and Germany to the line of Oder and Neiße River[14]. After World War II the districts located near the eastern bank of the river have became separate towns belonging to Poland.

In the context of divided cities one should notice that in terms of town planning, before 1945 both towns had been one city (see map 1). After the war both towns started to exists as separate organisms varied by culture, language and economy.

---

[14] J. Jańczak, *Społeczeństwo obywatelskie w polsko-niemieckim mieście podzielonym. Rola lokalnych organizacji pozarządowych w kreowaniu transgranicznych zachowań partycypacyjnych*, [in:] S. Michałowski, K. Kuć-Czajkowska (eds), *Przywództwo lokalne a kształtowanie demokracji partycypacyjnej*, Lublin 2008, p. 393.

Frankfurt (Oder)[15] is a city located on the western bank of the Odra River and on the eastern border of Germany. It is the easternmost University town in Germany. Frankfurt (Oder) is situated in the German state of Brandenburg and its population is ca. 60,000 people. It is worth mentioning that before the German reunification in 1990 about 86,000 inhabitants lived in Frankfurt (Oder). Around 1226 the town was founded by Frankish traders and was given market and settlement rights. In 1253 the town of Frankfurt (Oder) received its town charter. The early settlers lived on the western banks of the Oder. The trade character of the old Frankfurt (Oder) and its affiliation to the Association of Hanseatic Towns resulted in a significant position and wealth[16].

Today Frankfurt is most of all a University Town with its European University 'Viadrina' re-established on 15 July 1991. Viadrina European University maintains close cooperation with Adam Mickiewicz University in Poznań. Both universities jointly run the Collegium Polonicum, located just opposite the Viadrina on the Polish side of the Oder River. The University traces its history to Brandenburg's First University – Alma Mater Viadrina (1506-1811) and continues its traditions[17]. As a result of its geographical location, Frankfurt (Oder) became an international meeting ground of East and West, where trans-border cooperation seems to be the most visible and valuable element[18]. Frankfurt (Oder) lies directly opposite the Polish town of Słubice.

The Polish neighbor town of Słubice, which before 1945 was the Frankfurt suburb of Dammvorstadt, is a town in the western part of the Lubuskie Voivodship. Słubice's name derives from a Slavic settlement in the Middle Ages called Śliwice. Słubice was established in 1945 as part of the new border formation in line with the Potsdam Agreement. Previously located in the Gorzów Wielkopolski Voivodship the town is currently the capital of Słubice County. Słubice has only existed as an independent Polish town since 1945, but the shared history with Frankfurt is much older. Whereas the western Frankfurt developed into a trade, Hanseatic and exhibition centre, the eastern part stayed as an 'embankment suburb' until 1945[19]. The town of Słubice has a total population of ca. 17,000

In 1939 ca. 15,600 people lived in Słubice. After German re-unification, in 1991 there was an economic revival caused by the influx of German tourists to the town of Słubice[20].

---

[15] The full name – Frankfurt an-der-Oder is usually referred to simply as "Frankfurt". When it is necessary to distinguish it from Frankfurt am Main, the abbreviation "Frankfurt (Oder)" is used. For this article's purposes, I use the name Frankfurt (Oder).
[16] *Frankfurt Oder. Miasto poety Kleista*, http://www.frankfurt-oder.de/, 16.06.2008.
[17] "*The Alma Mater Viadrina enjoyed great repute as an institution of learning for persons who later played an important part in shaping and staffing the civil service of this principality as well as the Prussian state*"; European University Viadrina Frankfurt (Oder), http://www.euv-frankfurt-o.de/pl/ueber_uns/portrait/geschichte/index.html, 16.06.2008.
[18] *Frankfurt Oder. Miasto poety Kleista*, http://www.frankfurt-oder.de/, 16.06.2008.
[19] *Tourismusverein Frankfurt (Oder) e.V.*, http://www.tourismus-ffo.de/pl/index.php?k=2.3, 16.06.2008.
[20] Annually ca 11 million people and about 3 million cars cross the border bridge in Słubice.

Currently Słubice is a border town between Poland and The Federal Republic of Germany. The town's location determines the character of business in Słubice, where many businesses are connected with so called "service" tourism. Many citizens of Słubice work in the services of international tourism, border traffic, trade and craft[21].

From the beginning of the transition process in Poland and other East and Central European states, Słubice developed rapidly, especially since the town joined Frankfurt in the European region Pro Europe Viadrina. Today Słubice and Frankfurt work together in many areas; town development, tourism, transport, infrastructure, education and culture[22]. These fields of trans-border activities combine to increase the role of inter-communal and interpersonal relations in both towns.

Trans-border cooperation in a divided city

Considering the cooperation of Frankfurt (Oder) and Słubice it has to be stressed that two substantially different phases can be distinguished: before and after Poland's accession to the European Union.

Before analyzing contacts in divided cities it needs to be stressed that according to many scientists and political leaders the following types of cooperation can be distinguished: trans-national cooperation, trans-regional cooperation and cross-border cooperation.

Table 1. Types of cooperation

Trans-national cooperation	Inter-regional cooperation	Cross-border cooperation
– the highest level of cooperation	– the middle stage of cooperation	– the lowest level of cooperation
– cooperation between countries with regard to a special subject (for example regional development, education, culture)	– cooperation (between regional local authorities) mostly in single sectors (not in all areas of life) and with selected actors	– directly neighbourly cooperation in all areas of life between regional and local authorities along the border and involving all actors
– the interlinkage is rarely organized but there are certain approaches within the framework of international organizations (for example, Council of Europe, Nordic Council)	– interlinked within the framework of the Assembly of European Regions (AER)	– interlinked within the framework of the Association of European Border Regions (AEBR)

Source: *Practical Guide to Cross-border Cooperation*, Association of European Border Regions (AEBR), *Third Edition* 2000, p. 15.

[21] *Słubice City Hall*, http://www.slubice.pl/, 16.06.2008.
[22] Polsko-brandenburska strona internetowa dla miast kooperujących. Die brandenburgisch-polnische Website für Städtekooperationen, http://www.forum-grenzstaedte.net/index.htm, 13.06.2008.

The Polish-German cooperation during both of these periods has been determined by different factors and has taken different forms. Furthermore, the fields of cooperation are constantly evolving and expanding. In general, they can be divided into three categories that characterize three levels of common Polish-German undertakings.

As shown in Graph 1, there are different dimensions of international cooperation; Cooperation between every state within the EU, cooperation with both states – Germany and Poland, cooperation at the regional or local level – between German Land of Brandenburg and Polish Lubuskie Voivodship, and between communities from both countries.

Graph 1. Levels of transborder cooperation

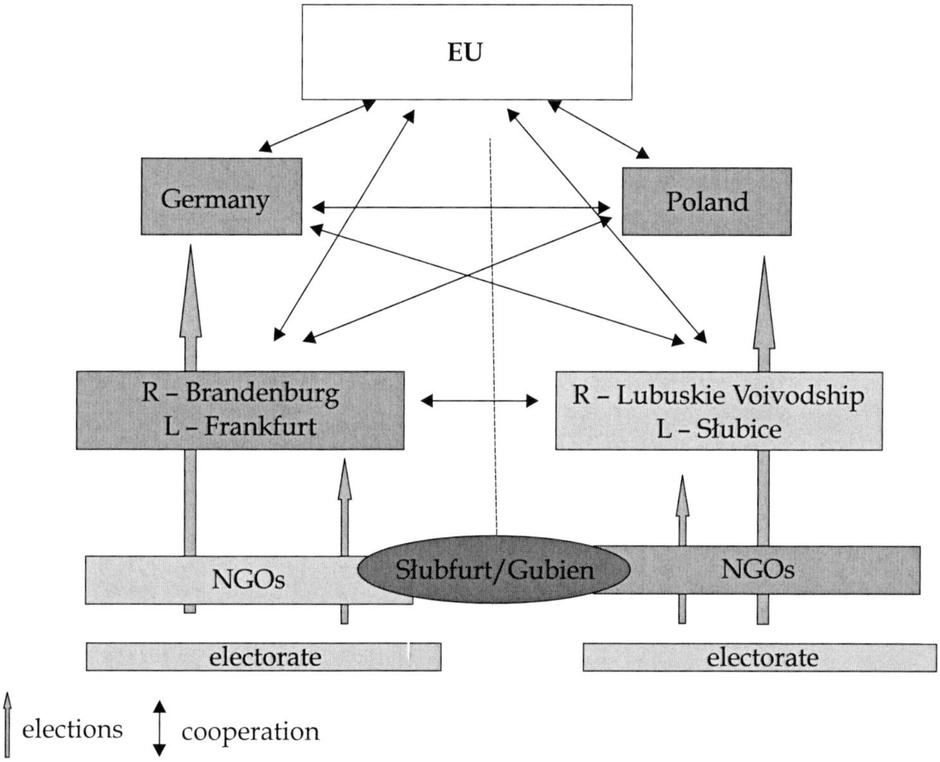

↑ elections   ↕ cooperation

Source: Magdalena Musiał-Karg.

Every participant in these international relations, as presented in Graph 1, has the possibility to conduct "business" with foreign partners of higher and lower administration levels. Additionally, the role of non-governmental organizations (NGOs) has to be stressed. NGOs are a kind of intermediary or connection between the society and institutions of local authorities.

NGOs have the potential to create and shape civil society, and through these processes they may influence the reduction of distance between politicians and members of the local community[23]. It seems to be very significant from Poland's point of view, because a real need exists for involvement of citizens in various activities for the interests of the local community. In the Polish-German borderland the need to activate the citizens assumes a wider dimension – it is related to working for the people from both the German and Polish side.

Considering transborder cooperation at national level, it has to be stressed that decisions on Polish-German undertakings are made by the central authorities, that is, by relevant institutions of the Polish Republic and Federal German Republic. It is worth emphasizing that in some cases final decisions are made by the relevant Ministry from the Polish side and relevant institutions at the regional level of Brandenburg (the reason for such a procedure is federal structure of Germany). The lower stage of cooperation in the borderland is regional assistance – the decision-making process involves institutions from neighboring regions – Polish Voivodship and German Lands and associations of communes or poviats from both countries. One should remember that in comparison to Polish Voivodships, German Lands are given wide autonomy (Land's bodies are responsible for most decisions on transborder cooperation) which causes some difficulties during the process of realizing many trans-border undertakings. Most decisions of Voivodships in Poland are dependent on decisions made by institutions at the higher state level (Ministries) which makes the Polish-German decision process much longer. Regional cooperation is led by the Lubuskie Voivodship and the Land of Brandenburg. Because of their proximity, the character of contacts and relations are much more intensive here. That is the reason why both regions consider themselves a most strategic and significant partner. Working contacts exist at every administration level. It is worth mentioning that the Euroregions play a very important role. From the very beginning they started to introduce many relevant programs to support regional institutions in their activities in many fields; education, culture, sport, science etc. From the perspective of this article – which is devoted to transborder cooperation in divided cities of Frankfurt and Słubice – the role of Euroregion Pro Europa Viadrina should be strongly emphasized as a support for both cities in the Polish-German borderland. Pro Europa Viadrina – like other Euroregions – is a trial of the creation of a new quality of life for citizens who are living in a territory of common history that is often very complicated and difficult. Financial donations for Polish-German projects as well as contacts of local authorities are extremely relevant for the transborder region. However, one should remember that the spontaneous, neighborly, cultural and commercial relations are also essential for further development of Polish-German borderland. Thanks to them – the key process for the united Europe has been taking place – the process of recognizing neighbors, reduction of negative stereotypes, improvement of mutual understanding, mutual sympathy and respect.

---

[23] J. Jańczak, *Społeczeństwo obywatelskie...*, op. cit., p. 393.

The third and the lowest stage of transborder cooperation is the local level where Polish-German partnership activities are initiated by local authorities, which in most cases are the decisive bodies when talking about common transborder undertakings. Thus, in practice – cooperation at the local level is first of all cooperation of two divided cities – Frankfurt (Oder) and Słubice.

Examples of cooperation

In this section I would like to present the most significant and effective examples of cooperation of Słubice and Frankfurt (Oder) as well as emphasize the features of mutual cooperation in divided cities.

Cross-border cooperation in adjacent border regions has a long tradition in Europe. It should be stressed that the Polish-German border areas have quickly learned from the experience of other countries' borderlands. One may list several key motives for cooperation in the Polish-German borderland: willingness to communicate with neighbors, overcoming of mutual animosities and prejudices between both nations, the strengthening of democracy and the development of operational regional/local administrative structures; overcoming of national peripherality and isolation; the rapid assimilation into an integrated Europe[24]. The idea of cross-border cooperation does not mean that one partner initially acts alone at the national level and later tries to involve or cooperate with the neighbor across the border. It encompasses all areas of daily life and development of joint programs, priorities and actions. It also includes extensive involvement of social groups, administrative levels and so on in cross-border cooperation.

Undoubtedly, Słubice and Frankfurt (Oder) are closely related to each other. It needs to be emphasized that both cities shared a common history: until the end of World War II, they hadn't been two separate cities at all and Słubice was a part of Frankfurt (Oder). The division into two separate units happened after World War II because it was decided that the river Oder would be the border between Germany and Poland. Subsequently, Frankfurt was located in East Germany until the iron curtain fell and Germany was reunited in 1990. Since that time Słubice is a town situated on the western border of Poland. One should remember that between 1945 and 1989 cooperation in both neighboring towns was mainly founded on personal contacts or took place while working together in Frankfurt's micro chip factory. After the collapse of the Soviet Union and due to the transition from a planned economy to a market economy a process of change started in both countries[25]. The decade after 1990 may be characterized as a period of great euphoria of common Europe – in particular on the Polish side. During that time both towns had a great

---

[24] *Practical Guide to Cross-border Cooperation*, Association of European Border Regions (AEBR), *Third Edition* 2000, p. 5.
[25] D. Eggert, S. Bentolila, C. Daumont, *Twin Cities: Frankfurt (Oder) – Slubice*, Scholarly Research Paper, 2006.

number of high expectations which was an engine for many efforts of both towns' authorities to prepare lots of common projects and undertakings. Currently, the citizens of the border regions of Central and Eastern Europe are optimistically embracing the future of a united Europe. The fall of the Iron Curtain has not only restored the freedom of movement between the citizens of Western and Eastern Europe, but also provoked a real wave of integrating activities and the restoration of cross-border relations between the authorities and the citizens.

Both Słubice and Frankfurt (Oder) play a major role in promoting and initiating cooperation across the border. Although it seems that in many transborder towns actors often fail to coordinate with their neighbors in an effort to achieve collaboration, Słubice and Frankfurt (Oder) appear to have very good (often even model) cross-border relations. Nowadays Słubice and Frankfurt (Oder) are leaders in cross-border integration activities, and – as A. D. Asher states – demonstrate a commitment by many local politicians. Particularly in the political field Słubice and Frankfurt (Oder) seem to have created a unique pairing to intensify cross-border collaboration. On many occasions they function as one "specific double town" to pursue their interests and to exchange ideas[26].

Graph 2 presents common Polish-German instruments that are affecting the cooperation of Słubice and Frankfurt (Oder). First an Executive Board composed of the Lord Mayor of Frankfurt (Oder) and the Mayor of Słubice is listed. This Board is responsible for bringing out the most important decisions on mutual collaboration, new agreements between the two towns as well as initiating common Polish-German undertakings and strengthening the cooperation. Furthermore, since 1993 both

Graph 2. Common cross-border bodies responsible for cooperation

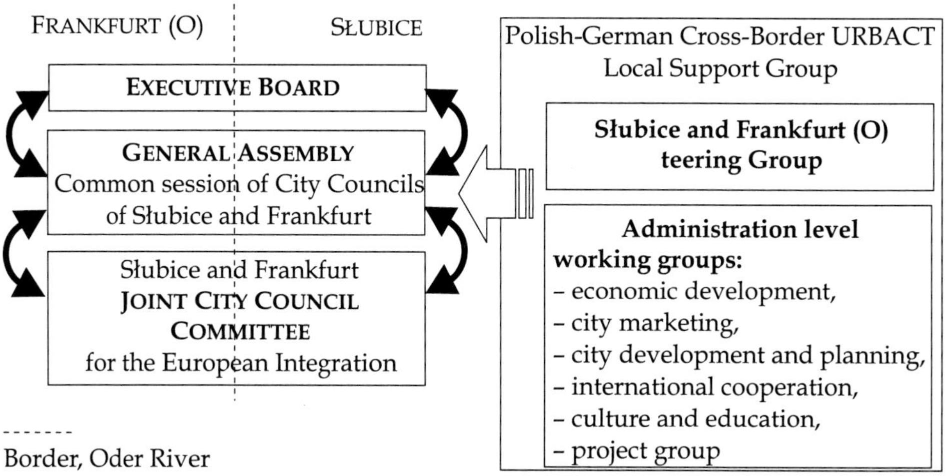

FRANKFURT (O) | SŁUBICE

- EXECUTIVE BOARD
- GENERAL ASSEMBLY — Common session of City Councils of Słubice and Frankfurt
- Słubice and Frankfurt JOINT CITY COUNCIL COMMITTEE for the European Integration

------ Border, Oder River

- Polish-German Cross-Border URBACT Local Support Group
- Słubice and Frankfurt (O) teering Group
- Administration level working groups:
  – economic development,
  – city marketing,
  – city development and planning,
  – international cooperation,
  – culture and education,
  – project group

Source: Magdalena Musiał-Karg basing on information of the Słubice City Hall.

---

[26] P. Joenniemi, A. Sergunin, *The Model of Twin Cities. Experiences from Northern Europe*, Barents Institute Reprint, no 2, 2008, p. 1.

City Councils meet once a year (as a General Assembly) to discuss the mutual cooperation and to hammer out a "joint vision of the future" for both towns.

The third body composed of representatives of both towns is a Joint City Council Committee (Słubice and Frankfurt Joint City Council Committee for the European Integration – Wspólna Komisja Integracji Europejskiej Rad Miejskich Słubic i Frankfurtu[27]), which meets about six times a year and its work is based on the common plan for the development of mutual cooperation and much deeper integration of Słubice and Frankfurt (Oder).

Concentrating on the political dimension of cooperation between Słubice and Frankfurt (Oder) it's worth stressing that next to the Polish-German governance institutions mentioned above we can enumerate other structures which are helpful in the process of shaping mutual good practices. These structures are a consequence of participation of both towns in the "EGTC"[28] URBACT project on the governance of cross-border conurbations in Europe[29]. The project brings together MOT[30] as the lead-partner and six cross-border conurbations in Europe[31] with the objective of exchanging experiences and promoting best practices of cooperation. As a result of being a partner in the framework of the URBACT project Słubice and Frankfurt established a Polish-German Cross-Border URBACT Local Support Group that co-exists with the other cross-border institutions (see graph 2). The Cross-Border URBACT Local Support Group consists of two main elements: a steering group composed of the head clerks of both City Hall's departments. They meet every two months and work on the local cross-border development plan of Frankfurt (Oder) and Słubice. The main objective of this group is to create a common development strategy for both towns through the year 2020 based on the grounds of prior experience. A significant component of the administration level is working groups that usually meet once a month. They base on the development plan and elaborate par-

---

[27] City Hall in Słubice.
[28] Expertising Governance for Transfrontier Conurbations.
[29] It is fundamental for cross-border agglomerations (that represent almost 25 million people in Europe) to define methods and tools to coordinate their policies in order to give concrete answers to the needs of their inhabitants in fields such as urban development, transport, employment, public services, health and environment; *The "EGTC" URBACT project officially launched on 19th November in Strasbourg, France. The cross-border agglomerations are networking at European level*, MOT Press Release, 21 November 2008, p. 1.
[30] Mission Operationnelle Transfrontaliere (MOT) – The objective of MOT is to facilitate the execution of cross-border projects. Its dual legitimacy (interministerial and as an association) enables it to encourage ongoing dialogue between national and community authorities and local project leaders. It exercises its role in three areas: operational assistance, networking and help with the definition of overall strategies; http://www.espaces-transfrontaliers.eu/, 13.04.2009.
[31] Eurometropole Lille-Kortrijk-Tournai (France/Belgium), Frankfurt on Oder/Słubice conurbation (Germany/Poland), Eurocidade Chaves-verin (Portugal/Spain), Ister-Granum EGTC (Hungary/Slovakia), Eurodistrict Strasbourg-Ortenau (France/Germany), Trinational Eurodistrict Basel (Switzerland/Germany/France).

ticular Polish-German projects and undertakings. Members of these groups also prepare new cross-border projects.

The experience provided by other European cross-border regions is a great help in the organization of the cooperation between the German Frankfurt and Polish Słubice authorities. Such an organization of Polish-German cross-border local institutions makes the process of cooperation easier and more effective and gives a new impulse to cross-border territory projects to intended to facilitate territorial cooperation.

The cross-border cooperation of the political authorities of twin cities of Słubice and Frankfurt may be described by the features listed in the table 2.

Table 2. Features of cross-border cooperation in Słubice and Frankfurt (Oder)

History	Structure	Cooperation
- Sister cities since 1991 - 1991 foundation of a common University: European University Viadrina and Collegium Polonicum (in partnership with Adam Mickiewicz University Poznań) - Founders of Euroregion Pro Europa Viadrina in 1993 - Since then more than 50 common projects in sectors of infrastructure, culture, youth exchange, tourism (ex. "European Garden" 2003)	- Common City Council Commission since 1993 - Regular Mayors' meetings since 1993 - URBACT-EGTC Frankfurt--Słubice Steering Group since August 2008 - Presidency of Euroregion Pro Europa Viadrina: Lord Mayor Martin Patzelt - Members in City Twin Association and EURO-MOT (since 2007)	- partners: Counties of Słubice (PL), Oder-Spree, Märkisch-Oderland (DE), Region Lubuskie and Brandenburg, Euroregion Pro Europa Viadrina - cross-border strategy: Common urban development plan - Agreement about close co--operation between both City administrations within project EGTC (signed 19.11.2008) - Involvement of citizens: co--operation between associations, schools etc., mainly in fields like culture, sport, education

Source: R. Bodziacki, M. Patzelt, *Słubice & Frankfurt (Oder)*, Presentation during the "EGTC" project launch conference, Strasbourg, 19th November 2008.

The most significant effect of trans-border cooperation is undoubtedly the joint educational institutions in Frankfurt and Słubice.

In 1991 a first declaration of partnership was signed, marking the determination of the two towns – Słubice and Frankfurt (Oder) to cooperate. The same year the university Europa Viadrina was established in Frankfurt (Oder), and two years later the Collegium Polonicum was created, which is the most distinctive building in Słubice and at the same time the most visible effect of transborder cooperation in Polish-German border area. The decision to establish higher education institutions in the Polish-German border area was probably the most important decision for Słubice and Frankfurt (Oder) history especially from the perspective of citizens living in this pair of towns. This decision may be considered as the first step in the development of the two border towns, which provoked further changes, deeper relations and more intensive contacts in the borderland.

Collegium Polonicum is a common higher education and research institution of Adam Mickiewicz University and European University Viadrina. It means that students are one of the most visible parts of both Frankfurt and Słubice. Collegium Polonicum as a Polish-German cross-border institution – has become an academic and cultural meeting place between Poland and Germany, open to teachers and students from all over Europe[32]. It creates an opportunity for thousands of young people to study together with classmates from Poland as well as other nations of Europe. This is regarded as a great improvement of both their academic and personal lives, as it leads to the development of close contacts, frequently deepening into friendships across European borders that are, in turn, often maintained in later life following the years at university.

In addition to the political and educational context of Polish-German cooperation in the border area there is a need to pay special attention to the social perspective of collaboration. One of the actors representing the cooperation at the social level is the Słubfurt association which was established in 1999, although earlier, members of a prototype Słubfurt association acted as an informal group. In the beginning they wanted to establish one organization but due to legal reasons they founded twin associations: one in Frankfurt (Oder) and one in Słubice. Both associations have the same goals, statutes and boards. The main idea of the creation of the Słubfurt associations was to conduct actions for joining both towns (Słubice and Frankfurt (Oder)) and regions into a one urban and culture place. That is the reason for the name of the associations: SŁUBice and frankFURT. At first Słubfurt members concentrated their efforts on cultural and arts events. Afterwards they focused much more on "work from scratch", cooperation and development. Today, next to supporting cooperation, both associations realize projects that are mostly related to the needs of local societies and even claim that Słubfurt is just one city[33].

The second example of such an approach to cross-border cooperation is an idea of Słubfurt city which is strongly supported by Michael Kurzwelly. According to

---

[32] The idea of Collegium Polonicum was born on September 6, 1991, when the Minister of National Education of the Polish Republic, Robert Glebocki, and the Minister of Science, Research and Culture of the Federal German State of Brandenburg, Hinrich Enderlein, signed a "Joint Declaration of Cooperation". In December 1991, the Vice-Minister of National Education, Prof. Roman Duda, confirmed the Consultation Council's resolution for the founding of the Collegium Polonicum in Słubice. The legal frameworks for the Collegium Polonicum were established on October 2, 2002 with signing an international agreement – *Umowa między Ministrem Edukacji Narodowej i Sportu Rzeczypospolitej Polskiej a Ministerstwem Nauki, Badań i Kultury Kraju Związkowego Brandenburgii w sprawie Collegium Polonicum w Słubicach, sporządzona w Warszawie dnia 2 października 2002 r.*, "Monitor Polski" z dnia 15 września 2003 r., nr 43, poz. 647.

[33] M. Garand, K. Kowala-Stamm, *Percepcja przestrzenna granicy i obszaru przygranicznego na przykładzie Słubfurtu*, [in:] B. Breysach, A. Paszek, A. Tölle (eds), *Grenze-Granica*, Berlin 2003, pp. 375–387.

him Słubfurt is the first city worldwide being located partly in Poland and partly in Germany.

In 1999 Kurzwelly started to run a project called *SŁUBFURT CITY? at the border of two countries that do not exist*. *Słuburt City* is an idea of creation of one urban area of Słubice and Frankfurt. Citizens of both towns took part in the project as well as students of the Viadrina University and artists, who had presented their works in the town area. "The Słubfurt city was made of two parts – Słub and Furt that were located by the Polish-German border. It was born from two cultures and two languages. On 8 November 1999 during the session of city council Słubfurt city was established and on 29 November 2000 it was inscribed to the European City Index, what means that Słubfurt is the world's youngest town"[34]. This town which does not exist in reality, has its own institutions (for example – a mayor), its own coat of arms and bugle. It is worth noting that a lot of projects realized were closely related to the process of building a common identity of citizens of Frankfurt (Oder) and Słubice – Słubfurters.

However, considering the cooperation of Słubice and Frankurt (Oder) one should be aware that next to many successful undertakings like Collegium Polonicum, non-governmental organizations, common political institutions and innovative trans-border projects, sometimes the cooperation is difficult and occasionally fails to reach success. An example of such an unsuccessful venture was an effort to connect both towns with a tram line. The idea of a common tramline was reasonable historically. It was in 1898 when the first tram went over the bridge on the Oder. The whole infrastructure survived World War II and the rails connecting Słubice and Frankfurt (Oder) were removed while rebuilding the bridge. On 20 May 2003, Słubice City Council adopted an act on the will of accession to the project on a local traffic connection between Słubice and Frankfurt (Oder). A parallel act was adopted by the City Council of Frankfurt (Oder). In November 2004 both councils specified that both towns would be connected with the tram. As usual, the biggest controversy arose when talking about the costs. The Frankfurt (Oder) costs were about 3 million euro, but 75% of this amount was to be covered from the INTERREG IIA Program. The City Council of Frankfurt (Oder) decided to submit this controversial issue to citizens and held a local referendum asking people if they wanted a Polish-German tram line to be built. About 17,000 of those eligible to vote took part in the referendum (less then 30%). 17% (3000) of voters supported the idea of the tram, while 83% of them answered "No". Although the referendum was not binding, the local authorities decided not to hold another referendum[35]. According to many local politicians, citizens and observers, the failed tram project may be perceived as one of the biggest disappointments and failures of the process of cooperation in

---

[34] *Słubfurt pierwsze polsko-niemieckie miasto nad Odrą. Rozmowa Piotra Streka z Michaelem Kurzwelly*, http://www.slubfurt.net/pl_start.html, 16.08.2008.
[35] *Tramwajowi NIE*, "Gazeta Słubicka", no. 1, 2006, p. 1; P. Jendroszyk, *Niemcy przestraszyli się Polaków*, "Rzeczpospolita", 31.01.2006; *Niemcy nie chcą tramwaju do Słubic*, "Gazeta Wyborcza", 21.01.2006.

Frankfurt and Słubice. The common Polish-German tram line was supposed to be a symbol of European aspirations of citizens of both towns. As "Rzeczpospolita" reported, such a tram could be the very first undertaking of such character in the Europea Union[36].

Conclusions

This paper aimed to answer some of the questions about forms, features and results of trans-border cooperation that may be observed in a divided city – Słubice and Frankfurt (Oder).

Cross-border relations like the link between Słubice and Frankfurt (Oder) may not only provide connectivity between two neighboring municipalities, but can also be used to provide examples of good practices for other border areas. Literature on trans-border relations handles existence and development of transborder ties with different reasons. It suggests for instance that such connections may exist due to economic reasons, initiatives of international organizations or neighboring countries and regions and towns that try to collaborate in many fields.

The decision to establish a Polish-German higher education institution – Collegium Polonicum was a very important milestone for the integration of the urban areas of Frankfurt (Oder) and Słubice. This university institution plays a very significant role in the integration and cooperation processes and is an important example of good practice in so called divided cities. It is considered to be an important symbol of Polish-German transborder cooperation.

Nongovernmental organizations such as the Słubfurt Association may be treated as key elements that deepen collaboration (not at an institutional level, but in the social dimension). One of the results of citizens' involvement in cross-border cooperation may be the feeling of the common citizens' responsibility not only for Słubice or Frankfurt (Oder) separately but for Słubfurt as a whole. What's more locals from both sides of the river have dubbed the two cities with the single name of Słubfurt to reflect and celebrate their shared situation and history.

On the grounds of cooperation of local authorities in both towns several efforts to harmonize procedures or to shape new institutional forms were undertaken. Without any doubt, proof of this is the common sessions of city councils, common committees and many other things. Next to these positive effects of collaboration there are some difficulties that hamper mutual relations: the language barrier (more Polish people speak German, fewer Germans speak Polish, discrepancies in legal provisions, different procedures in the decision making process (which prolongs the time of final decisions), lack of human resources (mainly on Polish side), and a lack of common strategic documents. Despite these disadvantages or unsuccessful projects (like the Polish-German tram line), authorities from both towns still do

---

[36] P. Jendroszyk, *Niemcy przestraszyli się Polaków*, "Rzeczpospolita", 31.01.2006.

their best to improve cooperation between Frankfurt (Oder) and Słubice in many fields.

These processes have a direct effect not only on Słubice and Frankfurt (Oder) area but also on other border regions and on the current and future internal and external borders of the EU. They have led to a substantial intensification of cross-border cooperation.

Copenhagen-Malmö
Different Sides of Integration in a Hybrid City?
Agnieszka Wójcicka

Introduction.
Investigation perspective, theoretical framework and assumptions

This paper analyzes the special form of a united city. The case study of Copenhagen-Malmö requires the definition of a "hybrid city". One possible meaning of a hybrid is: *"a composite of mixed origin"*[1]. Therefore, the phrase, a "hybrid city", coined for this investigation, can symbolize the creation process of a united urban agglomeration, composed of two cities of two different states, which have various historical and cultural backgrounds or political, economic and legal systems and are based both on the processes of cooperation building and conflict management/resolution. It can be a unique example of a united city because Copenhagen and Malmö could be physically "integrated" more as a result of technological progress – the Øresund/Öresund Bridge (from Danish: *Øresundsbroen*, from Swedish: *Öresundsbron*, joint hybrid name: *Øresundsbron*) was opened to traffic in 2000 – than by political breakthrough. *Øresundsbron* is the longest combined road and rail bridge in Europe and connects the two metropolitan areas of the Øresund/Öresund Region: the Danish capital of Copenhagen and the Swedish city of Malmö. Moreover, these neighboring cities were not divided by political borders, lines of demarcation, fences, walls, informal rules or so called invisible lines but by the state borders formed naturally on the Øresund/Öresund strait[2]. Conflict in general, especially military conflict, was not present between these entities – except for Danish-Swedish rivalry over Scania[3] (from the Swedish: *Skåne*) mainly in 17th century. The solution of conflict(s) was therefore not the basis of this integration.

The theories of integration, combined with the constructivist approach and the theory of non-zero summation, create the theoretical framework for this analysis.

---

[1] S. Wehmeier, a keyword: hybrid – *Cambridge Advanced Learner's Dictionary*, Oxford 2000, p. 638.
[2] Denmark and Sweden were connected once again. 7000 years after increasing sea levels at the end of the Ice Age severed the dry-land link between the two countries. See more: K. Lidmar-Bergström, J.O. Näslund, *Uplands and Lowlands in Southern Sweden*, [in:] M. Seppälä (ed.), *The Physical Geography of Fennoscandia*, Oxford 2005, pp. 255-261.
[3] Scania is the region on the southernmost end of the Scandinavian peninsula.

Firstly, theories of integration, mainly European, stress that integration is a closer form of relations than interdependence because it is hardly reversible, more exclusive, and has stricter legal bonds[4]. In general, states, regions, cities are choosing different forms of integration because interdependence turned out to be inadequate in realizing the crucial aims of regional, subregional or international politics. These acts of integration – combining two or more entities into a new whole – were particularly observed in the 20th century. Secondly, the constructivist approach enables the comprehension of integration as a flexible process – a practice that evolves with diverse intensity and concerns various sectors of public life. This methodology also allows an increased focus on the social norms and values or identities-building processes than on legal or materialist issues. What is more, it is possible to rethink the observed unification of Copenhagen and Malmö by emphasizing that this process of integration is not equal to a cooperation. Conflict is an important factor of integration and should not be omitted. This assumption indicates that the link to the theory of a non-zero summation is also noticeable. The logic of a non-zero game[5] should not be equalized to the intentional and conscious form of cooperation. It can also appear as mutual interdependence per se[6]. Moreover, two logics intervene in social or international reality: nonzero and zero games. The nonzero summation of one entity can be a zero summation of another one. It is therefore also necessary to examine the processes of integration also through the aspects of a conflict.

It is assumed that these two cities: Copenhagen and Malmö are becoming one urban agglomeration and a centre hub mainly as a result of the opening of the Øresund/Öresund Bridge to traffic in 2000. What is more, these cities and the bridge/tunnel link between them became a good example to follow in the region. There is a strong support for a new Øresund/Öresund tunnel from Helsingborg in Sweden to Helsingör in Denmark – the so-called HH link. 62% of those polled by SIFO Research International in a survey for local newspaper Helsingborgs Dagblad declared their support for a permanent link across the strait[7]. Additionally, the region of Scania is special in Sweden because of its dynamic history entwined with a close neighborhood to Denmark and even more so with continental Europe. It can thus be assumed that Scåne, in representing the decentralization and regionalization processes, is typical and different to the rest of Sweden and that is why the unique process of Copenhagen and Malmö growing into one common metropolitan area can be observed nowadays. These processes of integration of the cities analyzed us-

---

[4] A.S. Milward, V. Sørensen, *Interdependence or integration? A national choice*, [in:] A.S. Milward (ed.), *The Fronties of national sovereingnty, history and theory 1945-1992*, London–New York 1993, p. 19.
[5] R. Wright, *Nonzero. The logic of human destiny*, Warszawa 2000, pp. 124 and 371.
[6] Genes in chromosomes, for instance, cooperate following the logic of nonzero summation without conscious agreement to such actions. See more: R. Wright, *Nonzero. The logic of…*, op. cit., p. 371.
[7] P. Vinthagen Simpson, *Strong support for new Öresund tunnel*, http://www.thelocal.se/12140/20080531/, 31.05.2008.

ing the social constructivist methodology gives a broader approach towards highlighting how identities of these two states are being formed.

Presentation of Copenhagen and Malmö – a hybrid city

Copenhagen (from Danish: *København*) is the capital and biggest city of Denmark. It is situated on the Eastern shore of the island of Zealand (from Danish: *Sjælland*) and partly on Amager. The city faces the Øresund/Öresund strait to the East which divides Denmark from Sweden and links the North Sea with the Baltic Sea. Malmö and Landskrona are placed on the Swedish side of the Sound exactly across from Copenhagen. The capital is also a part of the Øresund/Öresund Region, which includes the islands: Zealand, Lolland-Falster and Bornholm on the Danish side and Scania (from Swedish: *Scåne*) on the Swedish side. The area can be divided into the metropolitan area of Copenhagen, the Danish periphery and Scania, where Malmö and its suburbs represent a main part of the Swedish side of Øresund/Öresund[8].

Map 1. The Øresund/Öresund Region and the main cities

Source: *Fakta om regionen. Øresundsregionen og nogle af de største byer*, http://www.oresundsbron.com/documents/document.php?obj=4928, 4.03.2009.

[8] *Øresund. General facts and figures*, http://www.oresundsregionen.org/3d200029, 11.03.2009.

Copenhagen Municipality is an administrative unit that covers the central part of the actual city. Copenhagen consists of boroughs and areas such as: Indre By, Østerbro, Nørrebro, Vesterbro, Amagerbro, Nordhavnen (North Habour), Valby, Kongens Enghave (King's Meadow Garden), also known as Sydhavnen (South Harbour), Christianshavn, Christiania (Freetown), Sundbyvester (Sundby West), Sundbyøster (Sundby East), Ørestad, Islands Brygge, Bellahøj, Brønshøj, Ryparken, Bispebjerg, Vigerslev, Vestamager, Vanløse[9]. Moreover, suburban Copenhagen is arranged in accordance with the Finger Plan (from Danish: *fingerplanen*) started in 1947, which split the suburbs into five parts – "fingers"[10].

Map 2 and 3. The location of Copenhagen. Copenhagen Municipality

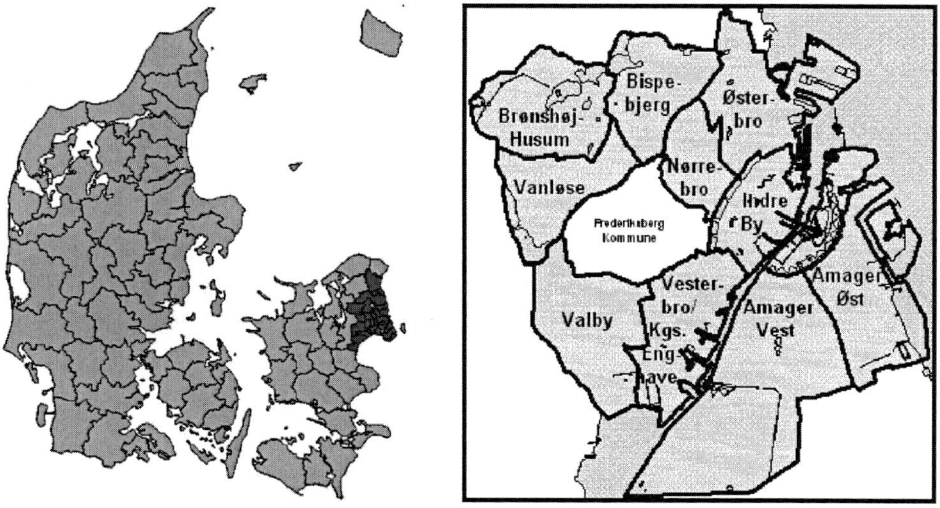

Source: *Kort over Københavns bydele*, http://www.sk.kk.dk/bydelsstatistik/bydelskort.htm, 13.03.2009.

The conurbation of Copenhagen contains a number of municipalities. After Copenhagen Municipality, the second largest is Frederiksberg Municipality which is an enclave inside Copenhagen Municipality. Both are a part of the larger capital region of Denmark (from Danish: *Hovedstaden*), which encompasses most of the Copenhagen metropolitan area. Before, the areas of Frederiksberg, Gentofte and Copenhagen municipalities used to define the city of Copenhagen, which was

---

[9] The suffix "bro" in the names: Østerbro, Nørrebro, Vesterbro and Amagerbro should not be mixed with the Danish word for: bridge, which is "bro" as well. The notion is considered to be an abbreviation or short form of the Danish word "brolagt" meaning "paved" concerning the streets paved with cobblestones – Copenhagen's former gates. See more: *Fakta om kommunen*, http://www.kk.dk/FaktaOmKommunen.aspx, 13.03.2009.

[10] The S-train lines are built in line with the Finger Plan, while green areas and highways are built in-between. See more: *The Finger Plan*, http://www.denmark.dk/en/menu/About-Denmark/Society/Economy-Production/Infrastructure/TheFingerPlan/, 13.03.2009.

changed after the latest Danish Municipal Reform at the beginning of 2007[11]. The area of the city of Copenhagen includes the municipalities of Copenhagen, Dragør, Frederiksberg and Tårnby, with a total population of 667,228 at the beginning of 2009[12]. The 2007 reform changed the traditional counties (from Danish: *amter*) into five larger regions. Smaller municipalities were merged into larger units, reducing the number of municipalities from 271 to 98. The new capital region consists of the municipalities of Copenhagen and Frederiksberg, the former counties of Copenhagen and Frederiksberg, and the regional municipality of Bornholm[13] with a total population of 1,662,285 at the beginning of 2009[14].

Malmö (from Swedish: *Malmö stad*) is the third most densely inhabited city in Sweden located in the southernmost province of Scania (from Swedish: *Skåne*)[15]. It is the center of Malmö Municipality (from Swedish: *Malmö kommun*) and the capital of Skåne county. It is also a bimunicipal locality[16], as the small town of Arlöv in Burlöv Municipality (from Swedish: *Burlövs kommun*) is a part of it. Both municipalities consist of smaller urban and rural areas, such as the suburbs of Oxie and Åkarp. The

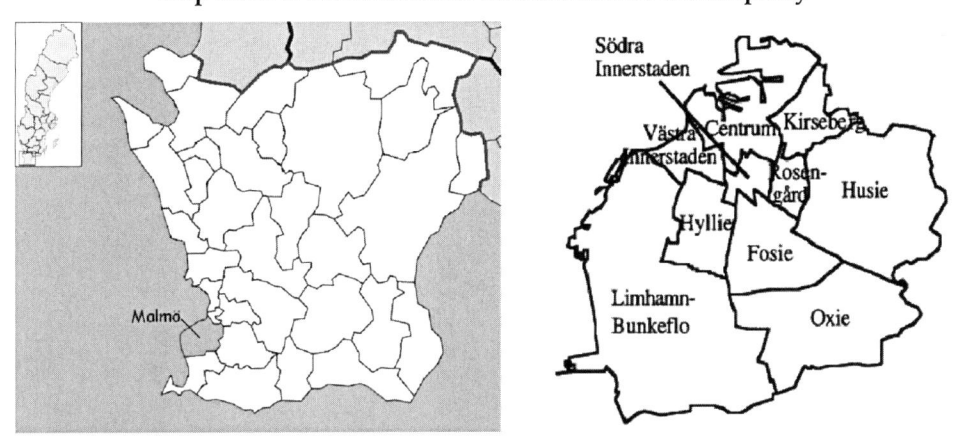

Map 4 and 5. The location of Malmö. Malmö Municipality

Source: Områdesfakta för Malmö 1998, http://www.malmo.se/download/18.d2883b1055feb9bec8000339/006.Malm%C3%B6.pdf+1998, 13.03.2009.

---

[11] To fulfill statistical needs after the Danish Municipal Reform from 2007, the "lands" (from Danish: *landsdele*) in Denmark were redefined. A land is a geographical and statistical definition, and the area is not thought to be an administrative unit.
[12] *Danmarks Statistik*, http://www.statistikbanken.dk/BEF1A07, 1.01.2009.
[13] *Om Region Hovedstaden*, http://www.regionh.dk/topmenu/omRegionH/, 13.03.2009.
[14] *Danmarks Statistik*, http://www.statistikbanken.dk/BEF1A07, 1.01.2009.
[15] Its location in southernmost Sweden makes it nearer to Milan in Italy than to the northernmost Kiruna in Sweden.
[16] *Report by Statistics Sweden*, Tätorter 2005, http://w41.scb.se/templates/Publikation____186288.asp, 13.03.2009.

total population of the urban area was almost 259,000 by the end of 2005, of which more than 9,000 were in Burlöv[17].

The Malmö urban area (from Swedish: *Malmö tätort*) is the third largest of the 1,400 localities or urban areas of Sweden. Malmö tätort is not the same as the city of Malmö, which is a semi-official name for the Malmö Municipality[18]. It is not the equivalent of Metropolitan Malmö – Greater Malmö (from Swedish: *Stormalmö*), which is a much bigger area. With regard to the definition of Statistics Sweden – Statistiska centralbyrån (SCB)[19], Metropolitan Malmö is one of Sweden's three formally acknowledged metropolitan areas and since 2005 is characterized by four districts: the municipalities of Malmö, Lund, Trelleborg, and a fourth area including the remaining municipalities: Burlöv, Eslöv, Höör, Kävlinge, Lomma, Skurup, Staffanstorp, Svedala and Vellinge[20]. In 2008, its population was noted to be 628,388[21]. Lund, with a municipal population of over 100,000[22] and one of Scandinavia's most notable university cities, is together with Malmö the region's economic and educational hub. The metropolitan area of the cities of Malmö and Lund in southern Sweden are named the South-Western Scania (from Swedish: *Sydvästra Skåne*) or Metropolitan Malmö[23]. It is also a part of the transnational Øresund/Öresund Region.

An integral part of this analysis is the presentation of the Øresund/Öresund Bridge which is the joined two-track rail and four-lane road bridge/tunnel across the Øresund/Öresund strait. In 2000, it linked Copenhagen and Malmö and started to create the largest Scandinavian conurbation. The international European route, E20, crosses the bridge and the tunnel via a two-lane motorway, as does the Öresund Railway Line. The bridge is the longest border-crossing bridge in the world[24]. The integration project obtained funding from the European Union (EU)

---

[17] Report by Statistics Sweden, *Folkmängd i riket, län och kommuner 30 juni 2008 och befolkningsförändringar första halvåret 2008*, http://www.scb.se/templates/tableOrChart____244147.asp, 13.03.2009.
[18] Officially, the town Malmö is named: "Malmö stad" (city of Malmö), as does some of other Swedish municipalities, and particularly the other two metropolitans of Sweden: Stockholm and Gothenburg. However, the term "city" has administratively been withdrawn in Sweden.
[19] *Storstadsområden. Definitions of metropolitan areas in Sweden*, http://www.scb.se/Grupp/regionalt/rg0104/Storstadsomr.xls, 13.03.2009.
[20] *Report by Statistics Sweden* – Statistiska centralbyrån (SCB), Kommunarealer den 1 January 2008. *Municipalities in Sweden and their areas*, www.scb.se/statistik/MI/M0802/2008A02/mi0802tab3_2008.xls, 13.03.2009.
[21] Report by Statistics Sweden – Statistiska centralbyrån (SCB), Folkmängd i riket, län och kommuner 30 juni 2008 och befolkningsförändringar första halvåret 2008, http://www.scb.se/templates/tableOrChart____244147.asp, 13.03.2009.
[22] Report by Statistics Sweden – Statistiska centralbyrån (SCB), Folkmängd i riket, län och kommuner 30 juni 2008 och befolkningsförändringar första halvåret 2008, http://www.scb.se/templates/tableOrChart____244147.asp, 13.03.2009.
[23] Region Scåne, http://www.skane.se, 25.03.2009
[24] Report by Øresundsbro Konsortiet, Facts worth knowing about the Øresund Bridge, Copenhagen 2008, p. 4.

and praise from the Organization for Economic Co-operation and Development (OECD)[25].

Photo 1 and 2. The Øresund/Öresund Bridge

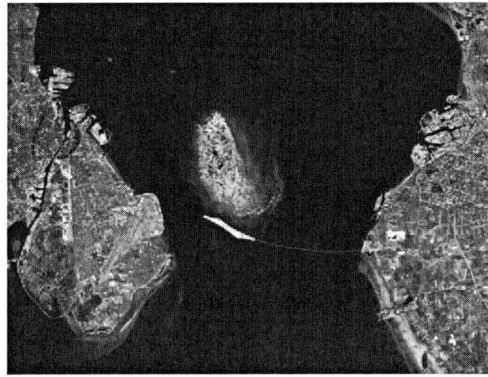

Source: P. Mens, *Bridge viewed from Sweden*, http://bridgephoto.dk/search/details.php?id= 2002112106, 4.03.2009.

Source: *The Øresund/Öresund Bridge*, http://www.nasa.gov/images/content/ 146928 main_image_feature_549_ys_full.jpg, 4.03.2009.

The fixed link across Øresund/Öresund includes a four kilometer long tunnel, an artificial island, Peberholm, which is four kilometers long, and an eight kilometer cable-stayed bridge. Its construction began in 1995 and was completed in 2000[26]. Within a broader perspective, this bridge is the crucial component in Northern Europe's infrastructure as the railway and motorway Scandinavian-continental European connector. Currently, this is assumed by the Great Belt Bridge, but from 2018 a new bridge across Fehmarnbelt will be completed, linking Fehmarn in Germany with the southern part of the Øresund/Öresund Region – Lolland in Denmark. This will create a future corridor on the Copenhagen/Malmö/Hamburg axis[27].

Study on the cooperation processes in the hybrid city

Inevitably, the opening of the Øresund/Öresund Bridge in 2000 started to foster the integration processes of Copenhagen and Malmö and the creation of the biggest

---

[25] P. Laurence, *Bridge shapes new Nordic hub*, http://news.bbc.co.uk/2/hi/europe/ 5339726.stm, 18.03.2009.
[26] Report by Øresundsbro Konsortiet, Facts worth knowing about..., op. cit., p. 7.
[27] The landworks on the Danish side included about 12 kilometers long electrified railway from the beginning of the link at the Øresund/Öresund coast to Copenhagen Central Railway Station together with a nine kilometers motorway from the coast to the existing motorway network on West Amager. On the other hand, the Swedish landworks involved around ten kilometers railway and motorway connection from Lernacken to Fosie (south east of Malmö) and an extension to selected railway parts from Lernacken towards Malmö. See more: *The Øresund Bridge – linking a region*, http://osb.oeresundsbron.dk/documents/document.php?obj=3922, 18.03.2009.

well-prospering Scandinavian conurbation. It has created new opportunities to establish the Copenhagen/Malmö axis, a new Nordic economy, logistics, transport and culture hub, the Northern European Centre or the so-called gateway to the Baltic and Scandinavia. In this paper, cooperation processes will be portrayed through the analysis of opportunities that the bridge has enabled in forms of enhanced business competitiveness, co-working labor and housing markets, commuting and transport advantages or education and science partnerships.

The number of inhabitants, the size of economies (gross regional product), research, labor markets, business attraction, traffic statistics or the number of students can be used to calculate the competitiveness of Copenhagen/Malmö. It is the only conurbation in Scandinavia with more than 2.6 million inhabitants. The total population in the Øresund/Öresund Region is 3.6 million[28]. In the Baltic Region, only Hamburg, Berlin, St Petersburg, Warszawa, Katowice, and Copenhagen/Malmö have more than 2.5 million inhabitants[29]. Moreover, with the enlargement of the European Union by ten new member states in 2004, this conurbation has gained a central position in the EU. Admittedly, its strategic location in the Baltic area, its highly developed infrastructure and the well-functioning Swedish and Danish states create a concrete foundation for the creation of a European powerhouse in the Baltic Region[30]. That is why the main targets of Øresundsbro Konsortiet[31] are linked to two significant development tendencies. Firstly, the Danish and Swedish parts of the region must be joined into one consistent region with one common labor and housing market. Secondly, the region must attract international investment in the form of company startups. The vision of Øresundsbro Konsortiet is to create one international region around Øresund/Öresund which is able to compete with the largest and most developed regions in Northern Europe[32].

---

[28] B. Greve, M. Rydbjerg (eds), *Cross-border commuting in EU: obstacles and barriers. Country report: Øresund Region*, Research Papers from the Department of Social Sciences Roskilde University no. 11/03, p. 12.

[29] In London, Dortmond/Cologne (Ruhr) and Paris, for example, which are geographically similar to the Copenhagen/Malmö area in terms of size, there are 10 million residents while 7 million live in the Amsterdam/Rotterdam area (Randstad) and 6 million in Manchester/Liverpool. These numbers are higher than those for the administrative groupings, where borders are nearer to city centers and neighboring cities, are not added. See more: *Report by Øresundsbro Konsortiet, Facts worth knowing about...*, op. cit., p. 28.

[30] *Report by Øresundsbro Konsortiet, Facts worth knowing about...*, op. cit., p. 28.

[31] The bridge is owned and operated by Øresundsbro Konsortiet, which is jointly owned by the Danish and Swedish states.

[32] This is also the view of 90% of the region's decision makers who participated in a survey in 2007 in which 265 business leaders, politicians, journalists, senior civil servants, stakeholders, and other interested parties answered a questionnaire about the Øresund/Öresund Region's future potential. An enhanced infrastructure is pointed out by the greater part of the decision makers as a significant target if the region is to be a leading Northern European centre. Improved international specialization in main proficiencies and stronger international marketing of the region are also thought to be dominating. 90% of the survey's repliers also stress the necessity to unite forces across Øresund/Öresund to gain the aim of establishing

There are facts that support this vision. A study by Oxford Research noted the region's high potential in 2005, with its advanced infrastructure and concentration of biotechnology and IT firms[33]. Furthermore, research by the Danish agency Copenhagen Capacity based on the Ernst&Young European Investment Monitor report from 2005 shows that this area increased its share of inward investment projects in Scandinavia in 2004[34]. In addition, the Economist Intelligence Unit (EIU) named Denmark as the world's best country for company startups, investment and doing business in 2006, 2007 and 2008. It reveals its stable economy, adaptable labor market, well-functioning transport and communication infrastructure and encourages financing opportunities for businesses. Sweden is ranked eleventh in this survey[35]. The EIU highlights that Denmark is extremely attractive for American and European investors concentrating on Scandinavia. Denmark's location near to the other Nordic states and continental Europe (especially Germany or the Baltic states) makes it a logistics hub. In the competition for international investment in Scandinavia between Stockholm and Copenhagen, one of Copenhagen's benefits is its closeness to both the Danish and Swedish markets[36].

Figure 1. Sales in Copenhagen and production in Scania

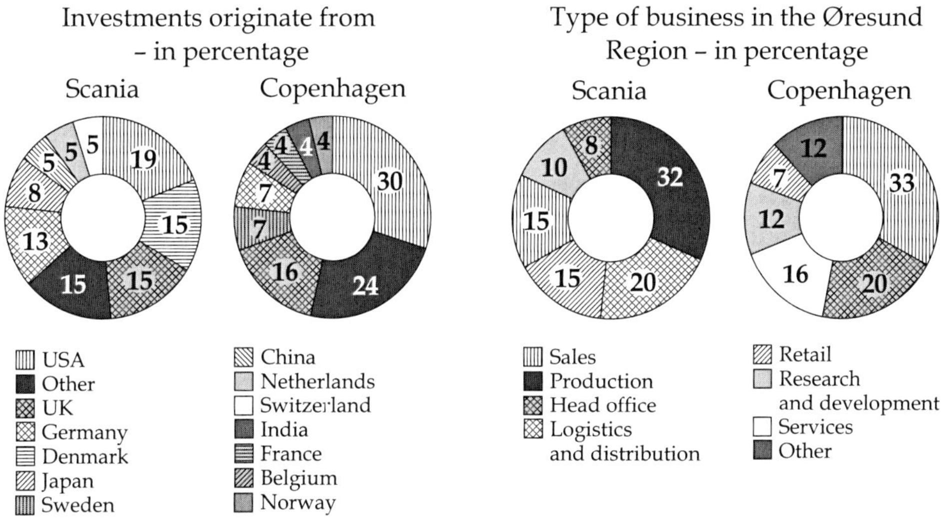

Investments originate from – in percentage

Scania: 5, 5, 5, 19, 15, 15, 15, 13, 8
Copenhagen: 4, 4, 4, 30, 15, 24, 16, 7, 7

Type of business in the Øresund Region – in percentage

Scania: 8, 32, 20, 15, 15, 10
Copenhagen: 12, 33, 20, 16, 12, 7

Legend:
- USA
- Other
- UK
- Germany
- Denmark
- Japan
- Sweden
- China
- Netherlands
- Switzerland
- India
- France
- Belgium
- Norway

- Sales
- Production
- Head office
- Logistics and distribution
- Retail
- Research and development
- Services
- Other

Source: *Report by Øresundsbro Konsortiet, Facts worth knowing about...*, op. cit., p. 44.

---

this region as a leading Northern European centre. See more: *Report by Øresundsbro Konsortiet, Facts worth knowing about...*, op. cit., p. 47.
[33] P. Laurence, *Bridge shapes new Nordic...*, op. cit.
[34] *Research by Danish Agency Copenhagen Capacity, based on the Ernst & Young European Investment Monitor report from 2005*, http://www.isa.se/templates/News___38544.aspx, 20.03.2009.
[35] *Country analysis and forecasts by the Economist Intelligence Unit*, http://country-analysis.eiu.com/country_coverage, 20.03.2009.
[36] *Report by Øresundsbro Konsortiet, Facts worth knowing about...*, op. cit., p. 43.

Foreign inward investment in the Øresund/Öresund Region is directed at different sectors. According to figure 1, in Scania, attention is paid to production, logistics and distribution and in Copenhagen more than half of the new companies target sales. This situation is also reflected in the labor market. There is higher employment in public administration and the financial and business sectors in Greater Copenhagen than in Greater Malmö, whereas employment in the health and social sectors is relatively high in Greater Malmö. Both have high employment in high-tech sectors such as IT and communication[37]. An analysis of foreign direct investments in the region between 2004 and 2006 by the Invest in Sweden Agency (ISA) shows that Copenhagen received 77% of the 174 foreign investment projects in the Øresund/Öresund Region over the period. In spite of this, Danish domination declined in 2006, when Scania kept the inward flow of foreign investment. These contrasts between Copenhagen and Scania demonstrate that the last one comprised 11% of the direct inward investments in Sweden, and Copenhagen 57% in Denmark, which explains the dominance of the Copenhagen area within Denmark[38]. There, especially the United States is the biggest foreign investor followed by investments from European countries. Denmark and Germany, for example, represent a considerable share of foreign investments in Scania. IT/electronics is the segment that invites most foreign investments to the region in general. The second largest sector in Copenhagen is the provision of services and logistics and in Scania it is transport[39]. Moreover, the Øresund/Öresund Bridge's business customers have constructive experiences on the both sides of the strait. In a survey from 2006, 75% of the companies prove that their expectations concerning their involvement on the other side of the strait have been fulfilled. Specifically, the expectations of the pharmaceutical and biotech industries, media and communication, and public and semipublic organizations have been met[40].

It can be claimed that Malmö gained more on the bridge opening to public. It still had a rather peripheral status in comparison with Stockholm or Copenhagen despite being the capital of Scania. Physically, in 2000, it became a part of the powerful Øresund/Öresund region. This fact revealed a crucial mutual dependence observable between Copenhagen and Malmö. Higher salaries and better career opportunities in Copenhagen attract Swedish citizens in Denmark and the lower costs of

---

[37] Report by Örestat, Slutrapport ÖRESTAT-II, http://www.orestat.scb.se/website/notice.aspx?CatId=40&NotId=221&Level=1, 20.03.2009.
[38] The database of the Invest in Sweden Agency, http://www.isa.se, 20.03.2009.
[39] The survey does not include acquisitions or mergers – only company startups or investments for expansion. See more: *Report by Øresundsbro Konsortiet, Facts worth knowing about…*, op. cit., p. 44.
[40] Those companies that have started up on the other side of strait have made a good decision. 70% of the Swedish companies that have set up themselves in Denmark and 60% of the Danish corporations that have done the same in Sweden have made a progress. The greater part of the companies have sales activities on the other side while 15% have established subsidiaries. See more: *Report by Øresundsbro Konsortiet, Facts worth knowing about…*, op. cit., p. 47.

living or house prices in Malmö (and in Scania in general) are a focus for Danes who prefer to keep their jobs in Copenhagen and commute[41]. The statistics prove this dependence. The number of Swedes who found jobs in Denmark set a new record in 2007. According to SkatØresund[42], there were 6,667 of Swedes who were employed for the first time in Denmark in 2007. This is an 85% growth in comparison with 2006. The manpower deficit in Danish companies and the higher unemployment rate in Malmö than in Copenhagen[43] led to an increase in employment of Swedes in 2006. It remained at a high level in 2007, and hit its peak in June 2007, when 800 Swedish citizens found employment with Danish companies[44].

Figure 2. What are the advantages of commuting across Øresund/Öresund?

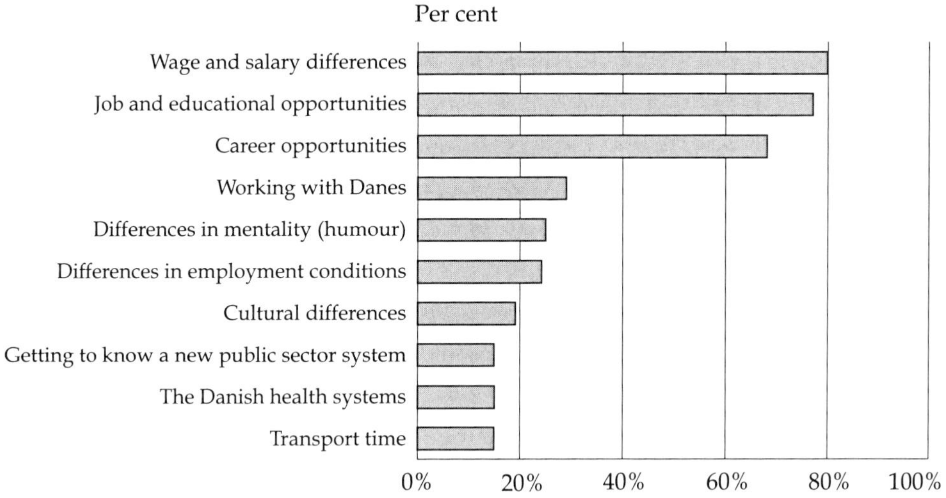

Per cent

Wage and salary differences	~80%
Job and educational opportunities	~78%
Career opportunities	~65%
Working with Danes	~28%
Differences in mentality (humour)	~22%
Differences in employment conditions	~22%
Cultural differences	~20%
Getting to know a new public sector system	~15%
The Danish health systems	~13%
Transport time	~10%

Source: *Report by Øresundsbro Konsortiet, Facts worth knowing about…, op. cit.*, p. 35.

---

[41] The region's population is approving the positive tendencies. A survey from 2007 proved that 56% of the Swedes in Scania and 40% of the inhabitants on the Danish side of Øresund/Öresund think that the region is already a reality. These figures are higher than in any earlier surveys since 2001. 84% of people questioned suppose that it is "good"/"very good" when more people are settling, studying or working on the other side of Øresund/Öresund. See more: *Report by Øresundsbro Konsortiet, Facts worth knowing about…, op. cit.*, p. 46.
[42] *SkatØresund is a joint tax office for the Øresund/Öresund Region*, http://www.skat.dk/data.aspx?oId=171311, 20.03.2009. When a Swede is employed on the Danish side of the strait, he/she is assigned a PAYE number as he/she is liable for tax in Denmark. People who have worked in Denmark before, have a PAYE registration number. Therefore, only Swedes who work in Denmark for the first time can be included in these statistics by SkatØresund.
[43] The Swedish unemployment rate is higher than the Danish. The difference was bigger in 1990s when Sweden was facing hard times. It is decreasing as especially Malmö (Scania in general) has experienced a high growth in recent years.
[44] The high level for June 2007 relates to the employment of seasonal staff when many Danish companies experience the deficit of workers, e.g. in Tivoli. See more: *Report by Øresundsbro Konsortiet, Facts worth knowing about…, op. cit.*, p. 34.

The data from a survey carried out by Øresundsbro Konsortiet among Øresund/Öresund commuters in 2006 support the statement that financial and career related factors are crucial for Malmö residents who commute to Copenhagen[45]. According to figure 2, 80% of those surveyed stress the advantage of higher wages/salaries and almost 80% of those examined highlight the job, educational and career opportunities. Benefits are seen as well in working with Danes, such as the differences in mentality or culture. Dissimilarities in weekly working time can influence cross-border movements as well. In Sweden, the normal working week is 40 hours, whereas in Denmark it is 37[46]. As a result, the time of commuting can be compensated for by the shorter working week. Moreover, shorter journey times, achieved since the bridge was opened to the public, is seen as an advantage to around 15% of those surveyed[47].

On the other hand, many Copenhagen inhabitants continue to move to Malmö. They resettle to improve their financial situation and housing conditions. What is more, they keep their employment in Copenhagen and commute to work. Regardless of decreasing house prices in Greater Copenhagen, many Danish citizens persist in moving to Malmö. In 2007, a new record was set regarding the amount of Danish arrivals which totaled 4,500, a 6% increase on 2006 figures. This is a result of years of enormous price increases in Copenhagen's housing market leading to a important rise in resettlements to Scania in 2006. On the other hand, many Danish citizens saw the reduction of the price difference in Danish and Swedish housing as a chance to return to Denmark. The amount of those who relocated from Scania to Zealand in 2007 increased by 39%. However, the influx from Zealand to Scania continued to be on a high level of 2,400[48]. This phenomenon is the result of the important price distinctions that still exist. A 140 square meter house, for instance, costs DKK 3,882,900 in Copenhagen and SEK 2,960,969 in Malmö[49].

Figure 3, representing the outcomes of a survey delivered by Øresundsbro Konsortiet among Øresund/Öresund commuters in 2005, confirms that it is beneficial for Danes – in terms of lower living costs and better housing standards – to settle in Scania and commute to their jobs in Copenhagen. What is more, lower car prices are also one of the three main reasons of the Danish influx to Scania. The additional savings made by Danes who exchange their Danish registration charges for

---

[45] Compare with: *Research by the European Urban Knowledge Network (EUKN), Copenhagen-Malmö: a bridge for employment, Denmark & Sweden*, http://www.eukn.org/eukn/themes/Urban_Policy/Economy_knowledge_and_employment/Urban_economy/Employment/Job_market/Eployment-bridge_1045.html, 22.03.2009.
[46] *Cross-border commuting in EU...*, op. cit., p. 29.
[47] Compare with: B. Greve, M. Rydbjerg (eds), *Cross-border commuting in EU: obstacles and barriers. Country report: Øresund Region*, Research Papers from the Department of Social Sciences Roskilde University, no. 11/03, pp. 35-36.
[48] *Report by Øresundsbro Konsortiet, Facts worth knowing about...*, op. cit., p. 37.
[49] *Report by Øresundsbro Konsortiet and Öresundskomiteen, Bostadsmarknaden i Öresundregionen*, København 2006, p. 4. Compare with: *Report by Øresund Trends, Bostadspriser*, http://tendensoresund.org/sv/download/11bostadspriser.pdf, 20.03.2009.

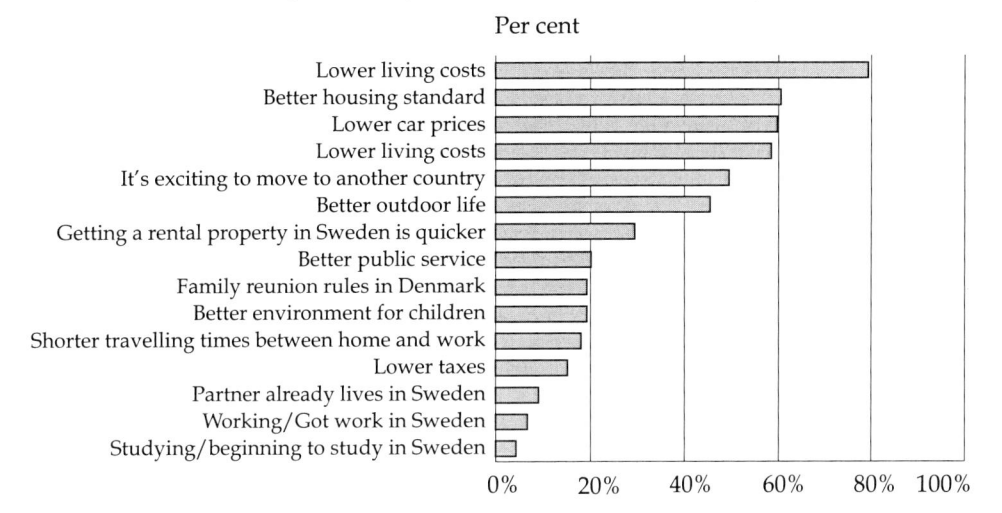

Figure 3. Why Danes are moving to Scania

Per cent

- Lower living costs
- Better housing standard
- Lower car prices
- Lower living costs
- It's exciting to move to another country
- Better outdoor life
- Getting a rental property in Sweden is quicker
- Better public service
- Family reunion rules in Denmark
- Better environment for children
- Shorter travelling times between home and work
- Lower taxes
- Partner already lives in Sweden
- Working/Got work in Sweden
- Studying/beginning to study in Sweden

0%   20%   40%   60%   80%   100%

Source: *Report by Øresundsbro Konsortiet, Facts worth knowing about…, op. cit.*, p. 38.

the Swedish VAT, are frequently used on a better car[50]. Better outdoor life is a reason to resettle for more than 40% of Danes surveyed. It supports the thesis that the advantages of migration can be both work- or leisure-oriented[51]. Moreover, cross-border marriages between Danes and Swedes are common. Around 10% of those surveyed justify the reason of their resettlement to Sweden with the fact that their partner already lives there. 318 Danes married Swedes in 2006. In 1996, there were only 153 marriages between citizens of the neighboring countries, according to Statistics Sweden[52].

The facts outlined above can also be confirmed by analyzing data on commuting, which rose considerably in 2007. 17,600 persons traveled across the bridge, together with 2,500 students. Commuting traffic was intensified by 3,900 persons in 2007 – establishing a new record. Figure 5 shows that car traffic increased by 17% in 2007. This is more than double the amount in comparison with 2001 and equates to 40,600 individuals traveling across the bridge by car or coach every day in 2007. What is more, rail traffic grew by 25% in 2007 and around 26,600 people took the train every day in 2007. All in all, almost 25 million commuters crossed the bridge in

---

[50] In general, Danes in Scania drive cars that, in Sweden, are for sale at between DKK 138,000 and 310,000 new. The ten best selling models in Denmark in 2006 have listed prices of between DKK 114,000 and DKK 325,000. In addition, VAT of 25% is payable on the whole value of the car, including the registration fee. See more: *Report by Øresundsbro Konsortiet, Facts worth knowing about…, op. cit.*, p. 40.
[51] P.A. Fischer, E. Holm, G. Malmberg, T. Straubhaar (eds), *Why do People Stay? Insider Advantages and Immobility*, http://opus.zbw-kiel.de/volltexte/2003/662/pdf/112.pdf, 20.03.2009, p. 8.
[52] D. Boman, *Swedes fall for Danes*, http://www.thelocal.se/8882/20071024/, 24.10.2008.

2007. This characterizes a 100% growth compared to 2001[53]. In addition, no less than 92% of travelers live in Sweden and work in Denmark. 41% of commuters go by car, while the rest take the train. Danes who have moved to Scania are more likely to take the car to go to work than the Swedes. 63% of all car commuters have Danish origins. The figure is 36% with regard to rail travelers. Certainly, students prefer to take the train[54].

Figure 4 and 5. Breakdown of passenger car traffic according to the place of residence and individual travelers by car or train across the Øresund/Öresund Bridge

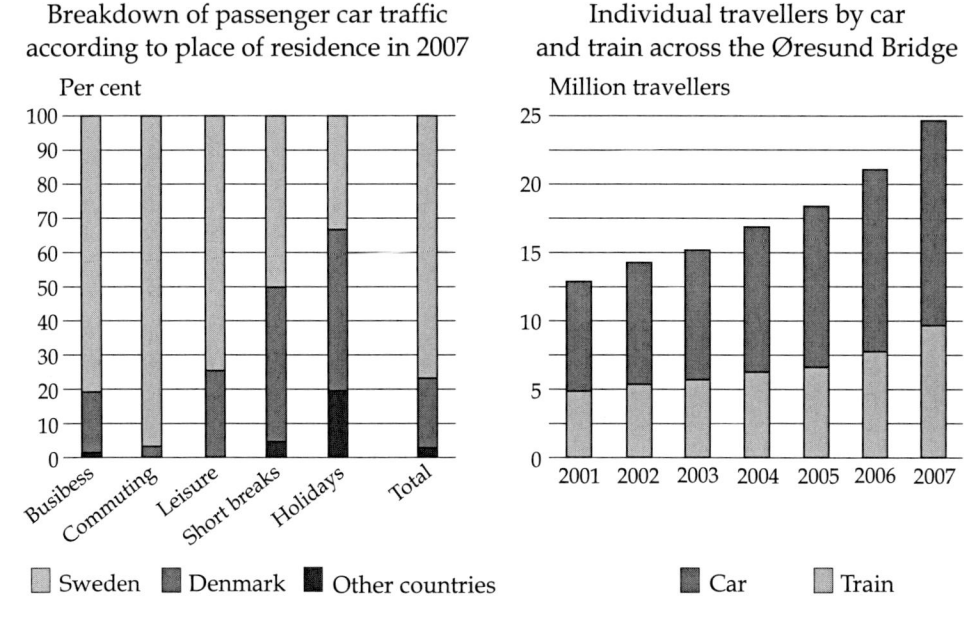

Breakdown of passenger car traffic according to place of residence in 2007

Individual travellers by car and train across the Øresund Bridge

☐ Sweden ■ Denmark ■ Other countries   ■ Car ☐ Train

Note: The data derives from surveys and is, therefore, subject to statistical uncertainties.

Source: *Report by Øresundsbro Konsortiet, Facts worth knowing about...*, op. cit., p. 10.

According to figure 4, international traffic across the bridge is inconsiderable. 73% of the bridge's traffic is regional between Copenhagen and Malmö. The regional

---

[53] The rise in the number of commuters was high both in 2006 and 2007 when a lack of manpower among Danish companies and price gaps in the residential property market intensified transfer across Øresund/Öresund. The amount of commuters is estimated on the basis of the number of full-time commuters (traveling five times a week). This definition has been chosen as it is based on the amount of crossings across the bridge by train or car and because there are no statistics accessible concerning the commuters' traveling regularity. See more: *Report by Øresundsbro Konsortiet, Facts worth knowing about...*, op. cit., p. 32.
[54] The results have been analyzed on the basis of the Øresund/Öresund bridge's customer panel which, in 2007, included 1,505 car commuters, and the replies to a survey from 435 rail commuters.

share of car traffic is increasing because of the enhanced integration between Copenhagen and Malmö (Scania in general). The distribution of travelers from Denmark and Sweden fluctuates along with the aims of traveling. The dominating goals of the traffic across the bridge are commuting and business. Nine out of ten commuters live in Sweden and seven out of ten leisure and business travelers are Swedes. Holiday traffic consists mostly of Danes.

Figure 6. Prices on the Øresund/Öresund Bridge in 2008

Prices incl. VAT	Standard price		BroPas[1)]		10-trip card	
	DKK	SEK	DKK	SEK	DKK	SEK
Passenger car	260	325	135	165	190	236
Motorcycle	145	180	60	74	105	130
Car with trailer/van/caravan	520	650	270	330	380	472
Prices excl. VAT						
Lorries over 9 metres	620	768				
Coaches over 9 metres	880	1,092				

Notes: All prices are per passage.
[1)] Annual charge for the BroPas is DKK 230 or SEK 280.
For further information and prices see www.oresundsbron.com.
Source: Information delivered by Øresundsbron, Priser, http://www.oresundsbron.com/documents/document.php?obj=5937, 22.03.2009.

In addition, the Øresund/Öresund Bridge pricing strategy, portrayed in figure 6, favors frequent customers and enables the integration processes between Copenhagen and Malmö. Clients can sign a contract with Øresundsbro Konsortiet, allowing them to take advantage of discounts and fast passage through the toll station's automatic lanes by having a so-called brobizz (an electronic transponder). In 2005, to simplify procedures for private customers, the BroPas product was introduced. By paying a subscription of DKK 230/SEK 280 once a year, BroPas purchasers can cross the bridge at a low, set price every time (DKK 135/SEK 165). BroPas is the good solution for private customers who use the bridge no less than once a year and not every day[55]. Commuters can sign a commuter contract which is the most advantageous for those who cross the bridge each day. Those who use the bridge 40 times per month pay DKK 2,827 or SEK 3,455 per month or DKK 71/SEK 86 per passage[56]. Commuters who are resident in Sweden and work in Denmark also get a particular

---

[55] BroPas purchasers have admittance to the Øresund/Öresund Bridge's program. It proposes deals on events and attractions on both sides of Øresund/Öresund at reasonable prices. See more: Information delivered by Øresundsbron, Priser, www.oresundsbron.com, 20.03.2009.
[56] The price depends on the number of crossings within one calendar month. See more: www.oresundsbron.com, 20.03.2009.

allowance of DKK 50 per passage when using their car or motorcycle as well as the normal transport allowance provided for in taxation legislation. Business purchasers who cross the bridge by passenger car, van, coach or lorry also can gain from a special business product[57]. Clients who do not wish to sign a contract can either get 10-trip cards at a discount of approximately 30% on the cash price or a single ticket with no discount at the toll station.

Integration of Copenhagen and Malmö has also been nurtured through cooperation in the field of science and education. A prime example is the Øresund University founded in 1992. It is a partnership between the region's eleven universities and consequently represents the biggest university in Scandanavia[58]. It has 150,000 students and 14,000 researchers and teachers[59]. There are five academic institutions from Copenhagen and one from Malmö within the partnership. Furthermore, Øresund Science Region has been established by the Foundation for Technology Transfer in Lund, the Danish Ministry for IT and Research and Øresund University as well as companies and research hospitals. The main aim is to support innovation and growth through cooperation[60]. These institutions unite two countries, form a platform of transnational dialogue and can be a stepping stone for a future enhanced cooperation between Copenhagen and Malmö.

In brief, the opening of the bridge cuts traveling time across the Sound to thirty minutes. This has definitely created new opportunities for creating one labor, housing or educational market across the strait and strengthening ties between companies and organizations in the region. The Øresund/Öresund Bridge integration index explains the phenomena per se. It measures the development in business and commuting related integration based on morning traffic on the bridge.

The integration index, illustrated in figure 7, reveals that an increasing number of people are separating their daily lives between the Swedish Malmö and Danish Copenhagen and that the Øresund/Öresund Region is becoming increasingly closer to reaching the aim of becoming one efficient and cohesive region. The integration index has more than quadrupled in seven years. In 2005, the region had

---

[57] According to the agreement on a fixed traffic volume, business customers can cross the bridge at a reduced price for the full year. By the end of a year, the final price is set on the basis of the number of passages undertaken for each vehicle category. The customer subsequently gets a final invoice for the full year. See more: www.oresundsbron.com, 20.03.2009.

[58] Among them – five are member schools from Copenhagen (Copenhagen Business School, IT University of Copenhagen, The Royal Academy of Fine Arts School of Architecture, The Royal School of Library and Information Science, University of Copenhagen) and one from Malmö (Malmö University). See more: *The Øresund University – the collaborating universities*, http://www.uni.oresund.org/sw5269.asp, 20.03.2009.

[59] *The Øresund University – the collaborating universities*, http://www.uni.oresund.org/sw5269.asp, 20.03.2009.

[60] It consists of four network organizations: Øresund IT, Øresund Food Network, Øresund Environment Academy, Øresund Logistics. See more: *The Øresund University – the collaborating universities*, http://www.uni.oresund.org/sw2379.asp, 20.03.2009.

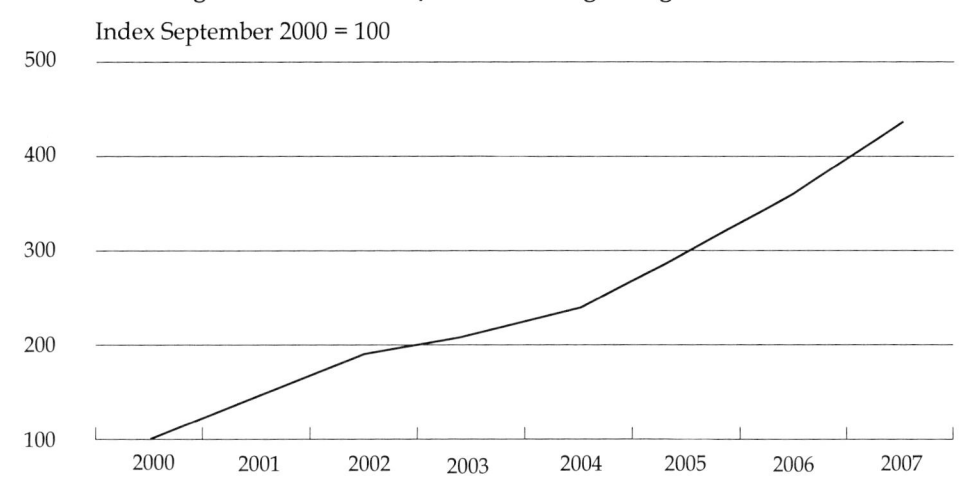

Figure 7. The Øresund/Öresund Bridge integration index

Index September 2000 = 100

Source: *Report by Øresundsbro Konsortiet, Facts worth knowing about…, op. cit.,* p. 30.

9,200 commuters using the bridge on a daily basis, the majority of them from Malmö to Copenhagen[61].

Analysis of the conflict-ridden phenomena in the hybrid city

The creation of the Copenhagen and Malmö conurbation, since the opening of the Øresund/Öresund Bridge in 2000, results as well in the conflict-ridden phenomena and significant barriers in parallel with cooperation and integration processes. The bridge links two states and has to overcome some important differences between them. Although from a continental perspective often acknowledged as identical models of well-prospering and high-developed welfare states, Denmark and Sweden still have various historical, political, economic or cultural backgrounds. Firstly, Sweden has led the neutrality policy (from Swedish: *alliansfrihet*) since 1815 and during World Wars I and II, this policy was kept. During World War I, Denmark was neutral but did not manage to maintain her neutrality in World War II. These facts formed different fundaments of those welfare states. Secondly, Denmark is the founding member state of NATO and joined the organization automatically in 1949; she became an EU member in 1973 together with Ireland and Great Britain. On the other hand, Sweden had totally different path of accession to the EU, joining together with Austria and Finland in 1995. She is still not a member of NATO. Hence, it can be claimed that Denmark is geopolitically closer to continental Europe than Sweden and that these states play different roles as well in Europe as in Scandinavia. Although, it cannot be seen as a simple demarcation of two states because

---

[61] P. Laurence, *Bridge shapes new Nordic…, op. cit.*

Scania – which includes Malmö – has a relatively strong regional identity and there is general support for decentralization and regionalization. Moreover, this province was under Danish rule until 1658[62] and many Scania people still feel more Danish than Swedish[63]. The Danish minorities on the Swedish side and vice versa can also cause conflicts[64]. Copenhagen and Malmö form the hybrid city that reflects these divisions and has to face problems related to the adjustment of legal solutions concerning e.g. unemployment benefits, taxation, pension, social and health systems, voting privileges, different languages and currency or national minorities as well as identity clashes. The conflict-ridden phenomena are to be shown through the analysis of these problems and barriers.

Figure 8. What are the disadvantages of commuting across Øresund/Öresund?

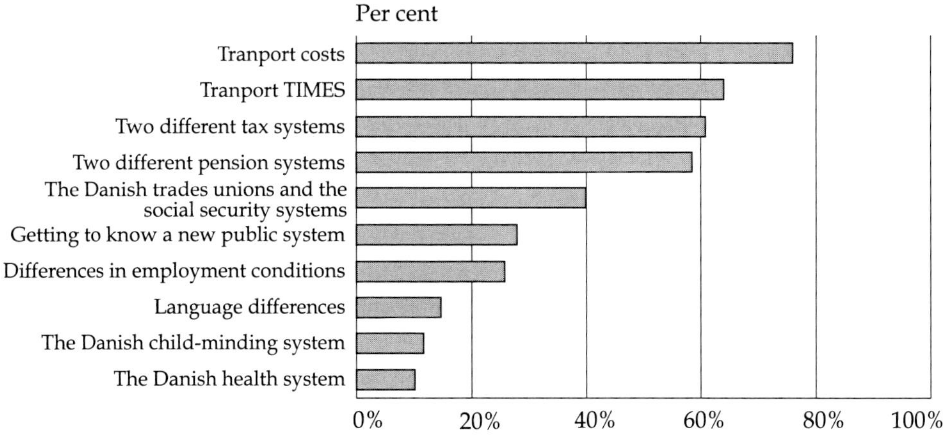

Source: *Report by Øresundsbro Konsortiet, Facts worth knowing about…, op. cit.*, p. 36.

---

[62] Scania and the eastern part of Danish territory on the other side of the strait were under control of the Swedish Crown in 1658 in accordance with the Treaty of Roskilde. See more: *Terra Scaniae. Skånes län efter 1658*, http://www.ts.skane.se/fakta/skaanes-lan-efter-1658, 22.03.2009. Scania's geographical location has encouraged strong political and economical ties with Denmark throughout the province's history. The strait splitting the cities as Helsingborg and Helsingør is only 4 kilometers wide, while the forests to the north through Småland were hard to traverse and created a natural barrier before the establishment of railways and other modern infrastructures. Since the breakdown of the Kalmar Union, Scania has been the key point of Danish-Swedish conflict and rivalry. By domination on both sides of the Øresund/Öresund strait, Denmark had effective control over the gateway to the Baltic Sea and could control trade through the sound. See more: K.J.V. Jespersen, *A History of Denmark*, Houndmills, Basingstoke, Hampshire, New York 2004, p. 3.
[63] S.Å. Olofsson, *Skåne blir danskt? (Scania becomes Danish?)*, "Helsingborgs Dagblad", http://hd.se/skane/2007/12/22/droemmar-om-stor-danmark/, 22.12.2007.
[64] In Sweden there are 44,000 Danish immigrants. See more: *Data of Statistiska centralbyrån*, http://www.scb.se/statistik/_publikationer/BE0801_2007K01_TI_02_A05ST0701.pdf, 24.03.2009.

According to figure 8, the main drawbacks of commuting are cost and time. Figure 2 which describes the advantages, supports these facts as well: the lowest proportion of people surveyed regard costs and time of transport as a benefit. Additionally, the two countries' tax, pension, social security and health systems create confusion which can also distract commuters.

The Øresund/Öresund Committee recognizes several co-related problems regarding the difference in tax systems although they are rather similar[65]. These are lack of transparency, problems concerning the difference in the relation between the tax system and the financing of social security and pensions, imbalance in the municipal budgets because of a one-sided flow of commuters and the fact that cross-border commuter definition[66] is not confronted with a modern working life. There are several barriers related to taxation regarding cross-border commuting to Denmark from Sweden[67]. Interest rates cannot be deducted by people with limited tax liability as well as expenses on unemployment insurance, trade union membership fees and private pension contributions. What is more, at macro-level, the larger share of commuters from Sweden to Denmark generates imbalance in Swedish municipal budgets as the taxes are not compatible with the expenses the municipalities have in relation with the commuters. As for incentives concerning cross-border commuting to Sweden from Denmark, it is impossible to deduct interests rates on student loans and trade union membership fees. The income for those who work both in Sweden and Denmark is unpredictable and fluctuates due to different tax levels. Individual tax allowance could be smaller in Sweden than in Denmark; this however depends on the size of earnings[68]. OECD has introduced international guidelines with the intention of avoiding double or discriminating taxation for cross-border commuters, which Denmark and Sweden have agreed to. In accordance with the OECD Double Taxation Agreement, the country of residence has the superior right to taxation of all the incomes of a person, while the employing country has the right to tax the earnings of a person within other taxes. Consequently, Copenhagen-Malmö commuters are liable to pay taxes in the residing country and limited taxes in the employing one. This indicates that only well-defined types of earnings can be taxed and only after six months full employment[69].

---

[65] The Danish and the Swedish tax systems are similar. In both states a distinction is made between government tax, country and municipality tax. Taxation is also progressive. There are even examples where the difference in tax systems have been beneficial for the commuters – i.e. those who live in Sweden but work on both sides of the border have been able to take advantage of both states' individual tax allowance and deduct interest rates in both states. See more: *Cross-border commuting in the EU...*, op. cit., pp. 20-21.
[66] Cross-border commuters are defined as those liable to pay tax in both countries. The rules, however, are created to eliminate double taxation, hence the distinction between limited and full liability for taxation is made. The definition of cross-border commuter does not encompass the variety and different degrees of commuting that exist nowadays.
[67] Report by Öresundskomiteen, *Debatoplag om en fremtidig skattemodel for Öresundsregionen*, http://www.oresundskomiteen.dk, 23.03.2009.
[68] *Cross-border commuting in EU...*, op. cit., pp. 22-25.
[69] *Ibidem*, pp. 19-20.

As for Danish and Swedish unemployment benefit, social security and pension systems, the differences are relatively small. Nevertheless, there are barriers concerning social insurance, unemployment benefit or pension. Employment in both countries triggers problems with regard to which social security and pension systems the employee is submitted to. Social security is associated with the work country, so these payments must be regulated there. However, in Denmark social security contributions in general are the responsibility of the employees who pay them via taxes, whereas in Sweden by employers. The interaction between the two systems is not problematic for the travelers only if they live in one country and work in the other one. Nevertheless, estimating the results of taking up employment on the other side of the border in terms of unemployment benefit is not straightforward. The eligibility criteria and duration period differs between the two states. The complexity is also intensified by the fact that commuters are subjected to both the Swedish and the Danish rules depending on whether they are in full-time or part-time employment. Moreover, troubles occur when an employee works in both countries. With regard to pension, the problems concern dissimilarities in taxation. In general, pensions are taxed in the country where the contributions have been made – despite the pension holders' country of residence[70].

There are also some problems with choosing between the Swedish and the Danish health services. More than 10% of people surveyed stress that the Danish health system can be the disadvantage of commuting. As a resident of one country with employment in another, Copenhagen-Malmö commuters can choose. However, using the health system in the country where you work can be problematic. A survey carried out by the Øresundsbro Konsortiet in 2007[71] showed that habit plays a key role for commuters when choosing the right health system. Danes prefer to be subjected to the Danish health system after their resettlement to Sweden, whereas Swedes mostly decide to stay in the Swedish system and work in Denmark. 38% of the survey's respondents who live in Sweden and use the Danish health system have encountered barriers. These problems concern the fact that neither the commuters nor the staff in the relevant health system are adequately well-informed about commuters' rights or about how to properly place the commuter patient into the system. It results in the fact that one in five has patients been refused treatment or rejected because they live in another country. An additional problem, which 15% of users of the Danish health service have met, is that they have been faced with a demand for payment in an otherwise free Danish system. Both problems are characteristic examples of the lack of knowledge about border commuters' rights and how they should be controlled within the administrative systems. Respondents

---

[70] Ibidem, pp. 27-28.
[71] The results are from a survey that was carried out in 2007 among the Øresund/Öresund Bridge's regional panel comprising 1,140 car and train commuters. 647 of the 1,140 participants answered the survey. See more: *Report by Øresundsbro Konsortiet, Facts worth knowing about...*, op. cit., p. 41.

who live in Sweden and use the Swedish health system do not have such problems to a similar extent[72].

Differences between these two states can negatively affect the Copenhagen-Malmö travelers; however it is important to note that these differences are not great when taking into account average gap among the OECD countries. Commuters also tackle problems with, for example, expensive text messaging and telephone rates across the strait and the two national banking systems which are not correlated. A survey delivered by the Øresundsbro Konsortiet in cooperation with Stepstone in 2006 demonstrated that challenges, excitement and higher wages/salaries are still more significant than job security and good conditions for paternity/maternity leave for jobseekers from Scania. The first three factors are typical of the Danish labor market while the two latter features refer more to the Swedish labor market. Among Swedes who do not take Denmark into their consideration, three out of five justify this with time-intensive journeys or that Denmark offers them no opportunities. The fact that different languages are spoken on each side of Øresund/Öresund is also seen as a problem by three out of ten persons[73].

The culture and identity clashes are also an important barrier to focus on, although the data showed in figure 2 points out such issues as differences in mentality or cultural diversity as advantages. Around 20% of those being surveyed stress these postive aspects. In those parts of Malmö and Copenhagen that are closest to the bridge, daily life is now characterized by a mixture of Danish and Swedish culture and nationality. In the Malmö district of Limhamn-Bunkeflo, 4% of the population is now Danish. One of the schools in the district has even introduced a class where Danish and Swedish children are taught both the Swedish and the Danish language in addition to the history and culture of the two states[74]. It can be stated that the closest neighborhoods to the bridge are quickly developing into a unique melting pot of Swedish and Danish culture. This issue is, however, more complex and reflects a constructivist approach, highlighting the evolution and process of social interactions and taking into consideration both cooperation and conflict-ridden issues. The Copenhagen-Malmö melting pot can reflect the regional divisions overall.

The culture and identity clashes can be traced back to pejorative nationalistic discourse. For instance, one of the Swedish nationalist parties – the Sweden Democrats (*Sverigedemokraterna*), is involved in Scania and has inaugurated numerous campaigns in the province under the motto: "Keep Sweden Swedish"[75]. It was an important slogan during the election campaign in 2006. As a reaction to this, a member of the nationalist Danish People's Party (*Dansk Folkeparti*) announced in 2007 that Scania, Halland and Blekinge should be reunited with Denmark, if a corre-

---

[72] *Report by Øresundsbro Konsortiet, Facts worth knowing about...*, op. cit., p. 41.
[73] *Ibidem*, p. 36.
[74] *Report by Øresundsbro Konsortiet, Facts worth knowing about...*, op. cit., p. 46.
[75] M. Can, *I Sveriges namn (In the name of Sweden)*, "Dagens Nyheter", http://www.dn.se/nyheter/politik/i-sveriges-namn-1.116641, 28.09.2002.

sponding referendum were to return such a result[76]. This far right-wing party is also afraid that freedom of residence within the Nordic states will make it too simple for immigrants with Swedish residency permits to establish themselves in Denmark[77]. In response to that debate, the major regional newspapers: Helsingborgs Dagblad, Kristianstad Bladet and Norra Skåne carried out polls asking its Scanian readership about their nationality and Swedes about their readiness to return Scania to Denmark. The results of these polls revealed that about half of those surveyed favored Sweden, half Denmark[78]. In the larger national polls carried out by the Swedish newspapers Expressen, Svenska Dagbladet and Aftonbladet, about 50% of surveyed supported the suggestion that Sweden should give Scania to Denmark and 50% were against[79]. The least number of votes in the Scanian newspaper polls supported the alternative "neither country"[80]. This vision is compatible with the idea of secession in Scania[81]. It was in this province that the anti-refugee referendum took place in Sjöbo in 1988[82], thereby representing the xenophobia and racism that appeared in Swedish society.

The culture and identity conflicts can also relate to the competitiveness between Denmark and Sweden to be a leader in the region in general and thus giving Copenhagen or Malmö respectively an adequately important role. There are two major areas competing for the unofficial capital status: the Stockholm region (including six counties surrounding Lake Mälaren) and the Øresund/Öresund Region (Copenhagen and Malmö)[83]. There has not been an official Scandinavian capital since the 16th century, when Copenhagen ruled the Kalmar Union[84]. It can be seen as the trademark. According to brand communications strategist J. Stubbs, it is a powerful tool

---

[76] C. Olsson, *Han vill ge Skåne till Danmark (He wants to give Scania to Denmark)*, "Aftonbladet", http://www.aftonbladet.se/nyheter/article1514813.ab, 22.12.2007.
[77] P. O'Mahony, *Danish People's Party fears influx of Swedish immigrants*, http://www.thelocal.se/6239/20070129/, 29.01.2007.
[78] S.Å. Olofsson, *Skåne blir danskt?, (Scania becomes Danish?)*, "Helsingborgs Dagblad", http://hd.se/skane/2007/12/22/droemmar-om-stor-danmark/, 22.12.2007.
[79] K. Lund, *Svenskerne: Skåne hører til Danmark (The Swedes: Scania belongs to Denmark)*, "Politiken", http://politiken.dk/indland/article450166.ece, 23.12.2007. Compare with: *Resultat: Tycker du att vi ska ge bort Skåne till Danmark? (Poll results: Do you think we should give away Scania to Denmark?)*, "Aftonbladet", http://wwwc.aftonbladet.se/vss/special/storfragan/visa/0,1937,31033,00.html, 22.12.2007.
[80] S.Å. Olofsson, *Skåne blir danskt?...*, op. cit.
[81] J. Sorens, *The Cross-Sectional Determinants of Secessionism in Advanced Democracies*, "Comparative Political Studies", vol. 38, no. 3, 2005, pp. 304-326.
[82] G. Alsmark, *The lessons of Sjöbo*, [in:] G. Rystad (ed.), *Encounter with strangers. Refugees and cultural confrontation in Sweden*, Lund 1992, pp. 37-55.
[83] Narrowly defined, Scandinavia consists of Sweden, Norway and Denmark. Finland does not belong to the region in the linguistic sense because it represents the finno-ugrain family of languages. However, the broader definition encompasses Finland and its autonomic territory Ålands islands, stressing the genealogical and economic bonds with Scandinavia.
[84] A. Eames, *Worlds apart: The Danish-Swedish culture clash*, http://www.thelocal.se/11874/20080519/, 19.05.2008.

to reach foreign investors[85]. Moreover, a standpoint that distinguishes the division between Scandinavian and European division can justify Copenhagen-Malmö identity clashes in the past. It can be claimed that Swedish demarcation from continental Europe can be observed while Denmark is supposed to have stronger bonds with the continent. According to L. Trägårdh this phenomenon is based on the theory called: the "four Cs"[86]. Scandinavia is juxtaposed or opposed to capitalistic, conservative, Catholic and historically colonial Europe and Scandinavia is described as liberal, progressive, Protestant, and praising solidarity, equality, peace-ridden and social-democratic values. *Norden* – as a construct of Scandinavian countries – is seen as non-European, non-Catholic, anti-Latin, anti-imperialistic, and anti-colonial. Within the perspective of the Øresund/Öresund Bridge that unites physically two cities and enhances cooperation, it cannot deny the dissimilarities within the Danish and the Swedish cultures in a broad meaning.

Conclusions

A hybrid city of Copenhagen-Malmö represents the integration processes leading to the creation of one urban agglomeration as a result of opening to traffic the Øresund/Öresund Bridge in 2000. The uniqueness of these processes can be seen in the fact that essentially, military conflict did not take place between these cities (excluding Danish-Swedish rivalry over Scania mainly in 17th century). Consequently, conflict solution was not the main fundament for this integration but the mutual benefits focusing on the creation of "joint forces" of the main advantages of both cities. The strength of the Copenhagen-Malmö agglomeration is mostly a result of the highly-developed Scandinavian welfare states they are part of, where a well-prospering economy, political stability and the lack of a bigger crisis have on the whole boosted interurban integration. Denmark and Sweden build a platform of so-called Nordic solutions concerning mainly economy and politics which often other European states wish to follow. Any serious economical or political state disorders could influence these integration processes negatively. In this case, interaction at state level can be more influential for the Copenhagen-Malmö integration than regional efforts. Furthermore, Copenhagen and Malmö could be physically "integrated" due to technological and not political developments. These neighboring cities were not divided by political borders, lines of demarcation, fences, walls, informal rules or invisible lines but by the state borders formed on the Øresund/Öresund strait.

The different facets of the Copenhagen-Malmö integration are distinguished by the fact that both cooperation and conflict intervene according to the logic of the non-zero game. Integration phenomena can not be a synonym of cooperation. What

---

[85] D. Boman, *Viking clash: Danes and Swedes battle to be biggest*, http://www.thelocal.se/8835/20071018/, 19.10.2007.
[86] L. Trägårdh, *Sweden and EU*, [in:] O. Wäver, L. Hansen (eds), *European integration and national identity: the challenge of the Nordic states*, London 2002, p. 154.

is more, conflict is a crucial component of integration and should not be ignored in this analysis. As M. Velde and H. Houtum point out, the state borders should not just be seen as a physical phenomenon but also as a socially constructed demarcation line between "us" and "them". That is why the labor market on the other side of the bridge, for example, can be physically near but perceived as distant[87].

These two foreign cities with dissimilar historical, cultural origins and political, economic or legal systems have been linked with a bridge since 2000. These cities inevitably have common interests but also a different national perspective concerning the role in the region. Cooperation processes are most visible in enhanced business competition, common working labor and housing markets, commuting and transport advantages or education and science partnerships. Conflicts and barriers remain: the adjustment of legal solutions concerning e.g. unemployment benefits, taxation, pension, social security and health systems, voting privileges, different languages and currency or national minorities as well as identity clashes.

The constructivist methodology allows the emphasis of integration as a flexible process – a practice that fluctuates and is concerned mainly with social norms and values or identities-building processes, as well as legal or materialist matters. Therefore, it is possible to redefine the observed unification of Copenhagen and Malmö underlining that a new "CopenMalm identity" is being established. It is composed of the key concepts such as a unique melting pot, an innovative Nordic hub in terms of economy, logistics and transport, the Northern European Centre or the gateway to the Baltic and Scandinavia. These components form a new level of social norms and values based on mutual dependence. The specific historical interdependence of Denmark and Scania or decentralization and regionalization processes observable in this province also reveal interesting fundamental aspects of the Copenhagen and Malmö integration and identity-building processes.

---

[87] M. Velde, H. Houtum, *The threshold of indifference. Rethinking immobility in explaining cross-border labor mobility*, "Review of Regional Research", vol. 24, no. 1, 2004, pp. 39-49.

Tornio-Haparanda
A Unique Result of Neighboring Towns' Collaboration
Tomasz Brańka

Two towns located on the border between Sweden and Finland – Haparanda and Tornio – can serve as a significant and unique example of cities' trans-border cooperation. The number of common procedures established between these communities has been continuously growing since the 1960s and is carried out in almost all administrative sectors and present in each aspect of everyday life. When facing some challenges resulting from belonging to two states, with three languages, two currencies, and different time zones – among other things – the authorities as well as common citizens tend to exploit the opportunity given by towns neighboring. The paper examines in brief the history of the region, basic facts about Tornio and Haparanda, and focuses on common initiatives undertaken between the two cities and major challenges they have to face.

Terms

In the literature different terms are used to describe the situation of cities (towns) separated by an international border. Reference is often made to "twin towns", "double towns" or "divided towns"[1]. "Twin towns" refer to the cities that may be geographically distant but engaged in various forms of cooperation; "double towns", sometimes also called "couple towns", are characterized by a relationship of complementarity and substitution, which is not necessary linked with the existence of an international border. "Divided towns" put an emphasis on *division*, which implies some enforced separateness[2]. However, the Haparanda and Tornio case can be best described by the term "neighboring towns". The cities in question are separated only by a narrow strip of grass and wetland yet they have never been united, even if now they are separated by an international border. Additionally, the border has become more "porous" and is not perceived as an obstacle any more due

---

[1] *Neighbouring Cities and Towns Divided by an International Border. Final activity report*, Steering Committee on Local and Regional Development, Council of Europe, Strasbourg, 1 October 2002, p. 6.

[2] Definition from: ibidem, p. 6. Depending on classification and authors the number of towns that could be treated as neighboring towns exceeds 100 across Europe. See: ibidem, p. 6.

to numerous bilateral agreements and complex political decisions (e.g. European integration)[3].

Basic facts

The cities of Tornio in Finland and Haparanda in Sweden are located in northern Scandinavia, within the area which is the essential part of the northern Gulf of Bothnia, extending from Raahe to Piteå, in its center. Tornio and Haparanda are situated on the opposite sides of the River Torne and are connected by a bridge. The peripheral position of the towns can be perceived as a positive factor affecting the establishment of closer cooperation as it forms the basis for the "need to unite"[4].

Haparanda in Finnish is known as Haaparanta, while Tornio in Swedish – as Torneå. The name Tornio is probably derived from Finnish word which means "tower-y". Haparanda is composed from words "aspen" and "river bank" and means "aspen beach".

As a result of historical processes ethnical composition of the region is quite complex. T. Lúnden and D. Zalamans distinguish four groups within the population of the southern part of the Torne Valley:
1) Finland Finns, living in Tornio and on the eastern side of the river, speaking a local dialect of modern Finnish, 'tornion murre'. They mostly have no or little knowledge of Swedish, with the exception of higher officials and people with particular jobs or interests across the border;
2) Sweden Swedes, living mainly in the urban area of Haparanda municipality. Some are descendants of the urban population of merchants and traders who were mainly Swedish-speaking, others are officials, teachers, etc. They mostly have no or little knowledge of Finnish;
3) Torne Valley inhabitants on the Sweden side, speaking Swedish and, more or less fluently, Finnish/Meänkieli. Some live in the urban area of Haparanda, but they are more numerous in the rural areas and municipalities further north;
4) Sweden Finns, living in the urban area of Haparanda, mostly immigrants from Northern Finland (including the Finnish part of the Torne Valley) who have settled in Haparanda having lived in southern Sweden as laborers. Many of them have little or no command of Swedish[5].

---

[3] Some authors claim that a border like that has changed into a *mere cartographic marker*. See: *Doing Research in Human Geography: Some ethical and methodological concerns*, A lecture given at Ylitornio, New Dynamics of ethnic and regional policy in the Nordic Periphery, 4th-15th of October 2004.
[4] R. Kosonen, K. Loikkanen, *Twin cities or paired border cities. Three case studies from the Finnish border*, Helsinki School of Economics, p. 26.
[5] T. Lundén, D. Zalamans, *Local co-operation, ethnic diversity and state territoriality – The case of Haparanda and Tornio on the Sweden – Finland border*, "Binational Cities" a special issue of "Geo Journal", vol. 54, no. 1, 2002, p. 36.

Figure 1. Basic figures on Haparanda and Tornio

Facts	Haparanda	Tornio
Founded	1842 (by Karl XIV Johan)	1621 (by Gustaf II Adolf)
Area	918 km²	1,348 km²
Inhabitants	10,200	22,500
Population density	11.1 per km²	16.7 per km²
Number of companies	App. 800	App. 1,150

Source: Statistic Sweden; Land Survey of Finland 2008; Population Register Center of Finland; Statistics Finland's; R. Nousiainen, *Haparanda-Tornio: International Meeting Place. From Vision to a Common City Centre with the Help of Urban Planning*, 2007 EFMD Conference on Public Sector Management Development, Madrid, 20-22 June 2007. Note: numbers counted for municipalities.

History

Tornio and Haparanda share a long history, even though they have never been united. The delta of the Tornio River has been inhabited since the end of the last ice age, and is one of the oldest stationary dwelling places found in all Scandinavia. Consequently, the theory that the region was only "colonized" in the Viking Age and inhabited since then was abandoned. A great written account of the blossoming place was given in 1519 by Olaus Magnus, a traveler, later a bishop of Sweden-Finland, who visited the market in Tornio. According to his description: "*This town has an extremely beautiful and advantageous position, and no other market place in the whole region as far as to the North Pole is as much visited as this town of Tornio. The Belorussians, the Laplanders, the Finns, the Swedes, hucksters from southern Finland and Sweden assemble here. Furthermore a great many of hucksters from Norway come here over the high mountains and across the wide wilderness*"[6].

Tornio got its town charter from Swedish King Gustaf II Adolf in 1621. The charter can serve as a proof that Tornio itself was the core of all trade in Lapland throughout the 16th century. At that time it was one of the largest merchant towns in the North and ranked as the richest in Swedish realm. During the 18th century Tornio gained international attention and was visited by several expeditions from Europe, who came to discover the Arctic.

The Lapland trade Tornio depended on started to decline in the 18th century and the Tornio harbor had to be moved downriver twice due to the rising of the land (post-glacial rebound), which made the river too shallow for navigation. However, the greatest blow to the town's wealth came with the war between Sweden and

---

[6] Translated in: R. Nousiainen, *Haparanda-Tornio: International Meeting Place. From Vision to a Common City Centre with the Help of Urban Planning*, 2007 EFMD Conference on Public Sector Management Development, Madrid, 20-22 June 2007.

Russia in 1808. Until 1809, Finland was an integral part of Sweden and the Torne River valley was situated within the Swedish Province of Västerbotten. With Sweden's defeat in the 1808-1809 war against Russia, one third of the country's territory was lost. According to the peace treaty, the whole of Finland, the Åland Islands and an area in the north defined by the Torne, Muonio and Könkämä rivers plus the town of Tornio (situated west of the Torne river) would form the new Grand Duchy of Finland with the Russian Czar as Grand Duke[7]. Consequently, the new border was not drawn following the ethnical but territorial principles along the Torne River.

The border was drawn across the deepest channel of two rivers: Muonio and Tornio, and split Lapland in two hurting the trade. The new territorial division also left an extensive area of Finnish speech on the Swedish side. The Finnish language, totally different from Swedish, was used for religious services and for the teaching by local priests (including teaching reading) in the Finnish-speaking areas. Public administration was entirely in Swedish, but this rarely affected ordinary people. Consequently, for more than half a century, the Swedish Government used the Finnish language for contacts with the local rural population, for education and for religious services. However, by the 1880s the Swedish attitude towards the area began to change. Integration into Sweden was seen as a goal then. The whole school system was reorganized, and the recommended language policy was one of 'Swedish only'[8].

As Tornio represented an important commerce center for the whole region the new border cut the connection to the western side. In order to guarantee the continuation of trade it was deemed necessary to build another town on the Swedish side of the new border. But – as Lundén and Zalamans put it – by 'voting with their feet' rather than by a political decision[9], the new town dwellers appeared in a small suburban village of Tornio – namely Haparanda, immediately south of the urban and state boundary. A new Swedish town received its city charter from the King in 1842.

On the other side of the border, Tornio was a sleepy garrison town during the Russian period. Trade only livened up during the Crimean War and the First World War, when Tornio became an important border crossing for goods and people.

After Finland won independence in 1917, Tornio lost its garrison and saw further decline although its population increased steadily. The town itself played no role of importance in the Finnish Civil War, but was the scene of some fierce street fighting at the onset of the Lapland War between Finland and Nazi-Germany. The quick liberation of the town by the Finnish forces probably saved it from being burned down like so many other towns in Lapland. With Finnish independence

---

[7] T. Lundén, D. Zalamans, *Local co-operation...*, op. cit., p. 35.
[8] T. Lundén, D. Zalamans, *The Northern dimension – Transboundary regionalization in the Torne Valley. A case of cultural, ethnic, national and political division*, http://www.ut.se/teaduskond/Sotsiaal/Politoloogia/english/border/dzt (January 19, 2009).
[9] *Ibidem*, p. 35.

leading personalities on the Swedish side feared that the new state would claim its 'ethnic territory' on the Swedish side, but no serious attempts were undertaken[10].

At the end of the Second World War, northern parts of Finland were completely destroyed, while the Swedish parts were untouched[11]. Haparanda created new employment opportunities with the success of a local brewery Lapin Kulta and a stainless steel factory Outokumpu. Tourism across the border was another growing industry. The town became the educational center for Western Lapland. However, in the 1970s, the differences between towns decreased and a new form of cooperation was introduced.

Cooperation

The contacts have been intense over the years but there were no official agreements in the 1950s. The change came in the 1960s when the authorities of Haparanda and Tornio agreed to introduce common economic measures[12]. At the beginning the municipalities concerned mainly cooperated in the realms of culture and education, but a joint campaign was broadened to include a variety of social, environmental and healthcare issues, as well as technical infrastructure[13].

However, it was not until 1986, that the authorities of both cities launched a study project to investigate the possibilities for cooperation between the municipalities. The decision-makers of the cities were far-sighted, and long before the debate on Finland and Sweden joining the EU started, they had understood what benefits cooperation would bring. As a result of this study, *Provincia Bothniensis* (PB), a supranational cooperation organization between Tornio and Haparanda was established in 1987[14]. The main aim of the new body was to develop, extend and finally deepen the cooperation between these border cities. It was done by means of coordination and preparation of joint projects and initiatives of the city councils and governments of each town. Each side appoints five members for a municipal electoral period. The actual work is performed in working groups, which cover different fields (Figure 2). A bilingual paper – Kranni (*Neighbors*) is distributed to all households with information about the common development of the towns several times a year.

---

[10] T. Lundén, D. Zalamans, *Local co-operation…, op. cit.,* p. 35.
[11] D. Zalamans, *Mental and Physical Borderlines in the Baltic Sea Region,* http://www.indeosocres.spb.ru/zalam_e.htm (January 22, 2009).
[12] T. Bagoly, N.H. Carcary, T. Malmgren, M. Opolka, E. Rozhkova, *Lesson on Collaboration and Learning (LOCAL). A political, economical and educational perspective,* Report paper Nordplus 2003, p. 15.
[13] O. Damsgaard, K. Lähteenmäki-Smith, *Towards a New Regionalism in the North,* Structural Change in Europe 5, Cities and Regions Facing up to Chance, October 2007, p. 3.
[14] R. Ronkainen, S.-E. Bucht, *Tornio-Haparanda: a Unique Result of City Twinning,* 4th NRF Open Meeting in Oulu, Finland and Luleå, Sweden, October 5-8, 2006, www.nrf.is/Open%Meetings/Oulu%Lulea2006/HaparandaTornio%presentation.pdf.

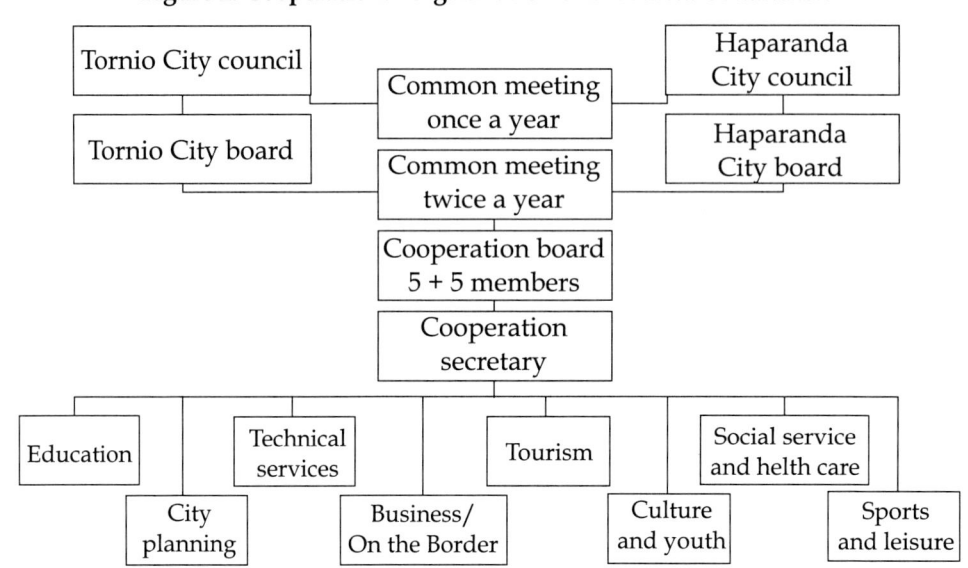

Figure 2. Cooperational organization of *Provincia Bothniensis*

```
Tornio City council                                    Haparanda City council
                        Common meeting once a year
Tornio City board                                      Haparanda City board
                        Common meeting twice a year
                        Cooperation board 5 + 5 members
                        Cooperation secretary

Education    Technical services    Tourism    Social service and helth care
      City planning    Business/On the Border    Culture and youth    Sports and leisure
```

Source: R. Nousiainen, *Haparanda-Tornio: International Meeting Place. From Vision to a Common City Centre with the Help of Urban Planning*, 2007 EFMD Conference on Public Sector Management Development, Madrid, 20-22 June 2007.

It is worth to mention that PB is by far not the only initiative in the region aimed at a closer connection of Nordic areas. During recent decades a number of organizations have been established in the Torne Valley with the aim of encouraging activities over the state boundaries[15].

One of those organizations is the *Bothnian Arc*, an organization uniting all the major towns from Luleå in the west to Oulu in the east with its offices now located in Haparanda. The body was established in 1998. The aim of the *Bothnian Arc* is to establish functioning regional cooperation between coastal towns and municipalities around the Gulf of Bothnia. This area contains the main industries of northern Sweden and Finland. The cooperation encompasses regional development in the fields of communication, environment and tourism, as well as the shared vision and community planning. The intent is to work towards increased exchange of goods, services and human contacts[16], and finally to develop a single unified competitive region.

Another organization, *The Torne Valley Council*, is the cooperation body for all the municipalities along the river boundary, including the Norwegian one. The Council is a discussion forum for all kinds of matters, especially the state decisions which will affect everyday life of the inhabitants in the Torne Valley. One spectacular outcome of these discussions is the fact that three Swedish municipalities (Haparanda,

---

[15] T. Lundén, D. Zalamans, *Local co-operation...*, op. cit., p. 37.
[16] *Setting up in Haparanda*, Haparanda Stad, www.haparanda.se/naring (20.01.2009).

Övertorneå and Pajala) 'illegally' declared they would join the European Monetary Union, something that the Swedish Government has not yet decided to do. The reason for this declaration was of course to facilitate the collaboration with the neighboring municipalities in Finland, but perhaps also to draw the news media attention to the problems of border exchange[17].

Finally, the Kemi-Tornio-Haparanda Development Agency (*Kotisatama* in Finnish) is a voluntary association formed by six municipalities at the base of the Gulf of Bothnia. The body focuses on the development of cooperation between these three cities and smaller neighboring municipalities.

Even if the cooperation within the region has been present for decades the membership in the European Union has created new conditions to implement concrete cross-border development projects and fasten further cooperation. In 1995, Haparanda and Tornio declared themselves to be one city, EuroCity[18], pointing at their strategically important geographical location in this cooperation across the northern national border[19]. The authorities of border towns were not troubled by the fact that there could be legal difficulties in joining two cities in two separate countries. "*We have always operated with the principle that first we do, then we see what Helsinki or Stockholm thinks about it*" Tornio mayor Raimo Ronkainen said[20]. One of the objectives is still to integrate the towns into a well-functioning whole, another is that the city center can develop a model for European cooperation between neighboring countries[21].

The cross-border cooperation is now oriented towards integrating the spatial framework and activities of the neighboring cities. Actually, even if EuroCity never became the success to the extent the authorities were hoping for, the list of several concrete results can be made, which also brought economic benefits to the towns (Figure 3).

The border cooperation focuses on five main areas:
– Vision and community planning;
– A cooperation organization;
– The labor market;
– Education facilities;
– Technical services[22].

---

[17] T. Lundén, D. Zalamans, *Local co-operation…, op. cit.*, p. 38. See also below.
[18] No formal name has been chosen for the united city so far, so the "EuroCity" has been used for the project's publicity. In other sources the name "Hapatornio" can also be found.
[19] *Setting up in Haparanda, op. cit.*
[20] Quotation in: *Tornio and Haparanda to join forces as Eurocity*, "Helsingin Sanomat", July 9, 2001.
[21] B. Brackhahn, R. Kärkkäinen, *Spatial planning as an instrument for promoting sustainable development in the Nordic countries. Action programme for 2001–2004*, Copenhagen 2001, http://www.lpa.dk/topmenuen/Publikationer/Andre_sprog/2002/planlaegning_som_instrument_i_Norden_uk.pdf, p. 16.
[22] *Setting up in Haparanda, op. cit.*

Figure 3. Agreements between Tornio and Haparanda

Joint use of Haparanda swimming pool, mid-1960s.
Agreement on joint sewage treatment plant, 1971.
Shared landfill, 1976-85.
Cross-border open school attendance at a comprehensive school level, 1978.
Provincia Bothniensis cooperation organization founded, 1987.
Joint language school, 1989.
Agreement on treatment of sludge from the sewage plant, 1990.
Fire and rescue service co-operation agreement, 1993.
Cooperation in ambulance services, 1993.
Agreement on the connection of district heating networks and deliveries of heat over the national frontier, 1993.
Agreement on joint use of ladder truck, 1994.
Privatization of the sewage treatment plant, 1996.
Merging of tourist offices, 1998.
Joint Euro senior secondary school, 1998.
Nursery agreement, 2002.
Refuse disposal, 2002.

Source: R. Nousiainen, *Haparanda-Tornio: International Meeting Place. From Vision to a Common City Centre with the Help of Urban Planning*, 2007 EFMD Conference on Public Sector Management Development, Madrid, 20-22 June 2007.

Concrete achievements include cooperation in cultural and leisure time activities; free school attendance across the border on all levels including vocational training, a common comprehensive school 'Language school' and an upper secondary Euro school; cooperation and joint investments in fire and rescue services; common sewage treatment plant; combining the district healing networks; combining tourist agencies; carrying out the redevelopment plan of the city bay.[23] It was estimated that thanks to joint initiatives in a public sector approximately 5 million Swedish crowns are saved every year[24].

Therefore, it can be said that local residents are already living in a united city as the cooperation is visible not only on an official level but also on a ground-level. There is a common bus crossing the border between Sweden and Finland, and both towns have installed letterboxes of the neighboring postal administration so that people can use them – with proper stamps – to send domestic rather than international mail[25].

---

[23] R. Ronkainen, S.-E. Bucht, *op. cit.*, p. 51.
[24] *Ibidem*, p. 20.
[25] T. Lundén, D. Zalamans, *Local co-operation...*, *op. cit.*, p. 38.

Undoubtedly, currently the most visible sign of close cooperation between the two towns is a construction of a new common city center in the border area. The project is known as a "På Gränsen" ("On the Border").

På Gränsen is a cooperative project to build a shopping and administrative center in the middle of the borderline between Haparanda and Tornio. Besides commercial services local residents will also find apartments, educational opportunities, jobs, culture and free-time options. The unique part of the project is also to build a common police station that would serve both towns. It would be the world's first police station between two independent states[26]. The process has been proceeding in phases, starting with an international architecture contest in 1996. The second phase was the development plan for the area, the third the implementation plan including both master plan and town plan. Construction started in spring 2005. The total area of the center is 12 ha, with 2/3 on Swedish and 1/3 on the Finnish side. It is expected that the shopping tourism will reach about 2 million yearly, and the new initiative will create approximately 1,800 new workplaces. The total budget of "On the Border" is EUR 200 million[27]. Only the infrastructure of the new downtown will be financed by the towns themselves. Funding has been sought from the European Union (through the INTERREG Programme) and private businesses, which should provide up to two thirds of financing[28].

However, it is important to mention that the project, initiated and mainly supported by the authorities of both communities, was not deeply welcomed warmly by in local residents on the Swedish side. In the fall of 2002, the plans were put at risk, when a slight majority of voters in Haparanda rejected the idea of a center to be shared with the town of Tornio in a referendum to accompany the Swedish Parliamentary elections. 53.1% of Haparanda inhabitants voted against the joint center with Tornio[29]. Those who opposed the "On the Border" initiative claimed that Haparanda should not afford to spend money on a project with a community in another country as long as important problems on the Swedish side need attention[30]. Despite the vote outcome, the local council still decided on pursuing the project. The authorities justified their decision with a low turnout: only about 50% of registered voters took part in the referendum, which meant that only about a quarter of the Haparanda population could be counted as opponents to the project[31].

---

[26] *Finnish Tornio and Swedish Haparanda to start building work on common city Centre*, "Helsingin Sanomat" April 28, 2004.
[27] P. Jukarainen, *The Attitudes of Youth towards the Other Side: The Finnish-Swedish and Finnish-Russian Borders*, [in:] D.E. Ganster (ed.), *Borders and Border Politics in a Globalizing World*, Lorey 2004, p. 139.
[28] *Tornio and Haparanda to join forces as Eurocity*, "Helsingin Sanomat" July 9, 2001.
[29] *Haparanda inhabitants do not want joint centre with Tornea*, "Nordic Business Report", September 16, 2002.
[30] *Finnish and Swedish border towns plan common city centre*, "Helsingin Sanomat", November 11, 2002.
[31] P. Jukarainen, *op. cit.*, p. 139.

The idea to construct a shared center is also based on strong economic assumptions. It was calculated that 14,000 vehicles cross the border line every day, meaning that the Customs station sees the passage of over 5 million vehicles and about 16 million persons annually[32]. In the whole area it is common to drive across the border to work, to do business or shopping. Even if the towns themselves have a total of 34,000 inhabitants, within the range of 150 km on both sides of the border half a million people live. When the range is stretched to 500 km it includes Russia and Norway. The total number of inhabitants in this area is over one million. The contacts should be facilitated thanks to the Barents Road opened in 2003. This 1,500 km road stretches from the Norwegian Atlantic coast to the Baltic Sea, and further to the north to Murmansk and the Barents Sea[33].

It is estimated that the total purchasing power in Haparanda and Tornio is approximately 2,200 million Swedish crowns (SEK) per annum (app. EUR 210,000). About 1,500 million SEK (app. EUR 145,000) is spent outside Haparanda and Tornio. Calculations show that purchasing power in the region is growing[34].

The success story can be observed on the example of IKEA, which in November 2006 set up its most northerly flatpack furniture store in Haparanda to attract the Finns, Norwegians and even the Russians. The effect has been described as *stunning*. Currently, the store is visited by 5,000 customers daily and the millionth customer crossed the threshold of IKEA 6.5 months after the opening. It is also worth to note that 75% of the customers come from Finland and the signage is both in Swedish and in Finnish[35]. Beforehand, Haparanda was struggling with 15% unemployment, a stagnant property market and a steady drift of its 10,000 residents to larger, more southern locations. Now, it is welcoming not only "shopping tourists" from northern Sweden, Finland, Norway and even Russia but also new companies and residents. Haparanda's economy grew by 10.8% in 2006, more than anywhere else in Sweden; unemployment has dropped to less than 4%; and house prices have climbed 40% in two years. IKEA[36] is followed by the most famous chains of stores in Sweden and Finland.

A challenge for economic cooperation between the neighboring towns emerged on January 1, 2002 with the introduction of Euro in Finland while Sweden rejected it in a referendum in 2003[37]. The fears that the change of the currency could negatively affect "shopping tourists" were soon dispelled. However, with typical Swedish attention to detail, the supermarket trolleys in some supermarkets were equipped with little calculators that helped customers navigate through the jungle of prices

---

[32] *Setting up in Haparanda*, op. cit.
[33] Barents Road, http://www.barentsroad.org/ (January 5, 2009).
[34] *Ibidem*.
[35] Haparanda Tourism, http://turism.haparanda.se/english/homepage.4.724fa9011b116c75428000324830.html (Januray 13, 2009).
[36] D. Lawrence, G. McIvor, T. Masters, *A thawing market*, "Financial Times", December 1, 2007.
[37] However, even before introducing Euro in Finland, there were two currencies: Swedish crown and Finnish marks.

during the transition period, as the prices were in three currencies – crowns, marks and euros.

At that time Haparanda gained wide attention as its Mayor Bengt Westman held a press conference in Brussels to announce that the euro would become a parallel currency, alongside the Swedish crown[38]. *"We will not wait for the rest of Sweden. Haparanda will move into the euro at the same time as the euro countries"* – said Westman in December 2001[39]. He was afraid that Sweden would suffer as a consequence of the wait-and-see policy. *"The crown has been a bigger currency than markka, but it will be a marginal currency compared with the euro"*. For obvious reasons Haparanda was not able to introduce euro individually, even though euro notes and coins are widely accepted in the town's shops. Haparanda also wanted to pay Finns working for the local council in euros, as they noticed that the Finns working in Haparanda had effectively taken a pay cut in 2001 because of the crowns' fall against the euro[40]. However, lawyers dissuaded the authorities from this solution, as it would breach an equality clause in the Swedish constitution[41]. However, the authorities and traders adapted to new conditions and currently the prices are displayed both in crowns and euros, and the town's budget is presented in the two currencies[42].

The "good practice" of trans-frontier cooperation is well illustrated in a sensitive area of education. Through a joint agreement between Tornio and Haparanda, there exists a comprehensive program of primary and secondary school education leading to bilingualism and open to residents of both towns[43]. Bilingualism is treated as a unique asset of Haparanda and Tornio. As the school says about itself: *"he clear focus of our school is in internationalism, a natural choice for a school located on the national border"*[44]. Free attendance to a comprehensive school has been possible since 1978 and the cities have a common language school in Haparanda, where instruction has been given in Finnish and Swedish since 1989. The curriculum of the school is a combination of the curricula of the Finnish and Swedish school systems. Thus, children grow up becoming bilingual and international at the same time as they develop roots in the community[45]. In autumn 1998, Eurolukio, the "Euro upper sec-

---

[38] Ch. Brown-Humes, *Swedish border town denied euro*, "Financial Times" (Special Reports), December 4, 2001.
[39] A. Petola, *Finally one currency*, Weiner Zeitung Online, www.weinerzaitung.au (December 21, 2001).
[40] On the Finish side, currency stability remains the main benefit of membership, D. Ibison, *Finland shows Sweden benefit of joining club*, "Financial Times", December 19, 2008.
[41] As the Swedish crown floats against the euro, staff might receive different pay for the same job.
[42] *Haparanda raises pirate flag over euro and Defies Swedish line*, "Helsingin Sanomat" July 5, 2001.
[43] However, for legal reasons the schools are located in Haparanda, as the Swedish school system is more liberal to commuters from abroad, see: T. Lundén, D. Zalamans, *Local co-operation…, op. cit.*, p. 36.
[44] http://www.suensaari.tornio.fi/lukio/index.php?Itemid=55&id=34&option=com_content&task=view (January 5, 2009).
[45] R. Ronkainen, S.-E. Bucht, *op. cit.*, p. 51.

ondary school", another unique institution started its activity. The aim is that students gain active skills in more than two languages and good opportunities for postgraduate studies both at Finnish, Swedish and European institutions of higher education and universities[46]. In 1998, the neighboring towns established the Eurocity Jobcenter, which provides private persons with information on employment and educational opportunities, and companies with information on operational opportunities and potential partners on the other side of the border[47].

Traditionally, sport is perceived as a strictly national issue that can draw visible borderlines. However, for practical purposes, Haparanda and Tornio share much of the sports and recreational infrastructure. When Haparanda and Tornio began developing their joint strategy for sports function, they agreed to avoid competitive investments[48]. As it was explained by Pekka Wimmer, sport services inspector for Finland's Province of Lapland: *"Here in Finland, in the Province of Lapland, we have such big municipalities in terms of area that it's not easy to organize the same sort of cooperation"*[49]. The best example can be observed on the "Green Zone" or "Tornio Golf Club". It is perhaps a unique golf course with 4 holes in one country, Finland, and the remaining 14 in another, Sweden. So, to hit all 18 holes players has to cross the border four times as the border follows the Tornio River which runs through the course.

Challenges

On the official side, the municipalities of the two towns show great willingness to cooperate in order to strengthen the position of the area. However, *Provincia Bothniensis* is sometimes criticized for being too hierarchical and top-bottom organized[50]. It was pointed out that even the key-project "On the Border" did not come from business itself, but was politically induced by the PB. In fact, the cooperation between private companies from Haparanda and Tornio is still weak. It can explained by the differences in tradition and size of companies, language problems, and personal antagonism[51]. The result of the Swedish referendum of 2002 could also serve as a proof that the Swedes living in Haparanda fear for being swallowed by larger Tornio and Finnish language and culture[52].

Despite Nordic peaceful coexistence the last 200 years of national politics have created nationalist and separatists consciousness expressed by youths[53]. Even if the

---

[46] In 2001 Eurolukio produced its first graduates, 19 Finns and 5 Swedes.
[47] R. Kosonen, K. Loikkanen, *op. cit.*, p. 11.
[48] K. Gerkman-Kemppainen, *Exercise without Borders*, Tornio Tourist Office 2003, p. 18.
[49] Quoted in: *ibidem*, p. 19.
[50] D. Zalamans, *Mental and Physical Borderlines...*, *op. cit.*
[51] D. Zalamans, *Transboundary regionalization. The case of Haparanda and Tornio*, [in:] G. Bucken-Knapp, M. Schack (eds.), *Borders Matter: Transfrontier Regions in Contemporary Europe*, "Border Studies Series", no. 2, Aabenraa 2001.
[52] L. Haininen, T. Rostoks, *Report from the Workshop on Governance in the North*, p. 7.
[53] P. Jukarainen, *op. cit.*, p. 138.

national border is becoming more and more porous, the mental one will pose a serious barrier to further cooperation and development of the border region identity. According to the research by Pirjo Jukarainen among the youth both in Haparanda and Tornio, the respondents found far more to complain about than to cherish in their neighbors. However, these attitudes were not based on any deep fundamental ethnic antagonism and the youths take the openness of the border for granted[54].

Consequently, the resistance to further cooperation comes both from the "above" and the "below". The "below" level operates on a traditional way of thinking 'what is good for them is bad for us'. In other words a win-lose model prevails. The cooperation is then limited by the lack of interest in politics in general. There can also be some remnants of thinking in national stereotypes as a result of earlier nationalist indoctrination, mentioned above with reference to the youths. The "above" resistance is however more structural. Much of the new state legislation is passed without consideration of its border effect[55]. It is emphasized that the decisions taken in Stockholm and Helsinki do not pay enough attention to special cases like the neighboring towns.

Despite a long history of cross-border cooperation, important obstacles to greater cross-border labor mobility exist, such as language problems and the lack of knowledge about employment systems. In response to these types of problems, as it was mentioned, employment offices in both towns have come together in a joint project to promote greater labor mobility. The project has resulted in a significant increase in two-way labor mobility. The employment offices have also organized seminars for employers and job seekers on tax legislation, unemployment benefit rules and social issues in both countries. The result of the project has been a 15% increase of job seekers finding a job abroad[56].

* * *

The Administration of Haparanda-Tornio has adopted a new vision up to 2010, according to which Haparanda-Tornio is about to become an international center in the Bothnian Arc and Barents Region; a meeting place for cultures, knowledge, logistics, innovation and people. The aim of decision-makers and officials in Tornio and in Haparanda is to be the forerunners of the frontier cooperation also in the future. As it was described by the Mayors of Tornio and Haparanda: *"We are now creating a new kind of working pattern in which the frontier, which used to be regarded as a barrier, has been turned into a resource, a resource which will offer new opportunities for the development of the regional"*[57].

---

[54] *Ibidem*, p. 140.
[55] T. Lundén, D. Zalamans, *Local co-operation…, op. cit.*, p. 42.
[56] *Eurocity, Practical Guide to Cross-border Cooperation, C6 Education*, Training and Labour Market Development, AEBR, 2000, www.aebr.net/publikationen/pdfs/Lace_guiden.ed.pdf, p. 146.
[57] R. Ronkainen, S.-E. Bucht, *op. cit.*, p. 51.

Map 1. Tornio-Haparanda

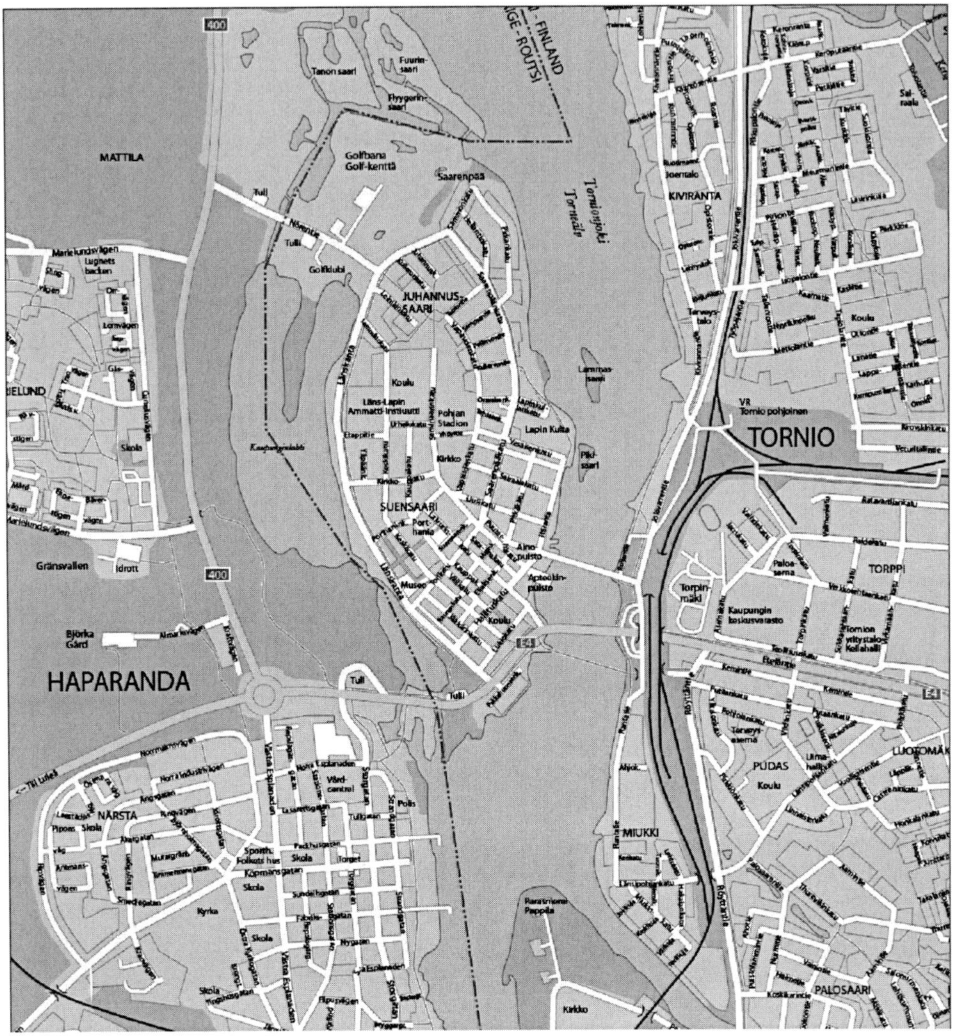

Source: www.eurotourism.com.

Berlin
Urban Imagery in a Former No-man's Land
– the Wall Strip Two Decades Later
Alexander Tölle

> *Wie oft hab ich mir die Sehnsucht, wie oft meinen Verstand,*
> *wie oft hab ich mir den Kopf an dieser Mauer eingerannt.*
> *Wie oft bin ich verzweifelt, wie oft stand ich sprachlos da,*
> *wie oft hab ich sie geseh'n, bis ich sie schließlich nicht mehr sah!*
>
> Mein Berlin, Reinhard Mey 1991[1]

Introduction: The Berlin Wall as an element of urban identity

Twenty years ago, on 9th November 1989, the Berlin Wall became passable for East German citizens, making obsolete what had until then been one of the most effective and appalling border control systems that has ever divided a city. The fall of the communist regime and the unification of Germany as well as of Berlin followed in the subsequent year, and the Berlin Wall as a physical structure quickly disappeared from the urban landscape, demanding decisions on how the resulting urban void was to be integrated into the cityscape. With the Berlin Wall having become inseparable from the city's identity during the more than 28 years of its existence[2], the interesting question is what its former space tells about the "new" unified Berlin today. While a place never has an identity in itself but is attributed an identity in people's minds, it may well be characterized by certain features that are recognized selectively by certain individuals or groups, thus influencing their process of identity building connected to a place[3]. As Ashworth has pointed out, the image-generating product is never a historic place in itself, but the experience of this place, which in turn is a result of interpretation[4]. Hence evoking or suppressing elements

---

[1] How often I have been running with my longing, how often with my sanity,
How often I have been running with my head against that wall.
How often I have felt desperate, how often I have been standing there at a loss for words,
How often I have seen it, until I finally stopped seeing it anymore!
[2] B. Ladd, *The Ghosts of Berlin. Confronting German History in the Urban Landscape*, Chicago–London 1997, p. 37.
[3] D. Ipsen, *Raumbilder. Kultur und Ökonomie räumlicher Entwicklung*, Pfaffenweiler 1997, p. 151; P. Weichhart, *Raumbezogene Identität. Bausteine zu einer Theorie räumlich-sozialer Kognition und Identifikation*, Stuttgart 1990, p. 22.
[4] G.J. Ashworth, *Realisable Potential but Hidden Problems: A Heritage Tale from Five Central European Cities*, [in:] J. Purchla (ed.), *The Historical Metropolis. A Hidden Potential*, Cracow 1996, p. 41.

of local history in urban revitalization processes always means the production of urban imagery determining urban images that represent a place in spatial, economic, social, and cultural terms. The crux lies, as Strauss has formulated it, in the time dimension of the interpretation process: urban images *"develop out of the contributed perspectives of various important sectors of the city's population as they have experienced the city during its past"*[5]. Due to the intertwined and subjective character of these processes, urban imagery production frequently results in conflicts[6] that may surface as clashes of interest between political decision makers, members of the business community, local elites, and different parts of the local community, and also as inconsistencies in the urban space.

This being a problem in any given pluralist urban society it becomes an even larger one in a city such as Berlin with a once split and even physically divided population, especially as its prominent situation on the world's political stage has in addition led to multiple forms of external perception. Hence this article – after having looked at what the construction of the Wall in 1961 meant for the city, its urban spaces, and its citizens – first elaborates on the extent to which the Wall dominated the ambiguous self-identity of the Berliners as well as the external images of the city evolving over time. The following chapter addresses the identity crisis of Wall-less Berlin as the city's development did not follow the expected "natural" track to quickly becoming the coherent heart of a happily unified nation. It looks then at chosen case studies of former Wall strip sites and discusses how far the urban imagery produced there reflects the conflicts and different concepts of identity in 21st-century Berlin.

Border spaces

The Berlin Wall was undoubtedly the most brutal and uncompromising of the demarcation lines of the Cold War. In 1945, when Berlin was divided into four occupation sectors by the victorious allied forces, once insignificant administration borders between city districts were transformed into borders between different ideological worlds. With tension increasing between the French, British and US governments on one side and the Soviet Union on the other, the demarcation line between West Berlin territory and the districts of East Berlin as well as the municipalities in the Soviet Occupation Zone bordering West Berlin (and becoming the German Democratic Republic in 1949) became more and more impermeable. In a climate of increasing aggression and confrontation any negotiations concerning border readjustments even on a minor local scale were impossible, so the line between the Western and the Eastern hemisphere cut right through different urban landscapes with no regard for historic traces or functional connections: through streets and places, waterways and bridges, parks and cemeteries.

---

[5] A.L. Strauss, *Images of the American City*, New York 1961, p. 33.
[6] W.G. Holt, *Distinguishing Metropolises: The Production of Urban Imagery*, [in:] R. Hutchison (ed.), *Constructions of Urban Space*, Stamford (Connecticut) 2000, p. 226.

On 13th August 1961, the East German regime turned this border into a physical one by building a wall along it, leaving only few very well guarded holes – checkpoints – in it. As a structure, the Berlin Wall was originally indeed just a barbed-wired wall of bricks, but it developed over time into a sophisticated system of border fortifications. By destroying existing urban structures, a parallel second wall was built (the hinterland wall), and in between the "death strip", a large corridor of land brightly illuminated at night, with no vegetation or built structures apart from watch towers, an asphalted border patrol road and trenches intended to prevent vehicles from breaking through. Any refugee who might have reached that area was in risk of being shot without warning. The Wall itself in its final version (the so-called "Border Wall 75", i.e. the fourth generation of the Wall that replaced its more primitive predecessors from 1976 on[7]) was made up of concrete segments 3.6 meters high, with a concrete tube on top to stop anyone from climbing it.

So the Berlin Wall "*was in its essence less a wall than a controlled sequence of empty, visible spaces*"[8]. From the East, with few exceptions, even access to the area adjacent to the border strip itself – a so-called "protection zone" of approximately 100 meters width – was limited to holders of a special permit, i.e. "reliable" residents. Indeed – by keeping a close eye on their fellow residents and any suspicious behavior or activity as so-called "Volunteer Helpers of the Border Troops", a significant number of those residents became an effective part of the border control system[9]. Any urban development and life was deliberately driven away from those areas. In West Berlin, however, no measures were taken to limit the drastic effects of confronting the Wall. As the irregular and jagged border line ran through the city, even West Berliners could be surprised sometimes when they unexpectedly bumped into the Wall, being warned possibly only by a laconic traffic sign stating "beware of dead-end street with no U-turn possibility for large vehicles". Nevertheless the sheer proximity of the Wall had a paralyzing effect on its adjacent city areas, turning even once central and vibrant city locations into peripheral and somewhat bizarrely forsaken areas.

Living in the divided city

In divided Berlin, through a process of "adaptation and repression"[10], people in East and West had no option but to come to terms with the realities and to organize their personal life in their respective halves of the city by turning their backs to the Wall and anything behind it. Still, there can be no doubt that it always dominated

---

[7] T. Fleming, H. Koch, *Die Berliner Mauer. Geschichte eines politischen Bauwerks*, Berlin 2001, p. 82.
[8] B. Ladd, *The Ghosts of...*, op. cit., p. 18.
[9] P. Feversham, L. Schmidt, *The Berlin Wall Today. Cultural Significance and Conservation Issues*, Berlin 1999, p. 112.
[10] T. Fleming, H. Koch, *Die Berliner Mauer...*, op. cit., p. 100.

people's minds – it simply was not possible to think "Berlin" without thinking "the Wall" at the same time. In effect its presence was to be felt in every place of the city: it gave an explanation to everything and above all to the city voids, i.e. all the places telling of a brighter past in both parts of the city. Gaps in West Berlin between once representative 19th-century houses at central city locations, derelict railway land in place of once vibrant and impressive railway terminuses, public transport stations either far to large for the current demand or closed and transformed into flee markets, or having become well-guarded ghost stations along West Berlin underground lines passing through East Berlin territory, or the area along the elegant boulevard of Kurfürstendamm which struggled to take over the function of a city centre for West Berlin – none of them had either flair or structure to be the heart of a big metropolis. In turn, the historic center of Berlin – the district of Mitte (Middle) – lay in the Eastern part of the city, yet bordered West Berlin on its western, northern and southern sides. As West Berlin was only a blank space on East Berlin maps – an *"Orwellian denial of reality [that] was symptomatic of attempts to normalize a bizarre situation through the suppression of any kind of comparison"*[11] – the East Berlin city center had the strange look of a peninsula, and the two targets of creating the vibrant heart of a "Socialist City" and of discouraging people from even coming any close to the Wall area collided in an awkward way. And there were voids also in the eastern part of Berlin: derelict houses and brownfield sites along apparently once vibrant city boulevards and squares were added to vast empty areas created by socialist building conditions (whether as a result of the lack of property value as a regulative force or of the lack of socialist building capacities).

The presence of the Wall in people's mind expressed itself also in the appearance of mental peculiarities. In 1973 an East German psychiatrist who had fled to the West published a book about "The Berlin Wall Disease" with case studies of former patients suffering from depression and other psychological disorders whose causes could be attributed to the very existence of the Wall perceived as a paramount symbol of control[12]. By East Berliners, the Wall was perceived less as a division of their city – as its Western half became an inaccessible and therefore unreal territory – but more as a structure to deprive them of the freedom to travel and thus to decide about fundamental issues of their personal life. They felt walled in, and so did the people of West Berlin – even though they had the possibility to calm down their colloquially called "Wall tantrum" by traveling West.

The Wall and the city's identity

City identity – or rather the lack of it – was an issue in Berlin long before the division. One may claim that Berlin lost its identity already after Prussia had been ab-

---
[11] P. Feversham, L. Schmidt, *The Berlin Wall...*, op. cit., p. 120.
[12] B. Ladd, *The Ghosts of...*, op. cit., p. 28; T. Fleming, H. Koch, *Die Berliner Mauer...*, op. cit., p. 100.

sorbed by Germany in 1871. The city may have risen to the capital of the German empire and to a metropolis of world standing, yet it never became a source of identity for the German people, and thus somehow remained *"without a firm shape or definition – an unfinished capital in the middle of an unfinished nation"*[13]. With the shift of the state borders in 1945, this always East- rather than West-looking city lost its ancestral hinterland (East Prussia, Silesia, Pomerania), which was once the predominant source of its population and vitality. This loss was at first plastered over by the quick sequence of dramatic events: the four-power control structure and its downfall, the blockade of West Berlin, and the following years with West Berlin being a front post of Western democracy in the Cold War as well as an open door in the Iron Curtain. So it was only after the construction of the Wall that some normalcy set in – yet, as Merrit rightly points out[14], this was no returning to a former state, but a new state being created after years of hyper-excitement. And with the construction of the Wall the search for a mission for the city turned into a permanent cause. As Engert described it back in 1985: *"Today the city is looking for a function. It knows what it was, but it still does not know what it is, let alone what it will be"*[15]. And in that process the Wall – the most famous structure of the city – played a decisive role: *"the wall became inseparable from the city's identity"*[16]. In the perception of a "front city" of Western democracy, the Wall was originally interpreted as a defeat: Western powers had not raised a finger to stop this violation of human rights. Yet over time, Berlin and the Wall developed into a symbol of justice for the cause of German unity. The interpretation was that it was only by force, i.e. by a cruel and absurd structure, that the "unnatural" division of Germany could be upheld, thus the "natural" state of Germany was that of a single nation[17]. The Wall signified both division and unity, of Germany as well as of Europe.

At the same time it was also a symbol of shame, figuring not only in frequently repeated official political statements from the West about the East German regime that had to wall in its citizens who would otherwise flee from them. The division of Germany was a result of the Second World War, which was a result of Nazi Germany's aggression. From this perspective, the Wall was a symbol of[18], and possibly even a just punishment for, German megalomania. The Nazi atrocities, unprecedented and inconceivable in their extent, were followed by the construction of an unprecedented and inconceivable border control system right across a city. In addition, the Wall was protected not by Red Army soldiers or any other foreign force, but by obliging Germans. And there was another point to feel ashamed of, especially on the Western side: a growing indifference towards the other half of the city.

---

[13] J. Engert, *Berlin between East and West: Lessons for a Confused World*, [in:] R.L. Merritt, A.J. Merritt (eds), *Living with the Wall. West Berlin, 1961-1985*, Durham 1985, p. 150.
[14] R.L. Merritt, *Living with the Wall*, [in:] R.L. Merritt, A.J. Merritt (eds), *Living with the Wall. West Berlin, 1961-1985*, Durham 1985, p. 193.
[15] J. Engert, *Berlin between…, op. cit.*, p. 153.
[16] B. Ladd, *The Ghosts of…, op. cit.*, p. 20.
[17] B. Ladd, *The Ghosts of…, op. cit.*, p. 30.
[18] *Ibidem*, p. 38.

While it became possible, on the strength of the Quadripartite Agreement, to visit the Eastern part of the city from the early 1970s on, the unpleasant bureaucratic procedures, queuing, and a compulsory exchange of Western into Eastern marks were enough to deter Westerners from traveling East if they had no family contacts. Thus, knowledge about the other side was in most cases rather embarrassingly low, even though most Westerners probably also felt a certain humbleness knowing that life just a few hundred meters away, across a coincidentally drawn border line, was much harder in various respects.

Hence there was a significant East-West ambiguity of perception of the dividing line. Westerners could physically interact with the Wall e.g. by touching it, painting on it, walking along it, looking over it, or traveling through it. The latter was even a familiar part of life to every West Berliner when using the transit routes to West Germany. Such a journey provided an awkward insight into East Germany: at its beginning and end was a passage through kilometers-long border fortification spaces at the checkpoints, and in between lay a trip through a land without a right either to turn off the carefully post-signed transit routes or to talk to casual Eastern travelers at rest stops (let alone to meet there with friends or families)[19]. By contrast, for Easterners even the territory adjacent to the border was a no-go area. To them the very existence of the Wall seemed unreal, just as the existence of a land beyond it.

Despite this East-West ambiguity of perception of the Wall, there was one aspect that Berliners on both sides had in common: something that may be best described as "*emotional comfort in relation to the Wall*"[20]. To understand it, one has to remember that the need for safety belongs to the basic social needs of people concerning their spatial environment. This refers to safety of life and health, but at the same time to a need for a familiar and predictable environment that despite certain changes and creative impulses remains easy to interpret. Objects in urban space induce the creation of cognitive maps in people's heads to allow orientation in a geographical but also a psychological sense: In a simply recognizable environment one quickly feels at home, and even a complex and large territory appears small and manageable if well-structured by spatial elements on the cognitive map[21]. In this sense, the Wall did not only define the margins of one's space in a physical way, but in a psychological sense it stood for clear parameters and gave orientation in space as well as in life. It represented the reassuring stability of the built environment and of defining relationships: "*The lines were drawn, the issues clear-cut*"[22]. In the East the Wall stood not only for a control and surveillance state, but also for a system guaranteeing the provision of basic needs from cradle to grave, and at the same time protecting against Western evils such as unemployment, crime or drugs. And the Wall stood also for the special function of each half of Berlin as a showcase of the respective political system, meaning that both city halves could rely on a constant stream of public in-

---

[19] F.C. Delius, P.J. Lapp, *Transit Westberlin. Erlebnisse im Zwischenraum*, Berlin 1999, p. 24.
[20] P. Feversham, L. Schmidt, *The Berlin Wall...*, op. cit., p. 124.
[21] K. Lynch, *The Image of the City*, Cambridge (Massachusetts) 1960, p. 5.
[22] P. Feversham, L. Schmidt, *The Berlin Wall...*, op. cit., p. 122.

vestment: West Berlin got lashings of subventions for economic activities not viable there in economic terms as well as for investments in the cultural and transport infrastructure, while "Berlin – the capital of the GDR" was always preferred to other East German territories in the supply of building resources as well as everyday goods. So living in the divided city had undoubtedly also its comfortable sides.

The former Wall strip between normalcy, integration, remembrance, and musealization

Yielding to public pressure, on 9th November 1989 the East German government decided to open its checkpoints, and the euphoria that followed is hard to put into words. As Ladd notes, already since the very end of 1989 references to the Wall were spoken and written in the past tense, even though the concrete structure still existed at that time. So *"the concrete and the symbol were no longer the same thing"*[23]. This became most apparent in the early 1990s, when excitement about having become one unified people again was increasingly replaced by a growing sense of difference between Easterners and Westerners ("Ossis" and "Wessis"): the "wall inside our heads" became the way to describe these problems. At the core of the problem lays what Taylor has called the *"theft of hope"* as the last treachery of the Communist regime: *"Manpower and productive capital resources lost to the West in the postwar period were not coming back"*[24]. The city was far from "retaking" its seat between the European metropolises such as London and Paris, it rather had to compete in economic terms with West German cities like Stuttgart and Düsseldorf[25]. Hence Berlin without the (physical) Wall was not a coherent heart of a united nation; on the contrary, the identity of the city was again in a limbo. And again the Wall was the symbol of that division of Berlin as well as of Germany.

It is in this context that the fate of the physical Wall is to be seen. After 9th November 1989, the no-man's land of the Wall strip was deprived of its threatening function and – by removing its draconic fortification edifices step by step in the following months – transferred into a peculiar transit space between two city parts which evidently belonged together and at the same time just as evidently represented two different worlds. Crossing this urban void became an unspectacular part of everyday life, even though this space was of course everything but ordinary: *"The crossing of this scar appeared like a cut in a film sequence: city – nothingness – city"*[26]. And it was not for long that it remained a simple transition place between recon-

---

[23] B. Ladd, *The Ghosts of...*, op. cit., p. 10.
[24] F. Taylor, *The Berlin Wall. 13 August 1961 – 9 November 1989*, London 2007, p. 660.
[25] A. Tölle, *Berlin – eine mitteleuropäische Metropole in Grenzlage*, [in:] B. Breysach, A. Paszek, A. Tölle (eds), *Grenze – Granica. Interdisziplinäre Betrachtungen zu Barrieren, Kontinuitäten und Gedankenhorizonten aus deutsch-polnischer Perspektive*, Berlin 2003, p. 195.
[26] N. Schüller, J. Klein, *Zeit zum Nachdenken. Der Mauerstreifen – Potenziale einer "prominenten" Stadtbrache*, "DISP", vol. 156, no. 1, 2004, p. 10.

nected streets as people started giving a new meaning to this space by integrating it into their everyday routine, e.g. by walking their dogs or dumping waste, by biking and promenading, or by sun-bathing. And due to the mostly still intact asphalted border patrol road, the Wall strip created new links through the city and around its Western half which had never existed previously.

The re-conquering of the border strip was an unorganized process. After 1989, most people just wanted to get rid of the hated Wall as quickly as possible and thus to forget about the painful division. "It was not until after its disappearance that the Berlin Wall was perceived and understood as an unwanted monument"[27]; originally early proposals to preserve parts of it for future generations or to mark its former course in the city received little support. It appears that the physical disappearance of the border strip was seen as just a natural process leading to normalcy. It is noteworthy in that context that the Berlin City Development Corporation decided in 1992 against the elaboration of any strategic planning document for the former border strip as a whole, even though by that time numerous renowned architects and urban planners – notably in the course of an exhibition organized in 1991 by the Museum of Architecture in Frankfurt-upon-Main – had already developed designing visions, like e.g. turning the whole strip into a public precinct integrating the two city halves[28]. As a result, the urban imagery produced in the former Wall strip reflects today the results of separate decisions and numerous processes – sometimes controversial, sometimes quiet – with different individual actors and decision makers.

Places of "critically reconstructed" normalcy

In numerous places along the former border strip any trace of it has simply vanished. Roads have been reconnected, real estate has been re-privatized, and new buildings have been erected filling gaps between the existing housing stock. No one who has not known the situation before 1989 would suspect today anything strange here, even though it may be amazing how many little remnants (such as posts in the streets, transformer boxes, lamps once illuminating the death strip and now left to innocently light the streets, hinterland wall stretches now just fencing off some private property) are still to be seen by "insiders"[29]. In the inner city area of Berlin, the policy of recreating pre-war city structures (whether along the Wall strip or in other parts) was implemented along the "Critical Reconstruction" lines. This catchphrase, which dominated urban discussions in Berlin during the 1990s, describes the target of creating an urban diversity by a mixture of functions and new urban structures oriented along traditional settlement forms, i.e. the dense block structure.

---

[27] *Gesamtkonzept zur Erinnerung an die Berliner Mauer: Dokumentation, Information und Gedenken*, Berlin 2006, p. 6.
[28] The presented projects are published in: V.M. Lampugnani, M. Mönninger, *Berlin morgen. Ideen für das Herz einer Groszstadt*, Stuttgart 1991.
[29] A remarkable travel guide to these relics is: A. Klausmeier, L. Schmidt, *Mauerreste. Mauerspuren. Der umfassende Führer zur Berliner Mauer*, Berlin–Bonn 2007.

The idea was not to invent some "new" Berlin, but to try to restore the old city's splendor, lost not only as a result of the war but also of the following reconstruction measures in the modernist style in both halves of the city[30]. Even though "Critical Reconstruction" has often been criticized as an unreasonable attempt to turn back the clock – as Ladd has pointedly formulated it, it seems to reflect "*a memory of the 1920s without Nazis, Communists, and overwhelming poverty*"[31] – this philosophy dictated the planning guidelines for the inner city. So the restoration of old street and square outlines and the adaptation of new buildings to the existing ones in form and architecture dominated the guidelines for the numerous urban competitions and workshops concerning key city areas, and eventually also the "Inner City Planning Framework", an overall strategic planning document for downtown Berlin adopted in 1999.

The arguably best-known worldwide symbol of divided Berlin (if not Europe) – the Brandenburg Gate in the middle of annihilated Pariser Platz situated in the death strip – is a point in case here. In the context of vehement discussions of experts and politicians as well as the broader public during the planning process of 1992-1996, the finally fixed guidelines defined a historic restoration of the square space itself and a height limitation deriving from the pre-war conditions for the adjacent buildings to be constructed[32]. Even most functions have returned, i.e. the luxury hotel "Adlon", the Academy of Sciences, and the embassies of France, the United States, and the United Kingdom. No one visiting this vibrant place today is likely to experience any of its dramatic history as a border point. The same may be said about the perhaps best-known urban project in reunified Berlin: the twin squares of Potsdamer Platz and Leipziger Platz. However, here the political guidelines to design these places in accordance with their pre-war function and character were significantly weakened by the economic boom processes of the early 1990s. Today, these places rather represent modern city development determined by visions of international star architects and by the economic interests of world firms and investors. The urban layout – apart from the octagonal form of Leipziger Platz – and functions are different from those of the pre-war times, and public life has largely shifted from public places to cosy malls and plazas[33].

The cases of Pariser Platz and Potsdamer and Leipziger Platz may stand here as two extreme examples of the numerous and much less-prominent places where the former city layout has been restored. There are few examples where the Wall strip has been used to create new structures – notably the recently-opened six-lane motorway connecting the inner-city ring road with the motorway to Dresden located on nearly 10 kilometers of the former death strip along the Teltow Canal is an example of a pragmatic and rather prosaic conversion of the former border strip.

---

[30] H. Stimmann, *Das Gedächtnis der europäischen Stadt*, [in:] H. Stimmann (ed.), *Von der Architektur- zur Stadtdebatte. Die Diskussion um das Planwerk Innenstadt*, Berlin 2001, p. 24.
[31] B. Ladd, *The Ghosts of…*, op. cit., p. 230.
[32] Senatsverwaltung für Stadtentwicklung (ed.), *The Capital City of Berlin. 15 Years of Development Measures*, Berlin 2007, p. 59.
[33] M. Pabsch, *Zweimal Weltstadt. Architektur und Städtebau am Potsdamer Platz*, Berlin 1998, p. 121.

Places of integration

As has been said, in the early 1990s there were several proposals of transforming the highly symbolic value of the former Wall strip into a visible urban space integrating both city halves. While this idea has not been realized, there are still places where it has influenced the design of post-Wall city spaces. The most significant example is the Mauerpark (Wall Park) located at the fringes of Wedding and Prenzlauer Berg, two densely-built inner-city tenement districts. Already in 1989 the paucity of greenery there led to the idea of converting the ancient military and railway land, which started to be turned into the death strip in 1961, into an urban park. Opened in 1994, its design by the landscape architect Gustav Lange in the form of an artificial necklace of green hills as *"a metaphor of the border that once was"* originally provoked rather sharp criticism by both experts and the public[34]. Yet over the years the Mauerpark has developed into an urban space accepted to an astonishing degree by the youth, attracting volleyball and soccer players, jugglers, musicians, and many other types of people and freaks that can be classified as belonging to the city's subculture. This in turn makes it an interesting spot for Berliners as well as tourists. Its attractiveness for all groups is certainly based to a significant degree on its rather run-down state, due to neglect in maintenance as well as to extensive use. Its *"destroyed rawness"*[35] leaves this former border strip in the state of a void again, but it is this very feature of the Mauerpark – never planned intentionally by its creators – that has turned it into a social space of high integrative power.

A less prominent example of a green urban space on the former Wall strip is the Engelbecken between the inner-city districts of Mitte and Kreuzberg. This decorative place was designed in the 1920s, after the Engelbecken basin and the 19th-century canal as its centerpiece had to be filled in, but it lost its splendor in the war destruction and in 1961 was turned into the death strip. In 1993 it started to be redesigned as a green space including water elements referring to the former canal. On the former East Berlin side new residential buildings were erected following the historic building line, thus restoring the ancient urban layout to the place. Thus, the Engelbecken has also developed into an open space along the former border that brings people from both neighborhoods together, but in contrast to the Mauerpark an allusion to its legacy as part of the death strip has been given up in favor of redesigning its 19th- and early 20th-century splendor.

Places of remembrance

The probably most prominent place in which the "Critical Reconstruction" concept of returning to normalcy clashed sharply with the legacy of the Wall is the former Checkpoint Charlie on Friedrichstraße. This was the only checkpoint between East

---

[34] C. Girot, *Eulogy of the Void. The Lost Power of Berlin Landscapes After the Wall*, "DISP", vol. 156, no. 1, 2004, p. 35.
[35] *Ibidem*, p. 36.

and West Berlin for allied forces, and it captured the world's attention as the often cited "focal point of the Cold War" when American and Soviet tanks confronted each other there at gunpoint in October 1961. Here in 1962 the human rights activist Rainer Hildebrandt founded the private museum "House at Checkpoint Charlie" as an *"island of freedom in the last building right at the border"*[36]. Here escaped agents as well as former political prisoners from East Germany could get help and advice, and the exhibition displayed the brutal history of the construction of the Wall as well as of imaginative escapes, including exhibits like hot-air balloons, cars with secret hiding places, or trucks that had crashed through the border barriers. The idea was to prevent the plight of those trapped behind the Iron Curtain from slipping out of attention. Until today the museum and museum shop continue to attract large crowds, while the former Wall strip and checkpoint have vanished. The ground has been sold to an investor who wanted to use the well-known location to create an "American Business Center" there, yet because of financial difficulties some lots of this "critically reconstructed" area remain undeveloped. References to the border situation are reduced to a double line of cobblestones that mark the Wall's course in the inner city and replicas of the former U.S. army control hut and the famous quadrilingual "You are leaving the American Sector" sign, as well as some information boards. In 2004, the still privately run "House at Checkpoint Charlie" stirred public upheaval by implementing an art project next to its premises consisting of the erection of 200 meters of a Wall replica and 1,065 black crosses (each three meters high) – one cross for each victim of the German-German border documented in the museum. While most passers-by and notably tourists liked this form of making history felt in the urban space, the not coincidental allusion of this Wall memorial to the Holocaust memorial, whose field of 2,700 black concrete slabs (by the way, also located on a former Wall strip site near the Brandenburg Gate) was at that time nearing completion, made it unacceptable for the official Berlin as well as most media representatives. Any equation of East German crimes against humanity with Nazi atrocities was regarded as impossible[37], and the memorial was finally abolished by the Berlin municipality – against active protests of former East German political prisoners – in 2005.

This strong reaction against the private Wall memorial also stemmed from the fact that by that time Berlin had already had an official Wall Memorial, whose history started back in 1990 when the German Historical Museum fenced off a 200-meter-long section of the border fortifications at Bernauer Straße. Bernauer Straße was a street with typical five-storey tenement houses on both sides, along which the border between the districts of Wedding and Mitte – i.e. between West and East Berlin – happened to run, so that the pavement of houses standing in East Berlin was already West Berlin territory. Pictures taken there on 13th August 1961 went around

---

[36] K. Liebhart, *Authentischer Ort, "DDR-Disneyland" oder "Pendant zum Holocaustdenkmal"? Checkpoint Charlie und das Berliner Mauermuseum*, [in:] R. Jaworski, P. Stachel (eds), *Die Besetzung des öffentlichen Raumes. Politische Plätze, Denkmäler und Straßennamen im europäischen Vergleich*, Berlin 2007, p. 265.
[37] *Ibidem*, p. 267.

the world, showing people jumping out of upper windows into rescue nets of a West Berlin fire brigade while lower windows were being bricked by East German border units. During the 1960s all houses were torn down to clear the way for the death strip, leaving only the bricked ground-floor front facades that served as an outer Wall, as well as the inaccessibly situated Church of Reconciliation. Bernauer Straße was probably the most brutal example of the Wall, until in the 1980s the facades were replaced by the standard Wall construction – and the neo-Gothic church finally blown up. Since in the course of an urban renewal scheme of the late 1960s the tenement houses on the Western side had also been torn down and replaced by modernist blocks, the street had lost its special visual aura.

The plan to keep parts of the former fortifications to build a Wall memorial was heatedly debated for years. Some were against preserving anything of the former Wall at all; others wanted to solemnly commemorate the Wall's victims or all the victims of East German human rights violations. Still others promoted the creation of a more triumphant memorial devoted to the "*unbreakable unity of the German people*"[38]. To make things more complicated, there were claims of former land owners to get back their property (including the Sophien Congregation to get back the part of their former cemetery that had been converted into the death strip) as well as plans by the city's transport unit for a six-lane inner-city by-pass. A design contest organized by the City of Berlin together with the Federal State in 1994 did not produce any laureate, yet in the coming years one of the few entries fulfilling the specifications and aspiring to retain the authenticity of the original site was carried out. The architects Kohlhoff and Kohlhoff reconstructed a 60-meter-long death strip with all fortification items between two gigantic steel oblongs (inevitably reminiscent of the Iron Curtain from the outside). The memorial's inside can only be perceived through shadow gaps, and it is this very inaccessibility which, as Feversham and Schmidt rightly point out, is probably the strongest element preventing it from becoming "*a somewhat banal assemblage*" and turning it into "*an emotional rather than antiquarian object*"[39]. Opened in 1998, the Wall Memorial is part of an ensemble including the tiny clay structure of the Chapel of Reconciliation built on the site of the former Church of Reconciliation, as well as a Documentation Center for the History of the Wall in the former congregation house built in 1965 for the Western part of the divided congregation. The engagement of the Reconciliation Congregation in the public debates of the 1990s had undoubtedly helped today's Wall Memorial Ensemble to come into being[40].

Places of musealization

Public discussions about the Wall Memorial, which then somewhat escalated in the context of the Checkpoint Charlie debate, were a clear indicator of evident deficits

---

[38] B. Ladd, *The Ghosts of…*, op. cit., p. 32.
[39] P. Feversham, L. Schmidt, *The Berlin Wall…*, op. cit., p. 164.
[40] U. Braun, *Versöhnungskirche. Kapelle der Versöhnung in Berlin*, Berlin 2003, p. 38.

in the way the city dealt with its Wall legacy. In addition, there were constant complains of tourist organizations that next to nothing had been left of the Berlin Wall, which throughout its existence represented a twisted mixture of tragedy and tourist attraction[41]. Undoubtedly, the demolishment of the Wall meant the destruction of Berlin's most famous structure[42]. With tourism being one of the few economic growth sectors in Berlin, these aspects had to be taken seriously when dealing with the Wall, as in general the major image factor is not Berlin as a historic capital – as this is closely connected with both Nazi and Communist dictatorship – but rather Berlin as a city making history, which is more connected with the constant changes in time and with the visibility of those changes in the cityscape[43]. Indeed, its demure and unspectacular form of documenting the Wall's history as well as its location just outside central Berlin have left the official Wall Memorial slightly off the routes of tourists, who rather turn to Checkpoint Charlie or to the "East Side Gallery", a 1.6-km-long piece of a higher-than-usual hinterland wall along a busy six-lane street in the district of Friedrichshain (parallel to the Spree river constituting the actual border line) that was turned into a gallery of over 100 murals by international artists in spring 1990. Even though the place tells nothing authentic about divided Berlin, it has been listed for preservation and reminds paradoxically strongly of what the Wall once looked like from the Western perspective. Another famous tourist spot is a section of the original Wall fenced off at Niederkirchnerstraße. It owes its protection to the location next to the ruins of the former Gestapo headquarters (former Prinz Albrecht Palais) and to the continuous public discussions about the future shape of this site, currently used by a temporary open-air exhibition under the title of "Topography of Terror". In its decaying state, this site offers for view two authentic sets of ruins embodying, as Ladd describes it, "*the essence of their respective states: on the right, the place were bureaucrats planned terror and genocide; on the left, the German Democratic Republic's most famous creation and most terrible obsession*"[44]. While this spatial closeness of remnants of two different dictatorships has been complicating the quest for an adequate sustainable way of designing this site for decades now, the site has a strong appeal to visitors rather taking liberties with the complicated German history.

The evident deficits led in 2004 to the creation of a working group by the City of Berlin with the task to elaborate what was eventually called an "Overall Concept of Memorial Plans for the Berlin Wall: Documentation, Information, and Remembrance"[45]. This document – while acknowledging the irrevocably decentralized and non-homogeneous structure of the existing remains and places associated with the Wall – aspires to set the ground for connecting them in substantive terms by allocat-

---

[41] *Gesamtkonzept...*, op. cit., p. 12.
[42] B. Ladd, *The Ghosts of...*, op. cit., p. 37.
[43] I.F. Hurtado, *Zukunft zum Greifen nah. Bedingungen, Semantik und Verortung des Berliner Stadtmarketing*, "Berliner Blätter", 37, 2005, p. 28.
[44] B. Ladd, *The Ghosts of...*, op. cit., p. 166.
[45] *Gesamtkonzept zur Erinnerung an die Berliner Mauer: Dokumentation, Information und Gedenken*, Berlin 2006.

ing to each of these places specific meanings complementing one another[46]. The working group defined its task in the context of the general issue of reflecting the legacy and remains of the East German communist regime, a task that with a time gap of nearly one generation has slowly grown to be a less emotional one. The "Overall Concept" as adopted in 2006 unambiguously defines the Wall Memorial in Bernauer Straße, which is to be significantly enlarged, as the central place commemorating the Wall and its victims, complemented only by individual remembrance of victims on the spots related to their fate. By contrast, Checkpoint Charlie is seen as the place to document the Berlin Wall in terms of world politics and notably the Cold War between the superpowers, possibly in the form of a new museum. In addition, different sights are to be connected by a Berlin Wall Trail, along which individual historic memorial places – such as the famous crosses for Wall victims next to the Reichstag building – are to be supplemented by quadrilingual (not coincidentally German, English, French, and Russian) information signs telling the story of these places. The double line of cobblestones that marks the Wall's course in the inner city is to be extended, and new aspects are to be addressed, e.g. the "ghost stations", or the main West Berlin motorway checkpoint on the transit routes to West Germany. In the course of a step-by-step implementation of the concept, the Berlin Wall has become much more visible again in the urban space, though mostly in the form of restored relics and information elements. In this way, looking for "authentic" traces gets reduced to chosen aspects, and the city image is fragmented into selected themes, the Berlin Wall being one of them together with, e.g., "Berlin in the roaring twenties" or "Third Reich Berlin"[47].

Conclusion: Incoherent urban imagery

The results of urban imagery production along the former Berlin Wall strip are above all non-homogeneous, which comes as no surprise in a city that has often been described as patchy and inconsistent. Today the Wall area tells a story of a struggle between destruction and forgetting, and preservation and commemoration. There is no question that the image of the Wall area – with the Wall until today the best-known symbol of Berlin – is representative of the image of the unified city. The Wall strip speaks of a wish for a hasty return to normalcy, a normalcy interpreted as a "critically reconstructed" urban landscape referring to pre-war times. It also speaks of this "European City" concept being distorted by contemporary city development features dominated by developers' malls and office towers, as well as of broken investors' dreams leaving undeveloped sites, which stand for the broken dream of Berlin returning to global significance and economic wealth. With the official Wall Memorial Ensemble and the Checkpoint Charlie area being the most poi-

---

[46] Ibidem, p. 17.
[47] U. Zitzlsperger, *ZeitGeschichten: Die Berliner Übergangsjahre. Zur Verortung der Stadt nach der Mauer*, Bern 2007, p. 185.

gnant points in case, the Wall strip represents the difficulties of interpreting the past and its physical remnants in a once bitterly divided community in which the perception of the Wall differed utterly not only between East and West, but also between people loyal to the East German regime and those oppressed by it, people with contacts on the other side and those without, people suffering under the border regime and those becoming indifferent. Added to that are political interpretations of the Berlin Wall, evolving over time and influencing what the city and its best-known building structure stood for. In this respect the former no-man's land between East and West is also expressive of the dissatisfaction that followed the euphoria of unification, and of the ephemeral hopes of becoming a coherent capital of a homogeneous nation replaced by the "the wall in our heads" symptoms.

Yet two decades after the Wall came down, and with it the communist regime in East Germany, the time span seems long enough to allow a new form of urban imagery production: a rather professional and unemotional musealization of this city space. Authentic remnants are being restored, put into a chosen context and complemented by new information and artistic elements as well as what may best be described as "heritage trails" and "heritage centers". It appears that urban imagery production by professionally creating traces of the past in this way – allocating individual significance to different urban spaces in order to create an overall picture – has entered a new phase. The need to streamline information, documentation, and remembrance is clearly intertwined with the target of catering to tourists, for whom the image of Berlin is above all that of the Wall city. Hoffmann-Axthelm has once called the Wall "*a coherent description of the city through via negationis*"[48]. It is perhaps due to the new failure to assume an identity that the former Wall strip steps in again to define Berlin by what it is not, and in this sense the former Wall as a space as well as a symbol remains connected to Berlin's identity – or a search for it.

---

[48] D. Hoffmann-Axthelm, *Berlin: Schönheit der Stadt*, "Kursbuch", vol. 137, 3, 1999, p. 93.

Brussels
Cooperation in Theory, Conflict in Practice?
Tom Vandenkendelaere, Lien Warmenbol

Introduction

Very recently, the state of Belgium has had to deal with a severe political crisis. Existential questions are not new for a country that is mainly inhabited by two ethnic groups, the Flemings and the Walloons. Its federal structure today is very much a product of the quest for an adequate response to previous crises between its two main ethnic groups. The country is made up of three regions, in which three communities live mainly separated (see fig. 1), except in Brussels. The series of state reforms, of which the most recent one was introduced in 2008 after a number of open conflicts between the Flemish and Walloon major political parties, prove that existential questions are indeed never far away in Belgium and Brussels was definitely not spared from these either.

It is not a surprise either to say that, throughout Belgium's past, the capital city Brussels has always occupied a very important place in the debates. The city has given *lieu* to the very first revolts against the Netherlands that eventually led to the creation of the Belgian state in 1830 and ever since, its character has always been marked by a great symbolic value. Hooghe and Fitzmaurice are but two of the many authors confirming the particular position of Brussels[1]. As will be described more closely below, the city is not only inhabited by the country's two main ethnic groups, but these are obviously at the very heart of the city's particular constitution and both also have their specific reasons to consider Brussels as crucial for their own development and future: *"The Brussels issue reveals all the dimensions of a community conflict in Belgium: linguistically, Brussels is approximately 80 per cent French-speaking; culturally, it is the capital city and the political centre of the national government; ethnically, many residents have direct family ties with both Flanders and Wallonia; territorially, it is located within the Flanders region, north of the linguistic border"*[2].

As the capital of Belgium, the Brussels Capital Region indeed forms an enclave in the Flemish region and has the bilingual status. As a product of the state reform of 1970, the *Wet houdende organisatie van de agglomeraties en federaties van gemeenten* of 1971[3] and

---

[1] See e.g. J. Fitzmaurice, *The Politics of Belgium – A Unique Federalism*, London 1996, p. 125; L. Hooghe, *Belgium: Hollowing the Center*, [in:] U.M. Amoretti, N. Bermeo (eds), *Federalism and Territorial Cleavages*, London 2004, p. 55.
[2] M. De Ridder, L.R. Fraga, *The Brussels issue in Belgian politics*, " West European Politics", vol. 9, no. 3, 1986, p. 376.
[3] Law regarding agglomerations and federations of cities, free translation.

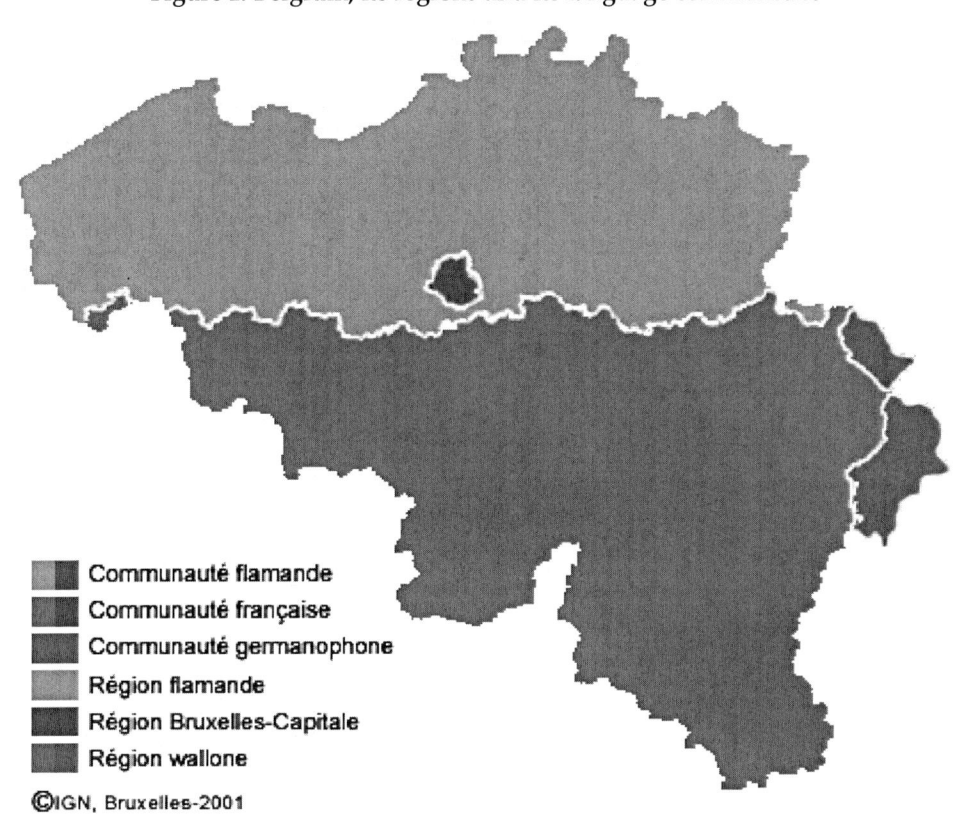

Figure 1. Belgium, its regions and its language communities

- Communauté flamande
- Communauté française
- Communauté germanophone
- Région flamande
- Région Bruxelles-Capitale
- Région wallone

©IGN, Bruxelles-2001

Source: Communauté française, *Présentation: Géographie*, http://www.cfwb.be/index.php?id=portail_geographie, 9.03.2009.

the *Bijzondere wet met betrekking tot de Brusselse Instellingen* of 1989[4], the Brussels Capital Region, to which we will further refer as 'Brussels' or the 'city', is made up of nineteen boroughs, each with a bilingual status[5].

The problems Brussels has been confronted with in the latter part of the twentieth century, are very much the product of its turbulent past. Brussels has been a Flemish city for long. Throughout the years, the city has been overruled by a French-speaking population, mainly in the 18th century under the influence of the French regime and in the 19th century due to the industrial revolution in Wallonia[6]. In the 1950s, Brussels was again at the centre of Flemish interests, as they had

---

[4] Special Law regarding the Brussels institutions, free translation – Belgisch Staatsblad, *De Brusselwet:* Bijzondere Wet van 12 januari 1989 met betrekking tot de Brusselse Instellingen.
[5] Centre de Recherche et d'Information Socio-Politiques, *Presentatie van het Gewest*, http://www.rbc.irisnet.be/crisp/nl/b3.htm, 4.02.2009.
[6] The industrial revolution took place earlier and was more successful in Wallonia than in Flanders; the latter relied on agriculture for a long time.

Figure 2. The Brussels Capital Region with its 19 boroughs

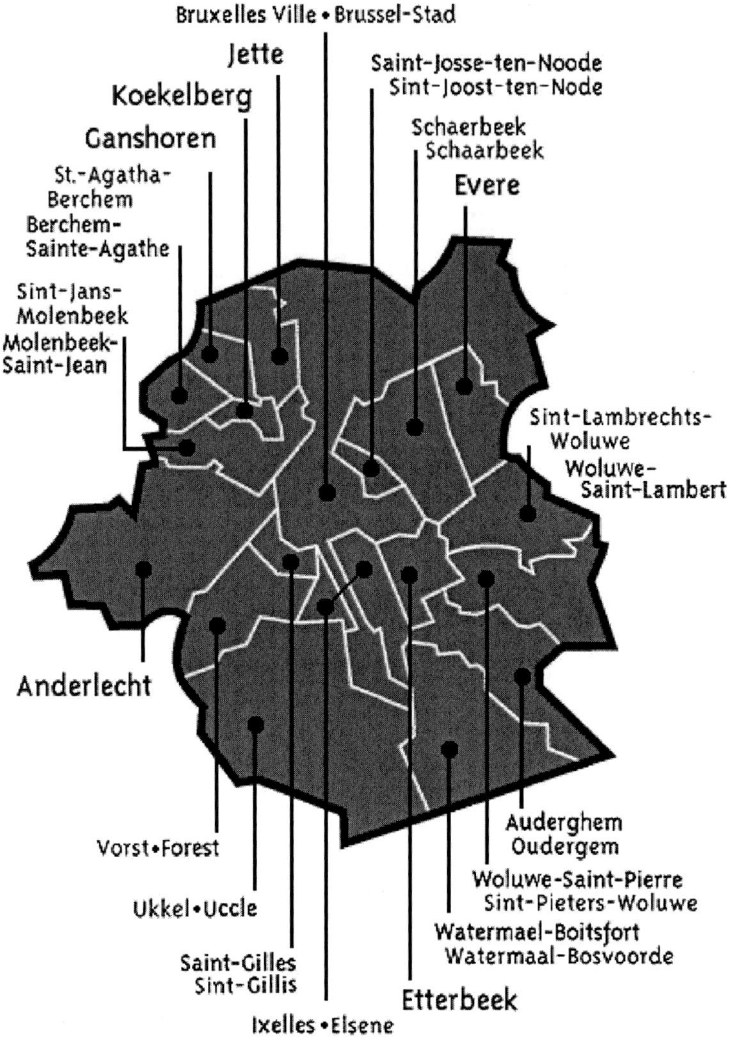

- Bruxelles Ville • Brussel-Stad
- Jette
- Koekelberg
- Ganshoren
- St.-Agatha-Berchem / Berchem-Sainte-Agathe
- Sint-Jans-Molenbeek / Molenbeek-Saint-Jean
- Saint-Josse-ten-Noode / Sint-Joost-ten-Node
- Schaerbeek / Schaarbeek
- Evere
- Sint-Lambrechts-Woluwe / Woluwe-Saint-Lambert
- Anderlecht
- Vorst • Forest
- Ukkel • Uccle
- Saint-Gilles / Sint-Gillis
- Ixelles • Elsene
- Etterbeek
- Auderghem / Oudergem
- Woluwe-Saint-Pierre / Sint-Pieters-Woluwe
- Watermael-Boitsfort / Watermaal-Bosvoorde

Source: Brussels Capital Region, *Territory and Population*, http://portail.irisnet.be/en/region/region_de_bruxelles-capitale/territoire_et_population.shtml, 9.03.2009.

started to develop an own, distinct identity and a consequent quest for recognition in the country[7]. Next to the fact that the city has a rich history being ruled by several groups, it also has a long tradition of immigration. The metropolis has always been attractive to inhabitants of the former colony, Congo, where they have formed

---

[7] M. De Ridder, L.R. Fraga, *The Brussels issue in Belgian politics*, "West European Politics", vol. 9, no. 3, 1986, pp. 376-392.

a community in certain neighbourhoods. Furthermore, in the sixties, a great deal of Italian, Spanish and Greek guest workers came to live in the Belgian capital, followed by Turks and Moroccans. More recently, Brussels has received immigrants of several other countries, predominantly Eastern European and African countries. Together with the immigrants from EU-countries (see below), these immigrants form together 46.3% of the Brussels' population[8]. This immigration is, naturally, not spread equally throughout the city, but concentrated in certain neighbourhoods and boroughs. In the sixties and seventies, the largest concentration of immigrants was located just outside the central inner-city Brussels borough[9]. Mostly, the boroughs of Anderlecht, Saint-Josse, Saint-Gilles and Schaerbeek hosted these guest workers. Still today, Moroccans, who are the main immigrant group, populate the north and west quarters of the city centre. The first guest workers (Italians, Spanish and Greeks) live in the south, while Schaerbeek and Saint-Josse are inhabited by the immigrants of a Turkish origin[10].

Meanwhile, as an important number of the EU institutions was being located in Brussels, the city received a wave of EU civil servants and consequently also a substantial number of expats, active in the private sector. These 'foreigners' are all EU-subjects and thus form another category of immigration in Brussels, which is more or less concentrated in certain neighbourhoods and boroughs as well. They are mainly concentrated in the eastern and southern parts of the city, and often display a suburban settlement pattern, although people from new EU member states prefer to live closer to the city in the same region[11].

Next to the EU and other governmental institutions, there is an important number of firms located in the city which attract thousands of commuters from all over the country every day.

Although the amount of both immigrants and commuters is high, an important number of indigenous inhabitants still live in the capital too, which, as already said, originate from the two main linguistic groups. This, combined with the geographic position of Brussels as a bilingual enclave in Flemish territory, has made the city a very complex case. There are reasons to believe the city, and perhaps consequently the country, is an example of cooperation between two ethnic groups, but there are equally many reasons to believe the city is still at the core of a conflict between ethnic groups. The *communes à facilité*[12] in the Brussels suburbs (see fig. 3), which have

---

[8] Observatorium, *Welzijns- en gezondheidsatlas van Brussel-Hoofdstad 2006*, Brussel 2006.
[9] W. De Lannoy, *Sociaal-geografische atlas van Brussel-hoofdstad*, Brussel 1978; D. Wijgaerts, *De bevolking van Brussel-hoofdstad: een sociaal-demografische analyse*, Brussel 1979.
[10] Observatorium, *Welzijns- en gezondheidsatlas van Brussel-Hoofdstad 2006*, Brussel 2006.
[11] Observatorium, *Welzijns- en gezondheidsatlas van Brussel-Hoofdstad 2006*, Brussel 2006.
[12] The *communes à facilité* are municipalities, formally belonging to the Flemish region (and therefore Dutch-speaking community) in which a substantial part of the population is French-speaking. For these inhabitants of the other language group, special facilities were created in order to enhance their integration. These facilities mainly include the possibility for French-speaking inhabitants to receive public communication and official documents in French and the possibility of French-speaking nurseries and primary education. Contrastingly,

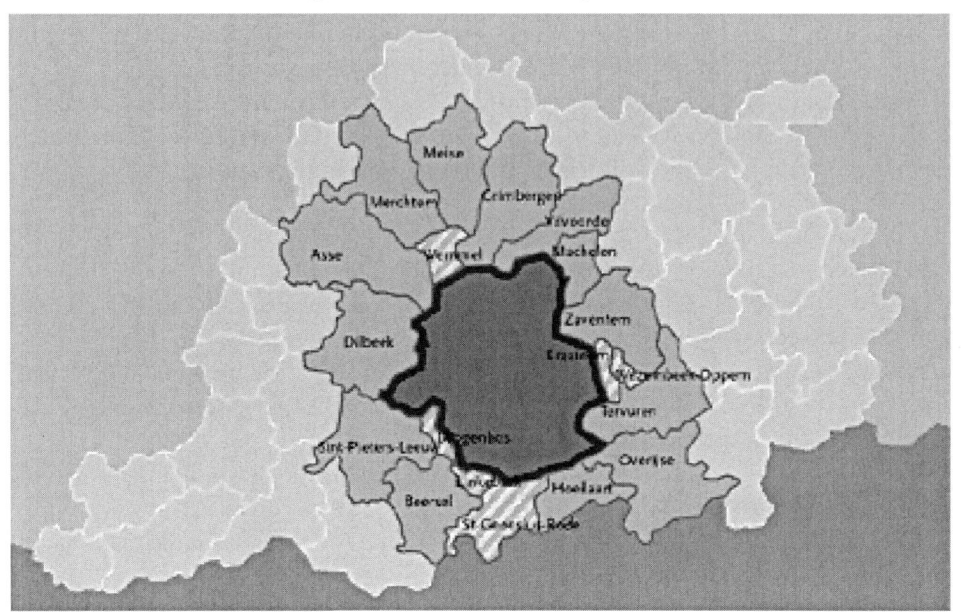

Figure 3. The *communes à facilité*

Source: Vlaamse Overheid, Steunpunt Taalwetwijzer, http://brussel.vlaanderen.be/terminologie.html, 18.12.2008.

been the subject of very heated debates up until today, can certainly not be excluded from this conflict, although doing so would bring the conflict to the national level, which is not our intention here. We will therefore only be looking at the nineteen towns that constitute the so-called Brussels Capital Region. As already stated, the particular character of the city has puzzled many authors already. The question whether Brussels really *'belong[s] on a list of divided cities'*, proposed by Murphy in particular, left us puzzled as well[13]. We therefore also used these as the starting point of our journey, constructed along the lines of conflict and cooperation. This being said, we felt important up-to-date additions could be made to Murphy's claims and believe we can develop the ideas introduced by him further.

---

these facilities now are at the very centre of the Flemish-Walloon language conflict, as their candidate-mayors were recently accused of calling for community election votes in French, which is to be done in Dutch, as stipulated in the *Omzendbrief Peeters* of 1997. Although the issue is based on diverging interpretations of the existing regulations, the Flemish Minister of the Interior has on the basis of these facts refused to acknowledge the elected candidate-mayors as actual mayors. See: Agentschap voor Binnenlands Bestuurvan de Vlaamse Overheid, *Omzendbrief Peeters*, http://www.binnenland.vlaanderen.be/regelgeving/omzendbrieven/omz16.12.1997.htm, 18.12.2008 & Steunpunt Taalwetwijzer, van de Vlaamse Overheid, *Het Taalgebruik in Bestuurszaken*, http://brussel.vlaanderen.be/bestuurszaken.html, 18.12.2008.
[13] A.B. Murphy, *Brussels: division in unity or unity in division?*, "Political geography", vol. 21, no. 2002, p. 695.

Interethnic relationships at the city level

In order to successfully tackle the Brussels case, it is of great importance to first define the nature of the Brussels conflict that arose in the past. Therefore, we will briefly focus on the debate on various sorts of relationships between two or more ethnic groups in the same spatial setting. To be clear, we consider the Flemings and the Walloons to be separate ethnic groups since they speak their own language and at least partly identify themselves with this group[14]. This does not imply they could not identify with a larger group, e.g. Belgians or Europeans, or a smaller group, i.e. inhabitants of Brussels. It does imply we can speak of 'interethnic relationships' when talking about the connections between Flemings and Walloons. Although a fair number of Brussels' inhabitants are bilingual, only a very small minority supposedly identifies with both language communities, i.e. those who are originally from bilingual families in Brussels.

Speaking of interethnic relationships then, we can discern several forms these relations can take in the particular spatial setting of a city. A distinction can be made between two forms of relations, which correspond to the two main traditions presented in the literature. On the one hand, there is the contact hypothesis and on the other hand, the competition theory developed under the tradition of the Chicago School. The latter was developed by Burgess among others, regarding the city as a whole of several concentric zones, with one 'zone in transition' where several ethnic groups meet[15]. From this point of view the idea that ethnic groups in the same spatial setting fight over shared interests like housing or jobs was developed by several authors. The key point is that through physical 'closeness', a (feeling of) competition or even rivalry can arise between these ethnic groups. When this situation occurs, we can already speak of an ethnic conflict, even when it remains restricted to some tensions. The conflict is called realistic when there is an actual state of competition between two groups (who have the same social status). The conflict can become unrealistic when it just deals with airing tensions and defining the other group in a negative sense to provide the own group with a positive social identification[16].

The contact hypothesis, on the other hand, was originally developed by Allport and stipulates that interethnic relationships will improve as contact between the ethnic groups increases[17]. Contrary to the competition theory, it assumes that a comparable status is a condition for a positive relationship. Empirically, hypotheses based on this contact approach do not really stand, certainly not when applied to ur-

---

[14] C. Timmerman, *Cultuurrelativisme: feit of fictie? Migratie en etnische minderheden in België*, Antwerpen 2003.
[15] E.W. Burgess, *The growth of the city: an introduction to a research project*, [in:] M. Janowicz (ed.), *The city*, Chicago 1974 [1925].
[16] H. Vermeulen, *De multi-etnische samenleving op buurtniveau*, [in:] H.B. Entzinger, P.J.J. Stijnen (eds), *Etnische minderheden in Nederland*, Boom 1990, pp. 216-243; T. Blokland-Potters, *Wat stadsbewoners bindt: sociale relaties in een achterstandswijk*, Kampen 1998.
[17] G. Allport, *The nature of prejudice: a comprehensive and penetrating study of the origin and nature of prejudice*, New York 1958.

ban settings: most authors see relationships worsen instead of improve when the ethnic groups are larger, and thus when there is more contact. Instead, interethnic relationships seem more relaxed in settings in which one ethnic group forms the clear majority and only a limited number of members from another group are present[18]. Given this, we would call a situation with neutral or positive contacts between members of several ethnic groups a situation of ethnic cooperation.

Both ethnic conflicts and ethnic cooperation can develop in certain degrees of intensity. Next to these two general categories, a situation of interethnic coexistence can exist. This is a condition in which two groups live together next to each other, i.e. without any connection. Each group is self-directed and does not come into cooperation nor in conflict with another group. This is often translated spatially in divided cities, where each group 'owns' its neighbourhood and groups are not mixed through their housing pattern.

Applying this theoretical knowledge to the Brussels case, we will firstly illustrate why we believe Brussels is a primary example of cooperation in theory, based on the delicate institutional framework that exists today and which is the fruit of a development that lasted throughout the 20th century. This section will then be followed by a description of the day-to-day situation of Brussels, which will examine whether the institutional modelling *vis-à-vis* the cooperation of the two language groups has indeed enhanced the cooperation, or whether we can still speak of two groups in conflict.

Brussels in theory

Examples of long-term peaceful cooperation of ethnic groups in one city are rare and the city of Brussels is no exception in this matter. On the positive side, it must be emphasised that the ethnic conflict has become less violent since the end of the 1960s. Compared to other cities with a multiethnic character, Brussels could indeed serve as model for non-violent coexistence and cooperation of different ethnic groups. This part of the paper will therefore focus on the institutional regulations and laws that have created such a framework for cooperation and coexistence, while having to deal with sensitive and mainly symbolic questions.

Remarkable about the Brussels case is the rather complex make-up of what can indeed be described as a conflict between ethnic groups. Different authors, however, do not agree on a univocal definition: Hooghe refers to it as a territorial conflict whereas Jacobs discusses the issues of Brussels as a polyethnic society connected with those of multinational institutional arrangements[19]. Murphy finally talks

---

[18] W.D. Chapin, *Explaining the electoral success of the New Right: the German case*, "West European Politics", vol. 20, no. 2, 1997, pp. 53-72; H. De Witte, *Contact met migranten en hun cultuur*, "Noord-Zuidcahier", vol. 21, no. 4, 1996, pp. 35-52.

[19] D. Jacobs, *Multinational and polyethnic politics entwined: minority representation in the region of Brussels-Capital*, "Journal of Ethnic and Migration Studies", vol. 26, no. 2, 2000, pp. 289-304; L. Hooghe, *Belgium: Hollowing the Center*, [in:] U.M. Amoretti, N. Bermeo (eds), *Federalism and Territorial Cleavages*, London 2004, p. 64.

about ethno-linguistic divisions[20]. As will be demonstrated, it is our belief that the institutional arrangements are very much based on the ethno-linguistic view. Questions Moreover, and perhaps most importantly, the Belgian identity as highest 'layer' of identity makes for the fact that the ethnic groups still have aspects in common, related to the Belgian federal state. It is for this reason we deemed Brussels as an example of cooperation between ethnic groups. A chronological overview of the major reforms and changes in Belgian history, as well as a detailed description of existing arrangements at the regional and the city level, will demonstrate this further. Having said this, as many have preceded us in providing detailed accounts of the key reforms and changes[21], we will only briefly describe the formal changes, to then turn to the effects this has had on the cooperation of the two main ethnic groups in Brussels today.

State reforms

The division of the country into four linguistic zones in the middle of the twentieth century and with it the official establishment of a bilingual Brussels seems to be the starting point of a complex quest for a balance between the Dutch- and French-speaking groups' rights. Indeed, the establishment of the language laws of 8 November 1962 and 2 August 1963[22] and with it, the indirect creation of a bilingual enclave in Flanders (see fig. 1), proved that Brussels could undoubtedly become the subject of ethno-linguistic discussions between the two ethnic groups. As it is well-described in the *Omzendbrief Peeters* of 1997, it was the government's intention to create a situation in which both language communities were guaranteed to keep their rights and to maintain their culture. In Brussels' case especially, this would prove to be a difficult exercise. As already pointed out, the Flemings, aware of their distinct identity, revolted against the increasing Frenchification in the 1950s. This led to violent demonstrations of the Flemish in Brussels in the beginning of the 1960s[23]. The Dutch-speaking and French-speaking media also chose sides, as well as the political parties, which ultimately resulted in a splitting of all national political parties. It was clear measures needed being taken, as the conflict was affecting virtually all spheres of society.

---

[20] A.B. Murphy, *Brussels: division in unity or unity in division?*, "Political geography", vol. 21, no. 5, 2002, pp. 695-700.
[21] See e.g. J. Fitzmaurice, *The Politics of Belgium – A Unique Federalism*, London 1996; L. Hooghe, *Belgium: Hollowing the Center*, [in:] U.M. Amoretti, N. Bermeo (eds), *Federalism and Territorial Cleavages*, London 2004, pp. 55-92; R. Senelle, *The Current Constitutional System*, [in:] M. Boudart, M. Boudart, R. Bryssinck (eds), *Modern Belgium*, Palo Alto 1990, pp. 166-200.
[22] And its adaptation by the law of 23 December 1970. R. Senelle, *The Current Constitutional System*, [in:] M. Boudart, M. Boudart, R. Bryssinck (eds), *Modern Belgium*, Palo Alto 1990, pp. 179-180.
[23] M. De Ridder, *The Brussels issue in Belgian politics*, " West European Politics", vol. 9, no. 3, 1986, pp. 378-179; E. Witte, H. Beardsmore Baetens, *The interdisciplinary study of urban bilingualism in Brussels*, Clevedon 1987, p. 53.

The regionalisation and division into communities under the first state reform of 1970-1971 made Brussels an independent region, in which both language groups were to be represented in a regional parliament and government[24]. The former was and still is made up of both Flemish and Walloon parties. It is currently composed of eighty-nine members, there are seventeen representatives for the Flemings and seventy-two for the French-speakers. The government is composed of five members, one president from the French-speaking community and two ministers from each language group. Next to that, there are three *secrétaires d'état*, among which one is Flemish.

A further major institutional change relevant for the coexistence of Dutch- and French-speaking people in Brussels was the *Bijzondere wet met betrekking tot de Brusselse Instellingen*[25], introduced during the second phase of the state reforms at the end of the 1980s. Until then, there was still no *'definite statute'* for the Brussels region, as Senelle describes it, and this was changed by the revision of Article 108*ter*, implemented by the above-mentioned Special Law[26]. With this law, not only were the parliamentary and governmental composition and competences stipulated, but also the link with the state structure and with the other communities and regions, as well as the budgetary provisions were established.

These important changes in the country's structure were in a sense consolidated in 1993 by the country's official federalisation. Contrary to Switzerland or Germany, though, the federalism was what Prime Minister Martens skilfully described as a *'fédéralisme d'union'*, a form of federalism which was to give more powers to the regions and communities and reinforced the central state at the same time[27]. This taken into account, it could be stated that Fitzmaurice's description of the situation in the 1970s still goes for today's situation when he said that „*simple 'geographical federalism' was clearly inadequate to meet the complicated reality of the Belgian situation*"[28]. Therefore, the important question to be tackled in this context is how this has facilitated coexistence and cooperation of the two language groups in Brussels. For that, an overview of the key tools that are intended to make coexistence possible is provided.

Regional and communal arrangements

The situation in which the bilingual Brussels Capital Region finds itself often leads to confusing and sometimes facetious situations, both for foreign visitors and for

---

[24] J. Fitzmaurice, *The Politics of Belgium – A Unique Federalism*, London 1996, p. 49.
[25] Special Law regarding the Brussels institutions, free translation – Belgisch Staatsblad, *De Brusselwet:* Bijzondere Wet van 12 januari 1989 met betrekking tot de Brusselse Instellingen.
[26] R. Senelle, *The Current Constitutional System*, [in:] M. Boudart, M. Boudart, R. Bryssinck (eds), *Modern Belgium*, Palo Alto 1990, pp. 181-183.
[27] J. Fitzmaurice, *The Politics of Belgium – A Unique Federalism*, London 1996, p. 145.
[28] J. Fitzmaurice, *The Politics of Belgium – A Unique Federalism*, London 1996, p. 123.

Belgian citizens. At the same time, it also confronts them with the reality of the conflict. This can be observed at both the regional and the communal level. Both are illustrated in the sections below.

Regional arrangements

With regards to Brussels as a region, the arrangements are strongly related to the key changes and reforms introduced above. Although recognised as one of the three regions, next to Flanders and Wallonia, the Brussels region obviously is more limited in size and it does not have the same powers as the two other regions. This is for example demonstrated by the fact that the legislative texts for the Brussels Region have been called *'ordonnanties'* and for the two others *'decreten'* or decrees. The *'ordonnanties'* have in a sense less power than the decrees, as they are subject to federal change, which is not the case for decrees[29]. This was considered as one of the measures taken to protect the Flemish minority in the region, as the French-speakers wanted it to become a fully-fledged region, which would make it more difficult for the Flemish community to have its say in Brussels affairs.

Furthermore, as was pointed out already, the Brussels region is made up of a council of eighty-nine directly elected members and a regional government of one Minister-President, four ministers and three *secrétaires d'état*. They deal with territorial matters, as usually happens with regions. For the personal matters, normally to be dealt with by the Communities, a Flemish, a French and a common community commission was established. They mainly deal with educational, cultural and personal affairs and their make-up corresponds very much to the division of the regional parliament and government, as the French-speaking members of the parliament and government seat in the French-speaking community commission and the Flemings in the Flemish community commission. In the common commission, all members of the Brussels council and government have a seat, except for the *secrétaires d'état*. This last commission deals with competences not affecting either of the language groups, mainly health and social-aid matters[30]. In this sense, a tool was created to guarantee an application of the community competences to the Brussels region. Voters in Brussels, voting on unilingual lists – the Flemings for the Flemish and the French-speakers on the French-speaking – therefore vote for representatives which are intended to represent them for both territorial and personal affairs[31]. This mechanism guarantees a fair representation of the groups and formally makes communication between them, in territorial and personal matters, possible.

---

[29] J. Fitzmaurice, *The Politics of Belgium – A Unique Federalism*, London 1996, pp. 136, 151.
[30] Brussels hoofdstedelijk gewest, *COCOM: Missions et Compétences*, http://www.bruxelles.irisnet.be/fr/region/region_de_bruxelles-capitale/institutions_communautaires/cocom/missions_et_competences.shtml, 7.01.2009.
[31] J. Fitzmaurice, *The Politics of Belgium – A Unique Federalism*, London 1996, pp. 131, 154.

Communal arrangements

With regards to the communal level, measures have also been taken to allow for coexistence and cooperation. The main idea behind Brussels' bilingual status is that each of the nineteen *boroughs'* governments and public services is bilingual in its representation and communication, in order to be able to address the citizen in the language of his or her preference. Due to the direct electoral system, however, it is possible that, at the council level, one of the two language groups is not represented if nobody of that group is elected[32]. Moreover, as Jacobs further adds: "*[T]here is no guarantee that Flemish politicians, who are elected into a city council, would gain a seat on the committee of the mayor and the aldermen*"[33]. This has, however, been overcome by a provision under the so-called Lombard agreements of 29 April 2001, where it is stipulated that, failing an alderman of one of the language groups, an extra alderman position can be created under article 279 of the new communal law, to allow for both language groups to be represented[34]. It appears that this has mainly been created for symbolic reasons, in order to appease mainly the Flemish community, which manifests itself actively with regards to its rights in an increasingly French-speaking environment.

Language laws and their relevance at the communal level

Looking at a more practical application of this bilingual policy, three specific language laws were put in place to organise educational, judicial and public matters respectively. With regards to the first, the structures put in place are as straightforward as possible. Education is organised along the language division, which means Brussels has both Flemish and French schools, which parents of either language groups can choose to send their children to. This being said, Brussels' schools are also forced to offer the other language in compulsory second-language courses during an increased number of hours compared to education in the other regions[35]. It must be said that this situation, often regarded as a disadvantage in the education system, must undoubtedly also be seen as a great asset given the possibilities to create bilingual children in unilingual families[36]. On Brussels' job market, knowledge of the two languages is of great importance.

---

[32] D. Jacobs, *Multinational and polyethnic politics entwined: minority representation in the region of Brussels-Capital*, "Journal of Ethnic and Migration Studies", vol. 26, no. 2, 2000, p. 291.

[33] D. Jacobs, *Multinational and polyethnic politics entwined: minority representation in the region of Brussels-Capital*, "Journal of Ethnic and Migration Studies", vol. 26, no. 2, 2000, p. 291.

[34] Vereniging van de Stad en de Gemeenten van het Brussels Hoofdstedelijk Gewest, *Nieuwe Gemeentewet: Titel XIII: bijzondere bepalingen betreffende de gemeenten van het Brussels Hoofdstedelijk Gewest*, http://www.avcb-vsgb.be/nl/publicaties/nieuwe-gemeentewet/gecoordineerde-tekst/bijzondere-bepalingen.html, 6.03.2009.

[35] See articles 5 & 10 of the language law on educational matters, Vlaamse Overheid, Steunpunt Taalwetwijzer, *Het Taalgebruik in het Onderwijs*, http://brussel.vlaanderen.be/onderwijs.html, 18.12.2008.

[36] N. Charkaoui, V. Huwé, *Brussel, een taalkundig en ethnisch-cultureel diverse stad*, [in:] C. Dewitte (ed.), *Wat met Brussel? Uitdagende perspectieven voor de hoofdstad*, Leuven 2008, p. 112.

Secondly, concerning the language law which organises the use of language in judicial matters, the provisions are more complicated, though also logical. In case of a record drafted by the police, the use of the language by the offender or, failing this, the *'necessity of the situation'* determines the choice of the language[37]. As for conflicts taking place in Brussels between two people of different language groups, the plaintiff has a right to choose his or her language of preference for the introductory legal act, but the defendant has an equal right to let the rest of the law suit be carried out in his or her language of preference[38].

Finally, as for the organisation of public matters in the bilingual region, it is stipulated that, on the one hand, the government must use both languages for public announcements such as newsletters or signposts and the citizen's language of preference for personalised communication such as permits or attestations. On the other hand, the authorities are expected to understand both languages when citizens wish to communicate in their language of preference[39]. To this effect, public officers employed in e.g. borough halls, hospitals or other public institutions are expected to pass a language test which demonstrates an elementary knowledge of the second language if they want to be permanently employed in a local administration[40].

Brussels in practice

In this part, we will look closer at how these institutional frameworks are applied in practice and to what extent they need to be used in the daily practice of living in Brussels. Rather than the above-discussed regional level, it will now be looked at the communal level, i.e. the 19 individual boroughs of the Brussels Capital Region (see fig. 2 above). We will first look at the election results, voting preferences and other political practices. Then, we will concentrate on the practice of language use in the daily life of Brussels, to conclude with the actual interethnic contact. In all three sections, we consider the importance of the spatial divisions of the phenomena, and the effects that mass immigration to Brussels has had on these practices.

---

[37] See article 11 of the language law on judicial matters, Vlaamse Overheid, Steunpunt Taalwetwijzer, *Veel Gestelde Vragen: Het Taalgebruik in Gerechtszaken*, http://brussel.vlaanderen.be/taalgebruikgerechtszaken.html, 18.12.2008.
[38] See article 4 of the language law on judicial matters, Vlaamse Overheid, Steunpunt Taalwetwijzer, *Veel Gestelde Vragen: Het Taalgebruik in Gerechtszaken*, http://brussel.vlaanderen.be/taalgebruikgerechtszaken.html, 18.12.2008.
[39] See articles 18-20 of the language law on public matters, Vlaamse Overheid, Steunpunt Taalwetwijzer, *Het Taalgebruik in Bestuurszaken*, http://brussel.vlaanderen.be/bestuurszaken.html, 18.12.2008.
[40] See article 21 § 2 of the language law on public matters, Vlaamse Overheid, Steunpunt Taalwetwijzer, *Het Taalgebruik in Bestuurszaken*, http://brussel.vlaanderen.be/bestuurszaken.html, 18.12.2008.

Political practices

As mentioned above, the Dutch-speaking community in Brussels is protected with some rules as far as the representation in the communal councils is concerned. In practice however, people from Flemish lists are not often elected in the nineteen Brussels boroughs, and in some of them even not at all. Still, the administration in these boroughs is officially bilingual.

At the local elections in 2000 for example, only eighty-four Flemish candidates were elected out of a total of 652. For the sake of comparison: ninety candidates with a non-EU origin were elected in the same election (see below). In certain boroughs, none or only one of those with a non-EU origin got elected, like in Uccle, Forest, Ixelles, Auderghem and Saint-Josse. They are best represented in boroughs like Anderlecht, Evere, Berchem-Saint-Agathe and Jette (more than 20%)[41]. At the elections of the Brussels' Capital Council in 2004, 83% of the Brussels' population cast votes for (a candidate of) a French-speaking list, whereas only 13.3% of them chose a Dutch-speaking list (3.8% of the votes were invalid). Looking at the division over the different quarters and boroughs, a large dispersal in these percentages can be observed. The Dutch-speaking lists receive more support in Anderlecht, the borough of Brussels and Molenbeek. They receive proportionally less in Uccle, Saint-Gilles, Ixelles and Saint-Josse[42].

Furthermore, these local councillors are not often represented in the majority. In the period 2000-2006 for example, in only one out of the nineteen boroughs a Flemish party was involved in a coalition, namely Agalev (the Greens) in the borough of Brussels. In nine out of nineteen boroughs a mixed list, mostly with the two parallel parties from the same family, got into a coalition together with some Walloon parties[43].

Because Brussels has become more and more a multicultural city with more than one third of the population of foreign origin, vote-seeking behaviour of political parties has changed as well. That is even more so since the voting right for non-nationals has been implemented in 2006, although a lot of the immigrants had acquired the Belgian nationality before. Gaining their votes has become a new objective in Brussels' politics, and influences the relationships between Flemish and Walloon lists as well[44].

It seems that, in line with their orientation to the French language (see above), immigrants are more inclined to vote for French-speaking lists. For example, this

---

[41] D. Jacobs, M. Swyngedouw, *Een nieuwe blik op achtergestelde buurten in het Brussels Hoofdstedelijk Gewest*, "Tijdschrift voor Sociologie", vol. 21, no. 3, 2000, pp. 197-228.
[42] Figures provided by responsible at Ministry of Home Affairs.
[43] J.-P. Nassaux, *La formation des coalitions dans les communes bruxelloises*, "Courrier hebdomadaire", vol. 55, no. 1770, 2002, p. 39.
[44] D. Jacobs, M. Swyngedouw, *Een nieuwe blik op achtergestelde buurten in het Brussels Hoofdstedelijk Gewest*, "Tijdschrift voor Sociologie", vol. 21, no. 3, 2000, pp. 197-228; D. Jacobs, *Multinational and polyethnic politics entwined: minority representation in the region of Brussels-Capital*, "Journal of Ethnic and Migration Studies", vol. 26, no. 2, 2000, pp. 289-304.

becomes clear through the number of elected immigrant candidates: in 1994, fourteen of them were elected, all on French-speaking lists. Six of them were on the list of the socialist party, six on the list of the Green party, and two on a centre-right party (FDF). All seats were gained in boroughs that are inhabited by a population that consists of more than 25% of immigrants[45]. In 2000, already 90 candidates with a foreign origin were elected. Again, all these candidates were elected on a French-speaking list, with exception of 3 candidates who were elected on the Flemish Green, socialist and Christian-democrat lists. The immigrants are best represented in boroughs like Saint-Josse, Molenbeek, Brussels borough and Saint-Gilles, boroughs that count indeed a lot of immigrants[46]. Of course, the relationship between the voting preference of immigrants and the election of foreign candidates is not rectilinear; presumably, a lot of indigenous voters have voted for these candidates as well to support the immigrant communities, to show their sympathy towards them. But these findings certainly indicate that French-speaking politicians gain more power through the preferences they receive from a part of the immigrant communities[47]. In addition, it seems that among the EU-immigrants there is also a division in the inclination to vote for a Walloon or a Flemish list. French-speaking lists are expected to rather attract immigrants from 'Latin' countries like France, Italy and Spain, whereas Dutch-speaking lists would do better among voters from 'Germanic' countries such as The Netherlands, Germany and Great-Britain[48].

The use of languages in the public sphere, then, can somewhat anecdotically be illustrated by the *'windows affair'* of 1975, in which the notorious mayor of Schaerbeek, Roger Nols, created *'ethnically separated windows'* in the borough hall for Dutch-speakers and foreign residents as supposedly no suitable candidates for the bilingual positions could be found[49]. It could be said that, over time, animosity has however been replaced by common sense. The introduction of the *taalhoffelijkheidsakkoord*[50] could be seen as an example of that. The core idea of this agreement, initially concluded in 1996 and revised afterwards, was that newly employed public officers could present a proof of passing the language test up until two years after

---

[45] M. Martiniello, *De politieke participatie van Belgen van vreemde origine in Brussel (1994-2000)*, [in:] M. Swyngedouw, P. Delwit, A. Rea (eds), *Culturele diversiteit en samenleven in Brussel en België*, Leuven 2005, pp. 145-157.
[46] D. Jacobs, M. Swyngedouw, *Het verenigingsleven van allochtonen van Marokkaanse en Turkse origine te Brussel*, [in:] B. Khader, M. Martiniello, A. Rea, C. Timmerman (eds), *Immigratie en integratie anders denken: een Belgisch interuniversitair initiatief*, Brussel 2006, pp. 131-152.
[47] M. Martiniello, *De politieke participatie van Belgen van vreemde origine in Brussel (1994-2000)*, [in:] M. Swyngedouw, P. Delwit, A. Rea (eds), *Culturele diversiteit en samenleven in Brussel en België*, Leuven 2005, pp. 145-157.
[48] H. Bousetta, M. Swyngedouw, *La citoyenneté de l'Union européenne et l'enjeu de Bruxelles*, "Courrier hebdomadaire", no. 1636, 1999, p. 43.
[49] U. Manço, M. Kanmaz, *From conflict to co-operation between muslims and local authorities in a Brussels borough: Schaerbeek*, "Journal of Ethnic and Migration Studies", vol. 31, no. 6, 2005, p. 1115.
[50] Agreement of language courtesy, free translation.

the start of their employment. Next to this, there would also be an easing of the language test as well as a liberalisation of the selection criteria regarding language knowledge[51]. Nevertheless, many organisations protecting the rights of the Flemish minority in Brussels assessed this to be to the advantage of French-speaking applicants, as French-speaking are generally considered to have more difficulties with learning Dutch than *vice-versa*. Findings in a report of the regional deputy-governor in charge of control over the correct application of the language laws confirm this trend, as in 2004, 83% of the city council's employees were French-speaking and 17% Dutch-speaking[52]. This, combined with the fact that the deputy-governor states in his conclusions that the agreement, and with it the easing of the language test have led to less ousters on the basis of insufficient language knowledge and that a *'sufficient'* number have indeed passed the test so far, could indeed point towards an imbalance between the opportunities of the two language groups[53]. A long procedural clash finally led to the abandonment of the *taalhoffelijkheidsakkoord* through a waiver by the Council of State in 2006[54]. This being said, in the introduction of his 2004 report, deputy-governor Nys already pointed out the fact that the reality did not match the legal provisions and that long-term legal changes are therefore a necessity[55].

Language practices

Having illustrated the important political character of the linguistic divisions, we will now turn to the daily reality as far as language use is concerned. As already pointed out, there are no official data that indicate the number of Dutch- and French-speaking inhabitants in Brussels since the language census was abolished in 1947. Apart from the voting data we presented above, we are therefore forced to rely on survey data. These data provide in a certain sense greater accuracy as people are being asked which language is being used at home most frequently. Janssens' data therefore allow us to compare survey data concerning language use at home of the Brussels' population from 2000 and 2006[56].

It appears that in 2006 56.8% speak only French at home, while only 7.0% speaks solely Dutch. The share of people who speak French together with another language is also larger than the share who speaks both Dutch and French. Then again,

---

[51] F. Vandendriessche, *Taalhoffelijkheidsakkoord: Synthesenota voor de locale mandataris*, http://www.brusselnl.be/downloads/verzoek_omzettingmandaat.pdf, 6.03.2009.
[52] H. Nys, *Verslag van de vice-gouvernerur van het administratief arondissement Brussel-Hoofdstad over het jaar 2004*, Brussel 2004.
[53] H. Nys, *Verslag van de vice-gouvernerur van het administratief arondissement Brussel-Hoofdstad over het jaar 2004*, Brussel 2004.
[54] Council of State, *Arrest nr. 161.084 van 7 juli 2006 in de zaak A.157.803/XII-4310*, http://www.brusselnl.be/downloads/arrest161084.pdf, 6.03.2009.
[55] H. Nys, *Verslag van de vice-gouvernerur van het administratief arondissement Brussel-Hoofdstad over het jaar 2004*, Brussel 2004.
[56] R. Janssens, *Van Brussel gesproken: taalgebruik, taalverschuivingen en taalidentiteit in het Brussels Hoofdstedelijk Gewest (Taalbarometer II)*, Brussel 2007.

a considerable percentage of Brussels (16.3%) speak another language at home. As we look at the developments between 2000 and 2006, we can discern a decrease of the Dutch language use and an even greater increase of the French language use. The share of people who only speak another language at home diminishes while more and more people use the combination of French with another language. This finding points in the direction of the expectation that immigrants use French as their first or second language, and Dutch not at all. This can be confirmed when we separately look at the immigrant group of the survey: Dutch only plays a marginal role (1.0%), most of them speak both their mother tongue and French at home (44.4%). Another large part of them only use their mother tongue (22.9%) while a smaller share (11.0%) only uses French. The evolution between 2000 and 2006 amplifies this trend[57]. Research by Phalet and Swyngedouw points out that the presence of immigrants indeed fortifies the French-speaking part of Brussels, but yet warns for a too optimistic view: a lot of immigrants, certainly those with a Turkish background, keep closely to their own language[58].

As far as knowledge of languages is concerned, it seems that more than 95% of the Brussels' population had a good or very good knowledge of French in 2006. Most surprisingly, English is the second language that is being spoken well or very well, before Dutch, while the order was reversed in 2000[59].

The phenomena described above indicate the growing importance of French as *lingua franca* and the belief in Brussels as a real bilingual city is indeed nothing more than an illusion. This can also be confirmed by data on language use in the public sphere: around 95% of the population speaks French to a stranger in the street, when their home language is French, another language or the combination. People who speak Dutch at home speak French to a stranger in only 68.2% of the cases, and Dutch in 22% of the cases.

Still, this image can be nuanced by the important presence of commuters travelling to their jobs in Brussels every day, from which a large part comes from Flanders[60]. Due to this mass phenomenon, the 'street image' during weekdays, especially in the city centre, changes drastically.

Social segregation at the neighbourhood level

As has already been pointed out in the introduction, the presence of the different ethnic groups in Brussels is not equally spread throughout the city but concentrated

---

[57] Ibidem.
[58] K. Phalet, M. Swyngedouw, *Grenzen aan integratie: perspectieven van Turkse, Marokkaanse en kansarme Belgische Brusselaars*, "Migrantenstudies", vol. 17, no. 4, 2001, pp. 207-225.
[59] R. Janssens, *Van Brussel gesproken: taalgebruik, taalverschuivingen en taalidentiteit in het Brussels Hoofdstedelijk Gewest (Taalbarometer II)*, Brussel 2007.
[60] F. Louckx, *L'intégration ethnolinguistique à Bruxelles*, [in:] E. Witte, M. De Metsenaere et al. (eds), *Le bilinguisme en Belgique: le cas de Bruxelles*, Bruxelles 1984, pp. 41-48; E. Witte, A. Mares, *19 keer Brussel - Brusselse thema's, 19 fois Bruxelles – Thèmes Bruxellois, 19 times Brussels – Brussels Themes*, Brussels 2001.

in particular boroughs. In this part, we will reflect on what the spatial segregation of the different ethnic groups implies for the interethnic relationships. In sum, the spatial dispersal of the different ethnic groups follows the traditional division of the city alongside the canal zone which splits the city in east and west. The eastern parts of the city were traditionally inhabited by a blue collar worker population rather than a white collar population. The last one has traditionally populated the western bank of the canal, where more suburban zones and more greenery can be found as well. This division is still visible in the settlement pattern of the immigrants: whereas the guest workers from the Mediterranean countries have populated the south, the more recent international immigration attracted by the EU institutions and international companies is roughly situated in the west[61].

Along the language borders, a spatial segregation can be discerned as well. We already described the spatial dispersal of voting preferences throughout the different boroughs. These findings are in line with an older estimation of the settlement pattern of the Dutch-speaking inhabitants of Brussels. Logie found indeed that Dutch-speaking inhabitants are concentrated in the boroughs of Anderlecht, Molenbeek, Berchem-Sainte-Agathe, Koekelberg, Jette, Brussels and Woluwe-Saint-Pierre[62]. These boroughs are all situated west of the canal except from the last two. However, this merely means that these areas are inhabited by a higher concentration of Dutch speakers and do therefore not exclude other language groups. It also means that this does not avoid other Dutch-speakers to settle down in other areas of the city. Moreover, since language is only a part of the identity and as many Brussels inhabitants speak several languages, the particular spatial divide is not of great importance in the interethnic relationship. We would therefore certainly not dare to say that the two ethnic groups live apart from each other.

Most of all, Brussels has the image of being a very tolerant place to live; people living there are used to other people with different (linguistic) backgrounds, social statuses and origins. Over the years, it became clear that entering into conflict with each other was of no use in Belgium's capital, given the massive immigration and internationalization of the city: *"Unlike thirty years ago, conflicts over language use in commercial establishments are relatively rare in Brussels today, and there is an apparent growing willingness among Brussels' residents speaking one language to learn the other major national language"*[63]. This confirms to a large extent the intentions behind the institutional measures taken in the latter half of the last century.

In the end, it seems that the inhabitants of Brussels find each other over boundaries of language and origin, in a common Brussels' identity. This identity is built upon the recognition that the city is a separate entity in the Belgian state, apart from

---

[61] Mort-Subite, *Barsten in België: een sociale geografie van de Belgische maatschappij*, Berchem 1990.
[62] F. Logie, *Ruimtelijke spreiding van de Nederlandstalige bevolking in Brussel-Hoofdstad*, "Taal en sociale integratie", vol. 3, Brussel 1981, pp. 87-109.
[63] A.B. Murphy, *Brussels: division in unity or unity in division?*, "Political geography", vol. 21, 2002, p. 699.

both Flanders and Wallonia. Concluding from Janssens' study, Brussels' inhabitants do not want to be associated with Wallonia, and certainly not with Flanders because of the supposedly racist and intolerant Flemish attitude. Instead, they construct (part of) their identity upon the multilingual and international character of the city, which they are proud of[64].

Conclusion

Through offering a contrasting view of the institutional arrangements, providing at least cooperation on paper and the day-to-day situation of Brussels, where we looked at the application of these institutional arrangements, we have attempted to discern whether Brussels can really be said to represent a hiatus between theoretical arrangements and the lived reality.

Our observations have led us to believe that the structural arrangements introduced via the different state reforms have not missed their target. In the case of Brussels, the dispute between the two language groups seems to belong ever more to the past. The language laws put in place therefore seem to have been a sensible reaction. Not only does the education system seem to be working flawlessly, also has the use of languages become less of a critical topic in Brussels' public institutions. At present, the city therefore presents an example of cooperation between two groups. The French-speakers clearly represent the majority of the Brussels populations, undoubtedly also due to the fact that Brussels gives home to a substantial number of immigrant groups which prefer to use French to Dutch. Nonetheless, it is also recognised that the Dutch-speaking commuters form a necessity for the future of Brussels as Belgium's capital. This further stimulates the mutual acceptance of both language groups and allows for a comparison with the theoretical cooperation model we presented at the beginning of this paper. Increasingly, the common sense among Brussels' citizens seems to prevail and the tolerant atmosphere allows for a particular coexistence of the two groups, which start to identify themselves more in a geographical way, rather than an ethno-linguistic way. It can be concluded that Brussels is indeed both in theory and in practice a good example of cooperation between ethnic groups.

This being said, the conflict is far from over yet. Nevertheless, it seems to have moved to other areas, such as the Brussels suburbs and the *communes à facilité*, briefly mentioned in the introduction. This means that still very little about the language dispute is being felt by Brussels' citizens in their everyday lives. However, despite the conflict having moved to a more federal level, Brussels is hardly ever to be left out of the language conflict. The *communes à facilité* and the *Brussel-Halle-Vilvoorde* election district issue are but two examples of that. Therefore, even though

---

[64] R. Janssens, *Taalgebruik in Brussel en de plaats van het Nederlands. Enkele recente bevindingen*, "Brussels Studies", vol. 13, 2008, p. 15.

there is no longer a conflict within Brussels, its position in the language dispute still is of primary importance and that is unlikely to cease being so in the short-term future.

We wish to thank Paolo Dardanelli as well as the participants of the 2009 Scientific Conference on Poland in the 21st century, for their extremely helpful comments and remarks on earlier versions of this paper.

Helsinki
A Divided City?
Emilia Palonen

Helsinki may appear as a most homogeneous city. Almost everyone looks the same and behaves the same. There appears not to be a massive gap in income between the citizen. Few show their wealth, there have been no beggars – until recently[1]. The public discourse in Finland presumes that the country is not divided. Consensus or unity is what is sought after: both for effective politics and for a strong sense of identity. Difference is harder to tolerate. Nevertheless, a number of subcultures mark urban life in Helsinki: multicultural art center, active gay night-life scene, a number of goth and heavy metal youth, and skaters inhabit public space. Recent debates about culture, identity and expression in public space in Helsinki have been on graffiti: the city had reversed its 1990s encouraging policy on the graffiti-art to a zero-tolerance approach to any tags or graffiti, and wiped out of the earlier city-sponsored urban art graffiti in 2000s. This article, however, focuses on more macro level political divisions. In short, it claims the following; Helsinki is an officially bilingual city where cooperation between the Swedish-speakers and Finnish-speakers has progressed far towards assimilation of the Swedish-speakers into the majority population, but a more urgent new conflict from other ethnic minorities looming. This takes up spatially the same division-lines as the one between the wealthy and the poor in Helsinki. Although Helsinki is thought of as a homogeneous city, it is in fact quite heterogeneous space of contrasts at a deeper glance.

From various perspectives, Helsinki has been a divided city for a long time. For the passing-by tourist the bilingual street names indicate a divide. Helsinki, indeed, is officially a bilingual city. Finland is an officially bilingual country, chosen to preserve Swedish language after having been part of imperial Sweden until 1809. Still today, Finland has a six percent strong Swedish-speaking minority, who according to the Finnish law, are provided in civil service in their mother tongue. Helsinki is one of 34 bilingual municipalities in Finland[2]. Municipalities are by law officially bi-

---

[1] The Romanian Roma beggars arrived in Helsinki in spring 2007, and sparked lively discussion about the use of public space (e.g. "Ydin", 2/2008).
[2] There are 348 municipalities in Finland as of 1.1.2009, 19 of them are Swedish-speaking, 20 bilingual with Finnish-speaking majority and 14 bilingual with Swedish-speaking majority. Source: Finnish municipalities web pages: http://www.kunnat.net/k_perussivu.asp?path=1;29;341;486;496;30278 (updated 11 January 2009, retrieved 27 March 2009).

lingual when eight percent or at least 3,000 people of the population have Swedish, or in Swedish minority communities Finnish, as their mother language. Helsinki has a population of circa 569,000, of whom Swedish-speakers constitute 6.1 percent in 2008. In comparison, speakers of other languages than Finnish or Swedish make up 9 percent of the population, and foreign citizens are 6.4 percent of the total population in Helsinki[3].

In practice, most Swedish-speakers usually use Finnish as the language of communication[4]. Unlike in those living in Swedish-majority municipalities, the Helsinki Swedish-speakers know Finnish well. Therefore one rarely hears Swedish in communication: most likely this would be in the west of the city – or the traditional inner-city department store Stockmann, the Swedish Theater or Swedish schools or higher- or popular-education units. In bilingual cities on the Finnish west coast one is greeted in two languages routinely at the cashier's of a supermarket. In Helsinki, instead of "Kiitos! Tack!", it is more likely to hear "Kiitos! Thank-you!" greeted at the end of the shopping in the center of the city.

However, the most multicultural areas are further away: a metro journey to eastern Helsinki would take one to areas where the most immigrants live. In the most eastern of the six greater districts of Helsinki live 29 percent of those who speak other than Finnish or Swedish as their mother tongue. In the eastern district they constitute 14 percent of the population in 2008. A tram journey takes one to the perhaps grunge-hippiest area of Helsinki, Kallio beyond the legendary Long Bridge that used to be the veritable frontier between the workers' and the bourgeois Helsinki. Beyond that one would take a metro to the eastern suburbs, passing by few wealthy coastal neighbourhoods. This paper suggests that the divide in Helsinki is no longer a Swedish-Finnish conflict, but increasingly becomes contested between the multicultural and monocultural Finland, i.e. immigrants between assimilated Swedish-speakers and Finns. It draws on earlier spatial-cultural conflict-lines. The methods of analysis include historical analysis and contemporary quantitative data.

Background

State of the Swedish-speakers today

Professor Erik Allardt has argued that the Swedish-speakers have created a problem for themselves in contemporary Helsinki by refusing to believe they would be served well in their mother tongue[5]. Against the view presented by the Canadian re-

---

[3] Data as of 1 January 2008. Source: official pages of the municipality http://www.hel.fi/wps/portal/Helsinki/Artikkeli?WCM_GLOBAL_CONTEXT=/helsinki/fi/Helsinki-tietoa+ja+linkkej_ (retrieved 27 March 2009).
[4] E. Allardt, *Svenska på stan; Stadin Ruotsi*, Helsinki 2000.
[5] E. Allardt, *Svenska på stan; Stadin Ruotsi*, Helsinki 2000.

searcher Kenneth D. McRae in what he considers an otherwise excellent book, *Conflict and Compromise in Multilingual Societies* from 1997, Allardt – Swedish-speaking Finn himself – found out in his study that Finnish-speakers' view Swedish-speakers sympathetically in Finland. Allardt points out that McRae's data that reveals a clearly negative attitude by Finnish-speakers to Swedish-speakers dates from the 1970s[6]. Today – or in 2000 when Allardt writes – the situation is very different. In fact, the transformation from the 1970s is indicative of a process of assimilation by the Swedish-speakers.

This can be seen as a positive development of cooperation over conflict, but Allardt points out the dangers assimilation. He asks whether Finnish-speakers have been spoiled by Swedish-speakers' readiness to use Finnish, that when they actually start a conversation in Swedish, Finnish-speakers are left puzzled – even though they in principle hold it good that Swedish-language service is an option in civil service, at least. In Allardt's study 81 percent of Swedish-speakers in Helsinki use always or mainly Finnish in their affairs in the city. In civil service 68 percent relies using Finnish. Those who use Finnish never, rarely or sometimes constitute 21 percent in affairs in the city, and 32 in civil service. *"It is of course not an ideal situation"*, notes Allardt, *"that Swedish-speaking Finns never use Finnish in bilingual metropolitan Helsinki region"*. Besides older people who have moved to Helsinki from areas that were only Swedish-speaking, six percent of Swedish-speaking Finns in their 30s never spoke Finnish in Helsinki, and eight percent rarely spoke it in the city. There are still those who are hostile to each other among both Finnish and Swedish-speakers[7]. Language, however, does not appear as a source of conflict for the wide majority of the population.

Positive attitudes seem to correlate with the knowledge of the language: those with the lowest level of education are more hostile, Allardt deducts[8]. Furthermore, it seems that Helsinki-based Swedish-speakers seem not to reveal their Swedish-speaking identity, but seek to appear equal with the Finnish-speaking majority. This, Allardt claims, poses a danger for keeping Swedish as a public language, and thus also for Swedish-speaking culture at large. Bilingualism could turn into Finnish-English bilingualism[9].

Cooperation has moved to wipe out unique and even productive cultural differences – perhaps some of the Swedish-speakers way of life, that could be maintained through friction. Particular identities need to express their claims *vis à vis* other identities, make their difference heard, whereas universalizing claims in the identity-politics of the majority may erode space for minorities and cultural difference[10].

---

[6] *Ibidem*, pp. 8, 16.
[7] *Ibidem*, pp. 7, 17.
[8] *Ibidem*, pp. 11, 19.
[9] *Ibidem*, pp. 13–14, 21–22.
[10] See e.g. E. Laclau, *Universalism, Particularism and the Question of Identity*, [in:] J. Rajchman, *Identity in Question*, Routledge, London–New York 1995, pp. 93–110.

Development of the bilingual city

Throughout its history Helsinki has been bi- or multilingual city. Founded in the middle of Swedish-speaking south coast in 1550 by the Swedish king Gustav Vasa, it attracted a lot of Finnish-speaking immigrants in the 17th and 18th centuries. The construction of the defense castle Viapori in 1748–1766, however, brought in Swedish-speaking immigrants, mainly artisans, from Sweden. The Baltic Sea trade brought in seamen from Sweden – as well as other Baltic countries. By 1780s Swedish language dominated. Even though a weekly Finnish-language sermon was held in the Lutheran Church, its necessity was under discussion, as the Finnish-speakers were practically bilingual. Swedish dominated in all ranks, and Finnish-speakers moving to Helsinki assimilated and adapted to the higher valued Swedish language, from whichever social background or area they were coming[11].

Swedish was the language in town far into the second part of 19th century, when major changes started to take place. First of all, Helsinki became the most important center in Finland, which in 1809, established itself as an administrative unit of its own, the Finnish Grand Duchy in Imperial Russia – the shop window for Enlightenment in Russia. Industrialization expanded the city beyond and more rapidly than other regional centers (most importantly Turku, Vyborg, Tampere, Pori, Oulu, Kuopio, and later Vaasa). The expansion brought in people also from the Finnish-speaking countryside. The new comers located themselves north east of the center of the city, beyond the Long Bridge (*Pitkäsilta*). By the turn of the century, in 1900, already 51 percent of the Helsinki citizen declared themselves as Finnish-speakers[12].

Swedish and Finnish were, however, not the only languages, Paunonen's charts reveal that in 1870, twelve percent of inhabitants were Russian-speakers and German was the native language of two percent in Helsinki. Finnish was spoken by 26 percent and Swedish by roughly 57 percent of Helsinki inhabitants. Polish became one of the minority languages also because of the presence of Poles in the imperial Russian army in Helsinki. The Jewish minority was some 200-person strong. During the 20th century this variety of languages was lost, but the 21st century presents a return to multilingualism[13].

Spatial and social differentiation started presenting themselves in Helsinki already in the late 19th century. Heikki Waris studied in the 1930s the emergence of working-class neighborhood in the north side of the Long Bridge (*Pitkäsilta*) in the 19th century[14]. "*Finns and Swedes were living in same areas north of Long Bridge as elsewhere in Helsinki*". Although from the 1860s and the 1870s there was rapid immigration into this area from the Finnish-speaking countryside, this Long Bridge

---

[11] H. Paunonen, *Vähemmistökielestä varioivaksi valtakieleksi*, [in:] K. Juusela, K. Nisula, *Helsinki kieliyhteisönä*, Helsinki 2006, pp. 19–21.
[12] *Ibidem*, pp. 22–23.
[13] *Ibidem*, p. 24.
[14] H. Waris, *Työläisyhteiskunnan syntyminen pitkän sillan toiselle puolelle*, 2. edition, Weilin+Göös, Helsinki 1973.

community remained bi- or multilingual. A third of those living in the workers quarters north of the Long Bridge were Swedish-speakers still in the turn of the century. Differentiation was made on class basis, or regionally in the case of local gangs where a new Helsinki dialect *Stadin slangi* was used. This language or dialect drew from a variety of languages around the Baltic Sea. In the course of the influx of Finnish immigrants and improvement of the status of Finnish, this neighborhood was also turning into a predominantly Finnish-speaking one. Language was not as important as pragmatism of getting-by. Mixed marriages and house-holds were relatively common.

Language was also not as important as class-struggle. From the start there were two Swedish-speaking political parties (Svenska partiet and Arbetarsförbunded) of which the workers' variant joined the social democrats already in the first universal elections for the Finnish parliament in 1906[15]. The task of representing Swedish voice in the parliament was divided, but class identity went before linguistic identity for those in the workers movement. The Swedish-speaking social democratic members of parliament would still into the second part of 20th century deliver their speeches in Swedish.

It was a different story among the intellectuals, upper class, and bourgeoisie, on the south side of the Long Bridge, where language was an important part of social engagement. Politics of language became predominant. The Fennoman movement since mid-19th century made a case for Finnish as the new dominant public language. By this they opposed besides Swedish also Russian – the language of the Empire. As a political act much of the intellectuals and bourgeoisie learned Finnish. Language wars took place verbally and socially between the Swedish and Finnish speakers. The two groups started to differentiate themselves through social acts. This included more manifested activity such as ritually meeting up by statues of literary figures associated to either the Fennoman or Swedish-speaking historical canon. Political symbolic landscape and its usage bore witness to the division between Swedish and Finnish speakers; Runeberg's statue and Lönnrot's statue were the poles drawing Swedish and Finnish speaking students. The choice of language at the University of Helsinki was debated. The political elite was also polarized, and each camp claiming power for themselves. This went parallel with the cultural life that was polarized. There were Swedish and Finnish as well as Workers' theaters. Particularly manifested in newly independent Finland in the 1920s and 1930s, was the struggle for public funding of arts: one the one hand, a battle between Finns and Swedes – but on the other hand, also between workers' cultural venues as opposed to the Finnish and Swedish ones[16].

The conflict is not a blood-based ethnic strife, but a political one. In fact there is no common genetic background between Swedish-speakers that would differenti-

---

[15] J. Sundberg, *Svenskhetens dilemma i Finland*, Helsinki 1985.
[16] See e.g. J. Varho, *Suomen valtion taiteelle osoittama rahoitus ja siitä käyty keskustelu sanomalehdissä vuosina 1925-1929*, extended MA thesis, University of Jyväskylä and University of Turku February 2009.

ate them from the Finnish speaking Finns: most Swedes moving to Finland were male and the languages of the "colonizers" or the urban majority were learned for pragmatic reasons by the population[17]. Many of the Fennomans were not originally Finnish-speakers but learned the language for their struggle. They changed, often translated, their Swedish names to Finnish ones. Families were often divided – and in some cases brothers ended up with different Finnified versions of their names.

Their politics was against the Swedish rule – that ended in 1809. The Enlightened ruler, Alexander I of Russia, had given Finland and autonomous status. Finland was the window to the West and a testing-ground for reforms in Russia. But it was neither the Russian rule that Fennomans longed for. They wanted an independent Finland, and based their claim on Herderian ethno-linguistic nationhood and the ideal of the nation-state. The choice of language used in public occasions was, therefore, a demonstration of a political ideology – rather than ethnic background. Another political position was that of the Russophiles, who saw the unity with Imperial Russia as an opportunity rather than a hindrance. Nevertheless, as the Fennomans learned Finnish, and even bourgeoisie and intellectuals moved from Finnish-speaking mainland to Helsinki, even the south of the city was becoming increasingly bilingual.

The dominant divide became that marked by the Long Bridge, the divide between red and white Helsinki. After the First World War and the independence afforded to Finland during the Russian revolution in December 1917, a bloody civil war broke out: workers and rural tenants versus bourgeoisie and small-holders. Sieges and inner city battles took place in major cities. On the north side of the Long Bridge, protecting the working-class neighborhood a defensible bastion of the workers' movement Paasitorni, was built in 1908 and badly damaged in the battles of the Civil War in 1918[18]. Again, what was at stake was not an ethnic battle, but a social one.

During the Interwar period there was a strong emphasis on Finnishness and nation-building. Fennoman national romantic revival turned into something more radical and openly conflict-driven. The Swedish-language usage faced critique from the popular xenophobic Academic Karelia Association (AKS) and the True Finns (Aitosuomalaiset) movement. It was no longer fashionable to claim Swedish-language as mother tongue in 20th century Helsinki. The growing capital city attracted also more and more Finnish speakers and Swedish-language lost its dominance. After the Second World War, Helsinki became clearly Finnish-speaking. One reason was the influx of refugees from behind the new Eastern border, Karelia, the region lost in war to the Soviet Union. Subsequently, the relatively late urbanization of Finnish countryside, the structural changes in 1960s and 1970s, also brought in

---

[17] See e.g. H. Nevanlinna, *Suomen ruotsinkielisten geneettinen tausta*, [in:] L. Huldén et. al., *Suomenruotsalaisuus suomalaisessa yhteiskunnassa*, Studia Generalia, University of Helsinki, Helsinki 1985, pp. 103-108.
[18] '100-Year-Old Paasitorni' (History), http://www.paasitorni.fi/en/ (retrieved 4 January 2010).

masses from Finnish speaking areas. Whereas, in 1910, 35 percent of the population were Swedish speakers, the figure was 29 percent in 1930, 19 percent in 1950, and only 11 percent in 1970[19].

Unsurprisingly, as the contemporary percentage of Swedish-speakers in Helsinki has moved to six percent, the Swedish-speakers feel marginalized and use Finnish in public. As already indicated, there is no longer apparent conflict, between the Swedish-speaking and Finnish-speaking Finns. Many Swedish-speakers become bi-lingual, as do the Finnish-speakers who seek an advantage for their children – training them to become fluent in an Indo-European rather than Fenno-Ugric language in popular Swedish-speaking kindergartens and schools. Allardt deducted from his study that as Swedish is a compulsory subject at Finnish schools, a better educated population implies a better knowledge of Swedish – and, as a consequence, readiness to accept linguistic difference[20]. Yet at the same time there are continuous debates on the issue of compulsory Swedish-studies. Some argue that English is much more relevant, others that Finnish-Swedish language and culture is dependent on the learning-requirement of the second national language.

All in all, the Swedish-speaking population articulate their distinct identity and maintain a cultural scene through newspapers, radio, TV, and theaters, even sports clubs, and cultural or political associations. The Swedish spoken in Finland is distinct from that spoken in Sweden and the *Finlandsvenska* culture also differs from Swedish culture. However, it is also not homogeneous: Swedish-speakers come from all social backgrounds. Furthermore, it is divided regionally. As John Westerholm points out: *"The Swedish-speaking bureaucrat living in Helsinki and fluent in Finnish, has little in common with the Swedish-speaking tomato farmer from Närpes* [in the Swedish-speaking West Coast]. *This is mutual"*[21]. The largest Swedish-language daily newspaper *Hufvudstadsbladet* is mainly for the Swedish-speakers in the south – the daily for the capital city as it is literally called. *Vasabladet* and *Åbounderrättelse* take care of the Vaasa and Turku regions. A cultural magazine *Ny Tid* caters weekly news for the left-wing Swedish-speaking Finns, and there are different forms of sub-cultures where Swedish-speakers have their own scene, unless they choose to integrate to the Finnish one. The advantage of this community, that amounts to circa six percent in Finland is the existing institutions and accumulated wealth. One of the most important forces for the Swedish-speaking identity is the Swedish People's Party, which has been closely connected to the Swedish-speaking voluntary associations. However, as Kreader and Sundberg have observed, as the voluntary associations become increasingly bilingual – operating pragmatically and saving resources – also the support of the SPP has been decreasing[22]. The party often takes

---

[19] H. Paunonen, *op. cit.*, p. 24.
[20] E. Allardt, *Svenska på stan; Stadin Ruotsi*, Helsinki 2000.
[21] J. Westerholm, *Onko Suomessa regionalismia?*, [in:] P. Raento (ed.), *Yhdessä erikseen: Kansalliset konfliktit Länsi-Euroopassa*, Gaudeamus, Helsinki 1993.
[22] M. Kreander, J. Sundberg, *Cultural autonomy in politics and in Swedish voluntary organizations*, "International Journal of the Sociology of Language", vol. 2007, issue 187188, pp. 55–73.

part in coalition governments: since the 2007 parliamentary elections the Swedish People's Party holds the posts of both Minister of Culture and Minister of Migration and European Affairs. Commonly, "duck pond" is a term used to describe the close-knittedness of Swedish-speaking community – or at least its elite, mainly based in Helsinki. Considering the relative size of the minority they are well represented in all levels of public administration.

Analysis: Mapping division-lines

Language and prosperity of neighborhoods

The Helsinki of 19th century was clearly divided into a 'prosperous' inner city and the 'backward' outer districts, the controlled and well-built south on Esplanadi, Erottaja, Bulevardi and the squares Senaatintori and Kauppatori. Language was used as a tool for reinforcing the communal barriers and sense of space. Swedish was the language of the centre in the late 19th century. Differences were clearly marked and manifested. As a sign of distinction, on the main boulevard, Esplanadi, the Finnish-minded Fennomans and others were walking on the north side and Swedish-speakers on the south side of the park. Also the place to live of the Helsinki inhabitants was clearly marked by class and social status, where differentiation was highly important in the turn of the previous century[23]. Sense of place and placing oneself was important for the identity.

This demonstrates, there are long-standing attempts by the elite to maintain the inner core of Helsinki for the elite. Various division-lines emerge that mark social differentiation at certain time. The spaces on the edges of the inner core inhabited by bureaucrats, artisans, Jews, and some workers were slowly in the course of the late 20th century turned into expensive center districts. Prior to that, from the Interwar period the bourgeoisie started relocating northwards to new districts Töölö and Munkkiniemi, whereas the upper classes remained in the south or moved to closer to the sea side.

Social housing projects brought the first workers' residencies were on the north side of the Long Bridge. Tiny flats in apartment blocks brought pride to the worker's movement: in city-developments in Hakaniemi and Kallio, people could move to more human-like conditions from the crowded huts. The 1920s and 1930s was the era of functional housing for the poor in the north side of the Long Bridge, especially in Vallila, and for the middle classes in Töölö, north of the inner core but west of the railway line, which still works as a social line of division in Helsinki[24]. Töölö was built on what used to be open space in the early 1900s. It attracted middle-classes, and those elites who longed for modern architecture, and spacious, stylish living in luxurious apartments or villas. The segregation and division-lines

---

[23] I. Uuskallio, *Arvostetut asuinsijat*, Helsinki 2001, pp. 45–46.
[24] I. Uuskallio, *Arvostetut asuinsijat*, Helsinki 2001.

were, as a consequence, clearly marked on the map of Helsinki. And they were made on grounds of social status.

As Waris has discovered Swedish was spoken in the working class neighborhoods. The Swedish-speakers in the working class neighborhoods in the east however assimilated better. In the census one could respond knowledge of the language that one sees as the most respected, and thus bilingualism did not become apparent in the statistics. In the interwar period the upper class southern districts remained bilingual, Töölö had 38 percent Swedish-speaking inhabitants in 1930, and Northwestern coastline, especially Munkkiniemi, was bilingual. The Swedish language dominated in the respected neighborhoods still in the interwar period[25].

By 1950s and 1960s respected neighborhoods were those marked by garden city character, space, increasing social mixture – also in terms of language, living-space, and low-rise buildings[26]. By 1960 especially Munkkiniemi, Lauttasaari and Haaga attracted the best of inhabitants. In those neighborhoods, the top two social sections made up roughly two thirds of the population, whereas in the inner city they were only 42 percent of the inhabitants[27]. These western neighborhoods and the centre are where today's Swedish-speakers mostly live. As the new neighborhoods were built in the early 20th century, the center districts became more socially mixed: the social differentiation was done on street-by street basis, argues Irma Uuskallio in her study of respected neighborhoods[28].

Contemporary conflicts: politics and prosperity

The political conflict between the East and West Helsinki based on the Long Bridge south of Hakaniemi still persists: there is a clear divide in the voting-patterns. East of that line, apart from few neighborhoods by the sea-front – including the garrison district Santahamina, the vote goes for the left parties and the Greens. The National Coalition party, main party of the political right wing gains high numbers of votes – along-side Swedish People's party in the western and southern part of the city, although this is not visible for the maps. Figure 1 shows the parliamentary elections in 2007 and Figure 2 local election results from 2008 (Figure 1 and 2: blue is National Coalition Party, red is SDP and green is the Greens). The Greens also hold the Vallila-Kallio-Alppila area with small apartments in what could be the geographical centre (not inner city) of Helsinki. The second map in figure 2 represents the voting activity, which is much lower in the eastern parts of the city than western Helsinki. The average yearly income levels closely correlate with that spatial differentiation in voting. (Figure 3) Similarly, the average income correlates with mother language of the residents.

---

[25] Waris, *op. cit.*, pp. 71–76.
[26] Uuskallio, *op. cit.*, p. 122.
[27] *Ibidem*, pp. 95–96.
[28] *Ibidem*, pp. 84–85, 95–96.

Figure 1. 'Greatest party in Helsinki', Social Democrats, National Coalition Party, Greens

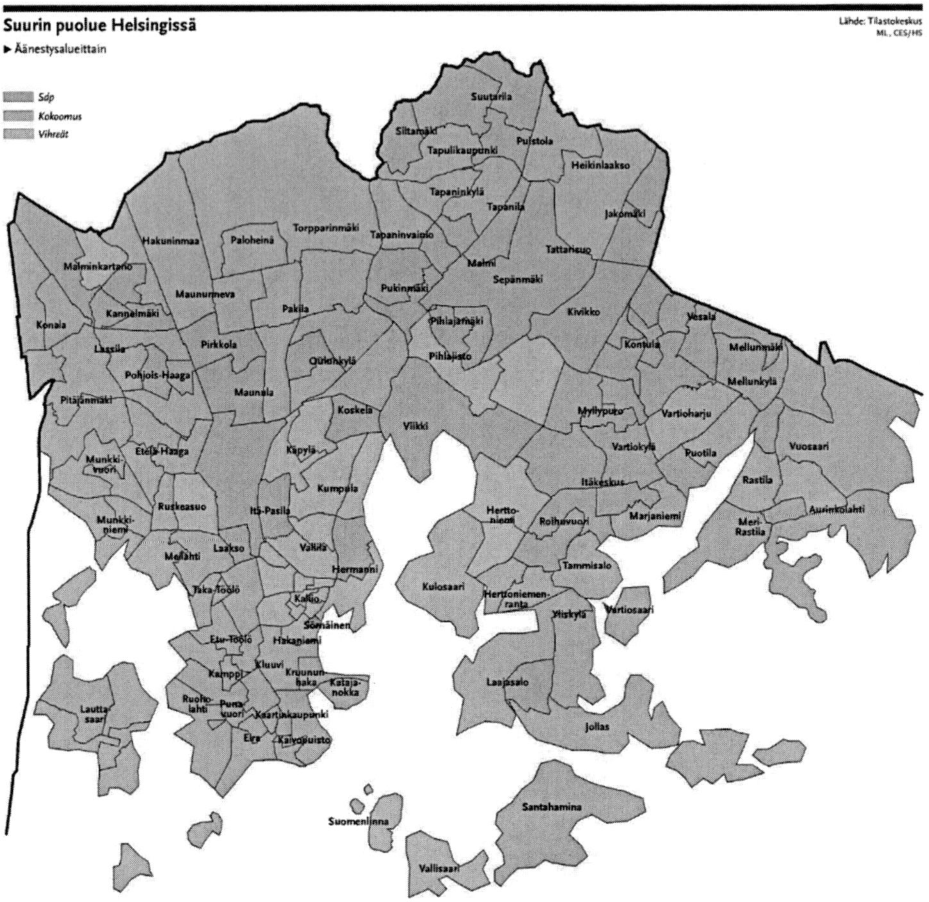

Source: "Helsingin Sanomat", 19 March 2007, http://www.fs.fi/nakoislehti/2007/03/19/, p. A7.

In addition to the larger difference between the three big parties, in which Greens belong in Helsinki, there's another interesting point of comparison. As one of the smaller parties, the Swedish People's Party has received a new rival: a radical right-wing party the True Finns. They run a migrant unfriendly, but usually not openly racist campaign. In the 2007 national elections who took 2.6 percent of the vote in the national elections in Helsinki, but already 4,1 nationwide. In the 2008 elections, however, they made a leap to 5.3 percent in Helsinki and 5.4 nationwide. In comparison to the 6.3 percent of the Swedish People's Party's gain in Helsinki and 4.7 nationwide in 2008, this is a significant figure in Finnish and local politics. Predominantly the figures are high on precisely the areas which tend to have low income levels.

There are vast amounts of socio-economic data about Helsinki that could be used in analyzing divisions. These figures are derived from Helsinki City online database (Aluesarjat). Helsinki is divided to different levels of analysis, there are seven

Figure 2. 'Party with largest share of votes and voting-activity in Helsinki', map 1: Party with most votes (SDP, Greens, National Coalition Party), map 2: Share of active eligible voters

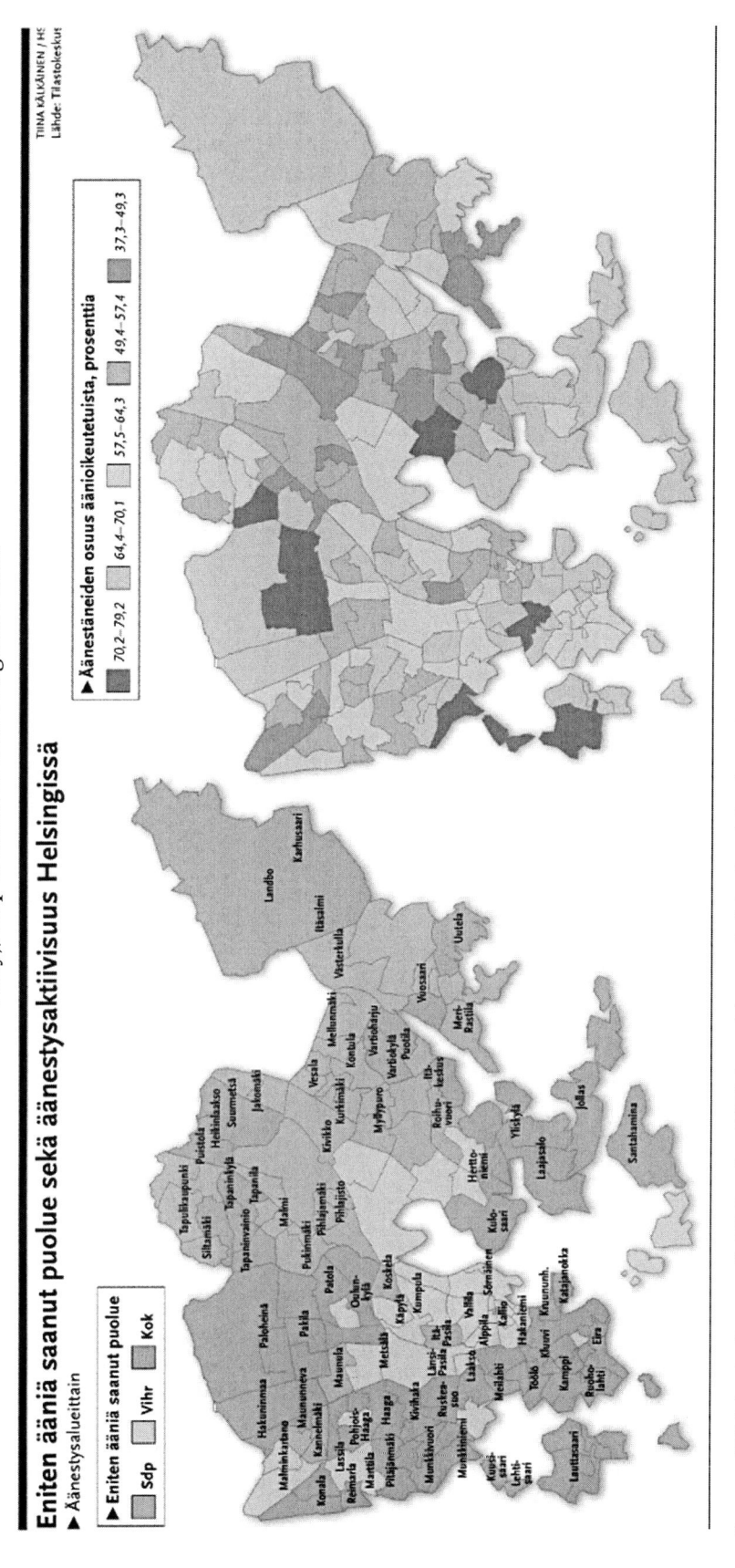

Source: "Helsingin Sanomat", 28 October 2008, http://www.fs.fi/nakoislehti/2008/10/28/, p. A6.

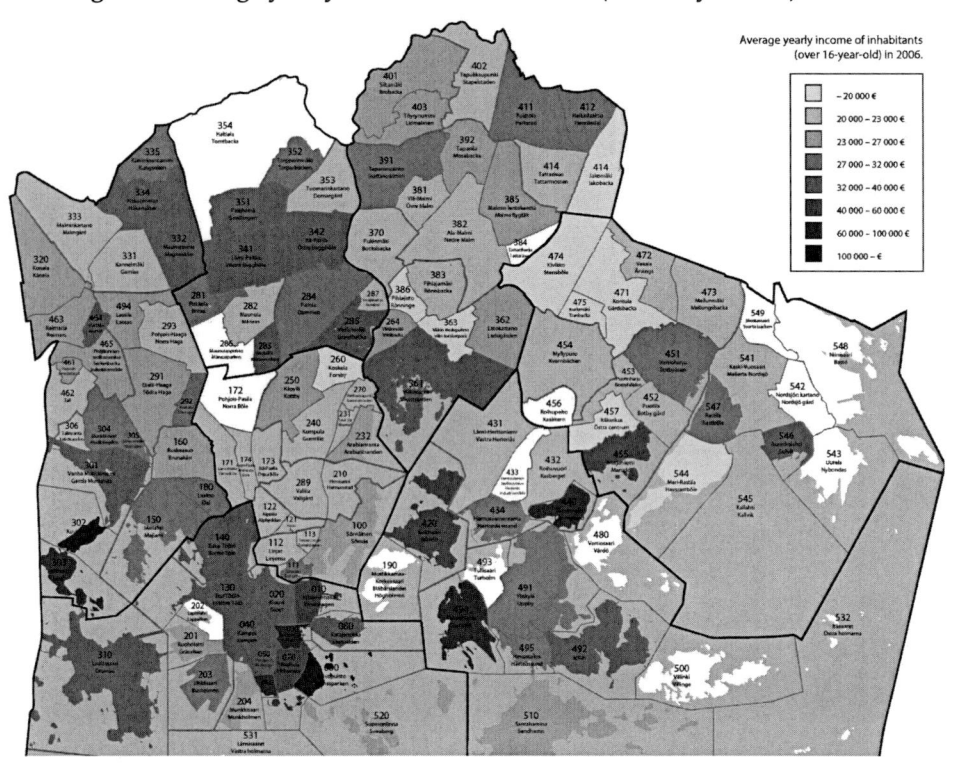

Figure 3. Average yearly income of inhabitants (over 16-year-old) in 2006

Source: Helsinki municipality: Regional series. Statistical database, http://www.aluesarjat.fi/. Graphics for maps: Jami Järvinen, 2009.

greater districts[29], 34 basic districts[30], and some 130 sub-district[31]. Looking at the data, however, the clearest differentiations between parts of Helsinki manifest at the sub-district. Perhaps as part of Nordic mixed housing projects, there are enclaves of wealth and poverty in Helsinki. These do not show on a comparison on larger district level and one could imagine that the equality-providing Nordic model has worked. However, looking at district-part level, the enclaves of wealth and poverty become visible. The division does not emerge between East and West or South and North in Helsinki. Rather there are four stripes of land crossing diagonally North-West to South-East. Furthermore, and more simplified perhaps, the closeness of water implies most often a wealthy neighborhood.

Despite the progressive taxation, there are districts in Helsinki, where income levels are extremely high, and extremely poor. While the average annual income level is 27,258 euro for those 15 years or older, each larger area does not deviate from

---

[29] See map on: http://www.aluesarjat.fi/aluejakokartat/.%5CHelsingin_suurpiirit.html.
[30] http://www.aluesarjat.fi/aluejakokartat/.%5CHelsingin_peruspiirit.html.
[31] http://www.aluesarjat.fi/aluejakokartat/.%5CHelsingin_osaalueet.html.

that margin for more than 10,400 euros per year, which nevertheless is over a third of the average income – and thus a significant sum.

Average income	2006
1. Souther greater district	37,626
2. Western	27,817
3. Central	22,443
4. Northern	30,718
5. North-eastern	23,754
6. South-eastern	30,288
7. Eastern	22,911
Average	27,258

Source: *Helsinki municipality: Regional series. Statistical database*, http://www.aluesarjat.fi/. (For a map of the numbered districts see lin on footnote 29.)

South is the best off, while Northern districts with mixed and mostly detached single-family housing is the second most prosperous, the coastal area of the South-east also hosts well of neighborhoods. Central, Eastern and North-eastern districts have clearly below average income levels, whereas West is around the average in Helsinki. Greatest distinctions, however emerge in the sub-district level. Just to list the polar opposites, Kuusisaari, an island in the West, has an average income level of 189,000, and Kaivopuisto in the South 159,000. Jakomäki in the North East has an average income level of 17,600 euros and Viikki Science Park only 12,050 euros yearly.

Contemporary conflicts: language

The differentiation on the basis of mother tongue shows a different kind of picture: The Swedish speakers are 34,500 out of 569,500 Helsinki citizens (2008), that is six percent of the population of the city. This might explain why there is little sense of division there. They are, however, mainly concentrated in the South 12,300, 36 percent of all Swedish-speakers live there, and constitute 12.6 percent of the population of this area, and West there are 6,700 Swedish-speakers, also 6.8 percent of the population. Mapping the mother language figures, it becomes clear that there are areas where Swedish-speakers have particularly concentrated on, mostly in the west and the center – but also some corners like the new acquisition by Helsinki from neighboring Sipoo – and while their numbers in Helsinki are in decline, there is a rise projected for 2018. Partly it is anticipating the return of many who moved to the countryside to Helsinki, partly it assumes that Swedish will be picked up by more Finnish speakers and new-comers to Helsinki. Looking at the city statistics today, both conflict and cooperation are clearly present in Helsinki.

Figures 4-5 demonstrate in which parts of Helsinki the Swedish-speakers lived in 1992 and 2008. One can distinguish the most Swedish-speaking neighbourhoods in the coastal areas: Kaivopuisto 36 percent, Ullanlinna and Eira 21 percent and Kaartinkaupunki 19 percent in the old and prosperous districts of the south, as well as the islands Kulosaari 20 percent and Lauttasaari 15 percent of Swedish-speaking inhabitants. Though there is a larger consentration in the South and West of the city, in coastal Tahvonlahti in the South-East there are 16 percent of Swedish-speaking inhabitants.

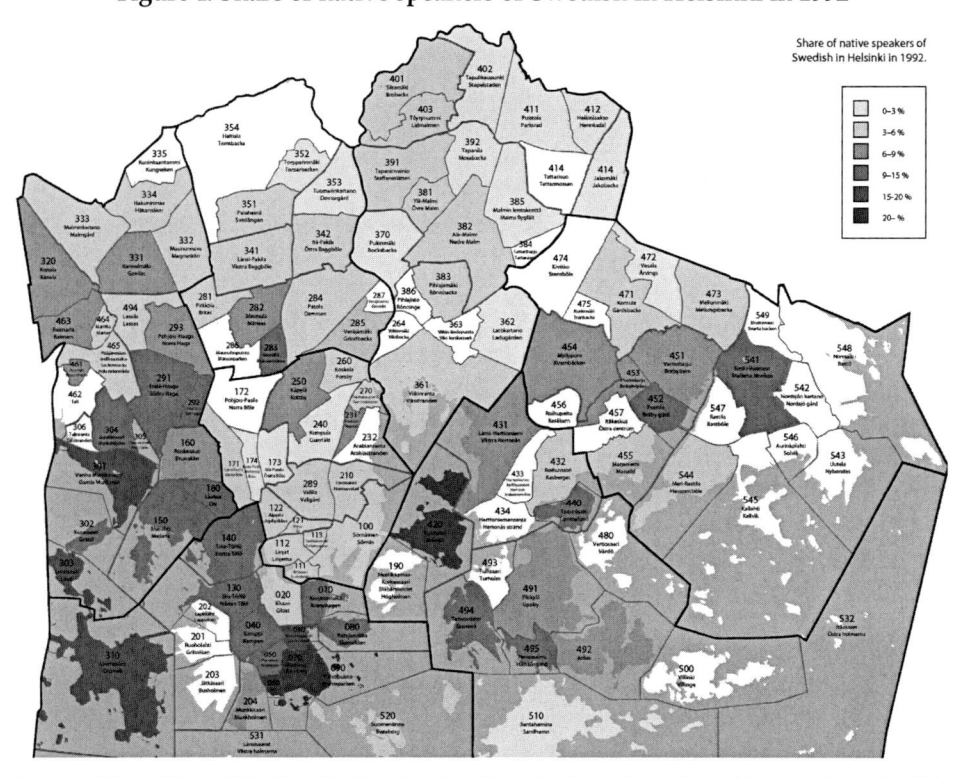

Figure 4. Share of native speakers of Swedish in Helsinki in 1992

Source: Helsinki municipality: Regional series. Statistical database, http://www.aluesarjat.fi/.

While the number of Swedish speakers drops slightly, less than ten percent in Helsinki from 1992 to 2008, the number of native languages other than Swedish or Finnish are on an increase. In fact, from 1992 to 2000 their number had tripled, whereas from 1992 to 2008, they increased almost five-fold, from 10,700 to 51,000. Their number in the South district had doubled, to six percent of the district's population, 6,000 in total. In the west, they are 7.6 percent, more than the Swedish-speakers, and their amount had increased almost four-fold. In the Center district they were 6.6 percent of the population, 5000 people. In the prosperous garden district of the North non-Finnish nor Swedish speakers are only four percent, but in North-East 9.6 percent and in the East 14 percent, increasing ten-fold to 14,600 from mere 1,500. A pattern starts to develop: East and North-East host significant

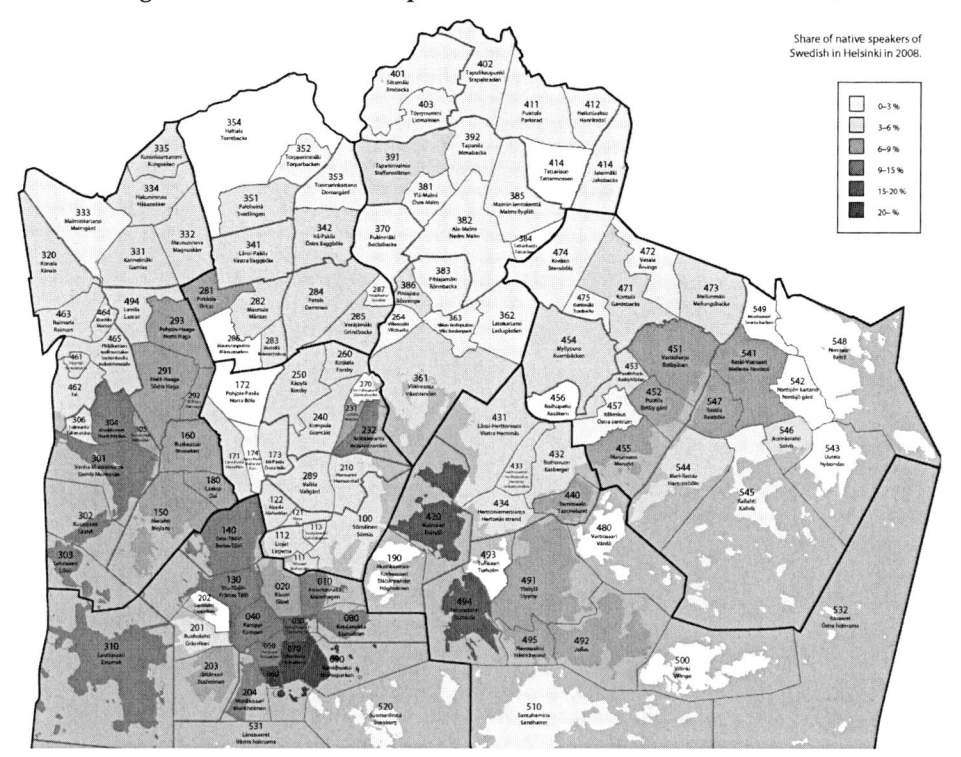

Figure 5. Share of native speakers of Swedish in Helsinki in 2008

Source: Helsinki municipality: Regional series. Statistical database, http://www.aluesarjat.fi/.

numbers of migrants, well exceeding the number of Swedish speakers in the West and Centre districts at large.

Why did this happen? First of all 1992 is a crucial year of comparison (the earliest one I could get as well), when the post-Soviet immigration started. The most spoken "other languages" are Russian, Somali, Estonian, English, Arabic, Chinese, Kurdish, Spanish, and Turkish[32]. Where did this segregation happen? Eastern districts are also areas where there has been housing-developments in the 1970s onwards, and especially in the 2000s. Social housing is available. On the sub-district level the immigration follows previous migrations of the poorest of the society: Jakomäki, a well known suburb already from the 1970s is poor and full of immigrants and has 21 percent of inhabitants whose native language is neither Finnish nor Swedish. There are five other district-parts that where more than a fifth of the population are migrant-based. Meri-Rastila, a poorer district in the East by the sea, with 25 percent, Kivikko 23 percent, Kallahti 22 percent, and Itäkeskus 21 percent as well as the Science Park of Viikki with 24 percent of inhabitants who speak other

---

[32] On 1.01.2005, P. Nuolijärvi, *Helsingin kieliolot 2000-luvun alussa*, [in:] K. Juusela, K. Nisula *Helsinki kieliyhteisönä*, Helsinki 2006, p. 328.

Figure 6. Share of those speaking other than Hinnish or Swedish as their native language in Helsinki in 2008

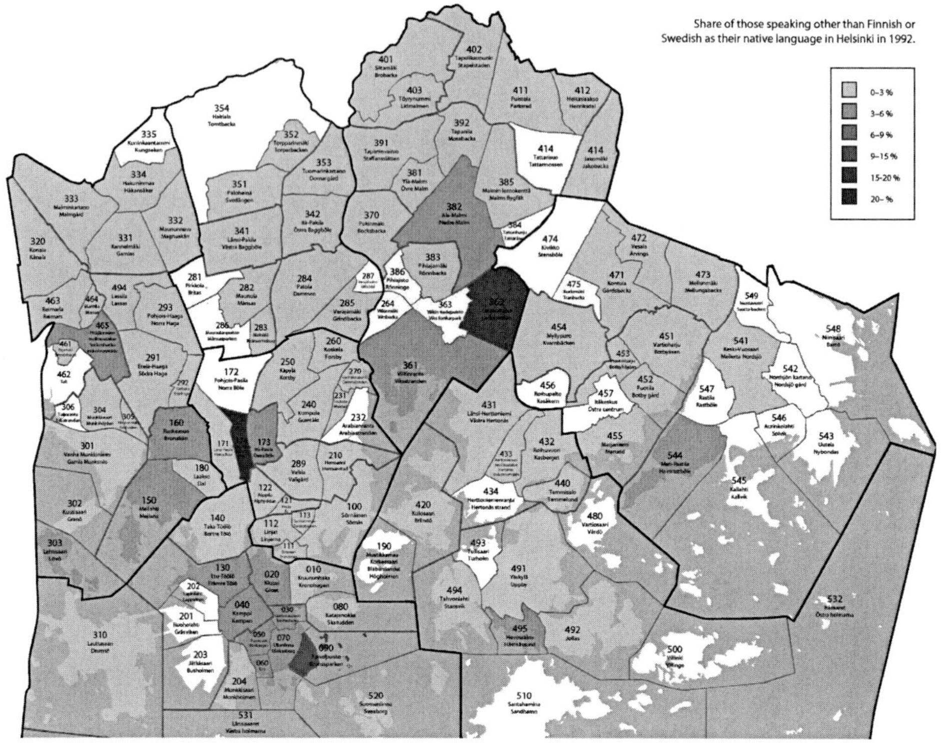

Source: Helsinki municipality: Regional series. Statistical database, http://www.aluesarjat.fi/.

than Finnish or Swedish as their native language. Just behind are Kurkimäki 19, Vesala 18 percent, Itä-Pasila in the Centre district 18 percent, Pihjalisto 16 percent and Roihuvuori industrial district 17 percent. In comparison, in the inner city, the diplomat district Kaivopuisto has only nine percent of non-Finnish or Swedish speakers, and Kluuvi, the commercial centre has 11 percent. Ruoholahti, a mixed district hosting council-housing but also private flats, has 12 percent. Only in Jätkäsaari, by the docks, Kluuvi, Kaivopuisto, and an eastern suburb Rastila, where a metroline was opened in 1998, there is both above average Swedish and foreign language-speakers population.

There are 35 neighborhoods out of 104 that have more than the average percentage of immigrants, 38 neighborhoods with more than average amount of Swedish-speakers. Swedish-speakers stick to themselves: Swedish-language schools are important institutions that maintain the distinctive Swedish-Finns culture, and there are services provided in Swedish in the neighborhoods where the schools and kindergartens are.

It is not quite the same with the immigrants. They often rely on short-term rentals or council-housing. In fact, it is surprising for a city like Helsinki that boasts hosting international IT companies, that the only places where its immigrants live are the least wealthy neighborhoods with the exception of Kluuvi and Kaivopuisto. Though some live in the more high-tech oriented western neighbour Espoo. Instead of being spread throughout the city – and also to those more valued neighborhoods discussed before – the immigrants live in ghetto-like environments, small districts, mainly in the East, North East and also in the Center. They also create their own culture. *Mogadishu Avenue* is a name for Meri-Rastila Street, present in the slang of the East[33]. The language, however, is not in the street signs that remain in Finnish and Swedish. Commercial signs, however, highliht the use of English and Russian alongside Finnish and Swedish in the city.

Conclusion

Each city hosts a multiplicity of division-lines. What appears as the most import one, sometimes depends on the onlooker. Interestingly, Swedish-speakers' role is not as dominant in the divide as one could expect from the bilingual street-name signs, and what it historically has been. This, especially for many Swedish-speakers is starting to present a problem. Some may say that it only demonstrates a successful case of cooperation. However, the conflict between these interpretations themselves poses a question on the ethics of cooperation. On what – or whose – rules and expectations does cooperation take place? To what extent would that have to imply assimilation of minority to majority culture? Is conflict the only way to manifest a particular identity? Is cultural conflict not a process of differentiation itself, which contests the legitimacy of the majority culture to present itself as the universal?

Cultural differentiation and sense of place are important parts of identity-creation. Some friction is needed for maintaining and articulating one's own culture, alongside or against something else. Multiculturalism present in Helsinki does not manifest itself in the center of the city, but it is dominantly present in the multicultural eastern neighborhoods. While this is not the place to discuss whether or not the immigrant dominated neighborhoods of Helsinki have created their own culture, what could it be, nor what it might become[34], it is vital to realize that this ghettoized culture is creating a counter-pole to the Swedish-speakers relatively assimilated into Finnish majority language and culture. Here, a future conflict is looming, as although much research is made into these migrant communities, they are not integrated into the city at large or the Finnish culture. Although the Prime Minister Matti Vanhanen launched in autumn 2007 a new term New Finn (*uussuomalainen*) singeling out Finnish citizens whose mother tongue is not Finnish, the emergence of a radical populist party True Finns and the issue of immigrants in Finland demonstrates there is more to be done politically and culturally to establish

---

[33] T. Ainiala, *Helsingin Bronks ja Monaco*, "Helsingin Sanomat", 4.02.2003.
[34] T. Joronen, *Similarities, differences and inteculturality*, [in:] T. Joronen (ed.), *Naahanmuuttajien vapaaaika ja kulttuuripalvelut pääkaupunkiseudulla*, Helsingin kaupungin tilastokeskus, Helsinki 2009.

in any way similar equality between the Finnish-speaking, Swedish-speaking and non-Finnish-nor-Swedish-speaking Finns.

A conclusion to be drawn from this article is the following: while Helsinki is returning to its multicultural roots, as the number of foreign speakers, *vis-à-vis* Swedish and Finnish speakers, is on the increase. However, as history has shown even in Helsinki, that plurality is easy to loose by pragmatically assimilating minority populations into the majority culture.

Luxembourg
Multiculturalism Revisited – The Case of the Labor Market
Monica Bajan

Luxembourg presents important cleavages among its different groups of residents on several societal levels including language skills, education, working class and political participation. According to Stuart Hall, such cleavages, although not tangible, tend to divide cities into different clusters. The present article analyzes how these different clusters interact in Luxembourg. In this respect, it operates with two categories of Luxembourgish residents: Luxembourgish citizens and foreign residents. The first part of the article addresses cooperation patterns in Luxembourg. A due emphasis is placed upon the city's successful multiculturalism-story. The lack of prior open conflict among Luxembourgers and foreign residents is explained through a double theoretical framework. This pins the Luxembourgers multicultural-orientation in the consensus-driven political culture of a small state, whereas coining down the laid-back attitude of foreign-residents in transnationalism. The second part of the article attempts to investigate potential conflict sources among the residents of Luxembourg. Henceforth, the direction of analysis turns towards a study case on the Luxembourgish labor market. It is argued that the segmentation of the labor market is favored by the incongruity between the Luxembourgish immigration policies and the dynamics of the Luxembourgish society.

Introduction

Luxembourg is not a divided city. At least not in the interpretation of the term as describing a territorial unity *"constituted of separate entities which resulted from political changes or border shifts"*[1]. An overview upon the local and national initiatives addressing the residents of Luxembourg instills the idea of an embraced multiculturalism through the adoption of integrative programs and a consensus-oriented public debate. In its 1995 European Capital of Culture manifesto, Luxembourg was presented as a *"city of all cultures"*[2], presumably in an attempted recognition of its long tradition of immigration and the successful co-existence of native Luxem-

---

[1] www.1809-border.net, 5.04.2009.
[2] See in this direction *Cahiers Européens d'Houjarray*, http://cahierseuropeens.net/cedh010/fra/actu.htm, 5.04.2009.

bourgers and foreign-residents. Regarding the latter aspect, both government's official sources, as well as social science studies[3] seem to concur that open ethnic or religious conflicts have never been a distinctive trace of the Luxembourgish society. Moreover, the Luxembourgish case has been quoted as an example of successful inter-ethnic exchange which could further inspire the European Union towards closer integration[4].

Bearing in mind the above given definition to a divided city, the lack of apparent conflict among the residents of Luxembourg correlated with the absence of visible territorial division lines may raise reasonable doubts upon the decision of including the Luxembourgish case among the rest of the study-cases brought together by the present publication. Nonetheless, such doubts would not be sustained, if one were to project the analysis beyond physical aspects of division within a city[5]. In this respect, Stuart Hall provides a more complex approach to the issue of city-division by drawing attention upon the fact that "*cities have always been divided [...] by class, by wealth, by rights to and over property, by occupation and use, by life-style and culture, by race and nationality, ethnicity and religion, and by gender and sexuality*"[6].

Hall's definition is further employed in the essay, whereas it helps portraying Luxembourg as a divided city, in spite of its multiculturalism claim. The choice is sustained by the observation of important cleavages among the different groups of Luxembourgish residents in terms of language skills, education, working class and political participation. As Stuart Hall argues, despite their intangibility such cleavages tend to divide cities into different clusters[7].

The present article analyzes how these different clusters interact in Luxembourg. In this respect, it suggests two categories of Luxembourgish residents: Luxembourgish citizens and foreign residents[8]. It aims at showing how the distribution of societal roles among these two categories has influenced their interactions and nonetheless the shaping of the Luxembourgish society. The paper claims that

---

[3] E.g. www.gouvernement.lu: *A propos…du Luxembourg multiculturel*, 5.04.2009; H. Willems, P. Milmeister, *Migration und Integration*, [in:] W.H. Lorig, M. Hirsch, *Das Politische System Luxembourgs*, VS Verlag fuer Sozialwissenschaften, Wiesbaden 2008, p. 81.
[4] *A propos…du Luxembourg multiculturel*, www.gouvernement.lu, 5.04.2009; http://www.cafebabel.com/eng/article/15945/luxembourg-three-languages-one-nation.html, 5.04.2009.
[5] E.g. spacial conditions, borderlines, districts etc.
[6] S. Hall, *Divided city: the crisis of London*, 2004, p. 2; www.openDemocracy.net, 5.04.2009.
[7] *Ibidem*.
[8] The first category includes citizens of both Luxembourgish and non-Luxembourgish origins. In the understanding of the present article, the second category is composed of Luxembourgish residents issued of both EU and non-EU countries, who have immigrated in Luxembourg for mainly economic reasons and who do not possess the country's citizenship. In certain cases the term is alternatively replaced by the word immigrant. Although cross-borders occupy an important segment of the total Luxembourgish labour market their status is very much different than that of any Luxembourgish resident. Whereas the article is primarily concerned with interaction within the Luxembourgish society, references to this latter category have been made where necessary, but have been kept brief.

the lack of real decision-making powers of foreign residents has contributed to the maintenance of a conflict-free Luxembourgish society, whereas leading to a deepening of social cleavages among Luxembourgers and foreigners, reflected e.g. in the segmentation of the Luxembourgish labor market.

The article is divided into four chapters including the introduction. The second chapter addresses cooperation patterns in Luxembourg. A due emphasis is placed upon Luxembourg's long tradition of successful immigration and harmonious integration of foreign residents. The lack of prior open conflict among Luxembourgers and foreign residents is explained through a double theoretical framework. This pins the Luxembourgers multicultural-orientation in the consensus-driven political culture of a small state, whereas coining down the laid-back attitude of foreign-residents in transnationalism. The third chapter attempts to investigate potential conflict sources among the residents of Luxembourg. Henceforth, the direction of analysis turns towards a study case on the Luxembourgish labor market. It is argued that the segmentation of the labor market is favored by the incongruity between the Luxembourgish immigration policies and the dynamics of the Luxembourgish society. The fourth chapter is reserved for concluding remarks. It summarizes the findings of the essay and it aims at offering alternative paths for a possible future grasp of the matter.

The research was primarily conducted through qualitative methods. Along with several social studies on the Luxembourgish society and press coverage stretching over the last 8 years, the official sites of several associations representing the foreign residents[9], as well as those of the Luxembourgish government, the city of Luxembourg, the national statistics office (STATEC) and the Luxembourgish Agency of Culture have been consulted. Additionally, in March and April 2009 three interviews on the developments and future prospects of the Luxembourgish society have been carried out[10]. An important difficulty encountered during the research process derived from the fact that most of the available literature referred to the Grand Duchy of Luxembourg, rather than to the Luxembourg city. In this respect, the article operated with elements of quantitative methodology applied to STATEC's published statistics on population, employment and territory in the Grand Duchy and within its administrative divisions. The results of the inference have been used as a support for the assumption that conclusions derived from the general observation of the Luxembourgish society can be used in the particularized analysis of the capital city.

---

[9] Association de Soutien aux Travailleurs Immigrés (ASTI) www.asti.lu, Centre Intercommunitaire (SESOPI) www.sesopi-ci.lu, Comité de Liaison des Associations d'Etrangers (CLAE) www.clae.lu.

[10] The author would like to thank Ms. Maryse Lanners, editor of Telecran Luxembourg, Mr. Jean Lichtfous, representative of ASTI and Prof. Michel Pauly, historian and professor at the University of Luxembourg for their time and kindness in answering the questionnaire, as well as for their suggestions regarding possible approaches to the topic and additional article documentation.

Cooperation Patterns in Luxembourg

The rich immigration history of the Grand Duchy of Luxembourg, combined with the geographical positioning of the country at the confluence of two major cultures, the German and the French, have had a considerable influence upon the development of a multicultural approach of the nowadays nation-state. National identity discourses have not given way to religious or ethnic conflicts, nonetheless due to a recognized inter-dependence between the country's wealth and its foreign residents. However, despite a harmonious cohabitation among individuals of various origins, cooperation patterns in Luxembourg have not always been clear[11]. This section aims at introducing the Luxembourgish society the context of immigration and at conceptualizing the interactions between Luxembourgers and foreign residents.

An overview upon the Luxembourgish society in the context of immigration

The Grand Duchy of Luxembourg is one of the smallest states in the world, situated in the Western Europe in between Belgium, France and Germany, stretching over 2,586 square kilometers and totalizing 493,500 inhabitants, out of which 44% are foreign residents[12]. From ancient until present times, the territory encapsulating the nowadays country has faced numerous waves of immigration and cultural mixing, which did not allow the formation of a purely Luxembourgish civilization[13]. While looking at the country's legally enforced multilingualism, the ethnic composition of its administrative units, as well as at its internationally constructed labor market, one may assume a continuous identity trade-off among endogenous and exogenous elements in the Luxembourgish society. A clear example of that is the nation's self-defined political culture by means of a comparison with the two major cultures neighboring it: *"We are like both of them [the French and the German], but not like one of the two"*[14].

Two main elements have been pointed out as contributing to the definition of a Luxembourgish identity throughout the 20th century. Firstly, the desire to distinguish from the German culture during and in the immediate aftermath of the World War II resulted into the emergence of a distinct national identity[15]. Subsequently, in

---

[11] E.g. the failure of the dialogue platform between the Luxembourgish government and the foreign residents provided by the National Council of Foreigners. See in this direction Kollwelter, Serge: *Active Civic Participation of Immigrants in Luxembourg*, Oldenburg IBKM, 2005, p. 18.

[12] Statnews no. 16/2009, http://www.statistiques.public.lu/fr/communiques/index.html, 8.04.2009.

[13] Forum fuer Politik, Gesellschaft und Kultur in Luxemburg: *Le Luxembourg, un pays pluriel. Un siècle d'immigration et d'intégration*, 2000, http://www.forum.lu/bibliothek/ausgaben/inhalt/artikel/?artikel=4832, 23.03.2009.

[14] J.C. Juncker, *Wir sind wie die beiden, aber nicht wie einer von beiden*, quoted by W.H. Lorig, *Politische Kultur*, [in:] W.H. Lorig, M. Hirsch, *Das Politische System Luxembourgs*, VS Verlag fuer Sozialwissenschaften, Wiesbaden 2008, p. 33.

[15] S. Kollwelter, *Immigration in Luxembourg: New Challenges for an Old Country*, 2007, p. 2; http://www.migrationinformation.org/Profiles/display.cfm?id=587, 8.04.2009.

the late '70s a second phase of identity definition has begun. According to Guy Kirsch[16], this phenomenon is rooted in both an assimilation of and an opposition to the foreign cultures gathered in Luxembourg. Despite the apparent need of defining the local culture against the exogenous factors impacting upon the Luxembourgish society, the interactions between Luxembourgers and foreign residents have not been marked by notable altercations.

The explanation draws upon the interdependence between Luxembourg's development as a wealthy country and the Luxembourgish labor force issued abroad. Two significant events in this direction are worth mentioning. In the first place, the discovery of iron mineral deposits in the 1870s has determined a large wave of work immigration from Germany and Italy, which lasted until the 1950s. This immigration wave is distinguishable from the others to come by the immigrants' lack of real interest towards establishing within the host country[17]. The second event previously announced, is the signing of a diplomatic agreement between Luxembourg and Portugal in the 1970s regarding the exportation of labor force from the latter country to the former[18]. Unlike the German and the Italian immigrants, the Portuguese came to Luxembourg together with the members of their families and settled in the host country. At the moment, 16% of the total Luxembourgish population is constituted of foreign residents having a Portuguese citizenship[19]. Inferring upon the data documenting migratory movements towards Luxembourg in the 19th and the 20th century, one may conclude that in all of them an essential role was played by a double economic component. On the one hand, Luxembourg whose population was mainly employed in agriculture required an influx of qualified immigrants, who could assume managerial roles in industrial activities, combined with a large amount of workers who would be accountable to the former. On the other hand, the qualified and less qualified immigrants turned towards Luxembourg due to petty wages and an increased rate of unemployment in their country of origin, as well as due to motivating recruitment policies and salaries initiated by the government and employers of the host country[20].

Although the studies focused on the Luxembourgish society only rarely address the capital city, and show preference to a more general approach encompassing the entire Grand Duchy, this article argues that several factors justify the application of deductions derived from such studies to the particular case of the Luxembourg city. A first argument draws on the duality Luxembourg country – Luxembourg capital city, sustained by the smallness of the state and by the concentration of economic,

---

[16] Quoted in *A propos...du Luxembourg multiculturel*, www.gouvernement.lu, 8.04.2009.
[17] Forum fuer Politik, Gesellschaft und Kultur in Luxemburg: *Le Luxembourg, un pays pluriel. Un siècle d'immigration et d'intégration*, 2000, http://www.forum.lu/bibliothek/ausgaben/inhalt/artikel/?artikel=4832, 12.04.2009.
[18] "Accord bilatéral entre le Luxembourg et le Portugal sur le recrutement de travailleurs portugais" quoted by A. Schiltz, *L'Emigration portugaise au Grand-Duché de Luxembourg. Analyse de l'impact local dans le village de Fiolhoso*, www.asti.lu/pdf/schiltz.pdf, 12.04.2009.
[19] Ibidem, p. 15.
[20] Ibidem, p. 16.

social and political life within the capital city. Starting with the '60s Luxembourg developed as one of the most important European financial centers, and subsequently as one of the main stages for European policies and politics, while hosting important European institutions. A next argument is based on the observation that from the country's total territory, only 8.9% constitute developed area. This percentage regards mainly the central-southern part of the Grand Duchy including Luxembourg city. Additionally, in 2008 a fifth of the total Luxembourgish population was concentrated in the capital, whereas Esch-sur-Alzette, as the next important town in the country, accommodated only a third part of Luxembourg city's total number of inhabitants[21]. Furthermore, in between 2000 and 2002 the capital gathered together more than a third of the country's total economic activity establishments, as well as almost a half of the total employed population[22]. In what concerns the city's position towards immigration the local data-bases indicate an unusual case of a capital city where the majority of the population is represented by foreigners and only 34.69% of the inhabitants possess Luxembourgish citizenship[23]. Contrary to what could be expected, the situation has not led to conflictive reactions towards the foreign residents. The observation is sustained by an interpretation of the results of the latest Luxembourgish legislative elections in 2004. From the four electing circumscriptions, the Centre including Luxembourg city has registered the lowest amount of votes given to the Alternative Democratic Reform Party (ADR), the only Luxembourgish party with a populist orientation[24]. The next sub-section presents the theoretical framework used at coining down the set of attitudes employed by Luxembourgish citizens in their interactions. Several examples of cooperation will be presented and analyzed.

The politics of a small state: theorizing the absence of conflict in Luxembourg

While attempting to explain the set of attitudes determining the interactions among various groups of residents within a city, one cannot ignore the city's political culture which offers the background for such interactions. In a similar manner it has to be kept in mind that foreign-residents, while bearing the political culture of their place of origin, are also conditioned in their actions by the process of immigration, which entails a constant transaction between their homeland and the host society.

In the case of Luxembourg, the political culture dominating the capital city is the same one that characterizes the entire Duchy. An overview upon its specificities reveals the society's tendency towards consensus and dialogue. It is somehow sur-

---

[21] *Le Luxembourg en chiffres*, 2008, pp. 6–11, www.statec.lu, 12.04.2009.
[22] http://www.statistiques.public.lu/fr/publications/horizontales/annuaireStatLux/index.html, 12.04.2009.
[23] http://www.vdl.lu/Mairie+et+services+centraux/Politique+communale/La+Ville.html, 12.04.2009.
[24] *Répartition des suffrages en % du total des voix exprimés par parti et par commune 1994–2004*, www.statec.lu, 12.04.2009.

prising that an open society would adopt as a national motto the concept of *mir wëlle bleiwen wat mir sin* – "we want to remain what we are". One could argue that a nation advocating such position tends much more towards closing itself in front of outside influences, than towards opening up to positive interactions with exogenous factors. In the case of a big state, which due to its economic and military resources is potentially capable of a considerable impact upon its international environment while acting alone, such assumption could be more easily sustained than in the case of a small state. Papadakis and Starr[25] observe that small states are provided with a different set of opportunities and constraints than larger states, they have different goals and interests and tend to adopt different manners of conducting their foreign and domestic policies. In the case of the Grand Duchy of Luxembourg the adoption of an isolationist path would most likely result into a loss of economic competitiveness on the national level, as well as in a loss of credibility on the European one[26].

In a 1977 comparative study Arend Lijphart[27] identifies Luxembourg as a consociational democracy, whose small size favors the augmentation of cooperativeness and accommodation within its society, whereas determining an accrued internal solidarity against the possible threats posed by other powers. While advancing the intra-society accommodation argument Lijphart refers predominantly to the relations between the political elites, which due to their often interactions on a small political stage are expected to adopt *coalescent instead of adversarial styles of decision-making*[28]. The cooperation between political elites in Luxembourg is confirmed by Bossaert[29] who notes that the country should be qualified as an exceptionally stable democracy, which has never be threatened by inner disruptions. In the same line, Govaert comments upon the specificities of the Luxembourgish institutions and political system, which favor coalition and prevent a party, either majoritarian or minoritarian, from imposing its views upon the others[30].

Political stability in Luxembourg is reflected also in the residents' response to questions of satisfaction with the Luxembourgish society. According to Eurobarometer 2006, 92% of the surveyed Luxembourgers claim to be very content with the society they live in and *do not expect that their personal situation will change in the*

---

[25] W.H. Lorig, M. Hirsch, *Einleitung: Luxembourg – "Small, beautiful, and successful"?*, [in:] W.H. Lorig, M. Hirsch, *Das Politische System Luxembourgs*, VS Verlag fuer Sozialwissenschaften, Wiesbaden 2008, p. 7.
[26] In fact, Luxembourg's participation in various international organizations as founding member demonstrates a distinguishable tendency of anchoring its political and economic development to supranational entities.
[27] A. Lijphart, *Democracy in Plural Societies A Comparative Exploration*, Yale University Press, New Haven–London 1977, pp. 15, 65–66.
[28] *Ibidem*, 27, p. 65.
[29] D. Bossaert, quoted by W.H. Lorig, *Politische Kultur*, [in:] W.H. Lorig, M. Hirsch, *Das Politische System...*, op. cit., p. 34.
[30] S. Govaert, quoted by W.H. Lorig, *Politische Kultur*, [in:] W.H. Lorig, M. Hirsch, *Das Politische System...*, op. cit., p. 35.

years to come[31]. This could be explained by a further application of Lijphart's claim of coalescence between political elites to the interactions between Luxembourgish residents. To both categories of residents immigration appears as a "win-win" situation, through which Luxembourgish citizens are reinsured of the preservation of Luxembourg's wealth and the foreign residents have access to higher living standards than the ones provided by their home country.

The particularities of the Luxembourg-oriented-immigration add up to the mentioned economic advantages towards preserving a conflict-free society. Thus, most of the foreign residents are white, European, catholic and coming from EU Member States. Their tradition and religious beliefs[32] do not differentiate them markedly from the Luxembourgish citizens. Only 6% of the foreign residents belong to countries outside the EU[33] and about 2.5% are Muslims[34]. Cultural and economic cooperation patterns among Luxembourgish residents seem to be successful. Each year the capital city hosts several cultural festivals[35] aimed at increasing the tolerance and interest among the different cultures. In what concerns economic cooperation, the Tripartite Coordination Committee, which provides a platform for regular consultations between the government and the social partners, offers a conclusive example coming from the field of labor relations[36].

Despite the existence of a number of organisms designed to facilitate the political integration of foreigners[37], the subject of their civic participation has been excluded for a long time from the Luxembourgish political agenda. Following the European Community Directive 94/80, starting with 1994 foreign residents[38] have gained the right to elect and stand for elections in local and national election rounds.

---

[31] Eurobarometer 66.1.: *La perception des politiques de l'UE et de ses institutions. L'opinion des habitants du Luxembourg*, 2006, http://ec.europa.eu/public_opinion/archives/eb/eb66/eb66_en.htm, 18.04.2009. The Eurobarometer refers specifically to the inhabitants of Luxembourg, which constitute a larger entity than the Luxembourgish citizens.

[32] Millmeister and Willems (*op. cit.*, p. 88) underline the fact that Luxembourg does not have a state religion and that other confessions besides catholic (Greek and Russian orthodoxism, Judaism and Protestantism) are as well represented and financially supported by the state.

[33] http://www.statistiques.public.lu/fr/communiques/population/population/2009/05/20090504/index.html, 18.04.2009.

[34] S. Kollwelter, *Immigration...*, *op. cit.*, http://www.migrationinformation.org/Profiles/display.cfm?id=587, 18.04.2009.

[35] One could note the *Festival des migrations, des cultures et de la citoyenneté* organised by CLAE, the charity manifestation *Bazar international de Luxembourg* and the *Fête des ateliers des cultures* organised by ASTI in collaboration with l'Action solidarité tiers monde (ASTM) and the Cultural meetings centre Neumünster Abbey.

[36] G. Falkner, S. Leiber, *A Europeanization of Governance Patterns in Smaller European Democracies?*, 2003, p. 14; http://www.mpi-fg-koeln.mpg.de/socialeurope/, 18.04.2009.

[37] E.g. the National Conference for Foreigners, aimed at encouraging a regular exchange between the Luxembourgish government, the associations of foreigners and the local commissions; the Government's Commission for foreigners aimed at facilitating the integration of foreigners in the Luxembourgish social, economical, political and cultural life; etc.

[38] It is important to distinguish within the category of foreign residents, a subcategory including citizens of non-EU countries, who are not allowed to candidate.

Important limitations to the foreign residents' involvement with Luxembourgish politics derive from residency conditions, which impose 5 years of residence in Luxembourg in order to be able to exert election rights. Additionally, election lists containing a majority of non-Luxembourgish citizens are not validated[39].

One could ask why the foreign residents did not fervently claim the recognition of their political rights in Luxembourg. In order to answer this question it is necessary to look again at the particularities of the migration waves, this time in what concerns the immigrants' expectations towards the host country. As stated before, the Portuguese represent the highest percentage of foreign residents in Luxembourg, namely approximately 38%[40]. Due to their predominance in this category, as well as due to the fact that they constitute the focus of political discourses and policies concerning foreigners in Luxembourg, the case of the Portuguese immigrants will be further employed as a landmark in responding to the above asked question. An overview of the Portuguese immigration in Luxembourg facilitates its characterization as a family immigration, implying that both partners of the Portuguese couple work in order to gain enough money, meant to secure their hypothetical return to the homeland. In a similar manner, Marques and Góis observe within the Portuguese community in Switzerland a tendency to turn towards the origins, which structures their social and economic activities[41]. They argue that this attitude is rooted in transnationalism, which as a theory explains how the immigrants redefine the connection with the country of origin, without giving it up entirely and how they respond to the process of assimilation within the host country. It is further sustained that a thorough incorporation never takes place. Instead one can notice the creation of multiple lines between the two societies originated from the immigrants' tendency to divide themselves in between the two spaces[42]. Transnational practices could offer an explanation[43] for the foreign residents' laid back attitude in what concerns the advancement of their political rights in Luxembourg. In a 2004 study Meyers and Willems show that only 15.4% of the Portuguese feel themselves Luxembourgish, by comparison with 14.3% of the Italian, 15.7% of the French, 18.8% of the Capverdiens and 23.7% of the rest of the foreign residents[44].

---

[39] As a consequence of these factors, in 1994 eight foreign residents stood for being elected, in 1999 six and in 2004 another eight. According to La Lettre de la Citoyenneté, in the 1999 elections foreign citizens amounted to only 1.2% of the total elected candidates, http://www.lettredelacitoyennete.org/luxembourg86.htm, 20.04.2009.
[40] *Ibidem*, 33.
[41] J.C. Marques, P. Góis, *Pratiques transnationales des Capverdiens au Portugal et des Portugais en Suisse*, "Revue européenne des migrations internationales", vol. 24, 2008, p. 150.
[42] *Ibidem*, 41, p. 152.
[43] For a further article, it could be worthwhile inquiring to what extent the foreign residents' lack of interest towards politics in general add up to transnational practices in the host country, as well as what is the role played by the gratitude they feel towards the latter in deciding not to interfere in local politics.
[44] Quoted in H. Willems, P. Milmeister, *Migration und...*, op. cit., p. 82.

The debate surrounding the active civic participation of foreign residents in Luxembourg outweighs the scope of the present article[45]. What should be kept in mind is the fact that an increased birth-rate among foreign residents, associated to a low birth-rate among Luxembourgish citizens, announces major transformations within the population distribution during the next two decades[46]. In the event of Luxembourgish citizens becoming a minority in Luxembourg one could assume that questions of foreign residents' active participation would transform in inquiries upon the state's legitimacy. In this direction, the following chapter attempts to explain a causality link between the Luxembourgish immigration policy framework and the dynamics of the society and its segmentation.

Diversity versus division within the Luxembourgish Labor Market

As pointed out before, Luxembourg presents important cleavages among its different groups of residents on several societal levels. Stuart Hall argues that *"intangible as these boundaries often are and maintained as they are by complex cultural and social codes, they tend nevertheless to divide the city into distinct clusters"*[47]. The observation of such clusters within the Luxembourgish society stirs Willems and Milmeister[48] towards suggesting that a negative corollary to multiculturalism is the development of parallel societies within the borders of the same state. Basing on this assumption the present article maintains that Luxembourg city, which hosts more than 120 different nationalities, as well as the biggest labor market in the country[49], has to face as well the development of parallel societies, this time within the borders of the same town.

The purpose of this section is two folded. Firstly, it aims at pointing out the specificities of the Luxembourgish labor market. Secondly, it envisages discussing the impact exerted by national immigration policies upon the maintenance of social cleavages between Luxembourgers and foreign residents.

The specificities of the Luxembourgish labor market

The Luxembourgish labor market is characterized by a low unemployment rate and high wages. The work force is composed almost equally of Luxembourgers, foreign residents and cross borders. As Hartmann Hirsch notes, the Grand Duchy is *"the EU Member State with the highest share of immigrants within the resident population, within*

---

[45] For further reading see: S. Kollwelter, *Immigration...*, op. cit.; Forum fuer Politik, Gesellschaft und Kultur in Luxembourg: *Le Luxembourg, un pays pluriel...*, op. cit.; S. Kollwelter, *Active Civic Participation of...*, op. cit.; S. Betch, *Les candidats portugais aux élections locales luxembourgeoises*, http://urmis.revues.org/document36.html.
[46] *Ibidem*, 14, p. 6.
[47] S. Hall, *Divided city: the crisis of London*, 2004, p. 2; www.openDemocracy.net, 22.04.2009.
[48] H. Willems, P. Milmeister, *Migration und Integration...*, op. cit., pp. 80-81.
[49] www.vld.lu, 22.04.2009.

the internal labor market (66%) and even more so within the competitive sector (73%); the last two figures include cross border commuters"[50]. From the residents who have reached the working age, Portuguese show the highest employment rate (72%), followed by foreign residents who are citizens of other EU Member States (67%) and by Luxembourgers born outside the country (65%). In contrast, foreign residents, citizens of non-EU member states, present the lowest employment rate (41%), as well as the highest unemployment rate (29%). The difference between this latter figure and the next unemployment rate, displayed by another group of residents, equals 23%[51].

Among cleavage patterns within the Luxembourgish labor market, the present essay chooses to mainly address *class segmentation*. To this purpose, it suggests firstly a definition of the concept with which it operates. In the understanding of the paper, labor market class segmentation refers to boundaries among different categories of jobs which derive from the existence of economic strata within the working class. The formation of strata is determined by standard labor market variables such as education and experience[52]. In the case of the Luxembourgish labor market, nationality is largely employed as a third essential variable. The observation is sustained by the almost equal division of the Luxembourgish workforce among three employment sectors: the public sector, the blue-collar sector and the white-collar sector. Thus, Luxembourgish citizens show an increased tendency towards employment in the public sector, which due to language proficiency requirements in all three administrative languages, as well as nationality conditions in several cases, is often closed to non-citizens. In what concerns the foreign residents, they are largely employed in the so-called blue-collar branches of industrial production and construction business. A particular case within this category is represented by the Portuguese population which, as already shown, totalizes 38% of the foreign residents of Luxembourg. According to CEPS Instead, Portuguese demonstrate the highest index of social reproduction within the Luxembourgish society. More than 80% of the employed Portuguese work in the same area as their fathers; this is frequently linked to the construction industry. Only 10% prove an ascendant mobility, whereas 8% demonstrate a descendant one[53]. Commuters from adjacent countries, which amount to a third of the total labor force employed in Luxem-

---

[50] C. Hartmann Hirsch, *Luxembourg's corporatist Scandinavian welfare system and incorporation of migrants*, 2009, p. 3; http://www.soc.kuleuven.be/ceso/impalla/ESPANET/docs/Hartman_paper.pdf, 29.04.2009.
[51] The figures are taken from a STATEC report on immigrant workers in Luxembourg published in April 2009, www.statistiques.public.lu/fr/communiques/population/emploi_chomage/2009/04/20090429/index.html, 29.04.2009.
[52] For further reading see B. Martin, *Understanding Class Segmentation in the Labour Market: An Empirical Study of Earnings Determination in Australia*, "Work, Employment and Society", vol. 8, no. 3, 1994.
[53] Figures taken from *A propos de l'immigration...*, "Zeitung Vum Lëtzebuerger Vollek", 19.10.2006, www.ces.etat.lu/Immigration_Zeitung%20Vum%20Letzebuerger%20Vollek.pdf, 29.04.2009.

bourg, occupy mostly white-collar jobs in real estates, business services, banking and insurance services[54].

With its 100,000 employment places, the capital represents the city with the largest labor market in the Duchy. According to the national statistics office, in Luxembourg is employed the highest number of workers and national bureaucrats[55]. Whereas it concentrates the main offices of the 220 financial institutions in the country, Luxembourg is also the working place of most of the cross borders. Additionally, due to its European dimension it gathers all bureaucrats working for the European institutions in the Grand Duchy[56]. Basing on this data, the paper observes a replication at city level of the class segmentation patterns within the country's total labor market. The following section argues that immigration policies contribute markedly to the maintenance of cleavages between Luxembourgers and foreign residents on the labor market.

The contribution of immigration policies to the maintenance of the segmentation between Luxembourgers and foreign residents on the labor market

In a 2005 speech to the national Chamber of Deputies, the Luxembourgish prime-minster expressed the necessity for the adoption of a new immigration law based on the idea of closer integration, which could appease the emergence of parallel societies within the Grand Duchy[57]. Until 2008 the legal framework regarding immigration was represented by a 1972 adopted law which linked the unperturbed entrance and residence of foreigners on the country's territory to the specificities of the existent economic situation. The law, which has been criticized for providing too-large-a margin of interpretation in what concerns the access of immigrants to the Luxembourgish labor market[58], has been replaced in 2008 by a new legislation which maintains different approaches towards EU and non-EU citizens. Hartmann Hirsch observes that although such distinctions are compatible with the EU regulation on free movement they favor the appearance and maintenance of gaps among different categories of residents, which in labour market terms are reflected in the unequal access to non contributory benefits[59].

---

[54] Of course the distribution of the three categories of Luxembourgish employees to the three identified employment sectors is only relative. According to their education and experience there are foreign residents employed in the white collar sector, as well as in the public sector there where Luxembourgish nationality is not a prerequisite. Similarly, there are cross border commuters employed in the blue collar sector and there are Luxembourgish citizens who work in baking and financial services. The above juxtaposition is based upon the observation of the main employment trends.

[55] *Emploi et chômage par canton et commune en 2007*, http://www.statistiques.public.lu/stat/TableViewer/tableView.aspx, 29.04.2009.

[56] http://www.vdl.lu/Mairie+et+services+centraux/Politique+communale/La+Ville/Historique.html, 29.04.2009.

[57] S. Kollwelter, *Immigration et économie*, 2006; www.forum.lu/pdf/artikel/5940_262_Kollwelter.pdf, 3.05.2009.

[58] H. Willems, P. Milmeister, *Migration und Integration...*, op. cit., p. 75.

[59] E.g. social assistance scheme, minimun guaranteed revenue etc. C. Hartmann Hirsch, *Luxembourg's corporatist...*, op. cit., p. 12; http://www.soc.kuleuven.be/ceso/impalla/ESPANET/docs/Hartman_paper.pdf, 3.05.2009.

The emergence of parallel societies in Luxembourg has not been solely determined by a weakly articulated legislative framework regarding immigration. Language policies, imposing trilingual proficiency within the education system and the administration, integration policies, linking naturalization to burdening residency and language knowledge conditions, together with the limitation of the foreign residents' participation to the decision making process have had an important contribution to the deepening of social cleavages among Luxembourgers.

In considering the named policies as part of a national immigration policy, the present article relies on the following reasoning in order to demonstrate the above assumption. The trilingual education system creates early separation lines between Luxembourgish citizens and foreign residents. This observation is confirmed by the 2003 PISA survey[60]. Although learning the Luxembourgish language is not part of the school curricula, a good knowledge of this language is required in most inter-schoolmate interactions, as well as teacher-pupil dialogues. Foreign residents enrolled in Luxembourgish schools are frequently faced with learning the three languages, out of which none is their mother tongue. Willems and Milmeister observe that throughout school development foreign residents tend more to register with technical high-schools which are skills-oriented, than with classical ones, which are knowledge-oriented[61]. Two deductions can be drawn from this observation. Firstly, the high number of foreign residents graduating technical high-schools determines their predominance in the blue-collar jobs sector. Secondly, lower level language expectations in high-school result in the students' non-proficiency in one or some of the official administrative languages, hence burdening their access to the public sector jobs.

In what concerns naturalization policies, Kollwelter notes that despite a steady increase in the number of naturalizations since 2001, foreign residents are generally characterized by a low rate of naturalization, as a consequence of restrictive national laws regulating this field[62]. The 2008 naturalization law presents significant modifications in comparison with its predecessors. Thus, for the first time it is stipulated the possibility to preserve one's nationality while acquiring the Luxembourgish citizenship. However, such privilege may be obtained only if the person introducing the naturalization request proves 7 years of residency in Luxembourg and a specific level of knowledge of oral and written Luxembourgish[63]. The new residency condition, which can be associated with the Luxembourgish society's attempt to avoid "benefit shopping" or "social tourism"[64] from the new comers, represents a hardening of the prior legal stipulations according to which foreigners could apply for naturalization after 5 years of residency. In the same line, the exigencies of Luxembourgish language knowledge imposed by the new legislation are

---

[60] H. Willems, P. Milmeister, *Migration und Integration...*, op. cit., p. 86.
[61] *Ibidem*, 60, p. 81.
[62] S. Kollwelter, *Immigration...*, op. cit., http://www.migrationinformation.org/Profiles/display.cfm?id=587, 4.05.2009.
[63] http://gouvernement.lu/salle_presse/actualite/2008/10-octobre/15-nationalite/index.html.
[64] C. Hartmann Hirsch, *Luxembourg's corporatist...*, op. cit., p. 12.

more severe than the ones contained by previous laws. Taking into consideration these factors, it can be assumed that Kollwelter's observation of a low naturalization rate among foreign residents will still be valid under the new regulation. Two important implications can be derived from this assumption. Firstly, a low naturalization rate of foreign residents results in a high homogeneity of the Luxembourgish administration, which in most cases allows only the employment of Luxembourgish citizens. Such homogeneity favors the maintenance of a *closed club* type of public administration from which an important part of the Luxembourgish society is excluded. Secondly, such low naturalization rate indirectly determines a low participation in the national decision-making process. As explained in the previous chapter, foreign residents still face a considerable exclusion from the Luxembourgish political stage. Due to the small percentage that they totalize among the elected politicians, one can deduce that they are able to exert only a limited influence upon the further development of immigration policies, which represent one of the important state tools for regulating labor market[65]. Maintained in their present form, these policies seem still far from being articulated with the dynamics of the Luxembourgish society and have the potential of deepening societal cleavages among Luxembourgish residents.

Conclusion

Retaining Stuart Hall's approach to city division, this article showed Luxembourg as a divided city along labor market cleavage lines among its residents. The chapters constituting the body of the article have linked the lack of conflict in the city to the consensus-driven Luxembourgish political culture and a laid back attitude of foreign residents regarding the assuming of important political roles in the host society. The study case on the Luxembourgish labor market has been chosen to portray a potentially conflictive background for the inter-residents interactions. An important factor supporting the choice was the visibility of class segmentation between the two categories of residents with which the article operated. Although no actual conflict was presented, it was shown that the lack of real decision-making powers of foreign residents can lead to further deepening of segmentation between Luxembourgish citizens and foreign residents.

Another way of looking at this subject could start from an observation of the residents' interests representation in the Luxembourgish Parliament. As the moment only 56% of the total population in Luxembourg are represented in the Parliament. In the event of Luxembourgish citizens becoming a minority in their own country one could inquire upon the relation between the foreign residents' political participation and the state's legitimacy.

---

[65] D. Groutsis, *The State, Immigration Policy and Labour Market Practices: The Case of Overseas-trained Doctors*, "Journal of Industrial Relations", vol. 45, pp. 67-86.

Personal Notes

Monica Bajan – researcher in doctoral formation with the Faculty of Law, Economics and Finance of the University of Luxembourg. Main areas of interest: Energy policy and regulation in Europe, EU-Russia Gas relationships, governance, foreign policy of EU Member States, political culture of EU Member States, immigration in Luxembourg

Péter Balogh, MA, is doctoral student in human geography at CBEES (Centre for Baltic and East European Studies), Södertörn University. His main field is political geography; and he is working as aresearcher for the project *The Influence of Political Territorial Hierarchies on Local Development and Relations in Cross-border Areas: The Central Role of Szczecin in Relation to the Divided Pomeranian Hinterland,* lead by professors Thomas Lundén and Anders Mellbourn.

Tomasz Brańka, Ph.D., researcher in Faculty of Political Sciences and Journalism at Adam Mickiewicz University in Poznań, Poland. His research interests are related to the Baltic Sea region, minorities and indigenous peoples' issues, regionalization and autonomous regions. In 2007 he defended his doctoral thesis concerning the autonomous regions of Nordic countries as non-sovereign actors of international relations. He is also the teacher of the Baltic University Programme.

Eda Derhemi (Ph.D. in Communications – UIUC) teaches in the Department of Media Studies (College of Media), and the Department of Spanish, Italian and Portuguese (Liberal Arts and Sciences), at the University of Illinois at Urbana-Champaign, USA. Her visit to Kosovo and Mitrovica in 2007 where the narrative section of this paper was written, was funded by IREX with an Advanvanced Research Grant. Her work and publications are about issues of old and new diasporas, linguistic and cultural endangerment, the role of local media for minorities, and the representation of ethnic conflict in the media. Her regions of interest are the Western Balkans and Italy. She also writes journalistic articles for Albanian and Kosovar newspapers and magazines.

Marcin Galent is an assisstant professor at the Institute of European Studies, Jagiellonian University, Poland. His Ph.D. research has been focused on immigration in the European Union. Specifically, he has been investigating reception of immigration through an example of English society. His current research focuses on relation between migration, Europeanisation, and identity formation processes. He is also the coordinator of the MA in Euroculture Programme at the Jagiellonian University.

Jarosław Jańczak, Ph.D., is an assistant at Adam Mickiewicz University, Poznań, Poland and European University Viadrina, Frankfurt (Oder), Germany. He has been collaborating in the field of research and didactics with several universities in Europe. His research has concentrated on border studies in the European context as well as the integration of Nordic Countries into the EU. He has been coordinating the Polish-German joint Master of Political Studies/Master of European Studies program.

Thomas Lundén is professor of human geography at CBEES (Centre for Baltic and East European Studies), Södertörn University. His major field of academic interest is political, social and linguistic geography. His publications include *On the boundary. About humans at the end of territory*, 2004, and as editor *Crossing the border. Boundary relations in a changing Europe*, 2006.

Michał Łuszczuk is the Assisting Professor in the International relations Department of Political Science Faculty in Maria Curie Sklodowska University in Lublin. His research interests cover political geography and international security.

Anders Mellbourn, Ph.D., is visiting professor at CBEES (Centre for Baltic and East European Studies), Södertörn University, and adjunct professor of politics and journalism at Halmstad University. He is a former director of the Swedish Institute of International Affairs and former editor-in-chief of the leading Swedish daily Dagens Nyheter. He is a regular commentator on international and public affairs in Swedish media.

Magdalena Musiał-Karg – doctor of political science at Adam Mickiewicz University in Poznań. Graduated in *political science* from Adam Mickiewicz University in Poznań and in *marketing and management* from Zielona Góra University. Also studied the *European Political Studies* at the European University Viadrina in Frankfurt Oder. Her academic interests concentrate on direct democracy, political participation, e-voting and cross-border cooperation.

Heino Nyyssönen is political scientist and teaches in the Universities of Jyväskylä and Tampere, Finland. He has particularly concentrated on world politics as East Central Europe, history's role in politics and politics of memory. Nyyssönen has held several academic positions in Finland, at the moment he is a senior assistant at the Department of Political Science and International Relations in Tampere. He has been a visiting scholar in Berlin and Budapest, in which he has lived several years since early 1990s. In 2007–2009 he has led an academic research group Nation and Their Others, comparing Finland and Hungary in the 20th century.

Przemysław Osiewicz – born in 1979, graduated in political science in the field of international relations from Adam Mickiewicz University in Poznań. He has a Ph.D. in political science. His doctoral thesis was dedicated to *Plans and Initiatives for a Peaceful Settlement of the Cyprus Question: Legal and Political Aspects*. Currently an Assist. Prof. at AMU in Poznań. Previous studies/guest researcher: Södertörns Högskola (Stockholm, Sweden); Eastern Mediterranean University (Famagusta, Cyprus); Chinese Culture University (Taipei, Taiwan). His scientific interests involve international conflicts and disputes, unrecognized states, security of energy supplies, Greek-Turkish relations, the Cyprus question, EU-Turkey relations, Iran's foreign policy and cross-strait relations between mainland China and Taiwan.

Emilia Palonen is a Senior Lecturer in Cultural Policy, Department of Social Sciences and Philosophy, University of Jyväskylä. She holds a Ph.D. in Ideology and Discourse

Analysis, and takes part in a comparative research project on identity-building in Finland and Hungary. *Nations and their others: Finns and Hungarians since 1900* received funding from the Academy of Finland, 2007-2009.

Anna Potyrała, works as a researcher in the Faculty of Political Science and Journalism of the Adam Mickiewicz University in Poznań, Poland. She graduated political science (1999) and law (2001) and defended Ph.D. thesis in political science in 2003. The author of several papers, the book *Współczesne uchodźstwo. Próby rozwiązania międzynarodowego problemu* (*Contemporary refugeesm. Attempts to solve the international problem*), Poznań 2005; and co-author of *Leksykon integracji europejskiej w obszarze 'Sprawiedliwość, Wolność, Bezpieczeństwo'* (*Lexicon of the European integration in the field of 'Justice, Freedom, Security'*), Poznań 2008. Her scientific interests comprise refugee and migration problems, international judicial system and EU Justice and Home Affairs.

Alexander Tölle; born 1970 in Berlin; Dr. Phil. (European University Viadrina Frankfurt-upon-Oder, 2005), MSc European Urban Studies (Bauhaus University Weimar, 2001), Dipl.-Ing. Urban & Regional Planning (Technical University Berlin, 1996); since 2005 Assistant Professor at the Institute of Socio-Economic Geography and Spatial Management of Adam Mickiewicz University, Poznan. Research interests: urban renewal, city management, urban cultural heritage, waterfront development, cross-border networking.

Cezary Trosiak, Ph.D., born in a Polish family in Komprachcice, Opole Silesia (Śląsk Opolski); assistant professor at the Faculty of Political Science and Journalism at the Adam Mickiewicz University in Poznań. His academic interests include: Polis-German relations, German minority in Poland, the processes of social and cultural transformation in the Eastern and Northern Lands, social consequences of Poland's membership in EU structures. He is the author of the study *Kształtowanie się pogranicza polsko-niemieckiego po II wojnie światowej* [*The shaping of Polish-German borderlands after Word War II*] and other papers devoted to this issue. He is a member of Collegium Polonicum research teams dealing with the issues of Polish-German borderlands.

Tom Vandenkendelaere is an MPhil student at the University of Kent at Canterbury and studies the effect of European enlargement on governmental bilateral relations between Germany and Poland. He also has a particular interest in Belgian politics and teaches both comparative politics and European politics on a part-time basis.

Lien Warmenbol is a Ph.D. student at the University of Antwerp (Political Science Department) and studies the success of radical right parties at the local and regional level. She is interested in interethnic relations and local politics in urban settings.

Joachim v. Wedel, Ph.D., has studied law in Passau, Wuerzburg and Washington and completed a Ph.D. in political science at the University of Siegen. Having worked as a lawyer in a rural area of Eastern Germany, he is currently affiliated to the Center of Baltic and East European Studies at Södertörn University, Huddinge/Stockholm.

Agnieszka Wójcicka (born in 1982) graduated from the Institute of Political Science and Journalism at Adam Mickiewicz University in Poznań in Poland (AMU). Currently she is a Ph.D. candidate in the Strategic Studies Department at AMU working on her doctoral thesis on the *Political identity of contemporary Sweden*. She received scholarships from the Węclewicz Foundation/Stockholm University (Stockholms universitet) in 2007/2008 and from the Scholarship and Training Fund/Norwegian University of Science and Technology in Trondheim (Norges teknisk-naturvitenskapelige universitet i Trondheim) in 2008/2009. Her academic interests concentrate on the field of International Relations (IR), European studies, processes of integration and globalization regarding the identities of the Scandinavian countries.